The Triple Helix of University–Government–Industry Partnerships and the Development of AI

Mohieddine Rahmouni
King Faisal University, Saudi Arabia

Mossab Saud Alholiby
https://orcid.org/0000-0002-8899-8770
King Faisal University, Saudi Arabia

Ben Othman Soufiene
King Faisal University, Saudi Arabia

IGI Global
Scientific Publishing
Publishing Tomorrow's Research Today

Vice President of Editorial Melissa Wagner
Director of Acquisitions Mikaela Felty
Director of Book Development Jocelynn Hessler
Production Manager Mike Brehm
Cover Design Jose Rosado

Published in the United States of America by
IGI Global Scientific Publishing
701 East Chocolate Avenue
Hershey, PA, 17033, USA
Tel: 717-533-8845 | Fax: 717-533-7115
Website: https://www.igi-global.com E-mail: cust@igi-global.com

Library of Congress Cataloging-in-Publication Data

LCCN: 2026002322 (CIP Data Pending)
ISBN13: 9798337376202
Isbn13Softcover: 9798337376219
EISBN13: 9798337376226
British Cataloguing in Publication Data
A Cataloguing in Publication record for this book is available from the British Library.

Table of Contents

Detailed Table of Contents

The chapter examines how universities and governments jointly shape the future of responsible AI through integrated knowledge production, policy formation, and ethical governance. It explores how academic research, interdisciplinary expertise, and talent development intersect with regulatory frameworks, national strategies, and public-sector oversight to create accountable and human-centered AI ecosystems. The analysis highlights global case studies, collaborative mechanisms such as advisory councils and regulatory sandboxes, and the challenges posed by bureaucratic gaps, rapid technological change, and geopolitical pressures. The chapter argues that co-creation, evidence-based policymaking, and inclusive governance are essential for ensuring transparent, fair, and socially aligned AI development.

The emergence of generative artificial intelligence (AI) has redefined authorship, creativity, and ownership in the digital economy, raising complex ethical and regulatory challenges. This chapter examines how university-government-industry collaboration, as outlined in the Triple Helix model, can strengthen ethical AI governance by redefining consent and creative labor. Using Indonesia as a focal point, the analysis examines how national and regional frameworks, particularly those of ASEAN, seek to align innovation with cultural and ethical accountability. By exploring case studies in education, policy, and creative industries, this chapter highlights how universities can operationalize ethical AI literacy and contribute to participatory governance. Ultimately, it argues that integrating creative consent into institutional collaboration provides a foundation for sustainable and inclusive AI ecosystems in Southeast Asia.

Preface

DESCRIPTION

The development of Artificial Intelligence (AI) is increasingly shaped by the dynamic interactions among universities, governments, and industry, commonly conceptualized through the **Triple Helix model**. Within this framework, universities generate foundational research and talent, governments establish ethical, legal, and regulatory directions, and industry translates innovation into scalable real-world applications. The convergence of these three sectors accelerates AI advancement while simultaneously addressing critical societal challenges related to governance, workforce development, sustainability, and the responsible use of technology.

The Triple Helix of University–Government–Industry Partnerships and the Development of AI examines how collaborative models among academia, public institutions, and private enterprises influence the research, governance, and deployment of AI technologies. The book explores AI's transformative role across innovation ecosystems, highlighting how coordinated partnerships shape policy design, project management practices, ethical oversight, and industrial implementation. By integrating theoretical perspectives with applied insights and global case examples, this volume serves as a valuable reference for educators, policymakers, industry leaders, researchers, and practitioners seeking to understand and strengthen cross-sector collaboration in the AI era.

COVERAGE

The many academic areas covered in this publication include, but are not limited to:

- Artificial Intelligence (AI)

- Business and Industry Innovation
- Economics and Economic Theory
- Ethics, Law, and AI Governance
- Government Policy and Regulation
- Higher Education and Research Systems
- Machine Learning
- Project and Innovation Management
- Public Policy
- Sustainable Development and Social Impact

Acknowledgement

Funding: This work was supported by the Deanship of Scientific Research, Vice Presidency for Graduate Studies and Scientific Research, King Faisal University, Saudi Arabia [Grant No. KFU260646].

Chapter 1
Theoretical Foundations of the Triple Helix Model in the Context of AI:
University, Government, Industry Partnerships for the Knowledge Economy

G. Silambarasan
https://orcid.org/0009-0004-6233-4943
Periyar University, India

Gautam Shivaraj
https://orcid.org/0009-0000-5184-8448
Adarsh Institute of Management and Information Technology, Chamarajpet, India

ABSTRACT

The Triple Helix Model, conceptualized as a dynamic interaction between universities, industry, and government, plays a critical role in fostering innovation, particularly in the context of Artificial Intelligence (AI). This model emphasizes the importance of collaboration among these three sectors to promote knowledge exchange, technological advancements, and economic growth. As AI continues to revolutionize various industries, the integration of academic research, government policy, and industry expertise becomes essential for building a sustainable knowledge economy. This chapter explores the theoretical foundations of the Triple Helix Model, highlighting its relevance to AI development. It examines how university-government-industry partnerships can accelerate AI innovation by providing a structured approach to resource sharing, policy development, and commercial application.

DOI: 10.4018/979-8-3373-7620-2.ch001

1. INTRODUCTION

Artificial Intelligence (AI) has come to be the meta-technology, i.e. a pervasive cognitive infrastructure with the ability of modulating industrial sectors, socio-economic formations and knowledge institutions together. Unlike previous technological paradigms that are based on closed industrial systems, AI is a general-purpose enabling substrate that changes cognitive, value creation logics and decision architectures and regulatory modalities. As economies move away from material production to develop knowledge-based growth patterns, the focus of innovation shifts toward epistemic production in which intellect, as well as information, analytic models, and learning architectures, are the focus of capital accumulation. Within this reconfigured landscape the Triple Helix Model emerges as a crucial form of interpreting the landscape, allowing for an understanding of the interplay of institutions upon which the formation of AI capabilities is built. AI destabilizes linear models of innovation where universities created knowledge, industry commercialized it and government-controlled results; it requires recursive knowledge flows, translational real-time research, reflexive regulatory forms and cyclic learning in many directions. Universities become centres of algorithms, of discovering knowledge, producing human capital, industries become translation machines converting esoteric research into computational markets and cyber-physical flows, and governments are the systemic orchestrators of mandatory regulation and envisioning regulatory ecosystems, sovereign investments into the infrastructure and ethical governance mandates. The environment of AI therefore forces structural interdependence between Helix's actors: in the absence of sustained talent pipelines, state mediated alignment and industrial absorptive capacity, the innovation in AI collapses.(Yu et al., 2025)

Simultaneously, AI exposes asymmetries and systemic vulnerabilities, which go beyond ordinary capacities of governance preparation - such as surveillance externalities, algorithmic prejudice, loss of livelihood, cyber-security fragilities, and failure risks through automated decision infrastructures. In this sense, the Triple Helix is changed from an innovation promotion heuristic to a socio-technical risk mitigation and institutional steering system. This chapter places the Triple Helix in the context of the emergent logic of AI-driven knowledge economies, raising the question as to how institutional behaviour is reorganised in the context of intelligence technologies, and how hybrid roles are constituted under co-evolutionary learning regimes. Rather than simply describing the course of AI, it clarifies the way AI helps change national competitiveness and how it shapes the redistribution of epistemic power and creates mandates for resilience for policymakers, for scholars, and for strategic actors attempting to architect viable innovation ecosystems. Ultimately, AI is not a satellite actor as part of the Triple Helix, it reconfigures its cognitive logic, its operational condition and its dependence relations. The maturation of the

AI capability overtime will depend on the dexterity with which universities develop talent and discovery, the industries turn intelligence into a sizeable infrastructure as well as the governments organize harmony, ethics and resilience to incidents that raise systems wide. Thus, it is the Triple Helix that emerges as the epistemic engine, governmental form and economic platform on which knowledge societies of the AI era will be built. (J. Huang et al., 2025)

2. THEORETICAL BACKGROUND

The Triple Helix Model offers meta-theoretical framework of understanding how knowledge institutions, regulatory systems and innovation based industrial structures co-evolve. Within the framework of artificial intelligence (AI), this framework gains even greater analytical significance, since the AI is turning the nature of innovation as it has traditionally belonged to the realm of material change into the realm of intelligence generation, computational rule, and the establishment of epistemic capital. In this section, the historical theories underlying the Triple Helix paradigm will be expounded and their developmental process will be discussed in the context of cognitive and techno-organizational processes caused by AI.(Matovu et al., 2025)

2.1 Knowledge Economy Foundations

The rise of the knowledge economy rearranges the theory of the economy by stating the idea that the knowledge is not some other factor of production, but the key building block of social value generation. As compared to the industrial era economies which prioritized land, labour and capital, the current modes of operation are based on cognitive assets and symbolic processing and the ability to abstract and infrastructures that facilitate learning. This change is accelerated by AI, which automates low-level cognition coupled with increasing the requirement of higher-order knowledge synthesis and algorithmic intelligence engineering. In this way, the Triple Helix will become an institutionalizing process of knowledge creation as a systemic economic role. the configuration, universities serve as epistemic engines, industries as innovation adapters and amplifiers, and governments as macro-regulatory stewards (stabilizing the risks and facilitating the formation of capabilities). This interaction forms a knowledge regenerative loop and makes the Triple Helix a self-reinforcing ecosystem of cognition-production.(Guevara et al., 2025)

2.2 Theoretical Foundations of the Triple Helix Model

The Triple Helix Model defines innovation as a natural by-product of organizational co-evolution, not a progressive result of individual organizational strengths. Theoretically, its basis is a synthesis of concepts of evolutionary economics, systems theory, sociology of knowledge and frameworks of institutional transformation. The main argument is that, universities, industries, and governments do not simply coexist in innovation systems, but they also constitute the identity, functionality, and development course to one another. One of the fundamental theoretical assumptions in the model is the institutional reflexivity where each helix adjusts to internalized roles that were previously played by other people. Start-ups are nurtured at universities, research chairs are funded by industries, and innovation accelerators and venture funds are created by government. This reactive adjustment brings about new forms of institutional combinations, which overrun the line between policy making, research writing, and commercial translation. The model also assumes that innovation is non-equilibrium, boundary-spanning, that is, it occurs at the interface regions, in the zones of technology park, digital hubs, AI accelerators, and regulatory sandboxes, but not in the interiors of organizations. These interface spaces are morphogenesis areas inside the institutions that emerge through repetitive engagement as the new knowledge structures, AI protocols, and norms of governance, and commercialization channels are crystallized. The Triple Helix proposes a radical ontology of governance, whereby the government is more than a rule-giver, more than an orchestration agent, industry is more than a profit-driven, more than a social capability provider, and universities emerge as innovation-focused, market savvy, strategic partners. These conceptual structures are in tune with AI that intelligence development, control, implementation, and ethical guarantee are decentralized functions that must be systemically co-produced.(Brodny & Tutak, 2025)

2.3 Artificial Intelligence as Triple Helix Logic Reinforcing

AI is an artefactual technology and a paradigm of governance, exacerbating the structural imperative of the Triple Helix. On contrary to the previous industrial technologies, AI requires Computational infrastructure: The computational infrastructure operates on the basis of a unified and standardized naming system. Computational infrastructure The computational structure works with a unified and standardized naming system.(Lim, 2026)

- o Training datasets
- o Ethical alignment systems.
- o Algorithmic verification and validation.

o Systems retraining on a regular basis.

In that way, no single institutional domain can serve as the preconditions of the AI innovation. The Triple Helix gets as a cognitive supply chain of universities generating algorithms and human talent, industry providing real-world problem problems as problem environments, deployment platforms and scaling infrastructure, and governments providing regulations, any grammars of risks, mission-oriented investment frameworks. The reinforcement of recursive feedback learning by AI also reinforces that the performance of deployed systems generates data that informs the further research agenda. This renders innovation non-linear, adaptive and path-dependent, establishing additional co-evolutionary processes among the institutional actors. Moreover, AI proposes systemic externalities, such as privacy risk, algorithmic bias, autonomous decision failure, and mandating shared governance over AI, i.e. not unidirectional control. In this regard, the Triple Helix becomes an ontological need of technological legitimacy by AI.(Uppuluri & Yang, 2025)

2.4 Century-Hybrid Institutional Forms Evolution

The pace of AI-based innovation architectures has helped to effect a structural metamorphosis of the Triple Helix ecosystem, where the conventional typologies of institutions are being dissolved into the hybridized socio-organizational formations. This has not been an incremental evolution, but rather a systemic re-engineering of knowledge governance, embodiment of capabilities as well as distribution of authority between universities, industries and governments. the past, universities had been in the epistemic space as knowledge creators, industries as knowledge implementers, and governments as enforcers of rules. Nonetheless, the complexity, dynamism and the socio-technical implications of AI make these simple categories insufficient. AI turns into a thinking platform, necessitating an inter-institutional expertise that cannot be held by an individual. As a result, institutional boundaries are curved, collided and merged forming what is theoretically known as para-institutional hybrids.(Tanveer et al., 2025)

Universities are becoming entrepreneurial cognitive ecosystems and are no longer confined in their historical role of knowledge making to algorithm translation into working prototypes, commercialization of research results, sovereign AI strategy design, and accelerators, incubators, and spin-out ecosystems. The resulting effect of this change is the emergence of the so-called entrepreneurial university, in which academic institutions have entrenched market-oriented capacities like venture offices, corporate research units, intellectual property clusters, and leading industrial consortia. In parallel, industries experience an inversion of their functional role as passive receivers of knowledge to actively generate and teach knowledge, through the establishment of corporate AI academies, skill transformation infrastructures, co-designed doctoral programmes, and public research funding processes, becoming learning-intensive institutional forms and absorbing educational and policy roles to new AI skill volatility and regulatory complexity. Parallel to this, governments move beyond the enforcement-based governance and become architecture of innovation, ecosystem facilitators by creating AI capability infrastructures of national missions, digital public goods, sovereign data platforms, multi-stakeholder ethics councils and regulatory sandbox, thus becoming institutional integrators in the coordination of identity formation across the scientific research, industrial performance, and societal welfare nexus. The overall impact of these changes is the emergence of para-institutional interface mechanisms national AI research centres, cyber-physical testbeds, government-industry-university data cooperatives, digital supervisory authorities, and AI manufacturing zones that represent institutional hybridity, neither academic nor regulatory nor commercial in their own right but as translational engines generating knowledge to capability, capability to governance and governance to socio-economic resiliency. Therefore, hybridization is less an organizational mutation, but a systemic resupination to AI-led interdependence, in which value creation is based on institutional overlaps, co-evolution, and a recursive knowledge transfer rather than individual skill.(X. Huang & Zhou, 2025)

2.5 Multi-Level Innovation Governance Theory

At the micro level, innovation governance involves cognitive and behavioural structures governing researcher behaviour, norms of knowledge creation, algorithmic accountability and ethical reflexivity as well as career trajectories of talent, which is expressed in the formation of academic culture, research evaluation procedures, incentive systems and informal epistemic legitimacy norms. At the meso level, governance gives way to networked ecosystem coordination such as among technology parks, particular Artificial Intelligence parks, regional centres and Public-Private alliances through a coherence of incentives, knowledge mobilization, and collaborative innovation platforms including shared norms, co-funding tools, institutional agreements and boundary spanning leadership architecture. On the macro level, governance becomes mission-driven stewardship that determines digital sovereignty, national AI policy, security regime, ethics law, and intellectual property geopolitics, the state turns to not the enforcement of regulations, but the development of strategic capability built into the infrastructure of power of the state. On all these scales AI requires the governance of a cybernetism, which involves ongoing sensing, recursive feedback integration, recalibration, and the active rule improvement and evolution, instead of the conventional fixed oversight frameworks, co-evolutionary supervisory structures that emerge with human-machine interfaces, institutional learning processes, and adaptive regulative structures. As a result of untenability issues, governance has become co-produced across the Triple Helix to include universities in terms of epistemic authority, industries in terms of technological trajectories and governments in terms of institutional order stabilisation, and governance does not commission or repatriate (monopolised) but is performed through oversight councils, policy-embedded research infrastructures, ethics-as-architecture frameworks and regulatory sandboxes included directly into industrial operations. This creates a meta-governance ecosystem, a layer of governance-of-governance which allows self-steering orders of innovation where economic competitiveness is a governance competency, the reformulation of sovereignty in data control, the infrastructure and regulatory sophistication, and the Triple Helix emerges as a governing organism rather than collaborative heuristic. Thereby, AI ecosystems shift government to an external oversight to an internal layer of intelligence embedded in the innovation fabric, defining how knowledge systems evolve, stabilise, grow and correct themselves along temporal and institutional barriers.(Tutak & Brodny, 2025)

2.6 Theoretical Implications on AI Innovation

Artificial Intelligence is an event that catalyzes a paradigm change in the ontological, epistemological, and institutional suppositions that form the basis of innovation theory. Its appearance requires the re-consideration of the nature of the knowledge production, regulation and dispersion, and valorization and hence the metamorphosis of the Triple Helix into both an abstract of collaboration in innovation and an operational design of systemic intelligence generation. The innovation of AI is not linear in its sequencing phases of previous industrial periods, but rather recursive in its system evolution, with outputs continuously having retrospective influences as new input, forming endless learning cycles within research organisations, industrial systems, and policies. A migration of the innovation authority across institutional areas is one of the most salient implications. Universities become less passive repositories of theoretical expertise and instead turn into entrepreneurial infrastructures of intelligence, which are able to shape markets, design regulatory logics, and to steer ethical discourse processes. Industries become cognitive governance actors with research agendas of their own, with workforce epistemologies, and they even engage in normative decisions concerning the directional orientation of technology. Governments, in their turn, shift the role of regulation to an orchestrator of innovations and introduce the formation of AI capability into the national identity, strategic competitiveness, and security doctrine. The Triple Helix therefore becomes a process involving the sharing of authority and not a hierarchical delegation of such authority.(Hoareau, 2025)

The theoretical implication is in regard to the reinvention of competitiveness theory. With AI economies, competitiveness is not about manufacturing capacity, possession of resources, or capital accumulation. In its place, it relies on epistemic density, institutional flexibility, learning speed, regulatory complexity and systemic capability building. Knowledge is not a by-product, governance is a determinant of value capture; and technological maturity is co-evolutionary between institutions, rather than simply existing as individual technological artefacts. The innovation of AIs, thus, entails a country building what can be called cognitive sovereignty, the capacity to create, control, scale and integrate intelligences technologies.A implication is that of convergence of ethical-governance. AI slips the scientific research, ethical philosophy, law, and organizational responsibility. The questions, which were historically considered to lie in the fringes of innovation such as bias, fairness, transparency, autonomy, surveillance, labour substitution take centre stage architecturally. This compels the innovation theory to broaden the idea of optimization of the economy to that of normative stewardship where value creation cannot be disconnected of responsibility systems, human rights and socio-technical resilience. Instead of becoming an external constraint of AI systems and institutions, governance is a design criterion endogenous to AI systems. The AI instigates a reflexive epistemology, in which institutions should learn not just what the machine tells them but also what the effect of their actions of governance is. The factors of regulation on innovation paths, innovation on social behaviour, social feedback processes on research agenda, and machine learning models on institutional blind spots are presented. This recursive entrapment makes innovation a self-monitoring and self-correcting ecosystem, which is aligned to the theory of cybernetic systems and organizational learning paradigms. The AI forces theoretical acknowledgment of the Triple Helix as a kind of quasi-living system, a dynamic organism, metabolizing knowledge, reorganizing institutional roles, and restructuring the system of identity according to environmental pressures. Innovation therefore becomes a biological like process of adaptation, mutation and renewal. Universities, industries and governments co-evolve using coevolutionary feedback architectures, and interactions among them create emergent system level intelligence that would not be possible to engineer alone.(Bozhikin et al., 2024)

3. LITERATURE REVIEW

The changing literature on AI innovation ecosystems illustrates a major theoretical and empirical paradigm shift in the ways of knowledge production, transfer, and institutionalization in the modern digital economies. The initial research in the field of industrial innovation was focusing on linear approaches of technology development whereby universities produced scientific knowledge, industrial applied it in the market, and the government stepped in afterwards by regulation and stabilization of policies. Nevertheless, current studies have found out that AI is fundamentally a disruptive phenomenon that necessitates recursive, co-evolutionary learning structures in which knowledge, governance, and commercialization systems engage with one another and are mutually dependent. One of the key threads of the literature emphasizes the ideas of the importance of the university-industry cooperation as the driver of the maturation of AI capabilities. The sources of epistemic capital in universities include the foundational algorithmic research, theoretical concepts and pipelines of talent, whereas the sources of empirical contexts of problems, computer hardware and translational routes are found in the industries. Research shows that this kind of collaboration can not only quicken innovation diffusion, but also improve responsible AI development through the introduction of ethical control, evaluation metrics, and deploying feedback loops in the initial phases of research translation. Simultaneous studies focus on the mediating aspect of the state as a structural facilitator and a guide to governance. According to the literature, institutional preparedness can be influenced by government intervention, which the state should fund sovereign research centres, providing access to compute based on public infrastructure, and creating regulatory sandboxes to empirically test algorithmic safety. Governments also play a growing role as meta-institutional stewards, setting the stage, SaFA in establishing standards for interoperability, ethical governance, data sovereignty and/or AI exports. It is theorized that these forms of governance are necessary to reduce systemic risk and bring outputs of innovation in line with societal preferences.(Balsalobre-Lorente et al., 2024)

There is also a consistent finding in the literature, that AI bases in regions, e.g. Silicon Valley, Shenzhen, Bengaluru, are developing in locations of high Triple Helix fit. Scientists single out typical structure conditions upon which the ecosystems are based:

- o intensive college research capability;
- o industrial culture of entrepreneurs;
- o strategic government programmes; and
- o long-term capital commitments.

These clusters are the example of how institutional proximity, learning spill overs and networked structures of trust contribute towards accelerated innovation cycles in AI.

The modern literature leaves the description of an institution to the conceptualization of the phenomenon of institutional hybridization. Colleges are increasingly building incubators, corporate innovation laboratories, technology transfer offices, and science parks. In turn, industries confirm and recompense through sponsorship of research chairs, co-sponsorship of PhD programmes, and placement of engineers in academic laboratories. Governments create sovereign cloud platforms, ministries of digital economy and innovation sandboxes to manage high-risk experimental technologies. It is hypothesized that such hybridization is a form of boundary-blurring, which reallocates responsibility of innovation among actors, and creates novel structural identities: entrepreneurial universities, learning corporations, and orchestrating governments. The literature also describes this evolution through open innovation models with the emergence of AI testbeds, shared laboratories, joint ventures, inter-sectoral consortia, as well as cross-domain research alliances as dominant operating architectures. They are models of moving away institutional silos of proprietorship to collaborative system of intelligence where value is created with ease of mobility of knowledge, interoperability and development of solutions together.(Miah et al., 2025)

A second prevalent research theme is the frameworks of AI competitiveness at the national level. According to scholars, the national leadership paths become more and more dependent on massive state investments in research infrastructure, talent formation, scale of industries, and ethical regulation. The literature recognises AI as a strategic geopolitical asset, which believes that innovation is associated with digital sovereignty, labour market transformation, and security constructions. According to new publications, it is argued that those nations which have triple helix maturity are characterized by greater innovation intensity, reduced technology-to-market time, and stronger governance ecosystems. The literature portends a paradigmatic change namely that of linear, transactional relationships of innovation to complex, recursive and hybrid system of knowledge co-production. AI does not represent a technological artefact, it transforms into a knowledge-structuring power, changing the institutional design, industrial logic, and statecraft. The notion of convergence between the scholarly domains places the Triple Helix framework as a lens of analysis and operational framework of the innovation economies based on AI.(Banad et al., 2025)

4. CASE STUDY: TRIPLE HELIX COLLABORATION AI INNOVATION

As it is reflected in this case study, the formation of AI capability becomes manifested in a Triple Helix-staged innovation ecosystem, showing the interdependencies among academic studies, industrial implementation pathways, and state-based governance. The national hypothetical context represents AI as a non-technological product but an outcome of an institutional co-production, in which the processes of knowledge creation, regulatory organization, infrastructural provisioning, and commercialization co-evolve.(Liao et al., 2024)

4.1 Case Context

The center of the ecosystem is a university-based AI research facility, which has high-tech labs in machine intelligence, natural language computation, cyber-physical modelling and predictive analytics. This scholarly setting brings forth algorithmic novelty, experimental architecture as well as highly skilled employees. With this academic epicentre, industrial actors play the role of capability amplifier in terms of offering cloud computing environments, high-volume databases, deployment testbeds, cybersecurity, and access to technology scaling in the market. As a supplement to these two helices, the government plays the role of a system architect, passing a national AI mission, mobilizing fiscal policy to accelerate R&D, develops cybersecurity policies, talent migration programs, and sets export-control norms to strategic AI uses. The mechanism of interaction between the helix and other keratin molecules is elucidated by three mechanisms: Van der Wals forces, cationic interactions, and hydrogen bonding . The mechanism of interaction between the helix and other molecules of keratin is explained by three mechanisms: Van der Wals forces, cationic interaction, and hydrogen bonding.(Lu et al., 2026)

4.1.1 Knowledge Generation

In the university sector, knowledge creation plays the role of epistemic driver of Triple Helix innovation where the scientific inquiry is converted into codified intelligence structures. Scholars interact in the problem decomposition of cognitive problems, development of base learning models, computational structures and theoretical advances in machine learning, symbolic reasoning and socio-technical modelling. The production of the knowledge is not limited to the algorithmic development; however, it is aimed at building ontology, data epistemology, the interpretability theory, and human-AI co-learning paradigm, which places the university in the role of the producer of deep conceptual infrastructure. Capability incubation systems are doctoral programmes, post-doctoral fellowships, or interdisciplinary research clusters, in which tacit knowledge, research field and sectoral literacy are developed. These structures do not just produce publications, models and prototypes but rather cognitive capital represented by highly trained human.(Golec et al., 2025)

4.1.2 Industrial Translation

Industrial translation is the metabolism of the AI innovation system at work where abstract academic knowledge is alchemized into economically useful, scalable and embedded artefacts in the society. In this circle, companies are adaptive cognitive structures that absorb the intellectual property generated in universities and repackages it into market-based technologies, production systems and service platforms. This translation process includes ontological transformation - algorithms mature into enterprise grade solutions, and interact with the real world, in terms of latency, safety certification, heterogeneity of supply chains and human usability. The industries take responsibility of maturation pathways of technologies in the form of iterative engineering, cloud deployment infrastructure, distributed inference pipelines, and cyber-physical systems integration. R&D units in corporations are interpreted brokers where academic research is broken down into design structures, technical standards, and workflows that can be made. Data pipelines provided by industry environments - healthcare records, financial transactions, edge sensor telemetry - these are holistic contextual learning substrates that hone down academic learning models to their applicability, robustness, and resilience in unfavourable (operational) conditions. Industrial translation is not technical conversion but it is institutional re-encoding. Firms internalisation of research is through have the features of, are designed as, namely, architectures of, are individual schemes of, are made up of and include “clouds of” stable, interactive corporate AI and individual identity infrastructures which are made up of, by, and facilitate “arches” of interacting methodologies, procedures, and process technologies in the form of, for example, “existing academies” “DIE companies” “what is an academy” and “academic” and “rainbow educational companies” which are further interactively managed and defined by, as part of multifaceted and multiple “arrays and scales”, Providing joint arrangements for patents, venture investment arms, and Artificial intelligence accelerator platforms which support start-ups that are based on university discoveries.(Mamès et al., 2025)

These conduits have the effect of making industry a co-producer of knowledge, as opposed to a passive consumer of it. It takes over academic epistemics and implants them into value chains, supply networks, and design cultures. The result of translation is reflected in production automation, predictive decision systems, adaptive manufacturing intelligence, platform economies and new business models and extending the national innovation frontier as well as reconfiguring labour systems, customer experience modalities and sectoral competitiveness.

Therefore, industrial translation is the dynamic component of the Triple Helix that converts a dormant academic ability into an institutional capacity, distributed utility and socio-economic change within industries such as healthcare, transportation, finance, intelligent infrastructure, and hi-tech manufacturing. It acts as the channel in which knowledge is transformed into praxis, technology is introduced into the society by the absorptive, reformulative and deployment capabilities of industry.(Almeida & Deutsch, 2025)

4.1.3 Governance and Alignment

The normative and structural intelligence layer of the Triple Helix system is called governance and alignment, as in this case, the state plays a meta-coordination role, which determines the speed, orientation, and moral permissibility of AI innovation. Government agencies act as the policy-makers and ecosystem stabilizers, which are in charge of building the institutional scaffold in which scientific competence is converted into socio-economic value. In this capacity, the state sets standards of technical integrity and threshold requirements for risk, auditability requirements and regulatory grammars to ensure the diffusion of AI works in line with national strategic priorities and collective welfare imperatives.(X. Zhang & Tan, 2025)

This level of governance is forward-looking, not responsive: regulators use innovation guidance tools like fiscal stimulus mechanisms, sovereign funding pools, models of public procurement, and human capital development models, and these incentivize responsible experimentation and market expansion. Simultaneously, governments design sovereign data governance systems, such as data localization systems, federated trust systems, identity authentication systems, and digital public goods, and thus epistemic sovereignty is institutionalized in the national system of innovation. The most important aspect of this role is risk mediation, where state agencies develop regulatory sandboxes, algorithmic audit boards, AI ethics commissions and adaptive oversight laboratories that will de-risk innovation without limiting discovery dynamics. These systems allow high-stakes technologies, including autonomous systems, health intelligence platforms, or financial AI, to develop as they experience monitored exposure, which is what allows them to be corrected and learn in an institutional way. Governance also involves harmonizing capabilities, harmonizing different institutional tempos and incentive systems in academia, industry and within civil society. This includes skills development ecosystem, STE(A)M workforce pipelines and competency frameworks that transform labour markets to reflect emergent techno economic realities. Ultimately, governance and alignment turn the state from the compliance enforcer to the strategic innovation orchestrator to the strategic sourcer of equilibriums between the system level risk, the level 2 opportunity and equally the level 3 sovereignty with a societal impact. This reduces government to not only a regulating force in the AI age, but also a thinking force that influences the development, morality and identity of national intelligence systems.(Ali et al., 2025)

4.2 Helix Synergy Outcomes

University, industry, and government interplay create new system processes that are not achieved by a uni-institutional one. The Triple Helix does not simply facilitate collaboration, this yield innovation externalities, deepening capabilities trajectories, and national competitiveness paths that multiply over time. Among the most prominent changes, one can distinguish the development of startup ecosystems that have an AI source. These organizations are offshoots of the scholarly epistemic repositories but are hastened by the repositories of industrial incubation like provisioning venture capital, access to cloud infrastructure, industrial mentorship, and go-to-market contingents. As opposed to being left behind in the realm of academic publications, algorithmic innovations are shifted into scalable companies. This process is institutionalized within the universities in the form of the translational research centres and intellectual property groups and technological transfer offices and the industry is available to offer acceleration resources, sharing risks models, and market signaling mechanisms. This AI startup generation helps to diversify the economy of a country, promote the culture of entrepreneurship, and renew industrial base knowledge. The second major consequence is the localization of the AI technological capability, which promotes the digital sovereignty and strategic autonomy. By generating knowledge and skills collaboratively and sharing such skills, countries can become less dependent on external AI systems, purchased computing systems, or externally developed government technologies. Local companies also start to create local AI, natural language models that are trained on local linguistics, domain-specific analytics engines, manufacturing edge intelligence, or healthcare diagnostics that are trained on local data. It produces the resilience against geopolitical disruption, technological dependency and intellectual property leakage, and allows transitioning to technology consumption to technology authorship.(Moldashev et al., 2025)

The harmonized regulatory and governance environment is also created through the triadic interaction. The universities add the empirical knowledge to the process of policy-making; the industry provides understanding of practical deployment; and government incorporates these two views into adapting rules. The resultant governance design incorporates safety, ethics, equity, risk reduction, and competitiveness throughout the whole AI innovation life cycle instead of seeing regulation as an after-thought. The standards of algorithmic auditability, cybersecurity compliance, responsible data processing, and the ethics-based risk scoring become institutional artefacts that are co-constructed to provide predictability, legitimacy, and stability to make investments. An ultimate, structurally relevant result is manifested in the workforce transformation and human capital upgrading. Industry back-end supported skill pathways, re-curriculum in academia and government-sponsored up-skilling programs create a multi-tiered skill pyramid of AI talent - from research scientists, to system architects, to data engineers, regulatory practitioners and skill-set of applied AI practitioners. Institutionalizing lifelong learning in the ecosystem takes place in the form of micro-credentials, degree-industry hybrid courses, apprenticeship schemes, and AI competency models. This unceasing ability enhancement compensates the obsolescence of skills, inclusive workforce, and speed up national preparation to algorithmic economies. A combination of these results demonstrates that Triple Helix synergy generates structural change as opposed to episodic breakthroughs. The AI innovation is a self-perpetuating ability system, with the production of knowledge, the growth of commercialization, stabilization of governance, and human creation developing as interconnected and mutually reinforcing systems. The ecosystem then transforms into an innovation cluster but turns into a national intelligence infrastructure, which contributes to economic renewal, institutional modernization, and a mature policy.(Chowdhury et al., 2025)

5. AI INNOVATION VIA TRIPLE HELIX COOPERATION

As it is reflected in this case study, the formation of AI capability becomes manifested in a Triple Helix-staged innovation ecosystem, showing the interdependencies among academic studies, industrial implementation pathways, and state-based governance. The hypothetical national context describes AI not as a stand-off technological product but as an institutional side effect, whose processes of knowledge creation, regulatory structure, infrastructural supplying, and commercialization change in tandem.(Nicoletti & Appolloni, 2025)

5.1 Case Context

The ecosystem has a university-based AI research complex, which consists of advanced machine intelligence, natural language computation, cyber-physical modelling, and predictive analytics laboratories. This scholarly setting brings forth algorithmic novelty, experimental architecture as well as highly skilled employees. With this academic epicentre, industrial actors play the role of capability amplifier in terms of offering cloud computing environments, high-volume databases, deployment testbeds, cybersecurity, and access to technology scaling in the market. As a supplement to these two helices, the government plays the role of a system architect, passing a national AI mission, mobilizing fiscal policy to accelerate R&D,

develops cybersecurity policies, talent migration programs, and sets export-control norms to strategic AI uses.(Nicoletti & Appolloni, 2025)

The mechanism of interaction between the helix and other keratin molecules is elucidated by three mechanisms: Van der Wals forces, cationic interactions, and hydrogen bonding.The mechanism of interaction between the helix and other molecules of keratin is explained by three mechanisms: Van der Wals forces, cationic interaction, and hydrogen bonding.(Nicoletti & Appolloni, 2025)

5.2 Knowledge Generation

In the university sector, knowledge creation plays the role of epistemic driver of Triple Helix innovation where the scientific inquiry is converted into codified intelligence structures. Scholars interact in the problem decomposition of cognitive problems, development of base learning models, computational structures and theoretical advances in machine learning, symbolic reasoning and socio-technical modelling. The production of the knowledge is not limited to the algorithmic development, however, it is aimed at building ontology, data epistemology, the interpretability theory, and human-AI co-learning paradigm, which places the university in the role of the producer of deep conceptual infrastructure. Capability incubation systems are doctoral programmes, post-doctoral fellowships, or interdisciplinary research clusters, in which tacit knowledge, research field and sectoral literacy are developed. These structures do not just produce publications, models and prototypes but rather cognitive capital represented by highly trained human.(L. Zhang et al., 2024)

5.3 Industrial Translation

Industrial translation is the operation metabolism of the AI innovation system whereby abstract academic information is transformed into economically useful, scalable, and social integrated artefacts. In this circle, companies are adaptive cognitive structures that absorb the intellectual property generated in universities and repackages it into market-based technologies, production systems and service platforms. This translation process includes ontological transformation - algorithms mature into enterprise grade solutions, and interact with the real world, in terms of latency, safety certification, heterogeneity of supply chains and human usability. The industries take responsibility of maturation pathways of technologies in the form of iterative engineering, cloud deployment infrastructure, distributed inference pipelines, and cyber-physical systems integration. Corporate R&D departments act as interpretive brokering institutions, translating academic knowledge into design/technical specifications/workflows, which can be implemented. Industry environments, such as healthcare records, financial transactions, edge-sensor telemetry, are data pipes that can be used as contextual learning substrates, which can be refined into academic models to be more applicable, resilient and robust to non-ideal conditions of operation.

It is not a simple technical conversion, industrial translation entails institutional re-encoding. Firms internalisation of research is through:

- company AI universities and learning systems,
- designed graduate programmes jointly

Research Topic Seminar paper 19 March 2012 - The research papers offered at i-ITI's joint research seminar in Stirling on 19 March, 'IPR Challenges in Practice' - many of them are being prepared at the i-ITI iConferences people have received they are: joint patenting arrangements,

- venture investment arms, and
- Artificial intelligence accelerator platforms which support start-ups that are based on university discoveries.

These conduits also enable industry to be a co-producer of knowledge, but not a passive consumer. It internalizes the world of scholastic epistemics, and transplant them into value systems, supply systems, and design cultures(Lim, 2026). The result of translation is reflected in production automation, predictive decision systems, adaptive manufacturing intelligence, platform economies and new business models and extending the national innovation frontier as well as reconfiguring labour systems, customer experience modalities and sectoral competitiveness. Industrial translation so is the kinetic stage of the Triple Helix, where latent academic intelligence is absorbed into institutional capacity, distributed utility and socio-economic change both within individual sectors (healthcare, transportation, finance, smart infrastructure and advanced manufacturing) and system-wide (sectoral). It acts as the channel in which knowledge is transformed into praxis, technology is introduced into the society by the absorptive, reformulative and deployment capabilities of industry.(Lubaba et al., 2025)

5.4 Governance and Alignment

Governance and alignment is the normative and structural intelligibility of the Triple Helix system that the state will play the role of a meta-coordinator, which influences the pace, the directionality, and how ethically acceptable AI innovation can be. Government agencies act as the policy-makers and ecosystem stabilizers, which are in charge of building the institutional scaffold in which scientific competence is converted into socio-economic value. Within this role, the state develops the standards of technical integrity, risk levels, audit requirements and regulatory grammars, which enable the AI diffusion to be in accordance with the national strategic priorities and collective welfare imperative(X. Huang & Zhou, 2025). This level of governance is forward-looking, not responsive: regulators use innovation guidance tools like fiscal stimulus mechanisms, sovereign funding pools, models of public procurement, and human capital development models, and these incentivize responsible experimentation and market expansion. Meanwhile, governments design sovereign data governance systems, such as data localization systems, federated trust systems, identity authentication systems, and digital public goods, and thus entrench epistemic sovereignty into the national system of innovation.(Liao et al., 2024)

The most important aspect of this role is risk mediation, where state agencies develop regulatory sandboxes, algorithmic audit boards, AI ethics commissions and adaptive oversight laboratories that will de-risk innovation without limiting discovery dynamics. These can be used to allow high-stakes technologies (i.e., autonomous systems or health intelligence platforms or financial AI) to innovate in a monitored exposure process, which enables the process of corrections and institutional learning. The Governance also involves harmonizing capabilities, harmonizing different institutional tempos and incentive systems in academia, industry and within civil society. This involves the skills development ecosystems and STEM-AI workforce pipelines, as well as competency frameworks that can re-organise the labour markets around the new techno-economic realities. The governance and alignment make the state a compliance enforcer instead of a strategic innovator, a curator of system wide balance among risk opportunity, sovereignty, and impact to the society. This reduces government to not only a regulating force in the AI age, but also a thinking force that influences the development, morality and identity of national intelligence systems.(Liao et al., 2024)

5.5 Expanded -Helix Synergy Outcomes.

University, industry, and government interplay create new system processes that are not achieved by a uni-institutional one. The Triple Helix is not simply a facilitator of collaboration, but it generates innovations externalities, strengthening capability, and national competitiveness paths, which accumulate over time. Creation of startup ecosystems of AI origin is one of the most salient outcomes. These organizations are offshoots of the scholarly epistemic repositories but are hastened by the repositories of industrial incubation like provisioning venture capital, access to cloud infrastructure, industrial mentorship, and go-to-market contingents. As opposed to being left behind in the realm of academic publications, algorithmic innovations are shifted into scalable companies(Tutak & Brodny, 2025). This process is institutionalized within the universities in the form of the translational research centres and intellectual property groups and technological transfer offices and the industry is available to offer acceleration resources, sharing risks models, and market signaling mechanisms. This AI startup generation helps to diversify the economy of a country, promote the culture of entrepreneurship, and renew industrial base knowledge.(Miah et al., 2025)

The second major consequence is the localization of the AI technological capability, which promotes the digital sovereignty and strategic autonomy. By generating knowledge and skills collaboratively and sharing such skills, countries can become less dependent on external AI systems, purchased computing systems, or externally developed government technologies. Local companies also start to create local AI, natural language models that are trained on local linguistics, domain-specific analytics engines, manufacturing edge intelligence, or healthcare diagnostics that are trained on local data. It produces the resilience against geopolitical disruption, technological dependency and intellectual property leakage, and allows transitioning to technology consumption to technology authorship. The harmonized regulatory and governance environment is also created through the triadic interaction.(Hoareau, 2025) The universities add the empirical knowledge to the process of policy-making; the industry provides understanding of practical deployment; and government incorporates these two views into adapting rules. The resultant governance design incorporates safety, ethics, equity, risk reduction, and competitiveness throughout the whole AI innovation life cycle instead of seeing regulation as an after-thought. The standards of algorithmic auditability, cybersecurity compliance, responsible data processing, and the ethics-based risk scoring become institutional artefacts that are co-constructed to provide predictability, legitimacy, and stability to make investments.(Wirz et al., 2025)

An ultimate, structurally relevant result is manifested in the workforce transformation and human capital upgrading. The multi-tiered AI talent pyramid, comprised of research scientists, system architects, data engineers, regulatory specialists and others involved in AI system development, is created through industry-sponsored skill paths, academic re-curriculum and government-funded up-skilling schemes. The ecosystem will institutionalize the lifelong learning by use of micro-credentials, degree-industry hybrid programs, apprenticeship models, and AI competency frameworks. This unceasing ability enhancement compensates the obsolescence of skills, inclusive workforce, and speed up national preparation to algorithmic economies(Wu et al., 2025). A combination of these results demonstrates that Triple Helix synergy generates structural change as opposed to episodic breakthroughs. The AI innovation is a self-perpetuating ability system, with the production of knowledge, the growth of commercialization, stabilization of governance, and human creation developing as interconnected and mutually reinforcing systems. The ecosystem then transforms into an innovation cluster but turns into a national intelligence infrastructure, which contributes to economic renewal, institutional modernization, and a mature policy. (J. Huang et al., 2025)

6. RESEARCH GAPS & LIMITATIONS

Although the advantages of the Triple Helix model in facilitating the formation of AI capability have been demonstrated, there are still large gaps in the structure, epistemic, and operational space that occur both in academic discussion and practice. These weaknesses indicate institutional interaction weaknesses, governance coherence weaknesses, and socio-technical evolution weakness, and suggests that existing models are not yet complete, not well integrated, and not theorized to meet the needs of rapidly scaling AI ecosystems. The most notable constraint has to do with disjointed coordination processes. As universities, industries and governments continue to participate more in the fields of innovation together, their interfaces tend to be loosely coupled and transaction oriented, instead of being deeply integrated or institutionally aligned. Intellectual property, information stewardship and talent mobility as well as risk responsibility governance structures do not often have an unified oversight, which generates operational frictions and non-optimal knowledge uptakes.(Matovu et al., 2025)

The second limitation is the disparity in the AI literacy and absorptive capacity within the three helices. Universities can comprehend the complexity of algorithms without market translation sensibility; industries can be practical in deployment but without the ethical governance insightfulness, governments can have power but without a depth of domain knowledge to implement adaptive regulation. This lack of epistemic maturity leads to mismatches of capabilities and slows the momentum of collaboration and the quality of innovation. The other structural shortfall is that of policy cycle lag in comparison to technological acceleration. The pace of development of AI technologies is exponential, and the structures of governmental decisions are tied to bureaucratic timeframes. Consequently, regulatory obsolescence, lack of oversight, and reactive as opposed to anticipatory governance are created, placing countries at systemic risks of safety, labour disruption, bias or security weakness. Also, academia experiences poor commercialization cultures and translational infrastructures especially in the public universities. Imposing incentive systems are geared towards publication and not patenting, impact on society and venture development. Therefore, the knowledge is confined in the silos of academia which slows down technology diffusion, limits entrepreneurial channels, and makes ecosystems less agile.

This is compounded by the ethical, epistemic, and sovereignty dilemmas. With the rise of AI as cognitive agency in the decision system, the issues of algorithmic legitimacy, surveillance risk, attribution of accountability and moral embeddedness become more disputable. (Guevara et al., 2025)Institutional systems of dealing with such tensions are, however, young, fragmented or normatively underdeveloped. There is more than just the operation blind spots, but scholarly literature also has substantive blind spots. Few enquiries into the long-term governance of AI learning feedback loops such as how institutions rectify, re-train or socially recalibrate AI systems across decades have been made.(Tutak & Brodny, 2025) On the same note, the topics of cross-border sovereignty in knowledge ownership, digital trade, and intellectual capital mobility, and AI supremacy will not be explored theoretically even though they have geopolitical relevance.

6.1 AI Learning Feedback Loop Governance Over the Long-Term

The major aspect of AI policy and innovation theory that is a critical frontier is the long-term governance of the feedback loops of algorithmic learning, which are not yet adequately conceptualized in mainstream scholarship. Compared to fixed technologies, AI is autopoietic, i.e., its performance, patterns of decisions, and risk groups are transformed in the course of interaction with data, environments and users. This makes outdated the traditional and episodic forms of regulation. Sustained governance needs to be cybernetic, recursive and anticipatory, it needs to entrench ongoing sensing structures, real-time auditing dynamics, behavioural drift, and post-implementation retraining commits. Institutional memory formation, i.e. the mechanisms by which the society learns about AI failures, biases and emergent harms will also be necessary in governance, embedding the lessons in redesign requirements, regulatory norms and the development of human capacities. Lack of such memory results in persistent recidivism and hidden system frailty. Moreover, the AI feedback loops generate path dependency, i.e. initial mistakes can multiply exponentially into society. Therefore, governance needs to build in temporal intelligence, i.e., the ability to provide retrospective correction, forward simulation, decommissioning rules, and the ethical sunsetting of obsolete models. In a sense, long term AI regulation will become a meta-regulatory adaptive system that is able to control the evolution of AI over decades, react to emergent risks and institutionalize the accountability in the evolving technological ontologies.(Brodny & Tutak, 2025)

6.2 Knowledge Production Cross-Border Sovereignty Conflicts

The AI is turning knowledge into a weapon of a geopolitical tool, increasing disagreements about data possession, calculating resources, intellectual property, talent flows, and digital trade regimes. The generation of knowledge is an arena of power struggle with countries aiming to gain strategic power via dominion over training datasets, chip fabrication ecosystems, cloud infrastructure, and algorithmic capabilities. This creates an effect of territorialization of cognition as cognitive capital is a space that is fought over just like natural resources or territory. The cross-border tensions can be observed in the export restrictions on semiconductor technologies, access to AI models, competing AI standards, research nationalism. Sovereignty issues are also escalating since countries are building sovereign clouds, national AI missions and data localization laws that split global innovation flows as they seek to secure control over AI socio-economic externalities.(Lim, 2026)

The theoretical implication is that knowledge itself emerges as an object of geo-political power projection, including AI research diplomacy, academic espionage, AI sanctions, and the formation of techno-blocs is an indicator of the development of a post-Westphalian order of knowledge, in which cognitive infrastructure, not land or arms, is the main commodity of national success. The only way forward of governance in the future is by being innovative in diplomacy of innovations, federal standards, ethical treaty frameworks, and distributed data sovereignty paradigms that can reconcile the security interests with the international scientific advancement. (Uppuluri & Yang, 2025)

6.3 Human Work Identity Psychosocial Effects of AI

Psychosocial implications of AI adoption are one of the least theoretically studied but most radically changing aspects of the technology development. AI does not simply automate work, it restructures the ontology of work breaking the meaning systems, identity structures, and cognitive agency. The humans are now found more in in-between positions as co-supervisors with the algorithmic cognition, or as operators of the intelligent assistants, or as workers who have been rendered obsolete and are not employed in productive activities.(Tutak & Brodny, 2025) The result of this is identity erosion phenomena, such as devaluation of tacit expertise, loss of vocational pride, uncertainty of purpose and reliance on machine-mediated decision making. At the same time, new thinking pressures arise, including algorithmic over-dependence, decision paralysis, anxiety about surveillance, deskilling, and hyper-intensification of labour, as labourers oversee, but not perform jobs. On the societal level, AI transforms the concept of dignity, competence, social value, and human sovereignty. Effective adaptation, consequently, requires psych technical reinvention, i.e., reconstructing the meaning of work, developing meta-cognitive abilities, building psychosocial safety nets, and the development of human-focused AI systems that would maintain identity continuity.(Matovu et al., 2025)

6. FUTURE DIRECTIONS

History of evolution of Triple Helix configurations of AI innovation suggests that we are about to move to multi-layered socio-technical assemblages, with value being created relative to more encompassing institutional ecologies, and not between domains. It is projected that the future governance systems will reorganize into Quadruple or Quintuple Helix forms in which the civil society, knowledge systems of citizens and the ecological custodians as constitutive forces of innovation are involved. These long helices are a manifestation of the understanding that AI legitimacy, ethics as well as sustainability cannot be coded in elite technocratic space, but require dialogics within the society, environmental responsibility and participation. Regulatory sandboxes Artificial intelligence regulatory sandboxes will be a systemic component of next-generation AI ecosystems as experimentations in AI accountability, AI-safety verification, and AI-policy prototyping will become systemic, rather than hoc. Simultaneously, the countries will consolidate independent cloud computing environments and federated computing platforms, which will enable safe data, digital independence and economic stability against geopolitical technological dependencies. These types of future talent production will probably manifest themselves in the form of joint AI academies, whose property belongs to the industry-academia, and are structured on the basis of the state regulations. Such academies will be cyber-physical pedagogical to possess a co-learning, co-design, co-evolution of learners, researchers, algorithms and robotic systems and asymmetry of expertise between theory and practice in the industry. Geographically, geographies of innovation will be obliterated, becoming infrastructures of distributed cognition, linking AI centres, cyber-protected knowledge networks, multi-node knowledge clusters and transnational digital knowledge zones, where research, policy and market translation become borderless.(Guevara et al., 2025)

This change in the doctrinal understanding of ethics-as-infrastructure will be a radical change in which the development of AI is no longer aligned with the use of ethical rationale but is architecturally included in system design, auditability, data ontologies, and feedback controllers. The governance-by-design will replace governance-after-deployment and produce self-regulating AI ecosystems capable of normative and behavioural adaptation. There will also be greater hybridization of institutional morphology. A trend that reflects an epistemic reorganisation is the emergence of corporate labs run by universities and AI manufacturing parks subsidised by states and academic supercomputing clusters subsidised by industry which is jointly present as an institutional artefact. These mixed-breed institutions coexist and perform as engines of research, regulative facades, learning, and commercialization booster simultaneously and disrupt the jurisdictional silos. Distributed intelligence will be more reflexive, more permeable and polycentric and changing the very definition of collaboration as such, the way to go, the future AI ecosystems will be. The Triple Helix is no longer a delimited model but a mobile meta-infrastructure, which becomes a post-Helix innovation architecture where human agency, artificial cognition and institutional capability are all created as a integrated socio-technical system.(Ahmad et al., 2025)

6.1 Distributed Innovation Networks Intercity and Intercountry Across The Physical Campus Borders

The distributed innovation networks will characterise the further shape of AI-enhanced knowledge ecosystems where the geographic position of the classical university campuses, industrial estates and national research parks will no longer be a condition. These networks are post-territorial infrastructure of learning, experimentation and commercialization, through which learning, experimentation and commercialization is practiced through cyber-physical networks, federated computing and transnational epistemics. Cities will no longer be closed systems of innovation, but they will be incorporated in a multi-node cognitive constellation, whose dynamics are being coordinated in high bandwidth cloud networks, sovereign data layers, and interoperable policy frameworks.(Brodny & Tutak, 2025)

The model redesigns the geography of innovation as centripetal as centrifugal circulation based on which the expertise, datasets, algorithmic models, and institutional capabilities are constantly re-distributed across urban-regional and cross-border spaces. Smart cities become routers of knowledge, new knowledge is relayed to metropolitan centres of AI, and industrial clusters in the area, and computational centres of higher education.(Wirz et al., 2025) Similarly, nation states transform into AI federations and organize shared standards, authentication schemes, regulatory basis, and scale supercomputer pools that permit to enable easy partnerships in research and scale innovation. This diffused government also alters epistemic government. Instead of the organizational walls being introduced around them, digital collaboration structures, such as blockchain-secured IP exchanges, interoperable data lakes, federated learning structures, and diplomatic AI corridors across national capabilities mediate innovation. The space proximity is substituted with the cognitive proximity as innovation integration is being maintained not through space proximity but through shared regulations, similar motivations and information stream with an algorithmic structure. In addition, the distributed innovation networks accelerate the ability sovereignty through which smaller cities and emerging economies can be linked to global value chains without the need to have the mega-infrastructures locally. They make high-performance computing, virtual laboratories, and experimentation platforms mediated via the cloud democratized to areas that have traditionally been marginalized by innovation. This gives rise to polycentric innovation governance where intellectual capital and technological agency are distributed network-based assets, rather than an elite-controlled asset or a city centre.(Tanveer et al., 2025)

7. CONCLUSION

Artificial Intelligence is a threshold technology a thought infrastructure that can restructure economic structures, social structures, epistemic structures, and planetary regimes. The sovereign digital agency. The nature of AI innovation is non-linear, recursive, and socio-technical, and requires the production of knowledge communities, in which the creation, implementation, control, and ethical bargaining of new technologies are distributed across universities, industries, and governments. The speed of AI makes it urgent to dramatically transform institutions. Higher education institutions need to move past their conventional role as closed knowledge factories and become entrepreneurial engines of epistemology, to encompass the logics of commercialization, translational innovation models, and responsive talent streams to dynamic technological paths. The industry needs to shift the participation in the market to ecosystem-defining cognitive infrastructures, internalising pedagogical roles, ethical custodianship and demands to be publicly innovative. Governments need to replace top-down rule making with adaptive innovation orchestration, mission directed capability systems, data sovereignty strata, and reflexive regulatory structures which are self-evolving rather than imposed. The AI, the Triple Helix is no longer a collaboration heuristic but is instead a survival architecture, the least governance substrate of which nations preserve autonomy, promote productivity, and develop human relevance when faced with pressure of algorithmic displacement. It is the institutional operating system in which societies establish computational sovereignty, talent sovereignty and knowledge sovereignty. AI makes people even more interdependent, i.e., there is no one field that has enough cognitive or infrastructural capital to plan, coordinate, or humanise intelligent systems by themselves. In this way, the Helix is a developing coordination schema to a constitutive model of statecraft, which determines the formation of national identities, innovation diplomacy, and socio-technical futures.(Miah et al., 2025)

Finally, the Triple Helix during the AI era signifies an ontological re-positioning of the institutional purpose in which academia is employed as a generator of capabilities, industry is re-positioned as a generator of knowledge and government is re-positioned as a distributor of intelligence. Its success will either make or break the humanity flourish or structural inequity, depending on its success. As AI is diffused to the decision-making, value creation, security structures, and human meaning systems, the Triple Helix framework facilitates adaptive co-evolution instead of competitive disintegration. It is thus no longer just a theoretical donation but a strategic requirement to the future of society and the next stage of planetary development a meta-institutional scaffolding according to which, however, humanity engineers the next stage of technological civilization.

REFERENCES

Ahmad, W., Khan, S., Mazhar, T., Shahzad, T., Jiang, W., & Hamam, H. (2025). Industry 4.0 for smart transport systems: Foundations and applications. *Telematics and Informatics Reports*, *20*, 100255. DOI: 10.1016/j.teler.2025.100255

Ali, Z. A., Hasan, R., Alsanad, A., Alhogail, A., & Gumaei, A. H. (2025). Multiple knowledge depiction of digital twin-driven circular economy: Concepts, integrated advanced technologies, triple bottom line of smart construction, and exploratory case studies. In *Journal of Engineering Research*. Elsevier B.V., DOI: 10.1016/j.jer.2025.08.018

Almeida, F., & Deutsch, N. (2025). Urban living labs as catalysts for innovation: Advancing urban ecosystems within the quintuple helix model. *Urban Governance*, *5*(2), 133–141. DOI: 10.1016/j.ugj.2025.05.005

Balsalobre-Lorente, D., Shah, S. A. R., & Huseynova, R. (2024). Do circular economy, public-private Partnership and carbon policy manage the environmental stress? Developed countries' situation under the Prism of COP27. *Heliyon*, *10*(13). Advance online publication. DOI: 10.1016/j.heliyon.2024.e33532

Banad, Y. M., Sharif, S. S., & Rezaei, Z. (2025). Artificial intelligence and machine learning for smart grids: from foundational paradigms to emerging technologies with digital twin and large language model-driven intelligence. In *Energy Conversion and Management: X* (Vol. 28). Elsevier Ltd., DOI: 10.1016/j.ecmx.2025.101329

Bozhikin, I., Macke, J., & Miri, D. (2024). Mapping creative territories with actors, partnerships, innovations, and regulatory mechanisms based on literature review. *Cleaner and Responsible Consumption*, *12*. Advance online publication. DOI: 10.1016/j.clrc.2024.100186

Brodny, J., & Tutak, M. (2025). Towards a sixfold helix model for green smart cities? A conceptual exploration of stakeholder collaboration, interaction mechanisms, and role allocation. *Journal of Open Innovation*, *11*(4). Advance online publication. DOI: 10.1016/j.joitmc.2025.100681

Chowdhury, P. P., Khan, M. M. A., Sayem, A., Asif, M. A. R., & Roy, A. (2025). Assessment of organizations' maturity towards circular economy practice in manufacturing industries: Evidence from a developing economy. *Cleaner Logistics and Supply Chain*, *17*, 100286. DOI: 10.1016/j.clscn.2025.100286

Golec, M., Hatay, E. S., Gill, S. S., & Buyya, R. (2025). Artificial Intelligence (AI): Foundations, trends and future directions. *Telematics and Informatics Reports*, *20*. Advance online publication. DOI: 10.1016/j.teler.2025.100265

Guevara, K. M., Martínez-Valenzuela, G., Sánchez-Vásquez, V., Guerrero-Ruiz, K., & Fiallos-Cárdenas, M. (2025). Trends and perspectives on bacterial nanocellulose: A comprehensive analysis from the three helixes of innovation. In *Materials Today Sustainability* (Vol. 30). Elsevier Ltd., DOI: 10.1016/j.mtsust.2025.101090

Hoareau, K. (2025). Knowledge, power and the blue economy: Breaking down barriers. *Marine Policy, 182*. Advance online publication. DOI: 10.1016/j.marpol.2025.106883

Huang, J., Xu, Y., Wang, Q., & Wang, Q. (Cheems), Liang, X., Wang, F., Zhang, Z., Wei, W., Zhang, B., Huang, L., Chang, J., Ma, L., Ma, T., Liang, Y., Zhang, J., Guo, J., Jiang, X., Fan, X., An, Z., … Fei, A. (2025). Foundation models and intelligent decision-making: Progress, challenges, and perspectives. In *Innovation* (Vol. 6, Issue 6). Cell Press. https://doi.org/DOI: 10.1016/j.xinn.2025.100948

Huang, X., & Zhou, Q. (2025). Knowledge management model in the integration of open innovation and circular economy driven by digital intelligence: A comparative multi-case study. *Journal of Innovation and Knowledge*, *10*(6). Advance online publication. DOI: 10.1016/j.jik.2025.100839

Liao, H. T., Pan, C. L., & Wu, Z. (2024). Digital transformation and innovation and business ecosystems: A bibliometric analysis for conceptual insights and collaborative practices for ecosystem innovation. *International Journal of Innovation Studies*, *8*(4), 406–431. DOI: 10.1016/j.ijis.2024.04.003

Lim, W. M. (2026). Theory and theory development: Guidelines for establishing theoretical gaps, foundations, contributions, and implications. *Journal of Business Research, 202*. Advance online publication. DOI: 10.1016/j.jbusres.2025.115745

Lu, Q., Zhao, D., Liu, Y., Zhang, H., Zhu, L., Xu, X., Shi, A., Tan, T., & Kazman, R. (2026). AgentArcEval: An architecture evaluation method for foundation model based agents. *Journal of Systems and Software*, *232*, 112656. DOI: 10.1016/j.jss.2025.112656

Lubaba, M., Hassan, S., Sultana, M., Morshed, S. M., & Bari, A. B. M. M. (2025). Assessment of the challenges to implementing green manufacturing in the food and beverage industry: An emerging economy perspective. *Waste Management Bulletin*, *3*(3). Advance online publication. DOI: 10.1016/j.wmb.2025.100225

Mamès, M., Donner, M., & de Vries, H. (2025). Partnerships for sustainable food and bioeconomy systems in Europe: Exploring the role of intermediaries. *Sustainable Futures : An Applied Journal of Technology, Environment and Society*, *10*. Advance online publication. DOI: 10.1016/j.sftr.2025.101361

Matovu, B., Mim, T. A., & Lutalo, B. (2025). Where and how can Africa and India leverage the blue economy opportunities of the Indian Ocean region as a driver for sustainable development and partnerships? In *Sustainable Futures* (Vol. 10). Elsevier Ltd., DOI: 10.1016/j.sftr.2025.101218

Miah, M. T., Aiupova, N., Erdei-Gally, S., & Fekete-Farkas, M. (2025). Digital entrepreneurship ecosystems: Then vs. now-a future perspectives. *Digital Business*, *5*(1). Advance online publication. DOI: 10.1016/j.digbus.2025.100110

Moldashev, K., Sahimbekov, B., & Kozhakhmet, S. (2025). The institutional logics of research commercialisation: Reform, misalignment, and hybridisation. *Social Sciences & Humanities Open*, *12*. Advance online publication. DOI: 10.1016/j.ssaho.2025.102000

Nicoletti, B., & Appolloni, A. (2025). The Impact of AI Foundation models on the future of digital engineering for logistics and supply Chain. *Digital Engineering*, *7*, 100058. DOI: 10.1016/j.dte.2025.100058

Tanveer, U., Hoang, T. G., Ishaq, S., & Khalid, R. U. (2025). Public-private partnerships as catalysts for digital transformation and circular economy: Insights from developing countries. *Technological Forecasting and Social Change*, *219*. Advance online publication. DOI: 10.1016/j.techfore.2025.124270

Tutak, M., & Brodny, J. (2025). Stakeholder collaboration and open innovation in smart cities: A Quattro Helix model for technological and social transformation. *Journal of Open Innovation*, *11*(3). Advance online publication. DOI: 10.1016/j.joitmc.2025.100594

Uppuluri, P. C., & Yang, C. W. (2025). The Emergence of Foundation Models in U.S. Radiology: A Narrative Review of Clinical Utility, Safety, and Evaluation. *Academic Radiology*. Advance online publication. DOI: 10.1016/j.acra.2025.10.063

Wirz, C. D., Demuth, J. L., Bostrom, A., Cains, M. G., Ebert-Uphoff, I., Gagne, D. J., Schumacher, A., McGovern, A., & Madlambayan, D. (2025). (Re)Conceptualizing trustworthy AI: A foundation for change. In *Artificial Intelligence* (Vol. 342). Elsevier B.V., DOI: 10.1016/j.artint.2025.104309

Wu, S., Shi, C., Leung, Y. F., Otake, Y., Konishi, C., Zhou, M., Tao, Y., Cao, Z., & Nakamura, T. (2025). Perspectives: LLM agents reshaping the foundation of geotechnical problem-solving. *Geodata and AI*, *4*, 100036. DOI: 10.1016/j.geoai.2025.100036

Yu, W., He, H., Song, S., Zhang, J., Dai, L., Zheng, L., & Letaief, K. B. (2025). AI and Deep Learning for Terahertz Ultra-Massive MIMO: From Model-Driven Approaches to Foundation Models. *Engineering*. Advance online publication. DOI: 10.1016/j.eng.2025.07.032

Zhang, L., Banihashemi, S., Zhu, L., Molavi, H., Odacioglu, E., & Shan, M. (2024). A scientometric analysis of knowledge transfer partnerships in digital transformation. In *Journal of Open Innovation: Technology, Market, and Complexity* (Vol. 10, Issue 3). Elsevier B.V. https://doi.org/DOI: 10.1016/j.joitmc.2024.100325

Zhang, X., & Tan, Y. (2025). Digital Empowerment: Unlocking the "synergy barrier" of government-enterprise-public air pollution control. *Energy Reports*, *13*, 4846–4865. DOI: 10.1016/j.egyr.2025.04.036

Chapter 2
The Innovation Spiral: How Universities, Governments, and Industries Co-Create the AI Future

Amrik Singh
https://orcid.org/0000-0003-3598-8787
Lovely Professional University, India

ABSTRACT

Artificial Intelligence (AI) has become the foundation of the innovation ecosystem of the 21st century. The dynamic interaction of the three pillars of the Triple Helix model of innovation, that is, universities, governments, and industries, has been the key contributor to the development of AI as a laboratory curiosity transforming into a rapidly changing global force. Based on world case studies and theories, the chapter evaluates the role that universities and similar institutions play in advancing underlying research and talent creation; how governments create facilitative policy networks and ethical systems; and how sectors can turn research into commercializable solutions. It brings into focus the problem of innovation and ethical responsibility, the increasing significance of the public-private partnership, and the future of collaborative ecosystems to create a sustainable AI-based society. The research finds that the future of AI does not lie in one stakeholder in particular, but in the overall collective intelligence and mutual trust the innovation spiral will promote.

INTRODUCTION

Artificial Intelligence (AI) is a technological revolution and a social change at the same time. It is transforming the nature of human interaction, work, learning,

DOI: 10.4018/979-8-3373-7620-2.ch002

and government. In contrast to the past waves of innovation, AI is based on the interplay of knowledge, data, and cross-sectoral cooperation. The most effective AI developments, like natural language processing, self-driving cars, predictive health care have not been the accomplishments of the lone innovator, but rather the synergistic ecosystems of academia, government, and business (Oliveira et al., 2024). This three-part cooperation is what can be called the "Innovation Spiral" - a complex process of co-evolution in which each party constantly informs and is informed by the other. Research and education in universities offer the mental and imaginative backgrounds. Governments provide regulation, sources of funding and guidance in society. The industries introduce agility, resources, and market implementation. They create a feedback loop together and continually revise and broaden the AI innovation scope. This chapter aims to discuss how this Innovation Spiral works as a co-creative framework of the AI future. It combines the theoretical knowledge of Triple Helix model with empirical data of global AI ecosystems. The discussion confirms that the future of sustainable AI development is based on the ability to balance exploration (academic curiosity), exploitation (industrial use), and governance (ethical regulation).

Figure 1. The Innovation Spiral

Sources: Author's own elaboration.

The Innovation Spiral

The innovation spiral represents a continuous, non-linear process through which ideas evolve into impactful solutions. Rather than following a fixed path, innovation emerges through repeated cycles of experimentation, feedback, learning, and refinement. Knowledge creation, application, and adaptation interact dynamically, allowing innovations to respond to changing social, technological, and economic contexts. The spiral emphasizes collaboration among diverse actors, integration of theory and practice, and the cumulative nature of progress. Each cycle builds on previous insights, leading to more sophisticated and sustainable outcomes. By viewing innovation as a spiral, organizations and institutions can better understand how creativity, resilience, and collaboration drive long-term transformation. The Innovation Spiral is conceptually distinct from the Triple Helix, Quadruple Helix, and innovation ecosystem models by emphasizing process, temporality, and feedback intensity rather than structural relationships alone. While helix models map actors and their interactions, the Innovation Spiral foregrounds how innovation unfolds over time through iterative cycles of experimentation, learning, and recalibration. It highlights acceleration, recursion, and path-dependence, showing how outcomes from one phase reshape subsequent trajectories. Unlike ecosystem models that stress coexistence and coordination, the spiral captures dynamic momentum how knowledge, policy, and practice continuously amplify or redirect innovation. This temporal, feedback-driven lens adds analytical depth to innovation theory. A clear empirical vignette of the Innovation Spiral is visible in the evolution of AI-enabled smart campuses. Universities first piloted AI systems for learning analytics and energy management. Government agencies then supported scale-up through digital education policies, funding schemes, and data-protection standards. Industry partners integrated these pilots into commercial platforms deployed across multiple institutions. Continuous feedback from students, faculty, and administrators led to refinements in algorithms, governance rules, and service models. Unlike one-time collaboration, each cycle generated new knowledge, policy adjustments, and market innovations, illustrating how the Innovation Spiral operates as a dynamic, feedback-driven process shaping sustainable and context-responsive AI adoption.

Triple Helix to the Innovation Spiral

The shift between the Triple Helix model and the Innovation Spiral is the indication of the radical changes in the way societies structure and create innovation in the age of Artificial Intelligence (AI). The concept of Triple Helix framework views innovation as a product of the dynamic and interrelational relationships between the universities, industries, and governments. Nevertheless, the dramatic rate of technological transformation, integration of the digital and material worlds, and increased complexity of the world problems have superseded the unchanging assumptions of the old model (Stephens, 2025). The Innovation Spiral therefore becomes a more developed model that reflects the iterative, self-catalysing, and developing concept of co-creation in the modern AI environment. It recognizes that innovation is not a one-dimensional process that is traversed through research to commercialization, but is a feedback loop of experimentation, learning and adaptation with a wider range of stakeholders. The Triple Helix framework gives the conceptual base to the way in which institutional co-operation can lead to innovation. The universities in this model are not merely places where knowledge is created, but they are also involved in the commercialization and entrepreneurship activity. The industries also interact outside the profit-making motive to co-create technologies and the infrastructure of research and the governments are the enabling players by giving the regulatory, financial and infrastructural scaffolding that support the innovation ecosystem (Fisk et al., 2019). According to the model, once the three actors intersect and interact, new knowledge and technologies are likely to flourish as a result of new types of organizations and new types of institutions that transpire as a result of mixing the three actors: hybrid organizations, and boundary-crossing institutions. The Triple Helix employs reflexivity and mutual adaptation i.e. that all actors learn and adjust to others. As examples, universities take an entrepreneurial attitude, industries take a long-term basic research attitude, and governments even test out policies that are more akin to venture capital strategies. The Triple Helix is even more important in the case of Artificial Intelligence (Fujii et al., 2018). Artificial intelligence innovation is both data intensive and interdisciplinary and ethically challenging, which demands intense cooperation across normal borders. Universities also make their contribution in terms of fundamental research in the field of machine learning, cognitive science, and ethics, which not only produces algorithms but also critical thinking about the social implications of AI. In the meantime, industry implements these lessons through AI being deployed into the real world; in healthcare diagnostics and self-driving cars, establishing feedback loops which, in turn, inform policy decisions and new research directions (Hsu et al., 2020). Although the Triple Helix model may have some strong points, the speed of the networked world of AI innovation restricts its implementation. Digital age has made knowledge creation and dissemination more democratic with new actors like startups, non-governmental organizations (NGOs), open-source communities, and international organizations being introduced. In addition, innovation is non-linear and iterative nowadays. Policy sets are informed by research, industry practices are influenced by policy, and applied industrial implementation is creating new data that is defining new priorities in research. This reflexive and cyclical quality of innovation requires a model that reflects dynamism, diversity and expansion- a requirement that spawned the Innovation Spiral. The concept of the Innovation Spiral is based on the logic of the Triple Helix yet it changes the model of a fixed structure to a model of the process. It presents innovation as an ever-growing spiral cycle in which one cycle of interactions between universities, governments, and industries gives rise to the next. The innovations in each iteration help not only to improve technologies and policies, but also increase the number of participants and the area of innovation. An example is that as an AI research initiative moves out of the educational laboratory and into industry, it creates information, feedback, and ethical issues that trigger additional scholarly investigation and policy changes. With time, this self-reinforcing cycle turns into a spiral, and it represents the growth, adjustment, and progressive progression (Blankesteijn & Ghorbani, 2025). Universities remain beings of knowledge creation and ethical facilitation in the Innovation Spiral, which bases AI innovation on science and humanity. As an example, the innovation anchored in the ethical and philosophical space of academic systems can be found in places like the Stanford Human-Centered AI Institute and the Oxford Future of Humanity Institute. In the spiral model, governments are the policy designers and government financiers who not only control but also co-create. They stratify innovations and implement them in various settings and accumulate empirical evidence that guides academia and policy. Google, Microsoft, and IBM are tech-companies that are in symbiotic relationships with universities and governments by establishing joint research laboratories, ethics councils, and national AI initiatives.

Table 1. Innovation Spiral in Practice: Roles, Actions, and Feedback

Actor	Primary Role in the Innovation Spiral	Key Actions in Practice	Feedback Generated
Universities	Knowledge creation & talent development	AI research, pilot projects, ethics frameworks, curriculum design	New theories, skilled graduates, ethical insights
Governments	Policy enablers & ethical regulators	Funding programs, AI policies, sandboxes, data governance	Regulatory refinement, trust, public accountability
Industries	Application & scale	Commercial deployment, product innovation, market feedback	Performance data, user insights, societal impact

Sources: Author's own elaboration

In this industrial involvement the innovation spiral is becoming an engine of change in society as the agility of the private sector is a supplement to the stewardship of the public sector and the curiosity of the academia. This cycle can also be increased by the presence of startups and SMEs as these actors tend to be the connective tissue between state-of-the-art research and the new market possibilities. The spiral dynamic is very different to the linear line of innovation of the olden times (Leung & Loo, 2022). Rather than proceeding stepwise between basic research, applied development and commercialization, innovation is now happening as a result of iterative learning and co-evolution. Limiting the spaces of research, regulation and implementation become unclear, forming a dynamic ecosystem of multi-stakeholder governance. The collaboration results in the feedback loops that enable each stakeholder to improve, as universities can improve the curriculum according to the industry need; governments can revise the policies according to the industry development; and industries can change strategies according to the social expectations and academic knowledge.

LITERATURE REVIEW

The Innovation Spiral accommodates new actors and values that have been extended in the original Triple Helix. The civil society organizations are organizations that promote ethical principles and digital rights; environmental organizations make AI development pursue the principles of sustainability; and global organizations such as the AI ethics framework by UNESCO provide global coordination of local innovation. The spiral then turns into a multi-layered ecosystem, which is sometimes called a Quadruple or Quintuple Helix encompassing societal and ecological levels. This inclusivity would make innovation to be of greater interests to the society and not of corporate or national interests (Leung & Loo, 2022). Put simply, the transition of the Triple Helix to the Innovation Spiral is a shift of the structure towards the process, the interaction towards the evolution and the coordination towards the co-creation. It summarizes the dynamic, recursive and expansive innovation during the AI era. The spiral metaphor insists on growth, but also learning and ethical reflexivity - each rotation of the spiral revisits more of what has been known, reevaluates values and incorporates new understandings. It reminds us that innovation does not simply mean technological improvement but rather it is the constant redefining of the meaning of progress in the human race. Therefore, moving deeper into the AI era, the Innovation Spiral will continue to be a more inclusive and flexible tool of thought as to how universities, governments and industries, or even societies as a whole, can co-design a more intelligent and inclusive future. With a feedback, ethical, and adaptable core, the spiral will make sure that the AI innovation keeps up with the changing requirements of humanity, not only changing economies but also the very essence of such collaboration.

Universities as the Brain of AI Innovation

Universities have long been the intellectual and cognitive center of the technological progress and nowhere can this be more evident than in processes of developing Artificial Intelligence (AI). Since the early days of John McCarthy at Stanford University and Marvin Minsky at MIT in the middle of the 20th century, universities have influenced AI at both theoretical and ethical levels, with the University of Toronto Vector Institute and Stanford Human-Centered AI Institute becoming two of the most influential AI powerhouses (Conruyt et al., 2014). They are not only learning institutions but learning systems of inquisitiveness, experimentation, and synthesis across the disciplines, whereby ideas are fostered into innovations that ultimately revolutionize the industries and societies. The universities as being the cognitive center of the Innovation Spiral undertake three main roles- creation of knowledge through interdisciplinary research, development of talent through education and training and transfer of knowledge through collaborative research with industry and government partners. All these roles will make universities not only providers of intellectual capital but active participants in determining the course of AI innovation.

Production of Knowledge and Interdisciplinary Research

It cannot be discussed outside of the context of growth in computer science, mathematics, psychology, neuroscience, linguistics, ethics, and philosophy. Contrary to the traditional forms of science that tend to operate within certain boundaries, AI research tends to blur them and require cross-pollination of approaches and viewpoints. It is the fertile ground of such intellectual convergence in universities. In case, the Vector Institute of Artificial Intelligence in Toronto partners with the University of Toronto in order to develop deep learning research and discuss its application in healthcare, finance, and education. Future of Humanity Institute based at Oxford University is an interdisciplinary initiative between philosophy, data science and policy regarding the long-term existential issues posed by AI. A culture of open inquiry and peer review assists the university ecosystem to encourage innovation by sharing research results, which are kept in publications, conferences, and on open-source platforms (Lee & Ma, 2020). Such a transparency is in contrast with the proprietary character of industrial R&D, which means that the roots of AI, including algorithms, datasets, and theories, should be open to a joint development. Indicatively, initial advances in neural networks, natural language processing, and reinforcement learning began in the university environment and, subsequently, were commercialized by business. Besides, new interdisciplinary scholarly activities center on AI to the social good with an investigation of how smart systems can fight climate change, healthcare disparity, and access to education. Ethics incorporated into research would make sure that AI development is developed in accordance with the welfare of the society, making innovation grounded on humanistic principles. Universities therefore serve as knowledge centers where concepts are created, discussed and perfected and then converted into practical uses. Their multidisciplinary framework enables AI to develop as a scientific enterprise as well as a moral enterprise that combines the accuracy of computation with the moral values. This transforms the universities into the cognitive and ethical heart of the flow of ideas, which becomes the seed in the Innovation Spiral.

Capacity Building and Development of Talents

Higher institutions of learning are the only institutions that can develop such talent by educating and mentoring in addition to providing experiential learning.

The contemporary process of AI education is much broader than coding and algorithmology. Upon realizing AI has social consequences, colleges have introduced new courses in data ethics, sustainability, human-computer interaction, and policy analysis. Degree programs and courses become more and more interdisciplinary and merge technical rigor with social and philosophical understanding. As an example, the course of AI Ethics and Society at Stanford and the program of Social and Ethical Responsibilities of Computing at MIT allow students to gain the skills to critically evaluate the effects of AI implementation. Capacity building is also a strategic focus in the emerging economies. The AI Academies of China, the National Programme on Artificial Intelligence of India, and the AI Research Institutes that are being sponsored in Africa are indications of how educational systems are being restructured to make the coming generation of innovators (Konno & Schillaci, 2021). There are usually programs that are based on a combination of classroom education, project-based learning, hackathons, and industry internships, overcoming the gap between theory and practice. Universities are therefore a form of talent accelerator, which feeds the national AI missions and allows countries to be part of the global digital economy. Moreover, universities are now adopting lifelong learning and upskilling programs, with the blistering attack of technological change. Online AI certifications and executive education programs will allow working professionals to refresh their abilities, which will guarantee inclusiveness during the digital transformation. University-based efforts have resulted in the creation of democratized AI education platforms like Coursera, edX and Udacity, among others that have attracted millions of users around the world. This democratization is a form of capacity building but also social empowerment as AI literacy will be the requisite to informed citizenship in the digital age. Universities promote critical thinking, creativity and ethical reasoning, as this way of thinking is what makes AI innovation human-centered. Their educational mission concurs with such a larger societal purpose as augmenting human potential instead of limiting it with the help of AI. Talent development guarantees continuity in the Innovation Spiral, with each new batch of graduated talent adding new insights and competencies to the spiral, driving it into new discovery, application cycles.

University-Industry Research Partnerships

One of the key aspects of Innovation Spiral is the smooth movement of innovation between the industry and the academia. The universities do not only create ideologies but also have partnerships with the commercial organizations to develop research into real innovations (Konno & Schillaci, 2021; Singh, 2025). Such a partnership makes the technology advance more quickly and strengthen the social contribution of a scholarly finding. MIT-IBM Watson AI Lab is a pioneer example of this kind of collaboration where academics and corporate scientists combine their efforts to solve the problem of AI reasoning, automation, and ethics. On the same note, Leverhulme Centre of the Future of Intelligence in Cambridge University collaborates with industry and policy organizations to examine the impact of AI on society to make sure that coverage of technologies is ethically managed. These alliances are good examples of how universities and industries can jointly develop both scientifically sound and socially responsible solutions. Cooperative research is also done in the form of innovation clusters, incubators, and technology parks which provide connection between the universities and startups as well as the established companies. Indicatively, the location of Stanford University close to Silicon Valley has formed its own self-sustaining ecosystem, whereby ideas taught in the university are easily translated into business directly. Indian Institutes of Technology (IITs) have innovation cells that provide the collaboration with technology corporations such as Intel, Google, and Tata Consultancy Services, and advanced the local-friendly AI solutions. These types of collaborations demonstrate the way in which universities become mechanisms of connecting theory and practice, or more precisely, make research results produce economic and social benefit. Nonetheless, such increasing integration causes serious concerns about intellectual property (IP) rights, academic freedom and ethical integrity (Singh & Sihmar, 2025; Singh & Kumar, 2024). Commercializing university research may create confusion between the social and personal interests, and it may undermine the concept of openness and academic integrity. An example could be where corporate sponsorship is used to shape the agendas of research and thus the focus is on short-term applications instead of basic inquiry. Colleges should thus have balanced benefits systems, open IP policies and governance systems that conserve academic virtues within the frameworks that encourage innovation. The most effective university-industry partnerships exist when they work on the basis of mutually understanding and mutual purpose. The academic creativity and credibility benefit the industry, whereas universities get access to actual world data, funding, and deployment platforms. This symbiotic association has turned universities to living laboratories, where knowledge is not just created but is put into constant test and improved through use.

DISCUSSION AND INTERPRETATION

Universities can supply both the conceptual and technical frameworks that form the basis of AI via interdisciplinary research. They do this through education and capacity building to develop the human expertise to maintain innovation. And in collaborations with industry and government, they can apply the theoretical breakthroughs to practical effect and also move through the ethical difficulties of commercialization. Universities in the Innovation Spiral start the stream of ideas that propagate a cycle of learning and co-evolution among all the stakeholders. They do not stand by but are active creators of the AI future as the technological development principles are informed by prudence, inclusivity, and a sense of the greater good. The old purpose of the university, which is to pursue truth, promote knowledge, and promote the happiness of humankind, is more than ever pertinent as AI continues to change societies.

Policies as Policy Enablers and Ethical Regulators

Governments worldwide are instrumental in defining the direction of the Artificial Intelligence (AI) innovation. The state operates as policy enabler and moral controlling agent in the Innovation Spiral where universities, industries, and governments create technologies together in the technological future. Its dualism is to provide a boost to innovation and protection of the interest of the population, such that the benefits of AI become fairly distributed and are in line with societal values (Singh & Bathla, 2023; Singh, 2025). With AI more deeply integrated into everyday life, as it assists governments in creating economies, healthcare, education, and national security, governments no longer have the responsibility of funding research or writing regulations. They need to create flexible ecosystems that look forward to technological advancement without interfering with human dignity, privacy and fairness. This part discusses three fundamental areas of government involvement, which include strategic AI agendas, regulatory frameworks and ethical oversight, and policy laboratories that promote collaborative governance.

Strategic AI Agendas

The world governments are recognizing the AI as a strategic platform of national competitiveness, innovation and security. National AI strategies adopted demonstrate a transition to the concept of AI as a means of technology but a vital ingredient of future economic and social systems. The EU (European Union) is now a leader in terms of human-centered AI policy. Its elaborate framework - it is rooted in the European AI Act - aims to unleash control over the application of AI depending on its threat to the citizens. This stance focuses on transparency, accountability, and basic rights and makes innovation one that complies with ethics. Several other complementary efforts such as Horizon Europe provide funding to interdisciplinary research on AI that combines ethics, law, and social science with technology development. The attitude of the EU is based on the perception that AI competitiveness cannot be obtained solely through technological excellence but also trust and social acceptability. Next Generation Artificial Intelligence Development

Plan (2017) of China, on the contrary, represents the case of state-driven innovation. The strategy will incorporate AI into every part of the economy- manufacturing, healthcare, transportation and defense, with the significant financial investment of the government and centralized organization. Chinese AI policy is considered to make the country become a global AI superpower by 2030 through the focus on the innovation power and social governance (Singh & Kumar, 2025b; Singh, 2024e). The National AI Mission in India (often referred to as AI for All) is a policy of AI developmentally oriented. The mission is under NITI Aayog, the planning body of India, and focuses on AI in social good, which consists of healthcare, agriculture, education, smart mobility, and governance. The plan also includes inclusivity, which will close digital gaps and use AI to enhance sustainable development. The United Arabs Emirates, Japan, Canada, other countries, such as the United States, have also implemented their own AI strategies. The U.S. National AI Initiative Act (2020) emphasizes the federal coordination, funding of research, and collaboration with other countries, whereas the Singapore National AI Strategy suggests to apply AI to real-world scenarios in urban problems, transport, and healthcare. One of the first positions of AI governance in the world, the UAE Minister of State for AI, represents institutionalization of AI governance across governmental systems. Governments work together across national boundaries via multilateral structures, including the Global Partnership on Artificial Intelligence (GPAI) which supports the research and policy discussion across countries. Notably, governments also invest and construct infrastructures. They also invest in AI studies, create national computing hubs, facilitate open data projects, and create digital literacy programs to create a fair access point. Governments facilitate the spread of innovation and, as a consequence, reduce regional inequalities and enable smaller businesses to join AI systems. Therefore, the strategic agenda of the state is not reduced to competitiveness, but includes also to social inclusion and sustainability, which should correlate the technological advancement of the nation with its welfare and the welfare of the world.

Regulatory Frame Works and Ethical Supervision

Due to the high rate of development of AI technologies, governments have to find a way to balance innovation and ethical responsibility. AI in its uncontrolled form may contribute to inequalities, bias, and loss of privacy (Singh & Sihmar, 2025; Singh & Kumar, 2024; Sharma & Singh, 2024a). Therefore, governments have a responsibility as custodians of popular trust and are expected to provide regulatory environments that promote transparency, accountability, and fairness of AI. On the global scale, the frameworks, including OECD Principles on AI (2019) and the Recommendation on the Ethics of Artificial Intelligence (UNESCO, 2021), have become the landmark of responsible AI. These guidelines are focused on human rights, sustainability, and inclusivity and promote the incorporation of ethics in the national laws by the member nations. The European Union AI Act, as one example, categorizes AI systems into the following risk groups: unacceptable, high-risk, limited, and minimal risk and requires a relevant protection over each. This is a risk-based model that has become a global model of AI regulation that has influenced the creation of similar frameworks in other jurisdictions. The act also requires transparency, explainability and human supervision of algorithms, raising the standard of AI usage throughout the globe. The Blueprint for an AI Bill of Rights (2022) also provides principles of safeguarding citizens against algorithmic discrimination and transparency in automated systems in the United States. The General Data Protection Regulation (GDPR) within Europe has been a world standard when it comes to data protection, affecting the laws all over the world. Equally, new policies in India, Japan, and Brazil integrate localization of data and user consent as a tool to safeguard personal data and allow AI-based innovation. An important aspect of governmental control is algorithmic accountability (Singh, 2022; Singh, 2024a; Singh, 2024b). Governments are placing more and more demands that AI systems be audited by organizations regarding bias, accuracy, and explainability. This control will have AI results conform to justice and equality principles. Furthermore, the regulations of digital trade and data flows across borders, place the geopolitical aspect of AI regulation in the focus of the negotiations between open collaboration and national sovereignty between states. Nevertheless, the dilemma is whether to be fast to innovate, or to be ethical. Surveillance can kill innovativeness, and deregulation can kill and invite criticism. It is thus important that governments adopt adaptive governance the solution that enables policies to transform with technology. The balance here is ensured through policy experimentation, consultation of stakeholders and transparency. Governments are not passive regulators in the Innovation Spiral but are active and continuously improve their governance mechanisms by learning about new things with universities and industries.

University-Industry-Government Policy Labs

Another unique aspect of the AI era is the emergence of policy laboratories and AI sandboxes, places of co-creation between regulations and technologies. These labs are a paradigm shift of top-down regulation to co-regulatory experimentation that captures the ethos of the Innovation Spiral that has two-way knowledge flows between research, policy, and industry. The Centre of Data Ethics and Innovation CDEI is a trailblazer in the UK. Singapore has developed AI Governance Testing Framework, which is a sandbox testing environment of AI systems in regulated conditions, through collaboration with international corporations and universities. The strategy will allow regulators to envision risks, and at the same time encourage innovations via experiments. Other countries are taking the same direction (Singh, 2024b; Singh, 2024c; Nuong Deri et al., 2024; Deri et al., 2024). The CIFAR AI Policy Lab links policy makers and the researchers of the top AI institutes such as Mila and Vector in Canada, bringing about evidence-based governance. The U.S. National Institute of Standards and Technology (NIST) has a cooperative structure of AI risk management, with academic and industrial partners in standards development. India In India, the Responsible AI for Youth and AI for All programs involve educational institutions and startups in policy development and ethical AI encouragement, which prove how the concept of participatory governance can be applied at the grassroots level. An example of agile governance is policy labs, a form of policymaking based on adaptation to uncertainty and complexity. They enable governments to experiment, model moral issues, and solicit stakeholder views prior to the implementation of regulations on a large-scale basis. Notably, they too render AI governance more democratic, by engaging different stakeholders such as academia, industry, and civil society in the process of determining the ethical boundaries of AI. Such collaborations help governments to move away as reactive regulators and become the facilitators of innovation. The governments are very instrumental in the coordinating and ethical role in the Innovation Spiral that sees to it that technological advancements are not taken to be in direct opposition to the people and their shared good. They facilitate policies as strategic agenda shapers, infrastructural investors, and inclusive innovation ecosystem enablers (Bhalla et al., 2023; Singh, 2024d; Singh & Hassan, 2024). Being ethical controllers, they protect the transparency, accountability, and justice in the application of AI. They combine scholarly knowledge and industrial experience into the policy-making process through policy laboratories and adaptive governance systems, so that they can be flexible to a fast-evolving digital world. Whether AI governance has a bright future remains to be seen and depends on whether governments will be able to restore this delicate equilibrium of encouraging innovation and not sacrificing human rights. By so doing, they can become more than managers, and they are co-creators of ethical intelligence, thus creating an AI-driven future that benefits not only their economies, but the entire species.

Industry as the Engine of Application and Scale

Industry plays the roles of an application engine, commercialization engine, and scaling engine in the Innovation Spiral. Although the foundational research may be created in the university and regulatory and infrastructural assistance may be fostered by the government, the industry is the one that makes theoretical breakthroughs a tangible product or service and societal impact. In addition, industry does not only scale technological innovation but also influences perception and ethical systems in the society by making decisions and acting in a certain way (Singh & Hassan, 2024; Singh, 2025). This part discusses the way that industry contributes to the AI future in three interdependent directions: converting research into solutions in the market, enabling startups and innovation creation, and integrating ethics into corporate responsibility models.

Market Solution Strategy: Translation Research to Market

Industry is the key player that converts what is found in academics to feasible market products. The history of the AI revolution, which started in the laboratories of the universities and now conquers the global markets is the best example of how knowledge can be easily transferred to the sphere of commercialization. As an example, the AI-driven innovation of the AlphaFold revolutionized the field of biological science by allowing the prediction of protein structure with exceptionally high accuracy, and illustrated how AI-based innovation can accelerate discovery of new areas entirely new. The uses of AI in the industrial field cut across all the key sectors of the world economy (Singh, 2022; Garg et al., 2024). Adaptive learning applications like personalized AI tutors of Coursera or reinforcement learning models of Duolingo are adaptive learning applications in the field of education that illustrate how AI can scale personal learning experiences. The industrial ecosystem is therefore the translational platform of the innovation spiral- whereby theoretical models are translatable technologies.

Startups and Innovation Acceleration

Startups are the entrepreneurial vigor of the innovation spiral that allows the AI applications to be quickly iterated and democratized. The universities are very instrumental in developing these entrepreneurial ventures via incubators, accelerators and innovation hubs. Indicatively, Stanford StartX, MIT The Engine and IIT Madras Incubation Cell are AI-oriented start-up accelerators that offer mentorship, capital, technical assistance, and research knowledge. These programs turn the university campuses into innovation systems, in which students, researchers and entrepreneurs work to turn ideas into market-ready solutions. Public-private partnerships are also a key ingredient of the startup ecosystem. Startup India, the Digital Innovation Hubs of the EU, and the AI Supercluster Program provided within Canada are government-funded projects that provide funding, infrastructure, and policy assistance to incentivize innovation at early stages. In its turn, startups contribute to national AI missions by implementing the academic research to the socially relevant problems, such as agricultural AI in India, smart mobility in Europe, or climate analytics in North America. Notably, startups generate inclusive innovation. Niche or underserved markets are being served by many new AI companies, taking into account the needs of a local or regional market that large corporations might miss (Sharma & Singh, 2024b; Sharma et al., 2024). As an example, rural healthcare diagnostics AI-based tools, language translation where underrepresented communities are concerned, and affordable chatbots in education are some examples of how small-scale businesses can increase the social coverage of AI. Additionally, startups become the points of knowledge transference between universities and large companies. They internalize leading research, trial prototypes in the real world and ultimately scale or merge with other larger organizations. This innovation cycle: idea to prototype to market is dynamic and self-reinforcing as it is the characteristic of the Innovation Spiral.

Ethical AI/Corporate Social Responsibility

The industry has an overwhelming moral accountability as the use of AI technologies evolves into a widespread occurrence. Corporate actors are not judged based on their economic performance only but also on how they deal with matters related to fairness, transparency, privacy, and social impact issues. This has spawned the paradigm of Responsible AI (RAI) in which businesses incorporate moral contemplation into the design, implementation, and management of AI-based solutions. As an example, the Model Cards of Google include comprehensive documentation of the AI model performance and bias factors, and the Responsible AI Standard of Microsoft presents the principles of fairness, reliability, inclusiveness, and privacy. On the same note, AI Ethics Board in IBM incorporates multidisciplinary views, i.e., the legal, technical and philosophical standpoints, to assess AI applications prior to implementation. The corporate ethics are also applicable to the supply chains, environmental conservation and data management. Besides, the emergence of algorithmic audits and transparency reports points to a new period of self-regulation and social responsibility. Most companies in the recent past have partnered with civil society organizations and academic scholars to assess the social effects of their technologies. Such co-regulatory will reduce reputational risks as well as increase public trust, which is also an important asset in the competitive AI economy. The use of ethical AI cannot be based only on voluntary actions, but there should be strong mechanisms of governance. The question of data bias, surveillance, displacing labor, and unequal access to AI resources remain the challenges to corporate responsibility (Singh & Sihmar, 2025; Singh et al., 2024; Bhalla et al., 2023). The Innovation Spiral will help industries to go beyond compliance to value-based innovation in how they operate, which essentially implies that the ethical principles become part and parcel of corporate DNA, rather than being seen as an afterthought. Industry is the pragmatic driver of the Innovation Spiral, so that the knowledge created in universities and aided by governments has a real-life effect. However, in the process, it also predetermines the moral environment of the AI era. As the industries push forward the boundaries of what AI is capable of, they should be equally determined to making sure that AI is used for the prosperity of humanity and not just market profit. The power of the Innovation Spiral therefore lies in its ability to help industry find the balance between profitability and purpose, efficiency and ethics, innovation and inclusion in the end turning AI into the technological revolution rather than a technological evolution of the society.

GLOBAL CASE STUDIES CO-CREATION

The Innovation Spiral - the co-creation of technological futures by universities, governments and industries - is reflected in different ways in the contexts of the world. The way all regions develop AI represents a specific set of institutional and cultural priorities and policy philosophies combined (Nuong Deri et al., 2024; Garg et al., 2024). This section will discuss four emblematic case studies that include the United States, Europe, China, and India and each of which illustrates a unique model of the functioning of the Innovation Spiral in practice.

Academic Foundations of the United States

The US is the home of the modern AI and a living case of the successful collaboration of academia, industry and government creating a synergized innovation system. There is no place where this can be seen further than in the Silicon Valley, an area that is the embodiment of the strength of closeness between universities, venture capital, and entrepreneurial culture. The innovation engine in Silicon Valley was triggered by academic industry nexus organized around the Stanford University. During the post-World War II period, Stanford was the first institution to promote faculty and student commercialisation of research, an unusual policy in the period which saw the establishment of companies like Hewlett-Packard, Sun Microsystems, and Cisco Systems. The practice went on in the AI age, where university research in machine learning, neural networks, and natural language processing directly had a commercial use (Sharma & Singh, 2024b; Sharma et al., 2024; Singh, 2025). The Stanford Artificial Intelligence Laboratory (SAIL) and the AI Research Lab at UC Berkeley then became factories and nurseries of ideas and talent, churning out AI leaders who would be founders or acquirees of AI-related companies such as Google, NVIDIA, and OpenAI. The U.S. federal government, via agencies like the DARPA (Defense Advanced Research Projects Agency) and the National Science Foundation (NSF) has in the past had a catalytic role in that it has funded early AI research that has had long-term societal impact. The initial funding of natural language processing and robotics by DARPA, such as provided to them, formed the basis of AI-based applications in defense, automation, and cybersecurity today. Besides, the innovative environment of the U.S. is more flexible and enables quick experimentation and optimization. This has created an entrepreneurial risk-taking culture and multi-disciplinary teamwork, which are typical of the Innovation Spiral. Silicon Valley is therefore not only a physical location, but also an ideological construct- a model in which academic interest, industrial prowess and governmental assistance reaffirm themselves by building a world technological dominance.

Europe: AI Ecosystem Policy-Driven

Unlike the dynamism of the market-based approach in the United States, the AI ecosystem in Europe is policy push and ethics focused. European Union (EU) has established itself as an international frontrunner in the marketing of the human-friendly and reliable AI, accentuating how innovation should correspond to the principles of democracy, human rights, and sustainability. The centre of the European strategy is Horizon Europe program, the EU flagship research and innovation program. It funds interdisciplinary research in AI at a significant level where technical development is combined with legal, ethical and social aspects (Konno & Schillaci, 2021; Singh & Hassan, 2024; Singh, 2024e; Ansari et al., 2024). The EU promotes cooperation among academia, industry, and civil society through the European AI Alliance and AI-on-Demand Platform, where various stakeholders have ensured that they are involved in the development of the digital future of the continent. The European AI Act, which was launched in 2021, is an important regulatory framework that is aimed to regulate the risks of AI and permit innovation. The Act defines the ethical and operational standards to be followed by designers and users of AI systems by classifying them according to their possible impacts on society that could be unacceptable, high, limited or minimal risk. Such a strategy not only protects citizens but also increases the trust of the populace which is an extremely important component in the sustainability of long-term innovation. European universities and research centres, including the Future of Humanity Institute of Oxford, the AI Center of ETH Zurich, and the Institute of Ethics in AI of TU Munich, work closely with businesses and policy makers (Sharma & Singh, 2024b; Sharma et al., 2024; Singh & Kumar, 2025a). SAP, Siemens, and DeepMind (London) are the types of corporate actors that actively interact with the public authorities in the co-development of ethical frameworks and open innovation ecosystems. To Europe, policy consistency and moral governance are considered as competitive benefits but not limitations. The focus on responsible, open, and socially responsible AI in the region reflects a particular model of the Innovation Spiral - the model that prioritizes the welfare of the group, rather than dominating the market.

China: State-Led Spiral of Innovation

The AI ecosystem in China is one of the examples of state-driven innovation, in which the orchestration of the government, academic quality, and corporate agility meet the national strategic objectives. The vision of becoming the global leader in Artificial Intelligence is expressed in Next Generation Artificial Intelligence Development Plan (2017) which introduces the integration of technological progress with social governance and economic modernization into the future of China. Located in the middle of the Innovation Spiral is the Chinese government which is actively involved in setting it up. It coordinates investments, determines priorities in research, and promotes the cooperation of universities, state-owned corporations, and private technology developing companies. The engines of commercialization are the so-called private corporations, such as the BAT trio (Baidu, Alibaba, Tencent) and even the new players, such as Huawei and SenseTime. They spend a lot of money on applied AI, including autonomous driving and fintech, smart cities, as well as in healthcare. These companies work in close cooperation with government ministries and academic laboratories and reflect the hybrid innovation model of integrating marketility with centralized coordination (Leung & Loo, 2022; Singh & Bathla, 2023; Singh, 2025). Another similarity between the model and China is the focus on AI and data-driven governance of the state, implementing intelligent solutions in urban management, education, and healthcare. Smart city management and AI-aided judicial decision-making are pilot projects that show how the state uses AI to achieve administrative efficiency and social control. Although this brings about some privacy and surveillance concerns, it also brings to light that AI can be used as a means to build the national capacity and implement policies. Overall, the Innovation Spiral in China is defined by both the top-down orientation and bottom-up implementation which result in a rapid cycle of innovation that helps to synchronise the technological ambition and the goals of the national policies.

India: Academic-Policy Convergence

The AI innovation ecosystem in India is an unparalleled case of academic-policy convergence, with its leadership being led by the government, involvement of universities, and entrepreneurial drive. The Indian strategy is anchored on the National Strategy on Artificial Intelligence (AI for All) led by NITI Aayog, which is premised on the idea of applying AI to inclusive and sustainable development, but not just on global competitiveness. The AI mission in India focuses on the key societal areas, which include, healthcare, agriculture, education, smart mobility and governance, since this is what the country is developing. The attempts to democratize access to AI and AI literacy include such state-funded institutions like the Centre for Artificial Intelligence and Robotics (CAIR) and the National AI Portal (INDIAi) among others. An important part of this ecosystem is played by universities. Top educational facilitys such as Indian Institutes of Technology, (IITs) and Indian Institute of Science (IISc), engage multinational corporations such as Intel, IBM and Google, in research and capacity-building courses on AI. Programs like Startup India, Atal Innovation Mission are helping thousands of AI-driven businesses that make technologies local to regional environments (Garg et al., 2024; Singh et al., 2024; Bhalla et al., 2023; Singh, 2024d; Singh & Hassan, 2024). These startups usually come out of the incubators at the academies, and they seek to solve the grassroots issues, which reflects the democratizing nature of the Indian AI mission. The Innovation Spiral in India is a bottom-up movement that is in tune with policy frameworks and is focused on ethics, inclusivity, and human development. It is the way in which the emerging economies can use the concept of co-creation to create an AI future that is technologically modernized and socially just (Sharma & Singh, 2024b; Sharma et al., 2024; Singh & Kumar, 2025a). Innovation Spiral has many faces across the globe- every one being an embodiment of its own local history, institutional culture and policy philosophies. The U.S. model is enabled by entrepreneurial freedom, university-industry synergy; European model grounded innovation on ethics and governance; Chinese model proved that state-coordination at such scale; and India paradigm, inclusive and policy-driven co-creation.

CHALLENGES IN CO-CREATING THE AI FUTURE

The idea of the Innovation Spiral when universities, governments, and industries build AI together promises to be the gigantic potential of technological development and changes in the life of society. The process is, however, not smooth. The field of co-creation in AI is associated with various structural, ethical, and operational issues that may impede innovation, slow down adoption, and, in certain instances, amplify social disparities. These barriers are important to understand so as to design governing structures, policies and collaborative practices that can facilitate technological advancements as well as confidence of the society.

Fragmented Collaboration

Fragmented collaboration is one of the major obstacles of co-creation. Whereas universities emphasize on the creation of knowledge, theoretical study, and long-term investigation, industries tend to emphasize on immediate solutions marketable and on the return on investment. To illustrate the above-mentioned, the most innovative

AI algorithms created in research centers might not be used due to being considered too experimental and expensive or unsuitable in business approaches by companies.

Ethical Dilemmas

Such problems as data privacy, algorithmic bias, surveillance, and workforce displacement present complicated ethical dilemmas which cannot be addressed on the level of an individual stakeholder. Universities can pursue ethical protection and openness, industries can be concerned with efficiency and profitability, and governments can strive to strike a balance between innovation and protection of society (Singh & Singh, 2024; Singh & Bathla, 2023; Singh, 2025). The collective responsibility needed to handle these ethical dilemmas is difficult to attain especially in multinational partnerships where cultures, regulatory procedures and civil expectations are different. In the absence of unified systems, AI innovations can eliminate honesty, foster inequality, or unintended damage.

Funding Inequality

Another significant problem is the allocation of resources. The developing nations do not have the research base, high-performance computing capabilities and experienced human resources to be involved in the full Innovation Spiral. This type of unequal funding introduces a world-wide innovation gap, with AI development being concentrated in a small set of developed economies and restricting other countries. The lack of balance is likely to cause technological dependence, loss of competitiveness, and moral blindness because AI systems developed in one area might not be applicable and accommodative to other groups (Singh et al., 2024).

Policy Lag

Laws often have a hard time keeping up with the fast development of AI technologies. The governments might not have the skills, information, or institutional dynamism to foresee the arising risks related to AI usage. Consequently, data governance and algorithmic transparency policies, and cross-border digital trade policies tend to fall behind technology. Such a policy lag creates uncertainty to industries and universities, which may stifle innovation or the stakeholders may be exposed to legal and reputation risks.

Conflicts in Intellectual Property

Lastly, the issue of intellectual property (IP) clashes during co-creation greatly. JV and collaborative research can easily lead to ownership demarcation boundary, and therefore, it is not clear which party owns the resultant algorithms, datasets, and AI products. IP litigation may stifle commercialization and business alliances and even inhibit risk-taking, which weakens the team spirit underlying the Innovation Spiral (Singh, 2024e; Singh & Singh, 2024; Singh & Bathla, 2023; Singh, 2025). These conflicts should be reduced by means of transparent contracts, balanced benefit-sharing schemes, and institutional provisions to ensure that the stakeholders do not distrust each other. The Innovation Spiral can be met with solidarity in AI worldwide, by using common AI guidelines, and cross-border cooperation, and inclusive policies in AI innovation to attain the promise of an AI future that is highly technological and socially responsible.

Innovative Versions of the Innovation

The Innovation Spiral has already focused on the three-way partnership between universities, governments, and industries which leads to the research, development, and implementation of AI. Nevertheless, with the rise of AI technologies in terms of pervasiveness and power, the decade to come promises to widen this spiral to incorporate societal and environmental aspects. The new models Quadruple Helix--including the civil society--and the Quintuple Helix, focusing on the ecological sustainability, are indicators of the changed view of how the innovation should be understood. According to this broadened model, the success is not determined by the technological performance or economic output but by the social inclusion, ethical accountability, environmental responsibility and human prosperity (Singh, 2024e; Ansari et al., 2024; Sharma & Singh, 2024b). The fundamental aspect of this evolution is the awareness of AI innovation as a socio-technical concept. Technologies are not located in a vacuum, they interact with communities, institutions and ecological systems. When the stakeholders align their AI applications with the SDGs of the United Nations, they will incorporate intentionality into their innovation spiral so that AI innovations will promote a greater common good in the society. On the same note, open science projects, where researchers emphasize transparency, reproducibility, and data disclosure, allow working across borders and democratize AI research and reducing differences between resource-abundant and resource-limited areas. The further manifestation of the spiral evolution is seen in responsible innovation ecosystems. These systems promote early ethical contemplation, participatory decisions and ongoing scrutiny of societal and environmental influence. Companies, research establishments, governments and civil society organizations are now expected to work together not only to improve technological output but also to forecast and address the unintended effects, whether it is algorithmic bias, loss of privacy or socio-economic disparity. In the future, AI innovation will rely on a number of driving factors. To begin with, collaborative research will be required to be interoperable data ecosystems (Ansari et al., 2024; Sharma & Singh, 2024b; Singh & Bathla, 2023; Singh, 2025).. The capability to easily transfer and merge the datasets across institutions, regions, and sectors will speed up the evolution of AI, as well as will allow more robust, diversified, and fair solutions. The international scientific community will be able to collaborate with the help of open, standardized, and privacy-compliant data structures that will not harm ethical protection. Second, responsible innovators will develop with the help of ethical AI education. Curricula in the future have to be more comprehensive and include philosophy, law, social sciences and computational ethics. Universities are able to produce a workforce that will be equally both technical ingenuous as it will be responsible to the society. Third, the mechanisms of international governance will inform the cross-border cooperation and make sure that the development of AI will be in line with common standards and human rights. The ethical, legal and strategic issues related to AI across national borders will necessitate global treaties, trans-national regulatory guidelines, and multilateral collaborations, similar to Global Partnership on Artificial Intelligence (GPAI). Lastly, the adaptability of innovation ecosystems will be determined by socio-technical resilience. The next-generation spiral should be in a position to absorb disruption, inequality and technology shock. This demands elastic policies, involving all stakeholders, and solid risk evaluation frameworks that are capable of predicting and alleviating the social, economic, as well as environmental effects of AI implementation (Sharma & Singh, 2024b; Sharma et al., 2024; Singh & Kumar, 2025a). To sum it up, the future of the Innovation Spiral should not only be concerned with the development of AI capabilities but a system that includes ethics, sustainability, and human-centered values into the innovation process.

CONCLUSION

In both international and local settings, the synergy among academia and industry in Silicon Valley, policy-oriented ethical models in Europe, the dynamism between the state and the academic sphere in China, and an integrative approach to policy and academia in India, it is clear that AI innovation flourishes in an environment of interaction between knowledge, resources, and regulation. The cognitive core is given by universities creating knowledge across disciplines and developing talent, the application and scale are the drivers of industry, making research available as solutions to the market, and policy and ethical controls set by governments so that innovation is in line with societal priorities and trust. The Innovation Spiral has its challenges even though it promises. The issue may be hindered by fragmented collaboration, ethical issues, disparities in funding, lag in policy, and conflicts of intellectual property thereby resulting in less inclusivity. To solve these problems, it is necessary to have flexible governance, transparent arrangement, ethical supervision, and international collaboration. The stakeholders can guarantee that AI can benefit humanity and not widen the inequalities or bring about unintended harm only in case of collective responsibility. In prospect, the spiral should become more detailed with the help of Quadruple and Quintuple Helix models, which will involve civil society and environmental friendliness in developing AI. Essentially, the Innovation Spiral points to the fact that AI is not an isolated creation of a single research or the market; but the result of a multi-stakeholder, ongoing, co-creation, based on knowledge, ethics, and purpose. Humanity can guarantee that AI develops not only the boundaries of technology, but also equity, sustainability, and overall blossoming of the society by creating adaptive, inclusive, and responsible ecosystems of innovation.

REFERENCES

Ansari, A. I., Singh, A., Pattanaik, S., Patnaik, R., & Suryawanshi, U. (2024). Exploring the Role of AI-Powered Virtual Assistants in Optimizing Self-Service Experiences for Customers Within the Service Sector. In Nadda, V., Tyagi, P., Singh, A., & Singh, V. (Eds.), *Integrating AI-Driven Technologies Into Service Marketing* (pp. 225–238). IGI Global., DOI: 10.4018/979-8-3693-7122-0.ch013

Bhalla, A., Singh, P., & Singh, A. (2023). Technological Advancement and Mechanization of the Hotel Industry. In Tailor, R. (Ed.), *Application and Adoption of Robotic Process Automation for Smart Cities* (pp. 57–76). IGI Global., DOI: 10.4018/978-1-6684-7193-7.ch004

Blankesteijn, M. L., & Ghorbani, A. (2025). Embracing the Digital Horizon: Future Scenarios for the Dutch Higher Education System. *Futures*, •••, 103702.

Conruyt, N., Sébastien, V., Sébastien, O., Sébastien, D., & Grosser, D. (2014, September). Sign management for the future of e-education: examples of collaborative e-services in a Living Lab. In *IFIP International Workshop on Artificial Intelligence for Knowledge Management* (pp. 1-20). Cham: Springer International Publishing.

Deri, M. N., Zaazie, P., & Singh, A. (2024). Digital Future of the Hospitality Industry and Hospitality Education Globally. In Sharma, A. (Ed.), *International Handbook of Skill, Education, Learning, and Research Development in Tourism and Hospitality. Springer International Handbooks of Education*. Springer., DOI: 10.1007/978-981-97-4318-6_14

Fisk, R., Fuessel, A., Laszlo, C., Struebi, P., Valera, A., & Weiss, C. (2019). Systemic social innovation: Co-creating a future where humans and all life thrive. *Humanistic Management Journal*, *4*(2), 191–214.

Fujii, T., Guo, T., & Kamoshida, A. (2018, August). A consideration of service strategy of Japanese electric manufacturers to realize super smart society (Society 5.0). In *International Conference on Knowledge Management in Organizations* (pp. 634-645). Cham: Springer International Publishing.

Garg, A., Singh, A., & Yanan, J. (2024). Exploring the Impact of Digital Detoxification on Higher Education Students' Learning. In Grima, S., Chaudhary, S., Sood, K., & Kumar, S. (Eds.), *Business Drivers in Promoting Digital Detoxification* (pp. 111–126). IGI Global Scientific Publishing., DOI: 10.4018/979-8-3693-1107-3.ch008

Hsu, S. C. J., Hsu, H. M., & Hwang, S. Y. (2020). Co-creating future of Artificial Intelligence of Things (AIoT) through ecosystem partnership: a case study of Advantech Co., Ltd. In *Business Innovation with New ICT in the Asia-Pacific: Case Studies* (pp. 111–132). Springer Nature Singapore.

Konno, N., & Schillaci, C. E. (2021). Intellectual capital in Society 5.0 by the lens of the knowledge creation theory. *Journal of Intellectual Capital*, *22*(3), 478–505.

Lee, C., & Ma, L. (2020). The role of policy labs in policy experiment and knowledge transfer: A comparison across the UK, Denmark, and Singapore. *Journal of Comparative Policy Analysis*, *22*(4), 281–297.

Leung, R., & Loo, P. T. (2022). Co-creating interactive dining experiences via interconnected and interoperable smart technology. *Asian Journal of Technology Innovation*, *30*(1), 45–67.

Nuong Deri, M., Singh, A., Zaazie, P., & Anandene, D. (2024). Leveraging Artificial Intelligence in Higher Educational Institutions: A Comprehensive Overview. *Education and Law Review*, (30). Advance online publication. DOI: 10.1344/REYD2024.30.45777

Oliveira, T., Alves, H., & Leitão, J. (2024). Co-creation and innovation in higher education institutions: A systematic literature review and research agenda. *International Journal of Educational Management*, *38*(3), 839–872.

Sharma, M., & Singh, A. (2024a). Embracing Technological Innovation: A Review of Hi-Tech Services in Hospitality Industry. *Evergreen*, *11*(4), 2818–2830. DOI: 10.5109/7326926

Sharma, R., Sachdeva, T., Singh, A., & Nadda, V. (2024). A New Era of Engagement and Satisfaction: Transforming Customer Experience With AI-Driven Technologies. In Nadda, V., Tyagi, P., Singh, A., & Singh, V. (Eds.), *AI Innovations in Service and Tourism Marketing* (pp. 1–16). IGI Global., DOI: 10.4018/979-8-3693-7909-7.ch001

Sharma, R., & Singh, A. (2024b). Use of Digital Technology in Improving Quality Education: A Global Perspectives and Trends. In Nadda, V., Tyagi, P., Moniz Vieira, R., & Tyagi, P. (Eds.), *Implementing Sustainable Development Goals in the Service Sector* (pp. 14–26). IGI Global., DOI: 10.4018/979-8-3693-2065-5.ch002

Singh, A. (2022). Conceptual framework on Smart Learning Environment- An Indian perspective. *Journal of Education and Law*, (25). Advance online publication. DOI: 10.1344/REYD2022.25.36706

Singh, A. (2024a). Virtual Research Collaboration and Technology Application: Drivers, Motivations, and Constraints. In Chakraborty, S. (Ed.), *Challenges of Globalization and Inclusivity in Academic Research* (pp. 250–258). IGI Global., DOI: 10.4018/979-8-3693-1371-8.ch016

Singh, A. (2024b). The Role of Digital Transformation and Its Effects on the Education Sector. In Chakraborty, S. (Ed.), *Challenges of Globalization and Inclusivity in Academic Research* (pp. 92–99). IGI Global Scientific Publishing., DOI: 10.4018/979-8-3693-1371-8.ch007

Singh, A. (2024c). Endorsing Gamification Pedagogy for Nurturing Employability Skills in Higher Education Institutions (HEI). In Membrive, V. (Ed.), *Practices and Implementation of Gamification in Higher Education* (pp. 172–183). IGI Global Scientific Publishing., DOI: 10.4018/979-8-3693-0716-8.ch008

Singh, A. (2024d). Impact of E-learning on Student Motivation in Higher Education Institutions: An Indian Perspective. *Journal of Education and Law*, (29). Advance online publication. DOI: 10.1344/REYD2024.29.43214

Singh, A. (2024e). Students Wellbeing and Performance in Higher Education Institutions. In Aloka, P. (Ed.), *Factors Impacting Student Well-Being and Coping Tactics* (pp. 1–12). IGI Global Scientific Publishing., DOI: 10.4018/979-8-3693-8860-0.ch001

Singh, A. (2025). Integrating Artificial Intelligence in Enhancing Cultural Tourism Experiences. In Albattat, A. (Ed.), *Technological Innovation in Global Cultural Tourism* (pp. 23–40). IGI Global Scientific Publishing., DOI: 10.4018/979-8-3693-3196-5.ch002

Singh, A., & Bathla, G. (2023). Fostering Creativity and Innovation: Tourism and Hospitality Perspective. In P. Tyagi, V. Nadda, V. Bharti, & E. Kemer (Eds.), Embracing Business Sustainability through Innovation and Creativity in the Service Sector (pp. 70-83). IGI Global.

Singh, A., & Hassan, S. C. (2024). Service Innovation Through Blockchain Technology in the Tourism and Hospitality Industry: Applications, Trends, and Benefits. In Singh, S. (Ed.), *Service Innovations in Tourism: Metaverse, Immersive Technologies, and Digital Twin* (pp. 205–214). IGI Global., DOI: 10.4018/979-8-3693-1103-5.ch010

Singh, A., & Kumar, P. (2024). E-Learning Ecosystem in Higher Education Institutions: Trends and Practices. In Al Husseiny, F., & Munna, A. (Eds.), *Preparing Students for the Future Educational Paradigm* (pp. 1–18). IGI Global Scientific Publishing., DOI: 10.4018/979-8-3693-1536-1.ch001

Singh, A., & Kumar, V. (2025a). Organizational Innovation and Adaptation in Hospitality and Tourism: Strategies for Resilience and Leadership. In C. Ramos, T. Costa, R. Madeira, & J. Ferreira do Rosário (Eds.), Open Innovation and Technology in Tourism and Hospitality (pp. 355-372). IGI Global Scientific Publishing. https://doi.org/DOI: 10.4018/979-8-3693-8633-0.ch018

Singh, A., & Kumar, V. (2025b). User-Centered Hospitality: UI/UX as the New Frontier in Hotel and Restaurant Innovation. In C. Ramos, T. Costa, R. Madeira, & J. Ferreira do Rosário (Eds.), Open Innovation and Technology in Tourism and Hospitality (pp. 395-410). IGI Global Scientific Publishing. https://doi.org/DOI: 10.4018/979-8-3693-8633-0.ch020

Singh, A., & Sihmar, P. (2025). Higher Education Institution Sustainability: Role of Green Human Resource Management. In Adu-Gyamfi, M., Boateng, F., & Atiku, S. (Eds.), *Green HRM Awareness and Training in Higher Education Institutions* (pp. 1–14). IGI Global Scientific Publishing., DOI: 10.4018/979-8-3693-2956-6.ch001

Singh, A., Singh, D., & Chhikara, S. (2024). Online Learning: Challenges and Suggestions to Enhance Student Engagement in Higher Education Institutions. In Naidoo, V., & Verma, R. (Eds.), *Reshaping Entrepreneurial Education Within an Industry 4.0 Context* (pp. 59–80). IGI Global Scientific Publishing., DOI: 10.4018/979-8-3693-0409-9.ch004

Singh, V., & Singh, A. (2024). Revolutionizing the Hospitality Industry: How chatGPT Empowers Future Hoteliers. In Bansal, R., Ngah, A., Chakir, A., & Pruthi, N. (Eds.), *Leveraging ChatGPT and Artificial Intelligence for Effective Customer Engagement* (pp. 192–203). IGI Global., DOI: 10.4018/979-8-3693-0815-8.ch011

Stephens, R. J. S. (2025). Quadruple Helix co-creation and cities: Behavioral and institutional changes in innovation capacities and cultures. *Cities (London, England)*, *157*, 105579.

Su, C. Y., Lin, B. W., & Chen, C. J. (2015). Technological knowledge co-creation strategies in the world of open innovation. *Innovation*, *17*(4), 485–507.

Chapter 3
Synergizing Innovation:
Cross-Sector Collaboration Frameworks for Accelerating AI Advancement

Ravikumar R. N.
https://orcid.org/0009-0009-3705-1681
Marwadi University, Rajkot, India

S. Aarthi
https://orcid.org/0009-0006-9064-2091
Marwadi University, Rajkot, India

ABSTRACT

The rapid advancement of Artificial Intelligence (AI) increasingly depends on coordinated collaboration among universities, governments, and industries. This chapter examines how the Triple Helix model accelerates AI innovation by integrating academic research, policy frameworks, and industrial deployment capacities. It highlights how universities contribute foundational knowledge and talent, governments shape ethical and strategic direction, and industries transform discoveries into scalable solutions. The chapter explores collaborative models such as public-private partnerships, national AI missions, and shared data infrastructures, while also addressing challenges including incentive misalignment, regulatory ambiguity, and data silos. Case studies from healthcare diagnostics and smart mobility demonstrate how cross-sector synergy drives societal impact. The chapter concludes by proposing a multi-tier framework for strengthening responsible AI ecosystems through joint vision-building, policy alignment, investment strategies, and talent development.

DOI: 10.4018/979-8-3373-7620-2.ch003

1. INTRODUCTION

The dynamic nature of the tri-sectoral interaction between universities, governments, and industries is gradually becoming influential in the accelerated development of Artificial Intelligence (AI), with the collaboration of the sectors playing a leading role in the innovation. Since AI is a revolutionary technology that is finding applications in the healthcare, financial, mobility, agricultural, and administrative sectors, no one industry has the overall capabilities necessary to catalyze responsible and scalable development. The intellectual base, methodological improvements, and talented capabilities needed in AI discovery are made in universities. Governments set up regulatory certainty, country policy, code of ethics, and financial rewards that guide the technological development (Olayinka, 2023). The industries turn theoretical knowledge into implementable applications, platform, and solutions in the market. This chapter delves into how the synergization of these three areas, or the Triple Helix, has come to be a strategic requirement as opposed to a voluntary avenue of expediting the growth of AI. It presents the theoretical foundations of collaborative structures, describes their applicability to innovation structures, and explains the urgency of reducing fragmentation within industries (Mikhaylov et al., 2018). The chapter preconditions the consideration of how integrated partnerships can become the driving force of innovation, responsible adoption, and a stronger position of the countries in the world AI environment through the analysis of the motivations and challenges of cross-sector collaboration.

1.1 Evolution of AI and the Emergence of Cross-Sector Collaboration

The evolvement of the AI has passed the rule-based expert systems to advanced machine learning, deep learning, and generative models which have offered opportunities and challenges unseen previously. The early history of AI was largely confined to research laboratories, although the increasing computational demands and the need to implement a particular technology in practice quickly revealed the limitations of the individual innovation. Once AI switched to data-driven and large-scale applications, it could not happen without the collaboration of universities, government organizations, and industries (Zhou, 2008). It began to be seen as a strategic resource by governments, and national missions, funds and morality schemes were initiated. The industry participants who also had access to large datasets and the implementation infrastructures became fundamental partners in commercializing AI innovations beyond prototypes. Meanwhile, colleges continued to produce simple theories, algorithms, and competent scholars. It has resulted in official cross-sector partnerships such as public-private research labs, innovation hubs, and information-sharing initiatives and regulatory sandboxes. As such, the science, policy, and entrepreneurial implementation have been linked through the collaborative ecosystems, which is related to the development of AI (Z. Chen et al., 2025). As shown in the figure 1, the evolution of the AI leads to the formation of the AI in the framework of both simple rule-driven systems and current applications functioning within the context of the data, which means that the cross-sector collaboration between the universities, governmental agencies and the industrial stakeholders is required.

Figure 1. AI's Evolution and Collaborative Ecosystems

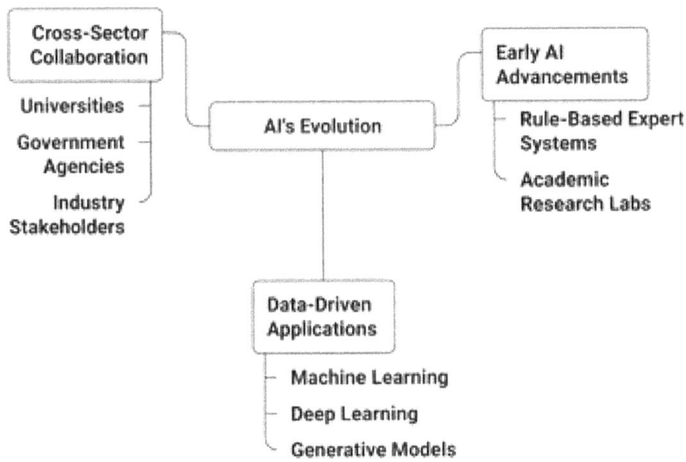

1.2 Importance of the Triple Helix in AI Development

The Triple Helix model is a comprehensive model that can be used to understand how mutual interactions between the universities, governments, and industries can speed up AI innovation. The individual sectors have their own distinct, but complementary role; universities conduct scientific research and produce talent; governments set the technological agenda through policy, funding and regulation; and industries transform academic discoveries into scalable solutions. This alignment is of utmost importance in AI development, as it has been highly demanded to operate with high demands of computational power, ethical safety, interdisciplinary knowledge, and sustained practical testing (Singla et al., 2025). The collaborative synergy will ensure that the research is not limited to the demands of the society, that innovations are not too far off the shifting demands of the governance, and new technologies have an answer and effect to reach the markets. The Triple Helix model contributes to accelerating, increasing the relevance, and social acceptability of AI systems through common resources, co-research centers, innovation missions, and data platforms. This synchronized ecosystem will reduce the distance between discovery and deployment to allow countries to be competitive in the global AI arena; this will encourage responsible technological advancement.

1.3 Problem Statement and Rationale for Synergizing Innovation

Although the advantages of cooperation are obvious, AI innovation has been fraught with fragmentation, lack of alignment between incentives, regulatory ambiguity, and uneven technological skill in a sector. Universities are often not able to have industry-level data sets and scalable computing infrastructure, and industries either have skills gaps or inadequate depth of research. Ethical control and protection of society by governments should engage in balancing innovation with risk management that may slow down the implementation of policies of the government or it may create uncertainty. Such gaps decrease the efficiency, add redundancy, and slow the implementation of powerful AI solutions (Poddar & Rao, 2024). The coordinated partnerships that aim at enhancing innovation through synergies will solve these issues by developing integrated opportunities of knowledge sharing, joint experimentation, and joint development of standards. The coherent collaboration model will make sure that the work of AI will be connected with the interests of the society, industry, and national missions. It creates a system through which ideas flow smoothly out of the conceptualization stage through testing and deployment (Chekanov, 2022). The synergy rationale can be made through the creation of trust, barriers minimization, exploitation of complementary advantages, and speedy responsible AI development in a multipolar world.

2. BACKGROUND TO THE STUDY

To establish the preconditions of cross-sector collaboration in AI, it is important to analyze the historical, technological, and geopolitical processes that determined the Triple Helix model. The model developed as a result of innovation research in the late 20th century and has viewed universities, governments, and industries as interdependent actors, the interactions of which lead to knowledge-based economic development. With the development of AI to have an overall-purpose technology that impacts the country and even the world in general, the applicability of the Triple Helix increased (Pique et al., 2018). The cycles of the historical innovation, such as the industrial revolutions and the digital transformation, proved that breakthroughs can be achieved when scientific research, policy of the government, and commercial innovation meet. The modern world is also marked by extremely fast international changes in data governance, national AI strategies, information infrastructure and global competitiveness, which are further motivating closer cooperation. Countries across the globe are committing to AI missions, regulatory standards, open-data environments, and talent pools to be on the forefront of the new AI economy (Mao et al., 2023). This context also puts the chapter into a wider theoretical and policy context, highlighting the reasons why integrated collaboration has ceased to be a choice, but a precondition to AI development, responsible governance, and sustainable technological ecosystems.

2.1 Historical Roots of the Triple Helix Model

Triple Helix Triple Helix model is a 1990s invention that describes the success of innovation whereby the universities, governments, and industries are not separate institutions but are co-evolutionary systems. Previously, the only institutions that were regarded as learning and research institutions were the universities, governments as regulators and industries as producers. However, in the advent of the knowledge-based economies, these functions started to alter and became more porous with the appearance of more fluidized relations and more hybrid forms of organization such as technology incubators, research park, and public-private constructions. The model is based on previous models of innovation ecosystems such as war-time research partnerships, national laboratories, and industrial R&D partnerships (Leydesdorff, 2012). These efforts emphasized that great scientific discoveries- such as aerospace engineering to biotechnology were a product of multipurpose work aided by policy leadership and industrial use. With digital technologies at the heart of economic development, the Triple Helix model offered an opportunity to interpret how cross-sector partnership can lead to competitiveness. This historical development provided the background of the application of the model to AI, where the interdisciplinary coordination and common areas of innovation are key to the development.

2.2 Transformative Role of Collaboration in Technological Revolutions

Technological revolutions have gone faster throughout history when there was collaboration bridging the gap between scientific discovery, policy support, and industrial implementation. Cooperative networks of academia, government agencies and private enterprises contributed to the creation of the steam engine, electrical systems, telecommunications, the internet and biotechnology. The pattern of these revolutions is clear: the universities are the first to form the fundamental ideas, governments are investing in infrastructural developments and protecting the people interest and industries are also commercializing the innovations into consumer products (Carayannis & Campbell, 2009). Cooperation in the framework of AI is even more essential because of the complexity, volume, and ethical aspects of the technology. Artificial intelligence systems demand large volumes of data, high-performance computing, years-long research, and strong regulatory systems, and a single industry is not capable of fulfilling each of these requirements. The cross-sector collaboration also establishes conditions of experimental testing, setting standards, and pooling of resources that hastens the technological maturity. It also makes the production of the prototype to deployment easier so that innovations can respond to actual societal needs (Campbell et al., 2004). Therefore, teamwork has always been a change technology driver, and AI follows the trend.

2.3 Global Shifts Driving AI Policies, Funding, and Innovation Ecosystems

Strategic policy actions, national competitive agenda and the fast-growing digital ecosystems are familiar to the world situation in the sphere of AI development. Countries in North America, Europe, and Asia have embarked on holistic AI actions regarding investment in research, employee training, data handling and ethical issues. These kinds of activities point to the growing value of AI as a driver of economic growth, national safety and technological dominance. At the same time, with the development of cloud computing, open-source platforms and the development of multi-national digital marketplaces, new forms of innovation and international collaboration have become feasible (Noya et al., 2024). In order to facilitate research and experimentation in AI, governments are investing in common AI infrastructure, such as compute clouds, national data platforms, and regulatory sandboxes. The industries are also collaborating with the universities in response to the scarcity of skills in an attempt to produce goods at a quicker pace. The competition of the countries on the international level has also contributed to solving the promotion of the AI ecosystems with the coordinated policy, investment, and multilateral alliances. The set of the changes helps to justify the applicability of integrative, interconnected systems of building responsible and scalable AI systems.

3. RESEARCH OBJECTIVES

To achieve the Artificial Intelligence, cooperation between the universities, governments, and even industries is becoming more dependent. Knowledge of how these sectors can manage, distribute resources, and coordinate their priorities is important in the quickening of innovation and being responsible in their adoption. This paper endeavors to discuss the processes, prerequisites, and directional approaches to make a successful cross-sector partnership through the Triple Helix model. The chapter has an analytical focus, which is based on the following objectives.

- To analyze cross-sector collaboration mechanisms that influence the speed, quality, and scalability of AI innovation across domains.
- To examine the evolving roles, responsibilities, and interdependencies of universities, governments, and industries in shaping AI ecosystems.
- To identify key barriers such as regulatory gaps, data silos, talent shortages, and incentive misalignment that hinder effective collaboration.
- To evaluate enabling factors, including shared infrastructure, policy support, innovation funding, and knowledge-exchange platforms that strengthen AI partnerships.
- To propose strategic pathways and a multi-tier collaboration model for fostering responsible, ethical, and sustainable AI development.

4. CONCEPTUAL MODEL

The hypothetical structure of this chapter reveals that the symbiotic linkages among the universities, governments, and industries encourage the responsible and speedy development of AI. It is built on the Triple Helix model and is premised on the reality that innovation is not linear but a dynamical cycle which is facilitated by a knowledge sharing process, coordinated governance, and a process of joint investment. It focuses on the bidirectional character of knowledge sharing and production between policy and research direction, financial resources and technology capabilities that all converge to establish national and global AI ecosystem (Miller et al., 2014). By mapping these interactions, the model provides a structured conceptualization of the value co-creation of various actors, ethical and regulatory challenges, and scaling AI solutions to the advantage of the society. The multi-tier model proposed in the present paper integrates the vision-setting, policy alignment, resource mobilization, data-sharing infrastructures and talent development into a single joint avenue. This comprehensive methodology contributes to the breakdown and makes AI innovations move between the stages of conceptualization and implementation effectively and responsibly (Yang et al., 2023). The conceptual framework can, therefore, be used as an analytical tool and a strategic roadmap to coming up with effective cross-sector collaboration mechanisms in the development of AI. Table 1 Sketches the key models of collaboration in the world that are employed to boost AI innovation.

Table 1. Cross-Sector Collaboration Mechanisms in AI

Collaboration Model	Participants	Purpose
Joint Research Labs	University–Industry	Co-create AI prototypes and conduct applied R&D
Public–Private Partnerships (PPP)	Government–Industry	Deploy AI solutions in national priority areas
Innovation Clusters	All three sectors	Foster ecosystem growth and shared experimentation
National AI Missions	Government–University–Industry	Align strategic goals and long-term investments

4.1 Triple Helix Innovation Synergy Model for AI

Triple Helix, Innovation Synergy Model is a representation of how universities, governments, and industries become interdependent forces to promote the development of AI. Universities provide both basic research and methodology and human talent needed in the development of algorithms and scientific discovery. Governments give guidance in terms of policies, regulatory systems, ethical provisions and strategic financing which dictate national interests and protect common interest. Research findings are complemented by industries by delivering research findings to deployable technology, scalable platforms and solutions that meet the needs of the market (H. Chen et al., 2025). In this model of synergy, there is the collaboration based on the sharing of laboratories, clusters of innovation, national missions of artificial intelligence, and joint research programs. The feedback loops make sure that academic research does not become irrelevant, policies are flexible, and technological innovations in the industry are based on scientific rigor and ethical standards. The model emphasizes that innovation does not arise in places with individual efforts but rather through the concerted efforts of integrating capabilities across industries (Global & Kazanskaia, 2025). The Triple Helix model enhances quicker AI technology creation, rollout, and responsible governance through the promotion of ongoing communication. Figure 2 shows the contribution made by universities, governments and industries towards complementary roles of research, policy and deployment of technologies, which intersect to lead AI innovation.

Figure 2. Triple Helix Synergy Model for AI Innovation

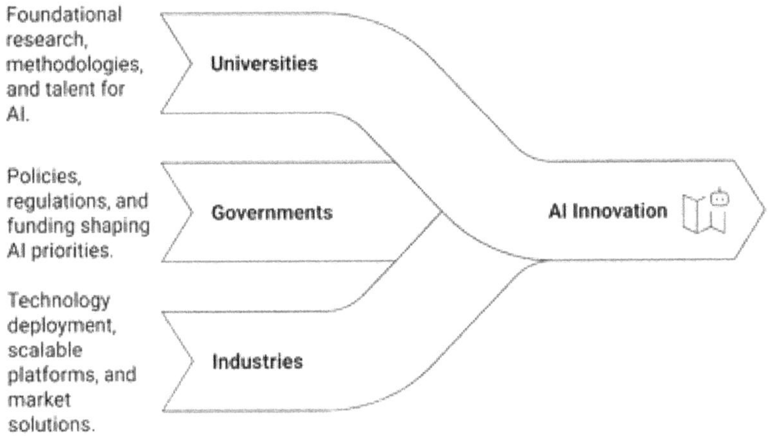

4.2 Flow of Knowledge, Resources, and Governance Across Sectors

AI innovation is based on the exchange mechanisms through fluid exchange in which knowledge, resources, and governance structures are transferred across sectors in a seamless manner. Universities produce scientific knowledge, data, and professional expertise that can fill the pipeline of industry research and make policy choices. Industries offer application data, test platforms, high-performance computing and market optimization which underpins research and government programs. Governments help in providing governance structures, ethical principles, regulatory sandboxes, and funding systems that help guarantee that innovation is done safe and fairly. This tri-directional flow establishes a pattern of constant learning, changes and co-creation (Etzkowitz & Klofsten, 2005). As a successful team, it is necessary to have common norm, interoperable systems, open communication lines and coordinated decision making. The other areas have the advantages of the other and overcome weaknesses through concerted efforts. These combined flows will minimize the repetition of the work, speed up the prototyping process, increase its adherence to regulations, and increase the confidence of society in AI technologies (Pearce et al., 2020). The combination of governance and scientific and industrial advancements is also achieved through this framework of collaborative flow, which is also efficient, responsible, and sustainable, thereby making AI innovations efficient and not careless.

4.3 Proposed Multi-Tier AI Collaboration Framework

The proposed partnership framework with a multi-tier is a methodology of the coordination of sector input to shared AI innovation goals. The Vision level establishes common long-term goals, which connect agendas of academic researchers, industrial roadmaps, and AI missions in countries. Policy tier harmonizes the regulatory requirements, ethical codes, and principles of operation to ensure the deployment is safe and responsible. The tier which organizes the sources of funding, resources allocation and shared infrastructural development to enable scalable experimentation and commercialization is the Investment tier (Laï et al., 2020). Data tier is an issue that revolves around common repositories, privileged access systems and interoperability systems that reduce the fragmentation and maximize the quality of research. Finally, the Talent level promotes the diversified education, training programs, movement plans and job skills development within industries. The layers form a solid partnership design when combined to enable the stable collaboration, the reduced number of obstacles, and the shorter development cycles (Larson et al., 2020). This hybrid structure would increase the stability of ecosystems, ensure the responsible development of AI, and ensure that the technological progress is appropriate to the economic, ethical, and social needs. Table 2 Generalizes the five-tier collaborative model.

Table 2. Proposed Multi-Tier AI Collaboration Framework

Framework Tier	Components	Purpose
Vision	Shared long-term goals	Aligns national, academic, and industrial priorities
Policy	Regulations, ethical standards	Ensures safe and responsible AI deployment
Investment	Funding, infrastructure	Supports scalable research and innovation
Data	Interoperable repositories, access protocols	Facilitates cross-sector knowledge exchange
Talent	Capacity building, interdisciplinary programs	Strengthens workforce and research capabilities

5. RESEARCH METHODOLOGY

The research methodology used in this chapter is qualitative, conceptual and case based research approach that would have been suitable to examine the dynamics of cross-sector cooperation in AI ecosystems. By taking into account the multi-layered structure of AI governance and the complexity of relationships between universities, governments, and industries, qualitative inquiry can provide complex insights into the actions of institutions, collaborative organizational structures and systems of innovation. To cover the two perspectives of the theory and make sure both are reflected in the research paper, the academic literature in the field, policy frameworks, and real-life case study were synthesized (McCradden, Sarker, et al., 2020). Such three-faceted process will enable the critical understanding of how the collaborative mechanisms operate, the issues that they encounter, and how they can be made to work. The methodology also involves the comparative analysis to establish the trends in different settings whether in the region or in the sector. The chapter provides a solid analytical foundation on the topic of explaining how the Triple Helix was able to create AI through the synthesis of both conceptual modeling and empirical observation. The research methodology suits well since it is deep, strict, and applicable in evaluating collaborative innovation ecosystems.

5.1 Research Design and Approach (Qualitative, Conceptual, Case-Based)

The research relies on both qualitative and conceptual orientation through the assistance of the evidence based on the cases. This approach is appropriate to analyze more complex relationships in the world of AI ecosystems when the variables are mutually dependent and cannot be examined in terms of quantitative measures. Qualitative lens allows the study to be, deep; change of contexts and interpretation of nuances to collaboration processes between universities, governments and industries. The sectors are evolved in the conceptual analysis that defines the interactions between them, the sharing of knowledge, and the joint development of the areas of innovation (Ms. Lolakshi P K et al., 2024). The other means of enhancing the research is through case studies whereby both successes and limitations of the collaborative structures are provided in practical terms. Through the assistance of the descriptive synthesis, thematic coding and comparative analysis, the study identifies similar patterns and frameworks of governance and strategic processes that characterize AI innovation. It is through this design integration that generates the validity of the findings and gives informative suggestions to the policymakers, academic leaders, and industry players.

5.2 Data Sources: Literature, Policy Documents, Industry Reports, Case Studies

The study is anchored on different and reliable sources of data to address the cross-sector collaboration in AI holistically. The academic articles, conferences, and theoretical structures provide background information about the systems of innovation, models of governance, and the trends of AI development. The policy reports of national and international bodies contribute to the information on the regulatory environment, ethics, and priorities of AI ecosystems. The reports of the two most successful technology companies, consultancies, and innovation agencies within the industry give practical information about the market trends and use of technology and challenges faced when undergoing the implementation process (Artyukhov et al., 2021). Case studies give the empirical examples of collaborative work of health sector, mobility, climate resilience and cybersecurity. All these sources have a triangulated evidence base that can be applied in investigating conceptual and operational aspects of collaboration (Ravikumar, et al., 2025). Having such a broad scope of data contributes to giving more credibility and legitimacy to the research results.

5.3 Analytical Framework for Synthesizing Cross-Sector Evidence

The analysis framework is a combination of thematic analysis, comparative evaluation and conceptual synthesis, which are used to analyze evidence within the Triple Helix sectors. Thematic analysis also finds common themes concerning the mechanisms of collaboration, governance practices, and issues of innovation. Comparison of case studies indicates variation in the role of the sector, support of policies, and mobilization of resources in different regions or areas. Conceptual synthesis is a union of theoretical concepts of the research in innovation with empirical data that will be used to refine the proposed model of collaboration (Joy et al., 2024). This framework helps in understanding multi-layered interactions in a systematic manner that is not simplified in terms of sectoral interdependencies. It also assists in developing strategic knowledge and practical recommendations as to the way the AI ecosystems can be improved. The framework would ensure that the conclusions and models presented in the chapter are analytic, context-relevant, and applicable in different institutional contexts through the links of theory and practice.

6. LITERATURE REVIEW

The facts in the literature about intersector collaboration in Artificial Intelligence (AI) are that the overall interaction between universities, governments and industries is the outcome of successful innovation. The players form a dynamic ecosystem where the research, policy, and commercialization collide so as to accelerate the pace of technology development. Studies highlight the value of complementation of its works: in universities, general theories and talent are created; in the government, the direction and the policies that regulate it are established; and in the industries, innovations are introduced on a large scale (Pinedo-López et al., 2025). The synthesis of the literature is performed in this section in compliance with the objectives of the research, the roles of the sector, the interdependent relations, and collaboration mechanisms that determine the development of AI. The review highlights the fact that the Triple Helix model can be used as a powerful analytical prism to comprehend how shared resources, collaborative efforts and integrated governance can generate more efficient and accountable AI ecosystems.

6.1 University Contributions: Basic Research, Talent Development, and Open Science

Universities are in the middle of the process of AI development, as they make significant contributions to fundamental research and theoretical innovation. Academic institutions are recognized by literature as the birthplace of basic algorithms, such as early machine learning models, neural networks and modern innovations in natural language processing and reinforcement learning (Mahetaji et al., 2025). Labs directed by universities tend to release innovative studies which influence the future of AI in the world. Talent development is another essential input that higher education institutions deliver capable graduates, researchers, and innovators that occupy the AI industry in the public and the private sector. Research also reveals the interest of universities in open science, consisting of open datasets, open-source tools, and more positive communication of findings, which enhances transparency, reproducibility and worldwide cooperation (University of Staffordshire et al., 2025). The open-access research also makes entry point less challenging, making smaller companies and countries in development contribute to AI innovation. Nonetheless, the literature reports the consistent obstacles, such as the lack of resources, the unavailability of industry-quality data, and the incompatibility between the academic literature and practical application, which support the necessity of systematic collaboration.

6.2 Government Roles: Policy, Regulation, Funding, and National AI Missions

The policies, ethical considerations and national strategies have been used by governments to increasingly influence AI development in order to ensure that innovation is promoted, whilst taking care of the interest of the people. The literature underscores the importance of governments in formulating regulatory frameworks on the area of data privacy, cybersecurity, AI ethics, and algorithmic transparency (Peddinti, 2025). The example of national AI missions can be seen in the United

States, European Union, China and India where policy direction can accelerate fundamental research, establish digital infrastructure and create incentive systems to spur innovation. Big funding Programs Big funding programs, research grants and public-private Partnerships serve as one of the main sources of funds to contribute to the large-scale research and experimentation. Another form of government enabling environments is through regulatory sandboxes, open-data projects and innovation clusters (Yelpaala et al., 2025). However, the literature suggests that the process of collaboration and innovativeness can be suppressed by the disintegration of the policy, slow regulating actions and uncertainty concerning the ethical norms. The literature has been unanimous in stating that moderate governance is not overly restrictive or permissive is a value that is at the core in ensuring that AI is created in a responsible manner and that people trust it.

6.3 Industry Roles: Technology Translation, Commercialization, and Innovation Scaling

It is at the industry sector that a decisive contribution is made in translating the scholarly discoveries in implementable AI technologies. It has been demonstrated in literature that industries have important assets, such as large volumes of data, computing resources, engineering skills, and access to real-world systems, which make possible quick prototyping and large-scale implementation. The concept of AI is operationalized into commercial products, platforms, and services available in healthcare diagnostics, autonomous mobility, financial, logistics, and customer engagement systems (Güneş & Kaban, 2025). Additional sources of experimentation capacity are provided by industry-supported innovation accelerator, corporate research labs and start-up ecosystems. Research points out that market relevance, scalability, and user-centered design are achieved through participation in the industry. Nonetheless, there are still issues related to proprietary information, lack of transparency of algorithms, and their incompatibility with societal or ethical aspects (Arora et al., 2025). These challenges are addressed through collaborative work with universities and governments that bring the issues of scientific rigor and the accountability of the government and business together. The literature finds that the involvement of industries is essential to facilitate practical effects, economic and scale-enhanced AI innovations. Table 3 Summarizes the different but not mutually exclusive functions of each of the Triple Helix actors in the development of AI.

Table 3. Comparative Roles of Triple Helix Actors in AI Innovation

Sector	Key Functions	Contribution to AI Ecosystem
University	Basic research, talent development, open science	Advances foundational algorithms and nurtures expertise
Government	Policy, regulation, funding, national AI missions	Provides direction, governance, and enabling infrastructure
Industry	Commercialization, deployment, engineering expertise	Converts research into scalable, market-ready solutions

7. CASE STUDY

Case studies give real examples of how universities, governments, and industries work together to enhance the innovation of AI and solve the real problems in society. They emphasize the working mechanism of the Triple Helix model and demonstrate how the common infrastructure, alignment of policy, and knowledge of technology come together to make AI implementation faster. The latest international projects show that successful cross-sector collaborations do not only increase the productivity of research, but also provide ethical and scaled ability, as well as acceptance of AI solutions in the society (Fernandes et al., 2023). These scenarios represent various fields including health care, mobility, and smart infrastructure; and they indicate the flexibility of collaborative models in different settings. This section reveals the huge potential of coordinated action in transformation by looking at successful implementations. The chosen case studies demonstrate that the combination of research, regulation support, and industrial engineering can yield effective results. All of them can inform future plans of resilient AI ecosystems based on collaboration, innovation, and responsible governance.

7.1 Case Study 1: Cross-Sector Collaboration in AI for Healthcare Diagnostics

Among the most successful cases of Triple Helix collaboration, the creation of AI-driven diagnostic tools to detect early diseases can be named. One of the recent efforts was the collaboration of major universities, national health organizations, and technology firms to create deep learning models to detect diabetic retinopathy, lung disease, and sepsis risk based on clinical images and electronic health records (Edmunds et al., 2019). Universities were involved in providing algorithmic innovation, clinical interpretation frameworks and annotated datasets obtained via academic-hospital research networks. The approval of regulatory approvals, ethical compliance and data-governance frameworks, all required by the government health departments, were enforced to align with the privacy and safety standards. Cloud infrastructure and engineering skills as well as real-time deployment platforms by technology firms helped in making hospitals and telemedicine systems scalable.

The partnership led to the implementation of AI tools that have been multisite clinically trialed and implemented into screening processes in various regions in India, Singapore, and the United States. This method minimized the diagnostic time, high rate of early detection and optimal clinical workloads. The case reflects on the speed of innovation in healthcare through cross-sector collaboration in terms of combining scientific rigor, policy assurance and industrial scalability. It also highlights the significance of ethical leadership and common data models in the ethical implementation of AI in a medical setting. Note that figure 3 shows how universities, technology companies and government health organizations can collaborate to provide research, infrastructure and regulatory control to create and implement AI-powered healthcare diagnostic systems.

Figure 3. AI Healthcare Diagnostics Collaboration Framework

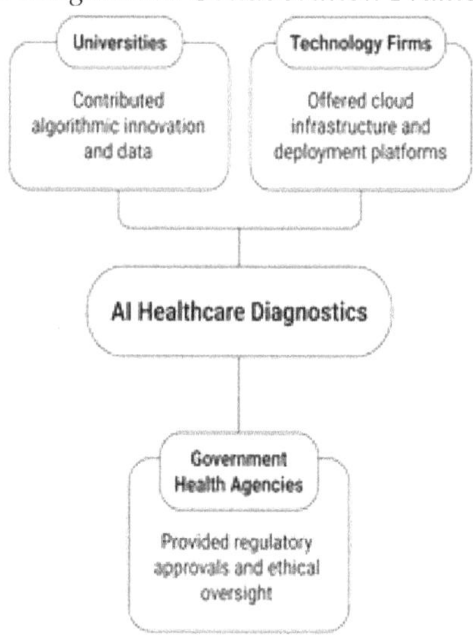

7.2 Case Study 2: Triple Helix Synergy in Smart Mobility and Intelligent Infrastructure

Another striking recent case of Triple Helix collaboration is the application of AI into smart mobility and smart transportation infrastructure. The universities collaborated with transport ministries and automotive technology companies to jointly come up with AI models to predict traffic, autonomous navigation, and roadway safety analytics(Evjemo et al., 2020). Researchers also provided superior computer vision, sensor fusion and optimization algorithms. The government agencies made urban mobility data available, also supported pilot environments, and created regulatory sandboxes to test the autonomous and semi-autonomous systems. Solutions based on edge AI were also implemented in industries, such as intelligent traffic lights, smart road sensors, Vehicle 2 Infrastructure (V2I) systems, predictive maintenance platforms, and intelligent maintenance systems.

The synergy allowed to roll out AI-driven mobility pilots in Singapore, Dubai, and Helsinki, resulting in the lessening of congestion, pedestrian safety, and optimization of the activities of the public transport. Start-ups in the area of micro-mobility analytics, fleet management, and environmental monitoring were also developed through the collaborative ecosystem. This example shows that a coordinated study, policy invention and industrial engineering can speed up the realization of intelligent infrastructure. It underscores the importance of government role in enabling testing safe conditions, the universities in developing analysis models and industry in providing scaling up. The figure 4 demonstrates the collaboration of universities, government agencies, and industries to develop, support, and deploy AI-driven mobility solutions, which will provide the growth of start-ups and allow real-life smart transport pilots.

Figure 4. Triple Helix Collaboration in Smart Mobility

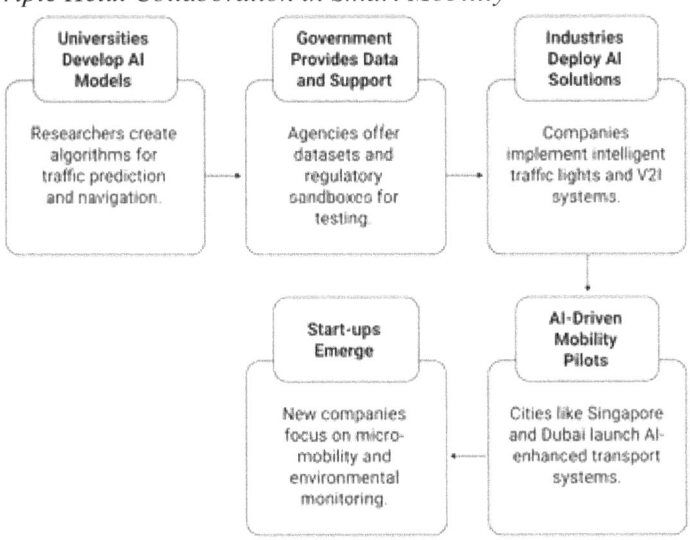

7.3 Lessons Learned from Successful Multi-Stakeholder AI Partnerships

In both of the case studies, a number of lessons are learned regarding the successful cross sector collaboration. To align the research interests, policy frameworks, and commercial approaches, first, there should be a shared vision and long-term commitment. Second, open data-governance systems create a sense of trust and facilitate a free flow of knowledge. Third, it is regulatory flexibility, i.e., sandboxes, pilot zones, and ethical rules that promote experimentation and ensure the safety of the people. Fourth, the natural experience of the industrial participation guarantees the real-world readiness and scalability to overcome the gap between prototypes and implementation (Ojo et al., 2016). Lastly, ongoing dialogue among sectors can be used to manage expectations, coordinate schedules and coordinate responses to new challenges. All these lessons together serve to support the fact that effective AI systems involve synchronized governance, interdisciplinary and coordinated infrastructure. The Triple Helix may still be used as a potent framework to organize such partnership and facilitate responsible and innovation-oriented development. Table 4 Provides a brief juxtaposition of both case studies as discussed in Section 7.

Table 4. Overview of Case Studies in AI Collaboration

Case Study	Sectors Involved	Focus Area	Key Outcomes
AI for Healthcare Diagnostics	University-Government-Industry	Early disease detection	Improved accuracy, faster screening, scalable deployment
Smart Mobility & Intelligent Infrastructure	University-Government-Industry	Traffic prediction, autonomous systems	Reduced congestion, enhanced safety, real-time analytics

8. RESULTS / DISCUSSION

The findings of this paper demonstrate the revolutionary nature of synergistic partnership between universities, governments and industries in order to drive AI innovation. If there is a cross-sector commitment, it has been proven that it leads to faster scaling solutions, decreases fragmentation, and facilitates the responsible utilization of AI technologies in the high-impact areas of the healthcare, mobility, and public administration (Lu et al., 2023). The collaborative structures give the opportunity to quickly experiment, share data and computational resources, and combine the scientific rigor and industrial engineering expertise. These advantages can however only be realized when governance frameworks, incentives and operational abilities in sectors are harmonized(Ravikumar & Aarthi, 2025a). The challenges that have remained throughout the discussion include: the lack of alignment of priorities, intellectual property conflicts, the lack of interoperability, and uncertainty in the regulatory environment, tend to hamper smooth collaboration. The barriers can be overcome through the coordinated policy tools, standard data ecosystems, and ethical design practices which can build trust and compliance (Jelovac et al., 2022). The findings demonstrate the significance of integrated ecosystem approach in which the governance, infrastructure, and multi-disciplinary talent work in harmony to sustain the momentum of innovations and benefit to the society.

8.1 Benefits of Synergistic Collaboration: Innovation Speed, Scalability, and Societal Impact

The synergistic collaboration may be regarded as the means of increasing the speed of innovation of the AI significantly because of the interplay of academic innovation, government regulations, and the execution of the industrial projects. Universities possess a research base and a pool of talent, which is relatively fixed over time, and industries possess huge datasets, platforms of deployment, and engineering experience. Regulatory transparency, national missions on AI, and financial initiatives are among the methods that encourage such initiatives by governments. A combination of these factors creates a powerful ecosystem where innovations are introduced in the concept to practice at a much faster rate (Zhu et al., 2019). Scalability enhances this because of shared infrastructure such as cloud resources, testbeds and open-data platforms which reduce redundancy of work and the cost of experimenting is lower. It is more meaningful when many stakeholders assume control and ensure that AI solutions are applied in order to address the actual problems, i.e. early detection of the disease or motion efficiency, or climate-resilience, and without reducing the degree of ethical standards. The ability to have such coordinated advantages proves the argument that a single sector cannot deliver the pace, reach, and worth of the people to enable AI adoption to be transformative in and of itself.

8.2 Challenges: Incentive Misalignment, Data Silos, IP Conflicts, and Regulatory Gaps

The cooperation in different structural issues is anchored in the dissimilarity of the interests of spheres and operational limitations despite the high potential. Situations where the incentives are incompatible typically occur when universities are concerned with publications, industries need to gain competitive edge, and governments are worried about risk reduction which in turn results in divided decision-making.

The existence of data silos is caused by privacy concern, proprietary ownership, and inability to exchange insights between institutions, which is due to the lack of interoperability. Intellectual Property (IP) issue is also a problem that baffles the opportunities of joint research, particularly in those instances where ambiguous agreements restrict the areas of commercialization or discouraging the potential of collaboration (Dooley & Kirk, 2007). The absence of regulation (the absence of explicit AI guidelines, slow regulatory process, non-homogenous data-governance policy) has an adverse impact on confidence and slows innovation process. These might reduce the degree of trust, slack operations and create technical ability gaps amongst industries. In order to alleviate these problems, conscious mechanisms are necessary, which should enable balancing the incentives, align the data structures, specify IP policies, and reduce regulatory processes (Ravikumar, et al., 2025). Table 5 Enlists major technical, regulatory and organizational threats to synergy.

Table 5. Barriers Affecting Triple Helix Collaboration

Barrier Category	Examples	Impact
Incentive Misalignment	Different KPIs across sectors	Slows decision-making and partnership sustainability
Data Silos	Fragmented datasets, privacy restrictions	Reduces model accuracy and experimentation
IP Conflicts	Unclear ownership, licensing disputes	Limits commercialization pathways
Regulatory Gaps	Ambiguous standards, slow approvals	Hinders deployment and public trust

8.3 Strategies for Strengthening AI Ecosystems: Governance, Shared Infrastructure, and Ethics

The formation of the AI ecosystems should be integrated; this should be based on good governance, shared infrastructure and practice of ethics. Defined governance frameworks; the joint committees, multi stakeholder councils and adaptive regulatory sandboxes can be handy in harmonizing priorities, and facilitate in making open decisions. The minimalization of this fragmentation can be performed through common infrastructure such as interoperable data platforms and national AI clouds and research testbeds to enable the attainment of regional and sectoral scale consistency (Ansell & Gash, 2008). The pillars are ethical frameworks, which potentially can help in promoting data stewardship, algorithmic fairness, transparency, and accountability. When ethics-by-design is used, the collaborative projects will be more compliant and trustful towards the regulatory laws in the society. Besides that, constant learning and interdisciplinary integration can be triggered by cross-sector training programs, mobility programs, as well as innovation centers. All these measures would likely result in resilience, equity, and AI ecosystems fit to facilitates long-term innovation that will be both compatible with the principles of the population and global benchmarks. Table 6 Finds some of the most efficient components that may be employed in the team work and innovation progress.

Table 6. Enablers of Effective Cross-Sector AI Collaboration

Enabler	Description	Expected Outcome
Shared Infrastructure	Common compute cloud, testbeds, data platforms	Faster experimentation and reduced costs
Aligned Governance	Joint steering committees, regulatory sandboxes	Transparent oversight and ethical compliance
Talent Mobility	Fellowships, exchange programs	Cross-pollination of skills and knowledge
Open-Science Practices	Open datasets, open-source tools	Inclusive and reproducible innovation

9. FUTURE RESEARCH

Future studies should advance on the cross-sector AI governance and enhance the models that help to develop sustainable collaboration. Towards the more penetration of AI systems in the work of society, more deep studies are required in the long term on the changing nature of governance structures and how partnerships respond to the change of technology, economic, and regulatory conditions. Studies also need to cover unresolved gaps in talent development, data access, and interdisciplinary coordination, with human capital and common knowledge being the focal point of AI development (Radaelli et al., 2024). The other fruitful avenue to pursue is the international collaboration models capable of balancing standards, data sharing culture, and ethical principles on the global scale. Since the AI innovation is accelerating, it should also be considered in the future through the lens of new paradigms, including open science, federated learning ecosystems, and global AI safety networks that can potentially reshape the way cross-sector cooperation occurs. Finally, future studies must focus on enhancing the theoretical framework, providing practical recommendations to professionals, as well as lead to the development of resilient, inclusive, and responsible AI ecosystems (Ravikumar & Aarthi, 2025b).

9.1 Need for Longitudinal Studies on Cross-Sector AI Governance

Cross-sector collaboration based on AI is a concept that requires longitudinal studies to comprehend how it evolves between periods. Recent research tends to focus on the short-term analysis of cases, which gives very little information on the sustainability, flexibility, and long-term outcomes of governance structures. Longitudinal studies may also indicate the impact of the changing policies, economic conditions and technological development on the outcomes of collaboration. They are also in a position to determine which mechanisms, including joint funding models, shared infrastructures, or regulatory sandboxes are able to support long-run innovation. Analyzing multiyear data enables researchers to observe the cyclic theme of collaboration in stages of development, stagnation and renewal (Villacis & Badruddoza, 2023). This kind of research will be critical in improving the Triple Helix model and will offer evidence-based recommendations to the policy makers and heads of institutions. Through the knowledge of the long-term trends, the stakeholders will be able to create smarter and more resilient AI governance systems.

9.2 Emerging Research Gaps in Talent, Data Ecosystems, and Multidisciplinary Collaboration

There are also still three fundamental areas of research gaps, including talent development, data ecosystems, and multidisciplinary collaboration. First, despite the fact that universities provide AI knowledge, there is a lack of research done on how cross-sector mobility programs, micro-credentialing, and lifelong learning programs can overcome workforce shortages. Second, data ecosystems are still fragmented with additional research needed to compare models of secure sharing of data, federated learning as well as interoperability standards that are innovative and privacy-aware (Kaur, 2024). Third, AI also requires multidisciplinary cooperation between computer science, ethics, law, economics, and social sciences, but the systems of integrating such a wide range of disciplines are inadequately developed. Future studies ought to examine processes that help in building interdisciplinary synergies and minimizing structural impediments to collaboration. Sealing these loopholes is crucial to creating innovative as well as socially-grounded AI ecosystems.

9.3 Prospective Trends: International AI Cooperation, Open Science, and Responsible AI

The further perspectives of AI collaboration are more global collaboration, more open science and more responsibility and ethics. International cooperation will become a must because countries will be trying to coordinate the rules, share experience, or address transnational challenges such as cybersecurity, climate change, global health (Ravikumar, et al., 2025). There is a high probability of the growing role of the open science practices which involve open datasets, open-source models, and transparent research in the democratization of AI innovation and the removal of inequalities among regions. Meanwhile, the idea of responsible AI will take a crucial place in the system design, implementation, and evaluation, which will set the trend of cooperation in industries. (Bengoa et al., 2021). Ethical auditing, AI safety measures, and human-centered AI models will become trendy ways that organizations will engage and innovate in their interactions. The above developments highlight the necessity of adaptive collaboration paradigms that are capable of reconciling scientific openness and governance as well as society expectations.

10. MANAGERIAL IMPLICATIONS

The research results of the current study provide paramount managerial implications to leaders in academia, government, and industry to develop successful ecosystem of AI collaborations. In the case of universities, findings highlight the necessity to match the research agendas to societal and industrial priorities and to promote interdisciplinary training and the open-science practices (Luo, 2020). The government agencies need to enhance regulatory transparency, simplify the governance, and develop incentive systems that promote responsible innovation. Leaders in the industry must embrace co-creation frameworks where academic knowledge and social control are incorporated in their development processes and they are not only scalable, but also ethical. In all industries, managers need to focus on communicating, developing common infrastructure and trust-building in order to decrease fragmentation and speed up its implementation. These implications point out the fact that collaboration is not an operation option alone but a strategic need to promote innovative, fair and socially beneficial AI systems.

10.1 Implications for University Leaders: Research Priorities and Collaboration Models

The leaders in Universities ought to strategically align the research agenda to the needs of the society and industry requirements. This means promoting cross disciplinary courses which are integrating computer science, ethics, policy and knowledge domain. The collaboration models should also encourage faculty-industry partnerships, visit researcher initiatives, and be involved in AI missions of the country. The leaders should also invest in open-science infrastructure e.g.

shared databases, reproducible research platforms, and collaborative laboratories (Wang et al., 2024). Improving the university-industry trust can also be achieved by improving the intellectual property management processes, which will help in commercialization. By creating a network between students, researchers, policy-makers and practitioners, universities will gain the ability to become the driving force behind responsible AI ecosystems.

10.2 Implications for Government Agencies: Policy Alignment and Innovation Incentives

The government agencies are key players in establishing AI innovation in the shape of policy consistency, ethical governance and strategic financing. The agencies must align national AI strategies to the requirements of the sector and develop regulatory infrastructures that do not compromise on the safety during experimentation processes. The collaborative projects can be stimulated with the assistance of the innovation incentives such as grants, tax breaks, and sandbox environments that can attract the industry (Aschhoff and Grimpe, 2014). Governments should also support shared digital infrastructure, open-data projects and standard protocols in an attempt to reduce fragmentation. Generally, the agencies may ensure that AI systems promote the good of the society and make the country more competitive by allowing the development of partnerships between the population and the private sector and maintaining the transparency of control.

10.3 Implications for Industry Leaders: Co-Creation Models and Ethical AI Deployment

The industry leaders should follow co-creation models whereby scientific research and policy guidelines are integrated in their innovation line. The cooperation with the institutions of higher learning will accelerate the course of the algorithms implementation realization, and the cooperation with the governmental organizations will ensure that the developed algorithms will be able to satisfy the stated regulatory and ethical requirements. The first position should be given to responsible AI implementation on an industry level, which involves the use of fairness checks, transparency systems, and routine risks evaluation (McCradden, Baba, et al., 2020). The capacity to be innovative in the long-term is supported through investment in interoperable platforms, safe data-sharing plans and workforce upskilling initiatives. This will allow industries to become competitive and socially responsible AI technologies by turning to proactive forms of governance and reduced participation in multi-stakeholder activities.

11. CONCLUSION

As shown in this chapter, the Triple Helix model, which connects universities, governments, and industries, is an effective and essential one that needs to be used to make AI innovation and implementation rapid and responsible, ethical, and scalable. The development of AI as a general-purpose technology requires collaborative mechanisms of combining both base research, policy management, and industrial engineering in a unified ecosystem that will be able to serve more complex needs of society. As the chapter demonstrates, higher education institutions generate scientific discovery, talent formation, and open knowledge; governments offer clarity in regulation, ethics protections, strategic investments and vision on the national level; and industries take what academics have developed and creates a real-world solution available on the market. These synergies allow innovating fast, accelerating growth, and achieving improved outcomes in the society in the areas of health care, mobility, climate resilience, and cybersecurity.

In the meantime, the chapter does not denounce the reality of the unherdable impediments, like misalignment of incentives, data fragmentation, IP dilemmas and regulatory confusion, and emphasizes the necessity to possess governance frameworks that foster transparency, interoperability, shared responsibility. The results support the idea of the need to maintain responsible AI futures through an integrated approach that cross-institutional and national divides. Since AI is becoming more relevant to the stability of economies in the world, social welfare, and ethical decision-making, cross-sector and international collaborations will need to become more profound to align the standards, exchange the best practices, and establish resilient infrastructures. Finally, this chapter recommends the proactive reinforcement of the global AI ecosystems based on collaboration, transparency, and responsibility to guarantee that the innovation does not merely make leaps forward but also reflects the values and overall human welfare.

REFERENCES

Ansell, C., & Gash, A. (2008). Collaborative governance in theory and practice. *Journal of Public Administration Research and Theory: J-PART, 18*(4), 543–571. DOI: 10.1093/jopart/mum032

Arora, A. S., Saboia, L., Arora, A., & McIntyre, J. R. (2025). Human-centric versus state-driven. *International Journal of Intelligent Information Technologies*, *21*(1), 1–13. DOI: 10.4018/ijiit.367471

Artyukhov, A., Krmela, J., Krmelova, V., & Volk, I. (2021). Quality of scientific activity, technology transfer and research integrity: Case of Ukrainian university. *Business Ethics and Leadership*, *5*(4), 101–109. DOI: 10.21272/bel.5(4).101-109.2021

Aschhoff, B., & Grimpe, C. (2014). Contemporaneous peer effects, career age and the industry involvement of academics in biotechnology. *Research Policy*, *43*(2), 367–381. DOI: 10.1016/j.respol.2013.11.002

Bengoa, A., Maseda, A., Iturralde, T., & Aparicio, G. (2021). A bibliometric review of the technology transfer literature. *The Journal of Technology Transfer*, *46*(5), 1514–1550. DOI: 10.1007/s10961-019-09774-5

Campbell, E. G., Powers, J. B., Blumenthal, D., & Biles, B. (2004). Inside the triple helix: Technology transfer and commercialization in the life sciences. *Health Affairs (Project Hope)*, *23*(1), 64–76. DOI: 10.1377/hlthaff.23.1.64

Carayannis, E. G., & Campbell, D. F. J. (2009). "Mode 3" and "Quadruple Helix": Toward a 21st century fractal innovation ecosystem. [International Journal of Technology Management]. *Journal International de La Gestion Technologique*, *46*(3/4), 201. DOI: 10.1504/ijtm.2009.023374

Chekanov, A. (2022). The Triple Helix in transition economies and Skolkovo: A Russian innovation ecosystem case. *Journal of Evolutionary Studies in Business*, *7*(2), 160–183. DOI: 10.1344/jesb2022.2.j110

Chen, H., Zeng, Y., & Cai, D. (2025). Deep learning for cardiovascular management: Optimizing pathways and cost control under diagnosis-related group models. *Frontiers in Artificial Intelligence*, *8*(1580445), 1580445. DOI: 10.3389/frai.2025.1580445

Chen, Z., Little, V. J., & Thuan, N. H. (2025). The evolving role of technology transfer offices in the entrepreneurial university: Go-betweens or playmakers? *The Journal of Technology Transfer*, *50*(3), 1060–1079. DOI: 10.1007/s10961-024-10123-4

Dooley, L., & Kirk, D. (2007). University-industry collaboration. *European Journal of Innovation Management, 10*(3), 316–332. DOI: 10.1108/14601060710776734

Edmunds, L. D., Gluderer, S., Ovseiko, P. V., Kamerling, R., Ton, J., Vis, L., Jenni, M., Tutton, G., Lawton-Smith, H., Nadabán, M. V., Rab, M., Rees, J., Anson, J., Rushforth, A. D., Allen, M., Buchan, A. M., Vendrell, M., Casta, A., Mehes, G., & Hassan, A. B. (2019). New indicators and indexes for benchmarking university-industry-government innovation in medical and life science clusters: Results from the European FP7 Regions of Knowledge HealthTIES project. *Health Research Policy and Systems, 17*(1), 10. DOI: 10.1186/s12961-019-0414-5

Etzkowitz, H., & Klofsten, M. (2005). The innovating region: Toward a theory of knowledge-based regional development. *R & D Management, 35*(3), 243–255. DOI: 10.1111/j.1467-9310.2005.00387.x

Evjemo, L. D., Gjerstad, T., Grøtli, E. I., & Sziebig, G. (2020). Trends in smart manufacturing: Role of humans and industrial robots in smart factories. *Current Robotics Reports, 1*(2), 35–41. DOI: 10.1007/s43154-020-00006-5

Fernandes, E. B., Wegner, D., & Möllering, G. (2023). Governance of interorganizational projects: A process-based approach applied to a Latin American–European case. *Project Management Journal, 54*(3), 219–234. DOI: 10.1177/87569728221145927

Global, N., & Kazanskaia, A. N. (2025). *Machine learning models and algorithms: Approaches, applications, and best practices*. NEYA Global Journal of Non-Profit Studies., DOI: 10.64357/neya-gjnps-ai-mch-lr-04

Güneş, A., & Kaban, A. L. (2025). A Delphi study on ethical challenges and ensuring academic integrity regarding AI research in higher education. *Higher Education Quarterly, 79*(4). Advance online publication. DOI: 10.1111/hequ.70057

Jelovac, D., Ljubojević, Č., & Ljubojević, L. (2022). HPC in business: The impact of corporate digital responsibility on building digital trust and responsible corporate digital governance. *Digital Policy Regulation and Governance, 24*(6), 485–497. DOI: 10.1108/dprg-11-2020-0164

Joy, Z. H., Master of Science in Business Analytics Michigan USA, T. U., Rahman, M. M., Uzzaman, A. U., Maraj, M. A. A., Master of Computer and Information Science Arkansas USA, S. A. U., Graduate Researcher College of Business Lamar University Beaumont Texas USA, M. I. S., & Graduate Researcher College of Business Lamar University Beaumont Texas USA, M. I. S. (2024). Integrating machine learning and big data analytics for real-time disease detection in smart healthcare systems. *Global Mainstream Journal, 1*(3), 16–27. DOI: 10.62304/ijhm.v1i3.162

Kaur, S. (2024). Advancements in artificial Intelligence: Machine Learning techniques and their real-world applications. *Journal of Sustainable Solutions*, *1*(4), 138–144. DOI: 10.36676/j.sust.sol.v1.i4.45

Laï, M.-C., Brian, M., & Mamzer, M.-F. (2020). Perceptions of artificial intelligence in healthcare: Findings from a qualitative survey study among actors in France. *Journal of Translational Medicine*, *18*(1), 14. DOI: 10.1186/s12967-019-02204-y

Larson, D. B., Magnus, D. C., Lungren, M. P., Shah, N. H., & Langlotz, C. P. (2020). Ethics of using and sharing clinical imaging data for artificial intelligence: A proposed framework. *Radiology*, *295*(3), 675–682. DOI: 10.1148/radiol.2020192536

Leydesdorff, L. (2012). The triple helix, quadruple helix, …, and an N-tuple of helices: Explanatory models for analyzing the knowledge-based economy? *Journal of the Knowledge Economy*, *3*(1), 25–35. DOI: 10.1007/s13132-011-0049-4

Lu, Q., Zhu, L., Xu, X., & Whittle, J. (2023). Responsible-AI-by-design: A pattern collection for designing responsible AI systems. *IEEE Software*, •••, 1–7. DOI: 10.1109/ms.2022.3233582

Luo, H. (2020). An emergency management system for government data security based on artificial intelligence. *Ingénierie Des Systèmes d Information*, *25*(2), 207–213. DOI: 10.18280/isi.250208

Mahetaji, K., Zogheib, C., & Spencer, R. (2025). Intersections between government data and AI strategies: A case study of technology policies in Canada's federal service. *Proceedings of the Association for Information Science and Technology*, *62*(1), 1024–1029. DOI: 10.1002/pra2.1333

Mao, Z., Wu, J., & Liu, M. (2023). A CIO-centric local government data-sharing leadership ecosystem in China. *Information Development*, *39*(4), 798–810. DOI: 10.1177/02666669211054176

McCradden, M. D., Baba, A., Saha, A., Ahmad, S., Boparai, K., Fadaiefard, P., & Cusimano, M. D. (2020). Ethical concerns around use of artificial intelligence in health care research from the perspective of patients with meningioma, caregivers and health care providers: A qualitative study. *CMAJ Open*, *8*(1), E90–E95. DOI: 10.9778/cmajo.20190151

McCradden, M. D., Sarker, T., & Paprica, P. A. (2020). Conditionally positive: A qualitative study of public perceptions about using health data for artificial intelligence research. *BMJ Open*, *10*(10), e039798. DOI: 10.1136/bmjopen-2020-039798

Mikhaylov, S. J., Esteve, M., & Campion, A. (2018). Artificial intelligence for the public sector: Opportunities and challenges of cross-sector collaboration. *Philosophical Transactions. Series A, Mathematical, Physical, and Engineering Sciences*, *376*(2128), 20170357. DOI: 10.1098/rsta.2017.0357

Miller, K., McAdam, M., & McAdam, R. (2014). The changing university business model: A stakeholder perspective. *R & D Management*, *44*(3), 265–287. DOI: 10.1111/radm.12064

Ms. Lolakshi, P. K., Satwik, K. D., Rai, S. R., Patgar, S. M., & Poojary, S. R. (2024). A review on A study of impact of technological advancement of intellectual property and research methodologies. International Journal of Advanced Research in Science. *Tongxin Jishu*, *389–393*. Advance online publication. DOI: 10.48175/ijarsct-19259

Noya, S., Taneo, S. Y. M., Melany, M., & Widyaningrum, S. (2024). Collaboration with Triple Helix: The mediating effect of mass media in expanding SMEs' information access. *Quality Innovation Prosperity*, *28*(1), 67–87. DOI: 10.12776/qip.v28i1.1940

Ojo, A., Porwol, L., Waqar, M., Stasiewicz, A., Osagie, E., Hogan, M., Harney, O., & Zeleti, F. A. (2016). Realizing the innovation potentials from open data: Stakeholders' perspectives on the desired affordances of open data environment. In Collaboration in a Hyperconnected World (pp. 48–59). Springer International Publishing. https://doi.org/DOI: 10.1007/978-3-319-45390-3_5

Olayinka, A. (2023). Synergistic integration of Artificial Intelligence and machine learning in smart manufacturing (Industry 4.0). *World Journal of Advanced Engineering Technology and Sciences*, *10*(1), 255–263. DOI: 10.30574/wjaets.2023.10.1.0264

Pearce, T., Maple, M., Shakeshaft, A., Wayland, S., & McKay, K. (2020). What is the co-creation of new knowledge? A content analysis and proposed definition for health interventions. *International Journal of Environmental Research and Public Health*, *17*(7), 2229. DOI: 10.3390/ijerph17072229

Peddinti, S. R. (2025). AI and Federated Learning for cross-industry data collaboration: Applications in finance, E-commerce, and medical tech. *Journal of Information Systems Engineering & Management*, *10*(30s), 78–82. DOI: 10.52783/jisem.v10i30s.4777

Pinedo-López, J., Baena-Navarro, R., & Torres-Hoyos, F. (2025). Science, technology and innovation in Colombia: Impact of the relationships between enterprises, government and universities. *Science, Technology & Society*, *30*(2), 363–385. DOI: 10.1177/09717218251326826

Pique, J. M., Berbegal-Mirabent, J., & Etzkowitz, H. (2018). Triple Helix and the evolution of ecosystems of innovation: The case of Silicon Valley. *Triple Helix (Heidelberg)*, *5*(1). Advance online publication. DOI: 10.1186/s40604-018-0060-x

Poddar, A., & Rao, S. R. (2024). Evolving intellectual property landscape for AI-driven innovations in the biomedical sector: Opportunities in stable IP regime for shared success. *Frontiers in Artificial Intelligence*, *7*, 1372161. DOI: 10.3389/frai.2024.1372161

Radaelli, D., Di Maria, S., Jakovski, Z., Alempijevic, D., Al-Habash, I., Concato, M., Bolcato, M., & D'Errico, S. (2024). Advancing patient safety: The future of artificial intelligence in mitigating healthcare-associated infections: A systematic review. *Healthcare (Basel, Switzerland)*, *12*(19), 1996. DOI: 10.3390/healthcare12191996

Ravikumar, A. Olimbaevich, I. R., Mashkhura, S., & Musayeva, S. (2025). Transforming Healthcare with Large Language Models and AI agents. In Advances in Computational Intelligence and Robotics (pp. 51–82). IGI Global Scientific Publishing. https://doi.org/DOI: 10.4018/979-8-3373-2008-3.ch003

Ravikumar, R. S., Manujakshi, Aarthi, S., Urazbaeva, Y., & Tamilselvi, S. (2025). Navigating data privacy, security, and regulatory challenges in healthcare AI ensuring fairness, bias mitigation, interpretability, and trust. In Transformative Role of Transformer Models in Healthcare (pp. 25–54). IGI Global Scientific Publishing. https://doi.org/DOI: 10.4018/979-8-3373-2038-0.ch002

Ravikumar, R. N., & Aarthi, S. (2025a). AI-powered synergistic robotics and IoT ecosystems for predictive and preventive healthcare. In *Robotics and IoT Synergy in Next-Generation Healthcare* (pp. 1–32). IGI Global Scientific Publishing., DOI: 10.4018/979-8-3373-5447-7.ch001

Ravikumar, R. N., & Aarthi, S. (2025b). Federated Learning and privacy-preserving search. In *Role of Library Resources for Higher Education in the Digital Era* (pp. 71–108). IGI Global Scientific Publishing., DOI: 10.4018/979-8-3373-3005-1.ch004

Ravikumar, R. N., Aarthi, S., Nadarajan, S., Masharipova, G., Mamadiyarov, Z., & Tamilselvi, S. (2025). Big data and cloud computing for climate-oriented remote sensing. In *Advances in Geospatial Technologies* (pp. 165–196). IGI Global Scientific Publishing., DOI: 10.4018/979-8-3373-3501-8.ch006

Singla, B., Afridi, S., Vayolipoyil, S., Ahmed, T., Afzaal, S., Saleem, K., Zobia Malik, M. T., & Qudsia, M. (2025). The evolving role of artificial intelligence in medical science: Advancing diagnostics, clinical decision-making, and research. *Cureus*, *17*(9), e91514. DOI: 10.7759/cureus.91514

University of Staffordshire. U. K., Adebayo, A. S., Chukwurah, N., Dish Network CO USA, L., Oluwaseun Ajayi, O., & University of the Cumberlands, U. S. A. (2025). Artificial Intelligence and Machine Learning algorithms for advanced threat detection and cybersecurity risk mitigation strategies. Engineering and Technology Journal, 10(03). https://doi.org/DOI: 10.47191/etj/v10i03.18

Villacis, A. H., & Badruddoza, S. (2023). Using artificial intelligence to predict and prevent future food insecurity. *Georgetown Journal of International Affairs*, *24*(2), 191–197. DOI: 10.1353/gia.2023.a913645

Wang, L., Ni, Y., Zhao, Y., & Chen, Y. (2024). The triple helix collaboration: Lessons from a Chinese provincial innovation ecosystem. *Chinese Management Studies*, *18*(4), 1276–1289. DOI: 10.1108/cms-08-2023-0391

Yang, Z., Cui, X., & Song, Z. (2023). Predicting sepsis onset in ICU using machine learning models: A systematic review and meta-analysis. *BMC Infectious Diseases*, *23*(1), 635. DOI: 10.1186/s12879-023-08614-0

Yelpaala, K., Gibbons, M. C., Vigil, I. M., Leaño, J., McCall, T., Opara, I., Zink, A., Nunez-Smith, M., Mukherjee, B., & Ranney, M. (2025). The Role of data in Public Health and health Innovation: Perspectives on social determinants of health, community-based data approaches, and AI. Journal of Medical Internet Research, 27(v27i1e78794), e78794. https://doi.org/DOI: 10.2196/78794

Zhou, C. (2008). Emergence of the entrepreneurial university in evolution of the triple helix. *Journal of Technology Management in China*, *3*(1), 109–126. DOI: 10.1108/17468770810851539

Zhu, X., Weigel, P., Baloh, J., Nataliansyah, M., Gunn, N., & Mueller, K. (2019). Mobilising cross-sector collaborations to improve population health in US rural communities: A qualitative study. *BMJ Open*, *9*(11), e030983. DOI: 10.1136/bmjopen-2019-030983

KEY TERMS AND DEFINITIONS

Triple Helix Model: A collaborative innovation framework involving universities, governments, and industries working together to drive technological advancement and societal progress.

Artificial Intelligence (AI): A field of computer science focused on creating systems capable of performing tasks that normally require human intelligence, such as learning, reasoning, and decision-making.

Cross-Sector Collaboration: Cooperative efforts among different sectors (academic, public, and private) to share knowledge, resources, and capabilities for collective innovation.

Innovation Ecosystem: A network of interconnected institutions, policies, technologies, and people that support the development, scaling, and diffusion of innovations.

Public–Private Partnership (PPP): A structured collaboration between government bodies and private-sector entities to develop projects, services, or technologies.

Open Science: A movement that promotes transparency and accessibility in research through open data, open-source tools, and public dissemination of scientific results.

Regulatory Sandbox: A controlled environment established by governments where new technologies can be tested with relaxed regulations under monitored conditions.

AI Governance: Policies, frameworks, and mechanisms that guide responsible development, deployment, and monitoring of AI technologies.

Commercialization: The process of translating research outputs into market-ready products, services, or technologies.

Data Ecosystem: The interconnected systems, standards, and practices that manage data collection, sharing, storage, and use across different sectors.

Responsible AI: An approach to AI development that prioritizes fairness, transparency, accountability, safety, and respect for ethical and societal values.

National AI Mission: A government-led initiative designed to promote AI research, infrastructure, innovation, and workforce development at the national level.

Knowledge Transfer: The movement of expertise, research outputs, or technologies from universities to industry or government for application and scaling.

Innovation Cluster: A geographic or virtual grouping of institutions and companies that collaborate to advance technological development in a specific domain.

Co-Creation: A collaborative process where multiple stakeholders jointly design and develop solutions, combining their expertise and resources.

Chapter 4
Public Policy for Responsible AI: The Role of Government in Shaping Ethical Triple Helix Collaborations

Azamat Ali
https://orcid.org/0000-0003-2931-2166
Lovely Professional University, Phagwara, India

ABSTRACT

The chapter discusses the participation of the government in facilitating ethical and accountable Artificial Intelligence (AI) in the Triple Helix model of collaboration among institutions, industries, and universities. It examines the role of the public policy in the development of innovation ecosystems through the encouragement of transparency, accountability, and inclusivity when developing AI. The discussion identifies key policy instruments, regulatory frameworks, and national strategies that promote cross-sector collaboration in terms of responsible AI adoption. Case studies demonstrate the ability of providing a proper balance between innovation and ethical considerations, including data privacy, fairness, and social welfare, through proper governance. The chapter concludes with the recommendations to construct strong and cooperative AI ecosystems that should correspond to the global standards of responsible innovation.

DOI: 10.4018/979-8-3373-7620-2.ch004

1. INTRODUCTION

Artificial Intelligence (AI) has emerged as a potent technology that influences economies, societies and governments worldwide. It applies in numerous fields of healthcare, transport, education, and government. When AI keeps expanding, issues regarding its ethical, social, and legal consequences have gained greater relevance. Responsible AI has risen to prominence in the world as it entails ensuring that AI technologies are designed and applied in a manner that is just and respectful to human values, honourable of human rights and social well-being. Responsible AI emphasises the importance of fairness, transparency, accountability and inclusiveness in every AI development stage (Hosseini Tabaghdehi & Ayaz, 2025). Responsible AI is necessary due to the number of challenges posed by the rapid technological advancements. These are algorithmic bias, invasion of privacy, lack of transparency, misuse of data, and unfair access to AI systems. Otherwise, AI can strengthen discrimination, increase inequality, and lower the level of confidence people have in institutions. Ethical innovation assists in resolving these issues by making sure that the moral and social values are integrated into the AI design and implementation processes. It advances a vision in which technology aids human well-being as opposed to strapping people or disenfranchising them (Radanliev, 2025).

These goals have to be attained by working together with various sectors. The Triple Helix model offers an effective platform of comprehending such collaboration. It refers to the three main sectors which are the driving point of technological and social innovation: government, academia, and industry. The sectors are interrelated and each has a different role to play. Higher education institutions produce new knowledge and offer moral and technical skills. The industries apply this knowledge in designing products and services that are practical. To make sure that innovation is safe, ethical and socially beneficial, governments have policies, standards and regulations that guarantee it. These actors combined in a balanced ecosystem which facilitates responsible AI (de Lima Figueiredo et al., 2023). The government plays a significant role especially in the three sectors. Governments develop policies that are meant to benefit the masses, lay down ethical rules, and develop control and monitoring systems. They also contribute to the field of innovation by financing it, national AI missions, and policy frameworks. They include the AI Act of the European Union, the AI Principles of the OECD, and the National Programme on Artificial Intelligence of India. These policies are geared towards strike a balance between innovations and accountability, protection of human rights, and social trust. Governments provide another way of bringing academia and industry together giving a sense of innovation that is in tandem with societal interests (Biju & Gayathri, 2024).

Academia makes a huge contribution in form of research, ethical study, and qualified professionals. Universities also are significant in analysing the societal impacts of AI, suggesting policy options, as well as providing interdisciplinary education, which integrates technical and ethical expertise. Industry and government collaboration can make academic institutions fill the gap between theory and practice. The role of industry is also critical, since it transforms ideas into the reality. The ethical aspects that companies building AI should include are fairness testing, audit, and impact assessment. Ethical corporate governance builds on confidence to the public and encourages sustained economic growth. Industry working with academia and government makes it possible to establish trustful and socially responsible AI technologies (Pan & Guo, 2022).

Lastly, collaboration on the international level is the only way since the advancement of AI spans across countries. The world organization like UNESCO, United Nations and World Economic Forums are advocating mutual ethical standards such as human centred design and accountability. These international standards have to be embraced and changed by governments towards uniformity and collaboration (Banifatemi, 2025). In these regards, the Triple Helix model proves the idea that responsible AI needs constant cooperation. Government creates a control, academia gives moral direction and industry is the execution engine. The combination of these two enables the development of AI based systems that are innovative, trustworthy, and socially oriented.

2. THEORETICAL FOUNDATIONS: TRIPLE HELIX AND RESPONSIBLE INNOVATION

2.1 Evolution of the Triple Helix Model and Its Relevance to Technological Innovation

Triple Helix model was created by Etzkowitz and Leydesdorff in the 1990s as a theoretical model of how innovation arises as a result of interaction of three main spheres of institutions: government, academia and industry. The previous theories of innovation were to a great extent linear and under this model universities were the creators of knowledge, companies were the ones putting it into practice and governments were the regulators. As the technological development and most of the entire digital one became more complex, however, this linear structure became insufficient. The Triple Helix model established innovation as a network process, interactive and collaborative in which each sector brings complementary strengths as well as assuming mutating functions (Leydesdorff, 2021). In this system, universities no longer remain in the research and educational fields; they even assume an entrepreneurial role of joining with the industries and aid in policy creation. The industries, which used to be focused on the production and commercialization of goods, invest in research and develop technologies with academic partners. Governments do not merely regulate but now make active facilitators of innovation environments by funding, coordinating, and enabling policy environments. This interdependence makes technological development to be attuned to the needs of the society as opposed to the market interests or academic interests.

The issue of the model as it applies to AI innovation is extensive. The field of AI development needs the incorporation of a wide range of areas of knowledge computer science and data analytics, on the one hand, and ethics, law, and social science, on the other hand. The Triple Helix model enables these disciplines and domains to be more synergistic in speeding up the innovation process and maintaining ethical responsibility. As an example, AI research centres endorsed by the government, industry sponsored university laboratories, and government industry innovation collaborations can all reflect the principles of teamwork of this model. The Triple Helix promotes not only technological development but also the development of inclusive and responsible innovation ecosystems by creating interaction between sectors (Zadegan et al., 2025).

2.2 Integration of Responsible Research and Innovation (RRI) Principles within AI Ecosystems

Responsible Research and Innovation (RRI) is an addition of an ethical aspect to technologic development. RRI, which has been popularized by the European Commission, makes sure that research and innovation are in line with needs of the society, social values, and ethical standards. It promotes the early thinking about the possible effects, transparency, and inclusiveness of the decision making process. The inclusion of RRI in AI ecosystems is an assurance that the new technologies will not only be technically effective but also socially positive and ethically correct (Georgiou et al., 2025). RRI helps to be guided by four dimensions which are anticipation, reflection, inclusion and responsiveness.

- Anticipation is the ability to determine what changes the AI technologies may have in the future, what risks they may entail, and what social effects they may cause, anticipating them before they become a reality. This will enable policy makers and developers to act before these moral issues present themselves.
- Reflection involves the stakeholders reviewing the motivations, assumptions and possible implications of their research and innovation practices.
- Inclusion means that the different perspectives, including those of the marginalized or underrepresented groups are incorporated into the innovation process.

- Responsiveness highlights the ability of the innovation systems to respond to emerging ethical issues, social demands or regulatory developments.

RRI with regard to AI facilitates the cooperation of universities, industries and governments in the development of solutions that are co-created and that accommodates human rights as well as brings about trust in the minds of people. As an example, universities can carry out ethical evaluations of AI applications, industries can have fairness and accountability tools, and governments can introduce regulatory measures that can ensure compliance. It is this shared accountability, which promotes a multifaceted attitude to innovation that is social good technological. Integrating RRI with AI systems can be used to turn innovation into a participative and value oriented process (that is purely technical). It makes sure that there is a balance between the technological abilities and the moral accountability such that AI grows and develops in a manner that favours all layers of society. The adoption of RRI into Triple Helix model is therefore a step further to innovation is a profit to innovation with a purpose (Ten Holter, 2022).

2.3 Ethical Dimensions of AI: Transparency, Fairness, Privacy, and Accountability

The application of AI creates important ethical issues that have to be mitigated to uphold trust, legitimacy, and fairness in their use. Ethical AI practices are directed by four key principles including transparency, fairness, privacy, and accountability all of which are directly related to responsible innovation and governance (Radanliev, 2025). Transparency makes AI systems understandable and explainable. Stakeholders would be in a position to understand the way AI models work, the information they are fed on, and the decision making process. External checks and balances can be conducted through the use of transparent systems that minimize the possibility of manipulation and bias. Algorithms disclosure can be enforced by the government, whereas the industries may establish explainable AI models to boost user confidence. Fairness attempts to remove bias and discrimination of AI algorithms. The biases of the machine learning models are usually the biases of the training data and as such they may deliver unfair results. The solutions to fairness are inclusive data collection, regular audits of algorithms, and impact assessments. Academia, government, and industry can collaborate to provide a standard in detecting bias and a rational way of controlling data.

Ethical AI is based on privacy protection since the majority of AI mechanisms are based on large datasets, including sensitive and personal information. Misuse of data may result to identity theft, surveillance as well as undermining civil liberties. The role of governments is also extremely important as they apply the laws related to data protection, including the General Data Protection Regulation (GDPR) enacted in the European Union and the Digital Personal Data Protection Act (2023) enacted in India. Industries need a robust data governance framework, and the universities can study privacy promoting technologies such as federated learning and differential privacy (Malhotra & Malhotra, 2024). Accountability is the identification and allocation of responsibility of actions and results of AI systems. It makes sure that in case of any harm there are redress and correction mechanisms. It would need accountability, audit trails, and proper responsibility among developers and users and ethical review boards that would oversee compliance. Accountability can be imposed by the governments in the form of legal frameworks, whereas the industry and academia can promote ethical standards and certification programs. Combining these actions will guarantee the AI systems are aligned with human interests and the popular trust (Novelli et al., 2024).

2.4 Role of Governance in Harmonizing Innovation with Public Values and Social Responsibility

Governance is one of the key factors in the process of making AI development compliant with societal values and ethics. It is also concerned with laws and regulations but also with institutional practices and communal policies and collaborative mechanisms that influence the technology evolution. Good governance is a compromise of promoting creativity and safeguarding the well-being of the people (Camilleri, 2024). The policy tools that governments can use to influence innovation are national AI strategies, ethical principles, funding schemes, and regulatory sandboxes. These tools can be used to experiment and still have a protective mechanism. As an example, the AI Act of the European Union introduces a risk focused approach to regulation making AI applications subject to categorizing them based on their potential effects on human rights. Equally, NITI Aayog of India advocates AI for All, which focuses on inclusiveness and transparency of AI based development (Inampudi & Gaurav, 2024). In addition to regulation, governance involves cooperation and interaction among various stakeholders. Public consultations, ethics committees and citizen engagement platforms are all mechanisms that enable governments to use the societal perspective in formulating policies. Such participatory pattern also increases legitimacy and assists to harmonize technological goals and shared values. It also enhances a sense of responsibility, with the citizens able to shape the way the AI systems are made and implemented.

Another very important aspect of governance is international collaboration. AI technologies do not respect national boundaries and such ethical concerns as privacy, surveillance, and bias in the algorithms have international consequences. Universal frameworks that support human centred AI have been suggested by organizations such as the OECD, UNESCO, and G20 and are based on the importance of fairness, inclusivity, and accountability. The implementation of these international standards in national policies guarantees the coherence and minimizes the ethical disintegration in global AI governance (Chinen, 2025). Governance in Triple Helix is the integrating mechanism of balancing innovation with the values of the people. Regulatory oversight and incentives, ethical analysis and evidence based research are offered by governments, academia and ensuring real world implementation and compliance are offered by industries. Such reciprocal design secures the social responsibility of technology development being innovative, socially responsible and ethically based. By integrating the principles of governance into all stages of AI development, societies will be able to foster the trust of people and move toward the sustainable and human centred innovation (Carayannis et al., 2022).

3. PUBLIC POLICY INSTRUMENTS FOR ETHICAL AI

3.1 Legislative and Regulatory Frameworks

Laws and regulatory frameworks give the legal basis to make sure that the technologies of AI are created and applied in a morally responsible way. These models specify the rights and responsibilities of governments, developers, and users and provide major principles: transparency, accountability, privacy, and fairness. Through this, they contribute to making sure that the technological development is not pulling out of the human rights and democracy. Numerous national and global policies today are intended to tackle the dangers of AI and at the same time promote social benefit innovation. This area has been in the forefront of the European Union by the European Union Artificial Intelligence Act (EU AI Act). This regulation is risk based and categorizes AI systems as unacceptable, high risk, limited risk, and minimal risk systems. The strict requirements of high risk AI systems, like the ones employed in healthcare, law enforcement, or recruitment, are connected with the aspects of safety, transparency, and human control. The EU AI Act is a large stride in both human centric and responsible AI in addition to legal certainty which facilitates accountable innovation among member states (Qiang and Jing, 2024).

The General Data Protection Regulation (GDPR) is a supplement to the EU AI Act as it deals with the security of personal data. It guarantees informed consent, provides people with the rights concerning automated decision making, and punishes violations of data. Even though it is a European law, the GDPR has impacted the data protection laws of various countries across the globe and has become a universal reference when it comes to the balancing of innovation and privacy (Lau, 2025). The Digital Personal Data Protection Act (DPDP) 2023 in India offers a contemporary data protection system in the country through the focus on transparency, consent related processing of data, and organizational responsibility. The National Strategy on Artificial Intelligence, known as AI for All, enhances the use of AI in the health care sector, agriculture, and education, supporting this legislation (Malhotra and Malhotra, 2024). Ethical AI strategies have also been adopted by other countries. The Pan-Canadian AI Strategy and the Blueprint of an AI Bill of Rights in Canada and the United States are signs of a more responsible approach to AI regulation in the world. These frameworks acknowledge that regulation ought to deal with risks and leave innovation to move forward. More specific regulations and tools, including algorithmic impact assessment and ethical audit, are another way of making sure that AI systems do not cross any legal and ethical limits during their lifetime (Ali, 2025).

3.2 Economic and Innovation Support Mechanisms

Governments also encourage responsible AI, besides regulation, using economic and innovation support mechanisms. These instruments offer funding, institutional backing as well as policy a stimulus that facilitates the production of AI technologies which would be in line with ethical and social goals. Economic processes assist in balancing regulation and innovation such that compliance is not a hindrance to innovation or technological advancement. The most widespread is the use of fiscal incentives, including tax incentives, research grants, and organizational subsidies, to organizations that implement ethical AI practices. The key aim of governments in funding projects is to be transparent, fair and inclusive in the design of AI. Indicatively, the Horizon Europe program by the European Union provides funding in the field of AI research with emphasis on ethics, human centred design, and trustful technology. On the same note, the Atal Innovation Mission and Start-up India Initiative in India offer grants and incubation services to start-ups focused on creating AI solutions to social and environmental problems (Bhushan, 2025).

To develop AI capabilities in academic and industrial places, governments also encourage government funding of research and development (R&D). This covers interdisciplinary research (a combination of computer science, social science, and ethics) to develop a well-rounded AI solution. The R&D programs should be conducted collaboratively between universities and companies to produce the projects, which should include ethical considerations in design, data protection, and inclusivity to the society. To illustrate, the AI research centres in Montreal, Edmonton, and Toronto in Canada are publicly funded and have made the responsible AI research one of their components of the mission (Salas-Pilco, 2021). Other mechanisms of innovation support are the development of AI hubs, research clusters, and innovation parks that assemble different stakeholders. These environments facilitate knowledge exchange, encourage experimentation and allow cross sector co-operation. Fatigue in responsible development of AI can be shared through these platforms by governments and training programs can be established to create digital literacy and ethical awareness. As an example, the Alan Turing Institute of the United Kingdom is a national data science and AI centre, which emphasizes ethics, governance, and public trust as its research themes (Dunleavy & Margetts, 2025).

As a strategy to be inclusive, marginalized or underrepresented groups are frequently the focus of economic instruments and promote diversity in AI studies and work. Women and minority groups may be assisted in education and entrepreneurship in AI with the help of grants and scholarships so that the innovation process can be beneficial to every layer of society. Additionally, governments can provide incentives to industries to implement corporate social responsibility (CSR) programs that support ethical AI, including through supporting communities and other social benefit open source AI, or even by creating open source AI. Governments can initiate responsible innovation culture by integrating both the use of financial incentives and policy direction. These economic tools are not only helpful to drive AI development, but they also incorporate ethics as a key principle of technology. Financing and regulation balance is necessary to form AI ecosystems that are dynamic and ethically responsible (Camilleri, 2024).

3.3 Collaborative and Standardization Measures

Governments alone cannot achieve the ethical governance of AI. The cooperation between the public institutions, business, academia, and international bodies is crucial in formulating uniform standards and common ethical standards. These partnerships facilitate trust, interoperability, and good use of AI across borders. One such tool that is useful in creating ethical AI is known as the public private partnership (PPP). Responsible AI design can be achieved through joint governmental and industrial research, creation of innovation laboratories, and policy think tanks, and can be a part of responsible AIs. Through these partnerships, sharing of resources, knowledge, and information is possible and ethical standards are used to drive technological innovations. To illustrate, the Partnership on AI, composed of academia, civil society, and large technological corporation's members, formulates the best practices and guidelines on responsible AI in the world. Likewise, the Fifth Industrial Revolution Centre in India, which is sponsored by the World Economic Forum, convenes policymakers, researchers, and leaders in the industry to create structures of responsible AI application (Prasad et al., 2024).

The other important policy tool is the establishment of ethical advisory boards and multi-stakeholder councils. These agencies have control over it and review policy suggestions and assess the social and ethical effects of AI. Countries like Canada, Singapore and France have set national AI ethics committees, which act as a guiding force in decision making, and also serve in balancing innovation and human rights. Such platforms increase the level of transparency and facilitate communication among developers, regulators and citizens. Harmonization of AI governance is also primarily achieved through standardization efforts. International entities such as the Organisation for Economic Co-operation and Development (OECD), UNESCO, and the International Organization for Standardization (ISO/IEC) have come up with international principles and technical standards of responsible AI (Tidjon & Khomh, 2022):

- The OECD AI Principles (2019) focus on shareholder values, transparency, and accountability.
- The Recommendation on the Ethics of Artificial Intelligence (2021) by UNESCO is aimed at fairness, environmental sustainability, and social inclusion.
- ISO/IEC JTC 1/SC 42 standards committee is engaged in technical recommendations of AI safety, risk management, and governance.

These programs support governments in creating national systems to go together and keep a uniform approach to moral AI advancement all over the world. International harmonization will eliminate regulatory dispersion and support collaboration in the development and implementation of AI. Besides that, cross border AI collaboration requires policy harmonization. Since AI systems will be applied in international markets, states must have common rules and ethical principles to trust each other. Knowledge sharing, joint R&D, and alignment in reaction to ethical issues like data sharing and algorithmic transparency may be encouraged by bilateral and multilateral agreements. As an illustration, Global Partnership on Artificial Intelligence (GPAI) is an initiative by more than 25 countries to discuss responsible AI and share best practices (Keith, 2024). With such collaborative and standardization initiatives, the governments and institutions can collaboratively develop an AI ecosystem that is based on ethical responsibility and trust by the people. The cooperation with other countries will guarantee the development of AI to fit the universal human values but give space to national priorities and contexts.

4. GOVERNMENT'S ROLE IN FOSTERING TRIPLE HELIX COLLABORATIONS

4.1 Policy Design for Cross Sector Collaboration

The policy design is one of the strongest tools that the governments have to facilitate collaboration between the academia and industry with the government institutions. Good policies generate environments of knowledge sharing, common research and collective innovation. This Triple Helix model underlines the fact that where innovation is encouraged is in the way these sectors relate to each other on a vibrant basis within a well laid policy environment (George & Tarr, 2024). Governments come up with mechanisms that promote interaction between the universities, industries and the populace agencies. These systems frequently involve national innovation missions, technology clusters, and sectoral councils which bring researchers into contact with the private enterprise. Governments make academic research translate into practice and industries enjoy the benefit of scientific discoveries through facilitation of collaboration. India, as an example, has made a national strategy to use artificial intelligence (AI for All) through NITI Aayog, aimed at linking the academic research institutions and industry stakeholders with the government departments. It promotes collective work in agriculture, healthcare, education and smart cities, applying the principles of ethical and inclusive innovation to the national development objectives (Parekh, 2024).

Inter-ministerial coordination is another successful tool of work between the sectors. AI governance usually cuts across various areas education, health, defense, labour, and commerce, so it is necessary to coordinate these sectors. Governments also form inter-ministerial committees or task forces to make sure that there is coherent policy making and implementation. As an example, the AI policy coordination of the European Union implies the collaboration of the Directorate General for Communications Networks, Directorate General for Research and Innovation, and other agencies to coordinate research, ethics, and market goals. Likewise, in Canada, the Advisory Council on Artificial Intelligence is involved in a collective of scholars, in the industrial and governmental sphere and is tasked with establishing the responsible development of AI policies and ensuring that innovation is consistent with ethical principles (Escobar & Sciortino, 2022). There are also national innovation missions encouraged by governments and which incorporate AI as a constituent of a wider development strategy. The Digital India and Make in India programs, such as those, also have elements that foster AI supported technologies and encourage self-sufficiency and competitiveness on the international level. They are missions that urge the academia and the industry to engage in government led initiatives, which establish common objectives towards technological development.

Besides, the governments create policy frameworks that facilitate open innovation, where universities and companies share data, develop patents jointly and co-invent technology. This solution enhances the knowledge economy and creates a base to use AI applications with ethical consideration (Rossoni et al., 2024).

4.2 Building Data and Research Infrastructure

The AI innovation requires a strong data and research infrastructure. Governments have the roles in developing and sustaining systems that will allow safe sharing of data, collaborative research and development of technology without violating privacy and ethical values. Infrastructure serves as the foundation of the Triple Helix model as it links universities, research laboratories, industries, and policymakers via data, investment and technological networks. The development of open data ecosystems can be viewed as one of the initiatives of the government. Open data platforms enable researchers, entrepreneurs and public agencies to share and exploit datasets to develop AI, which promotes transparency and innovation. An example can be the European Open Data Portal and the Open Government Data Portal in India, which are open data platforms that support the innovation of research and service to the public. These initiatives aid in making sound decisions based on the data and maintain that information related to sensitive matters is kept confidential according to data protection laws such as the GDPR and DPDP Act (2023). The open data policies also foster inclusivity whereby small companies and academic establishments can drive the innovation processes that previously belonged to the domain of big businesses (Malhotra & Malhotra, 2024).

Governments also use significant funds in AI research labs and networks of innovation. Creating AI research centres It helps to establish collaboration between universities, industries, and public agencies by creating public AI research centres, including the Alan Turing Institute in the United Kingdom or AI Research Institutes in the United States. These centres offer common facilities, grants and training schemes combined with ethical, legal and technical knowledge. The government in India has facilitated the establishment of AI research centres within the National Mission on Interdisciplinary Cyber Physical Systems that encourages both academic scholars and technological companies to collaborate. Not only do these institutions advance the research, but also make sure that the innovation is ethical and satisfactory to the population (Gupta & Pandey, 2025). Data interoperability and governance is another aspect of infrastructure that is important. Since AI is based on various materials and multiple sources, governments should make sure that the systems are interoperable, i.e. they can share and read the data in a similar manner. The interoperability improves the cooperation between universities, industries, and the world community. Governments come up with structures of standardizing data formats and adherence to security protocols. They also use privacy protecting technologies in the form of encryption, anonymization and federated learning to protect personal data but still allow collaborative research. This is so that innovation is not at the expense of the rights or insecurity of the citizens (Nilsson et al., 2024).

Other pillars of data governance are transparency and accountability. A national AI observatory or data ethics councils can be created by governments to oversee the use of government data and the risks that the use of AI may have. These organizations are the ones that mediate between the state, academia, and the industry to make sure that all AI research follows the ethical standards, as well as social expectations. Governments create data infrastructures that are both transparent and trustful to build on the legitimacy of AI innovation and increase the involvement of academic and private actors (Sargiotis, 2024). Moreover, capacity building and digital literacy investments are also relevant in order to maximize the gains of AI infrastructure. Researchers, civil servants, and entrepreneurs can be trained by governments in AI ethics, data management and responsible innovation to better understand these important fields. These efforts can not only enhance the institutional capacity but also facilitate the digital divide between the large research establishments and the smaller institutions. A productive and knowledgeable workforce is an added value that improves the performance of the Triple Helix model as it makes teamwork both technical and ethical competent.

4.3 Ensuring Ethical Oversight and Public Trust

Innovation in the field of artificial intelligence (AI) requires technological and institutional infrastructure although it is not sufficient to guarantee ethical and sustainable results. The efficient use of AI systems also requires the application of the concept of public trust and ethical governance. In the absence of trust, the society can be resistant to AI technologies, even when such technologies are evident to bring obvious benefits. Governments thus have a role to play in putting up governance systems that would lead to ethical control, transparency, and involvement of citizens, in decisions concerning AI. One of the aspects of democratic AI governance is citizen involvement. To engage the public in the discussion about AI applications, governments can conduct public consultations, stakeholder meetings, and online platforms providing citizens with the ability to express their opinions. Such participatory methods aid to incorporate the varied views, particularly those of the marginalized groups of people on policy formulation. This kind of involvement enhances the legitimacy of policies, accountability, and consistency between the technological development and the expectations of the society (Pislaru et al., 2024).

There is also the need to enhance transparency and accountability measures by governments. Transparency reports may also ask the organization to reveal data about the AI systems, such as information sources, algorithms, and decision making procedures. This allows the researchers, auditors, and civil society to go through it independently. Periodic algorithmic audits and impact evaluation also contribute to the maintenance of the ethical, safety, and fairness of AI systems. As an illustration, the European Commission suggests that AI should be assessed in terms of algorithmic impact before its implementation to determine the risks associated with it (Balasubramaniam et al., 2022). Risk based frameworks of governance are also significant. The stricter oversight is needed on high risk AI systems, including those ones that are employed in healthcare or criminal justice. The further improvements of public trust and the enhancement of responsible AI usage may be provided through ethical certification and continuous education of the population (Tiernan et al., 2023).

5. CASE STUDIES: GLOBAL MODELS OF RESPONSIBLE AI GOVERNANCE

5.1 European Union: Human Centric Regulation and the AI Act

The European Union (EU) has proven its place as a world leader in creating a human focused and ethics oriented approach to the regulation of AI. The EU approach emphasizes on the value of trust, accountability, and human rights so that the advancement in technology does not harm the citizens in terms of their safety and privacy. The core of this is the European Union Artificial Intelligence Act (EU AI Act) which was first proposed in 2021 and approved in 2024. It is the first global legal framework on AI regulation, which aims at risk management, transparency, and monitoring. EU AI Act divides AI systems into four groups according to the threat they are likely to pose to the individuals and the society (Cabrera et al., 2025):

- Unacceptable risk (restricted systems, e.g. social scoring).
- High risk (highly controlled e.g. AI in the healthcare or police industry).
- Low risk (with transparency requirements, e.g. chatbots).
- Reduced risk (no regulation in particular, e.g. AI powered games or spam filters).

This precautionary measure implies that more stringent regulations are set on those AI systems that bear greater impact. High risk AI developers have to meet the data quality, documentation, human control, and transparency of algorithms requirements. The Act similarly requires the establishment of a European Artificial Intelligence Board as a coordination body among the member states so that they may have uniform standards. In addition to the AI Act, there is the General

Data Protection Regulation (GDPR) that offers strong protection against privacy and individual rights. Data minimization, limitation of purposes and the right to explanation of automated decisions were the concepts introduced by the GDPR. These legal tools have a collaborative effect in bringing accountability into the AI lifecycle (Lau, 2025). Furthermore, the Ethics Guidelines to Trustworthy AI by the European Commission in its High Level Expert Group on AI (2019) enumerates seven principles, namely human agency, technical robustness, privacy, transparency, diversity, accountability, and ecological sustainability. The principles guarantee a human centric and inclusive approach to innovation. The integration of regulatory and ethical frameworks by the EU establishes a global standard of responsible AI governance that can show how all three elements of law, ethics, and policy can harmoniously interact to establish trustful innovation (Nikolinakos, 2023).

5.2 India: Responsible AI for Inclusive Growth

India has taken a unique approach to governance of AI to be based on inclusivity, social good and digital empowerment. The government understands that AI can take care of the developmental problems and lead to fair growth provided it is used in a responsible manner. The policy vision is informed by the National Strategy of Artificial Intelligence (AI for All) by NITI Aayog that focuses on the application of AI in solving real life issues in fields like healthcare, education, agriculture, smart cities, and infrastructure. The major aspect of the Indian structure is the program called Responsible "AI for All", which was introduced in 2021. This project illustrates the importance of ethical, transparent and accountable AI and encourages innovation which can be beneficial to all sectors of the society. The strategy incorporates four principles on which it is based: inclusivity, accountability, reliability, and security. NITI Aayog works with the ministries, educational institutions, and other organizations to create use cases that would favour social well-being. As an illustration, government grants and collaborations with companies facilitate the use of AI application in crop management, prediction of diseases, and customized learning (Dadhich & Bansal, 2025).

The Digital India ecosystem of India offers the platform to apply AI in an ethical and efficient way. Digital identity (Aadhaar), Unified Payments Interface (UPI), and data sharing models have all built a digital governance ecosystem to provide effective digital governance to everyone. Nevertheless, the policymakers in India know the possible threats of AI in privacy, bias, and exclusion. To deal with such issues, the Digital Personal Data Protection Act (DPDP) 2023 has provided a legal background of privacy of data, consent and responsible data processing. It supplements the development of AI as it will provide citizens with the ability to control their personal data (Sasi, 2025). Also, the AI Research, Innovation, and

Ethics program in India facilitates academic-industry-government partnerships. India encourages AI education, entrepreneurship, and ethical business through such initiatives as the National AI Portal or AI Innovation Centres. Capacity building programs educate policymakers, researchers and students to use AI in a responsible manner. The attempt at the adoption of AI in the functioning of the government like in the health, agricultural and urban planning is indicative of the practical nature of India, prioritizing innovation and ethical protection. The model of India is interesting because it entailed the integration of the concept of ethical AI into the general digital development strategy. Through prioritizing accessibility, transparency and social inclusion, the Indian government shows how emerging economies could use responsible AI as a resource of sustainable and fair development (Pandey, 2025).

5.3 North America: Collaborative Governance in Canada and the U.S.

Both Canada and the United States have worked out their unique yet complementary models of AI regulation in North America that focus on collaboration, transparency, and human rights. Their strategies include regulatory direction and multi-level collaboration among federal, state and local organizations, academia and the private industry. In Canada, the Pan Canadian Artificial Intelligence Strategy was one of the earliest nations to introduce a national AI strategy, which was launched in 2017. The plan aims at the development of AI research, the encouragement of ethical principles, and the provision of social broad benefits. The three most popular AI institutes in Canada, including Vector Institute (Toronto), Mila (Montreal), and Amii (Edmonton) are seen as hubs of excellence between academia, government, and industry. Such institutes engage in research in the field of AI ethics, fairness and transparency and provide assistance in the innovation of the public sector. The introduced Government of Canada tool, The Algorithmic Impact Assessment (AIA), makes sure that the deployed AI systems of federal institutions are reviewed in terms of bias, privacy, and social impact. Such proactive position portrays the responsible governance of Canada (Salas-Pilco, 2021).

The United States has been more decentralized, with the Blueprint for an AI Bill of Rights (2022) defining five principles, namely: (1) safe and effective systems, (2) algorithmic discrimination protections, (3) data privacy, (4) notice and explanation and (5) human alternatives, considerations, and fallback. The U.S. focuses on voluntary structures, sectoral regulation and policies that are friendly to innovations. Organizations have been advised to use informative guidelines to create reliable AI systems and this has been published by agencies such as National Institute of Standards and Technology (NIST) as the AI Risk Management Framework (2023). The U.S. also promotes the collaboration of academia and private technology firms by offering funding activities, such as the National AI Research Institutes, which are based on fairness, safety, and accountability (Law & McCall, 2024). Both nations have in common transparency, involvement of stakeholders and cross sector relationships. The Canadian approach is however more centralized and government oriented whereas the approach adopted by the U.S. is more market oriented and decentralized. They all demonstrate how regulation and flexibility of innovation should be balanced, so that the development of AI should remain in line with democratic principles and human rights.

5.4 Cross Regional Insights and Best Practices

Comparative study of EU, India and North America indicates that there are similarities as well as differences in governance. Transparency, accountability, and inclusivity are shared in all three, whereas the methods are different in their implementation. EU is dependent on the enforcement of the law and standardization. India is oriented on the developmental applications and social inclusivity, whereas North America is oriented on the collaborative and adaptive governance. These are the main differences and best practices that are summarized in the table 1 below.

Table 1. Comparative Overview of Global Responsible AI Governance Models

Region	Governance Model	Ethical Focus	Key Policy Instruments	Notable Features / Best Practices
European Union	Centralized, legal regulatory	Human centric, rights based	EU AI Act, GDPR, Ethics Guidelines for Trustworthy AI	Risk based regulation, strong privacy protection, institutional accountability
India	Inclusive, developmental	Social good, inclusivity, transparency	NITI Aayog's AI for All, DPDP 2023, Digital India Mission	Public private partnerships, AI for social welfare, focus on accessibility
Canada	Collaborative, research driven	Fairness, transparency, accountability	Pan Canadian AI Strategy, Algorithmic Impact Assessment	Ethical AI institutes, centralized review of federal AI use
United States	Market oriented, decentralized	Innovation ethics, privacy, fairness	AI Bill of Rights, NIST AI Risk Management Framework	Voluntary governance, flexible innovation environment

Based on these comparisons, there are a number of best practices that are identified:

- Risk based Regulation: The EU model shows that a successful risk classification system can be used to achieve balance between innovation and safety.

- Inclusive and Contextual Governance: The policy in India demonstrates the need to customize AI policies to the needs of the local population and make them available to all citizens.
- Transparency and Accountability Tools: The application of algorithmic impact assessments in Canada offers an example that can be used to conduct ethical monitoring.
- Voluntary and Flexible Structures to Innovation: The U.S. illustrates the fact that voluntary and adaptive structures can stimulate innovation and enhance ethical standards.
- International Collaboration: International collaboration is done on the international basis by organizations like OECD, UNESCO, and GPAI to harmonize standards and exchange the best practices.

These teachings highlight the need to integrate control, cooperation and training to have responsible AI governance. An ethical AI standard that incorporates the positive legal protection of the EU, inclusivity of India, and future driven governance of North America could be a universal benchmark of ethical AI. The effectiveness of such an approach will rely on how the governments will be able to coordinate the policies, engage various stakeholders and create the trust of the people by being transparent and accountable.

6. POLICY IMPLICATIONS AND RECOMMENDATIONS

6.1 Strategic Policy Directions for Responsible AI

Governments have to be on the frontline in ensuring that they come up with policies that make the development of AI to run in tandem with ethical guidelines and the interest of the people. To attain this balance, there is a need to strengthen ethical frameworks, institutional capacity and adaptive regulation. To begin with, ethical frameworks should be formulated and enforced. Transparency, fairness, accountability, and privacy are some of the principles according to which AI systems should be guided. National ethical standards and independent regulatory authorities need to be set up by governments to evaluate AI technologies prior to implementation. High risk AI systems can be implemented in the field of healthcare, finance, and law enforcement with the introduction of ethical audits and certification mechanisms. All these would aid in making sure that technological advancements do not undermine societal equality or the rights of people (Radanliev, 2025).

Second, the AI governance requires institutional capacity building. A large number of nations do not have proper infrastructure, skills, and regulatory bodies to manage

AI applications. Special training on the topics of AI ethics, data governance, and legal compliance should be provided to policy makers, regulators, and professionals. To create a workforce relevant in the future, universities and research body should make AI ethics and governance modules part of the academic courses. This will have the capacity of improving the institutions response to technological change and its social consequences. Further, governments would enable interdisciplinary research initiatives involving links between computer science and social sciences, law, and philosophy in such a way that innovation is human friendly (Hosseini Tabaghdehi & Ayaz, 2025).

Third, there is a need to adaptively regulate the rapid developments in AI. Conventional legal systems can have difficulties in keeping pace with the velocity and intricacy of technological advancement. The governments ought to thus adopt flexible evidence based regulations that are changing in accordance to the changes. Regulatory sandboxes can perhaps come in handy, i.e. controlled settings in which new AI systems are trialled with moderation before mass deployment. With these types of experimental spaces, governments are able to evaluate risks, as well as responsible innovation. There should also be regular reviews of the policies and feedback mechanisms that ensure the AI laws remain up to date (Inampudi & Gaurav, 2024). These policy directions (moral strictness, institutional reinforcement, and malleable regulation) are the ones that allow governments to facilitate a progressive and socially responsible innovation. All these measures will increase public trust, whose foundation is the ultimate acceptance and success of the AI systems.

6.2 Enhancing Triple Helix Synergy and Global Alignment

Government, academia and industry should closely collaborate on the responsible AI policies to effectively implement them. Triple Helix model provides the basis on which this synergy can be nurtured through mutual learning, joint problem solving, and joint accountability. Governments must promote AI literacy and popular awareness in all the spheres of society. Citizens, professionals, and policymakers can be better equipped to be involved in decision making when they know how their systems operate and what ethical issues they bring up. Digital literacy and fear or misinformation to AI can be eliminated or suppressed through public education campaigns, community workshops and online courses. Making such awareness will help in informed participation and also developing readiness to change in the society. Another significant measure of collaboration improvement is the promotion of open innovation. Governments can set up innovation centres, data sharing portals and research collaborations between government and industry, which enable various industries to develop AI solutions together. Universities can work with the industries to create the prototypes of ethical AI, whereas the industries can also offer the real life data and resources to be used in tests. Such collaborations must be informed by transparency, equity, and social responsibility with innovation being driven by the interests of the group and not a set of commercial interests (Pan & Guo, 2022).

The cross border character of AI technologies cannot be addressed at the national level, and globally, there is a need to harmonize policies. The issue of data privacy, statistical favouritism, and surveillance are ethical dilemmas that do not rely on national borders. Hence, it is important that international collaboration is made in order to be united in moral standards and technical principles. The policies used in countries ought to be in line with international guidelines like OECD AI Principles and recommendations on the ethics of artificial intelligence issued by the UNESCO. Through international forums, including the Global Partnership on Artificial Intelligence (GPAI), collaboration can improve communication organize studies and responsible innovation at the global scale (Chinen, 2025). The construction of synergy in the Triple Helix also implies the establishment of a mechanism of continuous dialogue between the three sectors. Governments are capable of conducting multi-stakeholder forums and AI ethics councils in which researchers, business leaders, and policymakers debate on the emerging ethical problems. This participatory pattern will make sure that the decisions regarding the development of AI are made based on the various opinions and societal values (Carayannis et al., 2022). Finally, the global alignment and Triple Helix cooperation can make the countries exchange their experience, coordinate ethical principles, and solve the shared problems together. These measures can make AI ecosystem more inclusive and more trustworthy to support innovation without harming human dignity and social wellbeing.

7. IMPLICATIONS

The chapter has a number of significant policy implications, institutional practice implications, and implications on the academic research in the field of responsible AI. A significant implication is associated with the government involvement in AI governance. The results suggest that the governments are supposed to stop being purely regulative and play an active role in encouraging cooperation between academia and industry. This suggests that there must be adaptable, comprehensive, and technological change policy frameworks. The governments must support ethical values like transparency, fairness, accountability and privacy and at the same time foster innovation by providing funding schemes and collaborative platforms.

The analysis also draws significant aspects to the academic institutions. Universities have been placed as the important players in responsible AI through research, education, and ethical counselling. This means that institutions of higher learning must incorporate ethical, legal and social aspects of AI in technical programs. There is a need to introduce interdisciplinary education that integrates computer science with ethics, law, and social sciences to develop responsible AI systems in the future. Evidence based policymaking should also be backed by academic research on the effects of AI on society and the effectiveness of the governing frameworks.

To the stakeholders in the industry, the study would suggest that responsible AI practices are the key to building up of the trust and long term sustainability of the people. The ethical design behaviours that companies should adopt when developing and deploying AI systems include fairness testing, explainable algorithms, and responsible data management. These practices have the potential of minimizing the risks of prejudice, discrimination, and violation of privacy. The conclusion also indicates that the industry involvement in the public private partnerships and standard setting programs can assist in aligning commercial innovation to the societal values and regulatory demands.

On the greater scale, the chapter highlights the significance of global collaboration in the governance of AI. Given the fact that AI technologies are not limited by national boundaries, such ethical issues as data protection, algorithmic bias, and accountability cannot be successfully addressed by single countries only. This means that national policies should be set in line with the international ethical standards and governments can be engaged in the international forums on common standards and common learning.

Also, the research has implications on institutional capacity building. The policymakers, regulators, and professionals need to undergo on-going training in the AI ethics, data governance, and assessment of risks. Enhanced institutional knowledge and skill will help governments and organizations better address the emerging ethical issues. In general, the chapter highlights that the issue of responsible AI requires the concerted actions of the government, academia, and industry to make the technological development in accordance with social values and population trust.

8. CONCLUSION, LIMITATIONS AND FUTURE SCOPE

8.1 Conclusion

Government intervention takes centre stage in ensuring that artificial intelligence has been developed and used in a manner that is ethical, inclusive and socially beneficial. In the Triple Helix model, governments act as controllers, facilitators and enablers that bridge the academia, industry and society with policies and institutional structures in place. Such a combined role will facilitate a balanced approach whereby as the technological innovation goes so does the ethical responsibility.

Governments can ensure that AI systems promote transparency, fairness, responsibility, and respect of fundamental rights by creating clear legal frameworks and ethical principles. Responsible AI development is further enhanced by investment into research infrastructure and capacity building. Funding of scholarly studies and industry development allows ethical considerations of AI technologies to be implemented during their development, implementation, and regulation. The mechanisms of funding, programs of innovation, and partnerships between the government and business inspire collaboration and sharing of experiences across industries, to be sure that AI solutions consider the needs of society, and not reflect the limited commercial interests. Audits and review bodies are examples of ethical management mechanisms that ensure the confidence of the people and avoid misuse or detrimental consequences. In addition, the coordination by the government assists in the alignment of innovation with the wider social values. Governments can instil a sense of ethical accountability in the national AI strategies and governance systems, thereby creating a sense of accountability by all involved parties. This partnership model helps achieve trustworthy, accountable, and socially responsive AI ecosystems that will ensure that the growth of technology serves human interests and social justice.

8.2 Limitations

There are some limitations that can be identified in this study. First, it is conceptual and descriptive in nature mostly based on secondary sources like the policy documents and academic literature. Consequently, it lacks empirical information to support the effectiveness of certain models of governance. Second, the analysis primarily targets specific areas and policy frameworks, and this could restrict the ability to generalize the study results to other contexts. Also, given the fact that AI technologies are rapidly evolving, certain regulatory and ethical debates may evolve with time. Such restrictions indicate that the findings should be used with care when generalizing them to all populations.

8.3 Future Scope

The future research prospects of the current work are the expansion of the scope of the empirical and comparative studies related to the responsible AI governance in various national and institutional environments. It is possible to study how Triple Helix collaborations operate in practice by relying on case studies, surveys, or interviews with policymakers, researchers, and leaders in the industry in future research. It is also possible to investigate the new AI technologies, including generative AI and autonomous systems, and determine whether the current ethical and governance principles are still applicable. Additional studies can be oriented toward the quantification of the social effect of responsible AI policies and best practices to make AI ecosystems more inclusive, trustworthy, and sustainable.

REFERENCES

Ali, A. (2025). Ethical Implications of Artificial Intelligence: Ensuring Patient Data Security. In *Transforming Healthcare Sector through Artificial Intelligence and Environmental Sustainability* (pp. 149-164). Singapore: Springer Nature Singapore. https://doi.org/DOI: 10.1007/978-981-97-9555-0_8

Balasubramaniam, N., Kauppinen, M., Hiekkanen, K., & Kujala, S. (2022, March). Transparency and explainability of AI systems: ethical guidelines in practice. In *International working conference on requirements engineering: foundation for software quality* (pp. 3-18). Cham: Springer International Publishing. https://doi .org/DOI: 10.1007/978-3-030-98464-9_1

Banifatemi, A. (2025). Human Agency and AI. In *AI for Community* (pp. 122–158). Chapman and Hall/CRC.

Bhushan, S. (2025). The Rise of India's Start-up Ecosystem: Transforming into an Entrepreneurial Powerhouse. *The Indian Journal of Public Administration*, *71*(3), 463–479. DOI: 10.1177/00195561251368730

Biju, P. R., & Gayathri, O. (2024). The Indian approach to Artificial Intelligence: An analysis of policy discussions, constitutional values, and regulation. *AI & Society*, *39*(5), 2321–2335. DOI: 10.1007/s00146-023-01685-2

Cabrera, B. M., Luiz, L. E., & Teixeira, J. P. (2025). The Artificial Intelligence Act: Insights regarding its application and implications. *Procedia Computer Science*, *256*, 230–237. DOI: 10.1016/j.procs.2025.02.116

Camilleri, M. A. (2024). Artificial intelligence governance: Ethical considerations and implications for social responsibility. *Expert Systems: International Journal of Knowledge Engineering and Neural Networks*, *41*(7), e13406. DOI: 10.1111/exsy.13406

Carayannis, E. G., Campbell, D. F., & Grigoroudis, E. (2022). Helix trilogy: The triple, quadruple, and quintuple innovation helices from a theory, policy, and practice set of perspectives. *Journal of the Knowledge Economy*, *13*(3), 2272–2301. DOI: 10.1007/s13132-021-00813-x

Chinen, M. (2025). International Governance of AI. In *Handbook of Human-Centered Artificial Intelligence* (pp. 1–37). Springer Nature Singapore., DOI: 10.1007/978-981-97-8440-0_83-1

Dadhich, A., & Bansal, Y. (2025). Implementing Responsible and Ethical Artificial Intelligence in India: Balancing Innovation and Regulation for Sustainable AI Development. In *AI Ethics in Practice: Navigating Academic Insight, Managerial Expertise, and Philosophical Inquiry* (pp. 23-40). Cham: Springer Nature Switzerland. https://doi.org/DOI: 10.1007/978-3-031-87023-1_3

de Lima Figueiredo, N., Fernandes, C. I., & Abrantes, J. L. (2023). Triple helix model: Cooperation in knowledge creation. *Journal of the Knowledge Economy*, *14*(2), 854–878. DOI: 10.1007/s13132-022-00930-1

Dunleavy, P., & Margetts, H. (2025). Data science, artificial intelligence and the third wave of digital era governance. *Public Policy and Administration*, *40*(2), 185–214. DOI: 10.1177/09520767231198737

Escobar, S., & Sciortino, D. (2022). *Artificial intelligence in Canada. International perspectives on artificial intelligence, 13*. Anthem Press.

George, A. J., & Tarr, J. A. (2024). A case study in innovation policymaking: Standard contracts as a tool to improve university–industry collaboration. *Journal of Science and Technology Policy Management*, *15*(5), 1085–1109. DOI: 10.1108/JSTPM-11-2021-0175

Georgiou, O., Maksymenko, M., & Russo, S. (2025). Responsible Research and Innovation. In *R&D Management and Technology Commercialization: Practical Concepts, Innovation, and Case Studies* (pp. 247-255). Cham: Springer Nature Switzerland. https://doi.org/DOI: 10.1007/978-3-031-86789-7_15

Gupta, C., & Pandey, P. (2025). Catalysing sustainable development: the role of DST in attaining SDGs in India and the way forward. *Proceedings of the Indian National Science Academy*, 1 14. https://doi.org/DOI: 10.1007/s43538-025-00398-y

Hosseini Tabaghdehi, S. A., & Ayaz, Ö. (2025). AI ethics in action: A circular model for transparency, accountability and inclusivity. *Journal of Managerial Psychology*. Advance online publication. DOI: 10.1108/JMP-03-2024-0177

Inampudi, S., & Gaurav, A. K. (2024). Transforming Institutions for Inclusive and Sustainable Governance: An Empirical Analysis of NITI Aayog's Role in India. In *Governance and Sustainable Development in South Asia: Bridging the Gap* (pp. 177-195). Cham: Springer Nature Switzerland. https://doi.org/DOI: 10.1007/978-3-031-67616-1_10

Keith, A. J. (2024). Governance of artificial intelligence in Southeast Asia. *Global Policy*, *15*(5), 937–954. DOI: 10.1111/1758-5899.13458

Lau, P. L. (2025). The AI Act and Data Protection: The Interplay Between Artificial Intelligence and Data: The AI Act and the GDPR. In *The European Artificial Intelligence Act: Promises and Perils?* (pp. 289-313). Cham: Springer Nature Switzerland. https://doi.org/DOI: 10.1007/978-3-031-98406-8_12

Law, T., & McCall, L. (2024). Artificial intelligence policymaking: An agenda for sociological research. *Socius: Sociological Research for a Dynamic World, 10,* 23780231241261596. DOI: 10.1177/23780231241261596

Leydesdorff, L. (2021). Evolutionary and institutional triple helix models. In *The Evolutionary Dynamics of Discursive Knowledge: Communication-Theoretical Perspectives on an Empirical Philosophy of Science* (pp. 89–113). Springer International Publishing., DOI: 10.1007/978-3-030-59951-5_5

Malhotra, C., & Malhotra, U. (2024). Putting interests of digital nagriks first: Digital personal data protection (dpdp) act 2023 of India. *The Indian Journal of Public Administration, 70*(3), 516–531. DOI: 10.1177/00195561241271575

Nikolinakos, N. T. (2023). Ethical principles for trustworthy AI. In *EU policy and legal framework for artificial intelligence, robotics and related technologies-the AI Act* (pp. 101–166). Springer International Publishing., DOI: 10.1007/978-3-031-27953-9_3

Nilsson, J., Javed, S., Albertsson, K., Delsing, J., Liwicki, M., & Sandin, F. (2024). Ai concepts for system of systems dynamic interoperability. *Sensors (Basel), 24*(9), 2921. DOI: 10.3390/s24092921

Novelli, C., Taddeo, M., & Floridi, L. (2024). Accountability in artificial intelligence: What it is and how it works. *AI & Society, 39*(4), 1871–1882. DOI: 10.1007/s00146-023-01635-y

Pallett, H., Price, C., Chilvers, J., & Burall, S. (2024). Just public algorithms: Mapping public engagement with the use of algorithms in UK public services. *Big Data & Society, 11*(1), 20539517241235867. DOI: 10.1177/20539517241235867

Pan, J., & Guo, J. (2022). Innovative collaboration and acceleration: An integrated framework based on knowledge transfer and triple helix. *Journal of the Knowledge Economy, 13*(4), 3223–3247. DOI: 10.1007/s13132-021-00852-4

Pandey, P. (2025). Digital Sovereignty and AI: Developing India's National AI Stack for Strategic Autonomy. *Procedia Computer Science, 254*, 250–259. DOI: 10.1016/j.procs.2025.02.084

Parekh, P. (2024). Analytics for Public Governance: A Case of Aspirational Districts Program of NITI Aayog. In *Integrating Advancements in Education, and Society for Achieving Sustainability* (pp. 57-64). Routledge.

Pislaru, M., Vlad, C. S., Ivascu, L., & Mircea, I. I. (2024). Citizen-centric governance: Enhancing citizen engagement through artificial intelligence tools. *Sustainability*, *16*(7), 2686. DOI: 10.3390/su16072686

Prasad, K. R., Karanam, S. R., Ganesh, D., Liyakat, K. K. S., Talasila, V., & Purushotham, P. (2024). AI in public-private partnership for IT infrastructure development. *The Journal of High Technology Management Research*, *35*(1), 100496. DOI: 10.1016/j.hitech.2024.100496

Qiang, R. E. N., & Jing, D. U. (2024). Harmonizing innovation and regulation: The EU Artificial Intelligence Act in the international trade context. *Computer Law & Security Review*, *54*, 106028. DOI: 10.1016/j.clsr.2024.106028

Radanliev, P. (2025). AI ethics: Integrating transparency, fairness, and privacy in AI development. *Applied Artificial Intelligence*, *39*(1), 2463722. DOI: 10.1080/08839514.2025.2463722

Rossoni, A. L., de Vasconcellos, E. P. G., & de Castilho Rossoni, R. L. (2024). Barriers and facilitators of university-industry collaboration for research, development and innovation: A systematic review. *Management Review Quarterly*, *74*(3), 1841–1877. DOI: 10.1007/s11301-023-00349-1

Salas-Pilco, S. Z. (2021). Comparison of national artificial intelligence (AI): Strategic policies and priorities. In *Towards an international political economy of artificial intelligence* (pp. 195–217). Springer International Publishing., DOI: 10.1007/978-3-030-74420-5_9

Sargiotis, D. (2024). Data Governance Frameworks: Models and Best Practices. In *Data Governance: A Guide* (pp. 165-195). Cham: Springer Nature Switzerland. https://doi.org/DOI: 10.1007/978-3-031-67268-2_4

Sasi, A. (2025). Decoding the Indian data governance model: Relooking at aadhaar. *Social Sciences & Humanities Open*, *11*, 101408. DOI: 10.1016/j.ssaho.2025.101408

Ten Holter, C. (2022). Participatory design: Lessons and directions for responsible research and innovation. *Journal of Responsible Innovation*, *9*(2), 275–290. DOI: 10.1080/23299460.2022.2041801

Tidjon, L. N., & Khomh, F. (2022). The different faces of AI ethics across the world: A principle-to-practice gap analysis. *IEEE Transactions on Artificial Intelligence*, *4*(4), 820–839. DOI: 10.1109/TAI.2022.3225132

Tiernan, P., Costello, E., Donlon, E., Parysz, M., & Scriney, M. (2023). Information and Media Literacy in the Age of AI: Options for the Future. *Education Sciences*, *13*(9), 906. DOI: 10.3390/educsci13090906

Zadegan, M. G., Ghazinoory, S., & Nasri, S. (2025). The triple helix model of innovation and sustainable development goals: A literature review. *Sustainable Development*. Advance online publication. DOI: 10.1002/sd.70041

Chapter 5
Bridging Knowledge and Policy:
How Universities and Governments Co-Create the Future of Responsible AI

Ravikumar R. N.
https://orcid.org/0009-0009-3705-1681
Marwadi University, Rajkot, India

S. Aarthi
https://orcid.org/0009-0006-9064-2091
Marwadi University, Rajkot, India

Nazira Kurbanova
Termez University of Economics and Service, Termez, Uzbekistan

Karimov Eyyub Sevdim
Azerbaijan Technical University, Baku, Azerbaijan

Bakhritdinova Dilobar Zaynitdinovna
Shakhrisabz State Pedagogical Institute, Shakhrisabz, Uzbekistan

Nasiba Jumaniyazova
Mamun University, Khiva, Uzbekistan

ABSTRACT

The chapter examines how universities and governments jointly shape the future of responsible AI through integrated knowledge production, policy formation, and ethical governance. It explores how academic research, interdisciplinary expertise, and talent development intersect with regulatory frameworks, national strategies, and public-sector oversight to create accountable and human-centered AI ecosystems. The analysis highlights global case studies, collaborative mechanisms such as advisory councils and regulatory sandboxes, and the challenges posed by bureaucratic gaps, rapid technological change, and geopolitical pressures. The chapter argues that co-creation, evidence-based policymaking, and inclusive governance are essential for ensuring transparent, fair, and socially aligned AI development.

DOI: 10.4018/979-8-3373-7620-2.ch005

1. INTRODUCTION

The exceptionally fast growth of Artificial Intelligence (AI) in the economic, social, and governance spheres of life has raised the concern that AI technologies should be established in a responsible manner and implemented in a manner that supports the values of society. With the rising role of AI systems in decision-making, the national level of competitiveness, and the sphere of providing services to the population, universities and governments are becoming vital contributors to determining its ethical, legal, and socio-technical premises (Atkinson-Toal & Guo, 2024). Universities can also play a role in terms of research, innovation and education as well as governments can offer a regulatory guidance, national strategies and institutional mechanism of oversight and accountability. They are all parts of a responsible AI ecosystem axis. This chapter discusses how the partnership between them creates knowledge, formulates policies, and governs ethically. It looks at the intertwining of technical expertise with the legislative frameworks and points out the infrastructures, which enable co-creation, e.g. advisory councils, ethical guidelines, regulatory sandboxes, and open science platforms. The (Караджоянни, 2021)new problems, such as geopolitics, bureaucracy, and the uncertainties of controlling generative and autonomous AI, are also described in the introduction. Together, they highlight the need to have effective, more cohesive methods that can influence the development of AI that can be social, open, and in the spirit of human values.

1.1 Emergence of Responsible AI as a Policy and Research Priority

Responsible AI is now a focal point on both the research and policy agendas of many countries across the world as countries acknowledge the transformative capability and risks of AI technologies. The growing complaints about algorithmic bias, privacy invasion, uncertainty in the decision-making process, and unfair effects on the society have increased the push towards creating AI systems that are ethically sound and reliable (Ravikumar et al., 2025). National AI strategies and regulatory frameworks are being developed by governments all over the world to guarantee accountability, safety and fairness, and academic institutions have broadened their research on explainability, human-centered design, risk reduction, and computational ethics (Edler & Fagerberg, 2017). The world has also advanced the norms and the principles of responsible AI by international committees like the OECD, UNESCO, and European Union that have enhanced responsible AI to be more than a policy dream. As a result, responsible AI currently exists at the nexus of technological innovation and government regulation, and needs to be aligned by both the efforts of universities that produce empirical data and governments that regulate the legislative landscape that, in turn, informs AI development and societal integration.

1.2 The Role of Knowledge Institutions in Shaping AI Governance

Universities have a facilitative role in determining AI governance through the production of scientific knowledge, ethical principles and technical protocols that guide the formulation of policy. Being concentration areas of research excellence, they explore the new AI threats, analyze the implications of AI on society, and create tools like fairness metrics, transparency models, and privacy-saving algorithms as the cornerstones of regulatory standards. Furthermore, universities are neutral arenas where multidisciplinary knowledge as computer science, law, social sciences, and philosophy come to play to form holistic understandings of responsible AI (Sigfrids et al., 2023). The other way that knowledge institutions impact governance is through expert involvement in advisory boards, white papers, pilot testing environments, and national AI councils. Such contributions enable policymakers to ground the regulations on empirical evidence and the state-of-the-art developments and not on speculative assumptions. Additionally, universities can be regarded as centers of talent improvement, providing the skills that future researchers, policymakers, and leaders of any industry may use to manage ethical AI ecosystems. By such functions, universities have a great influence on national and international AI governance paths.

1.2 Need for Strong University–Government Synergy in AI Ecosystems

The good working relationship between the universities and governments is imperative in the creation of the responsible AI ecosystem because none of them is capable of adequately addressing the dynamism and multi-faceted nature of AI technologies. The current scientific data, moral opinions, and technical discoveries should be available to the governments, so that they can be able to invent regulations that would be protective and at the same time innovation-friendly. The universities, in its turn, require positive policy environments, funding systems, and institutional structures that would make sure that the priorities of the research are aligned with the national needs (S. Sharma, 2024). Some of the ways through which this synergy is achieved are the joint advisory committees, regulatory sandboxes, policy laboratories, and co-funded innovation centers. It is through cooperation that the forms of governance become pliant, information-based, and realistic concerning technical constraints within the world. It also fosters shared accountability when it comes to the deliberation of the problems, which meet the rights of both data and accountability of algorithms alongside the impacts to the society. Without these concerted activities, AI regulations will turn redundant, fragmented, or under-trained, and scholarly researches might not be transformed into any policy. Through this means, synergy plays an important role in enabling trustful, equitable and socially compatible AI development.

2. BACKGROUND TO THE STUDY

The context that led to the study is the historical and theoretical premises that render university-government partnership to be crucial in developing responsible AI. The Triple Helix model that was originally developed to describe knowledge-based innovation by means of cooperation between universities and industries as well as governments has acquired a new significance in the field of AI. During the age of AI, scientific knowledge and the functioning of the society have become even more interdependent, with AI technologies affecting such vital spheres as healthcare, security, education, and government (Aarthi, et al., 2025). At the same time, the world regulatory environment has been significantly reshaped, with the European Union and other countries of Asia and North America moving towards elaborate laws such as the AI Act, and national approaches that focus on ethical and human-based AI ((OECD), 2021). Such changes emphasize the necessity to close the gap between the policy action and scientific knowledge. The policymakers will have to learn to balance where the new risks become apparent including generative AI misinformation, surveillance systems, and algorithmic inequalities, and universities will be required to create interdisciplinary research that can be utilized to inform future governance. All of these conditions collectively constitute the basis of the study of collaborative mechanisms that build responsible AI ecosystems.

2.1 Evolution of the Triple Helix Framework in the AI Era

Innovation, the conceptual framework of the Triple Helix assumes that it is a result of contact between universities, industries, and governments. This framework has changed in the age of AI to include more significant connections between academic research and the government policymaking because the social impact of AI requires integrated governance. In contrast to conventional innovation systems, AI ecosystems must be not only technologically developed but also ethically regulated, and their data must be governed and regulated by regulatory measures that react to the emergence of new risks ((OECD), 2023). Universities are also involved in the initial study of machine learning, ethics, and socio-technical systems, and governments also influence environments by legislation, national plans, and public investments.

Industry is also a significant participant and tends to be based on regulations and research findings generated by the other two spheres. The AI era has turned the Triple Helix into a more policy oriented and ethically focused concept, with knowledge generation and governance being closely interconnected. It is this development that underlines why university-government collaboration is especially essential to the process of making sure that AI development is in line with the values held by the people and long-term prosperity of the population (Farinha et al., 2016). As depicted in the figure 1, the responsible AI is crafted by universities, governments, and industry working together in the integrated roles of research, regulation, ethics, and technology development.

Figure 1. Evolution of the Triple Helix Framework in the AI Era

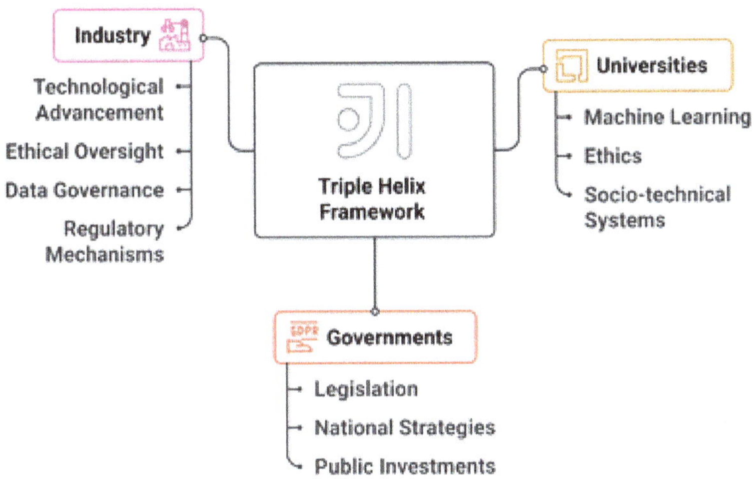

2.2 Global Shifts in AI Regulation and Ethical Standards

In recent years, the world witnessed a trend towards more systematic regulation of AI, as the world is increasingly aware of the dangers of autonomous decision-making, generative models of artificial intelligence, and massive data processing. European Union has taken the forefront in regulations with the AI act where they have focused on risk-based classification, transparency requirements, and outlawing detrimental AI activities. Equally, the Asian nations such as Singapore, Japan, and India have come up with governance systems that optimise innovation and rights protection of the citizens (Jobin et al., 2019). The regulatory activities in North America are focused on the accountability, algorithmic auditing, and industry-specific guidelines. Normative frameworks have been developed by international agencies like the UNESCO and the OECD that encourage fairness, inclusiveness and human centred design. These changes on a global level show that there is a gradual transition between voluntary ethical standards and mandatory systems of management. They also emphasize the necessity of evidence-based science and professional advice, which are particularly the prerogative of the universities. With the extensive application of AI systems to sensitive fields, including healthcare, finance, and national security, regulatory alignment gains more and more significance in protecting the trust of the population and ethical standards (Chintoh et al., 2024).

2.3 Rationale for Integrating Scientific Knowledge With Policymaking

It is crucial to incorporate scientific expertise into making of policies since AI technologies are associated with challenging technical, ethical, and social issues that demand evidence-based policy. The policymakers in most cases have to deal with fast changing innovations with very little technical knowledge and therefore it would be unwise of them to make decisions without the university. Empirical results, risk assessment, and methodological resources required to measure algorithmic fairness, system robustness, and impacts on society are offered by academic researchers (Zhang et al., 2021). This contribution of science assists in making sure that the regulations are not only conceptually good but also technically practical and future-directed. Also, by presenting interdisciplinary orientations, universities can add value to policy debates with the inclusion of law insight, ethics, sociology and public administration. In the absence of this form of integration, policy structures may become outdated, too restrictive or too protective. On the other hand, other scientific knowledge not related to governance may not be fully utilised and as such, their contribution to the society is limited. Thus, research and policy making combination will provide adaptive, transparent and responsible AI governance that can address the expectations of the populace and respond to upcoming threats in a rapidly changing technological environment.

3. RESEARCH OBJECTIVES

The swift development of AI technologies requires a concerted effort by the universities and the governments, which cannot resolve the issues of the digital age through the prism of ethical, technical, and governance issues on their own. This part summarizes the central goals driving the chapter, which is the necessity to learn about collaborative structures, co-creation processes, and policy-science interface. The objectives are designed to organize the investigation of the process of responsible AI ecosystems construction, maintenance, and regulation based on evidence-based, multidisciplinary collaboration.

- To examine the institutional and structural mechanisms through which universities and governments collaborate to shape responsible AI development.
- To identify the co-creation processes such as advisory committees, regulatory sandboxes, and joint policy labs that support ethical, transparent, and accountable AI ecosystems.
- To analyze the major challenges, constraints, and enabling conditions that influence the effectiveness of university government governance models.
- To evaluate the role of knowledge exchange, interdisciplinary research, and evidence-based policymaking in strengthening AI ethics and regulatory alignment.
- To propose strategic pathways for enhancing sustainable, participatory, and socially aligned responsible AI governance across national and global contexts.

4. CONCEPTUAL MODEL

The theoretical framework of this chapter portrays the process of co-designing the principles of responsible AI between universities and governments based on the combination of scientific knowledge and policy frameworks. It focuses on the ongoing interactions between knowledge-making and regulating needs as well as social expectations. This model puts universities, through which it is assumed they produce empirical data, moral systems, and new technology, as agents and governments, where they are thought to act as strategic facilitators by legislation, national AI missions, funding ecosystems, and regulatory supervision. Their combination creates a complex relationship that will establish AI governance as a cyclical process and not a linear chain (Ahmed et al., 2022). This model determines the feedback mechanisms by which the academic discoveries can be used to make adjustments in the policy, and vice versa, how the priorities in the policy affect the research agenda, career trajectories, and research ethics. It also puts a spotlight on multi-level governance channels, such as advisory groups, interdisciplinary AI ethics centers, and policy sandboxes, which facilitate the interactions between the two sectors. The conceptual model can offer an organized concept of how responsible AI ecosystems can develop and how the collaborative governance structures can ensure that AI development is based on the principles of human-centeredness, transparency, and accountability.

4.1 Framework Linking Knowledge Production and Policy Formation

The model that connects knowledge generation and policy development places the universities as the hubs of AI skills and empirical studies and identifies governments as the implementing institutions that would convert this knowledge into practical regulatory and strategic policies. Universities generate the baseline of research on algorithmic fairness, transparency, socio-technical risks, and ethical principles to be used as a source of the evidence in drafting national AI standards and governance tools. This learning is passed down in a formal manner like expert commissions, research consortia, white papers and advisory boards. The governments then incorporate the knowledge into the legislation, missions of the country and regulation sandbox, making sure that the policies are based on scientific reality and not on ideological presumptions (Brereton et al., 2023). The framework functions as a two-way interaction where governmental priorities encourage new scholarly research into new technologies in the sphere of generative AI, autonomous systems, and high-risk AI implementations. With the creation of knowledge being aligned to the policy imperative, the framework will make governance responsive, evidence-based, and socially accountable and ultimately result in the creation of AI systems that establish transparency, fairness, and social trust. The figure 2 illustrates the stratified approach of accumulating AI skills at the university level to government policy-making and adoption of adaptive evidence-based governance.

Figure 2. AI Governance Framework

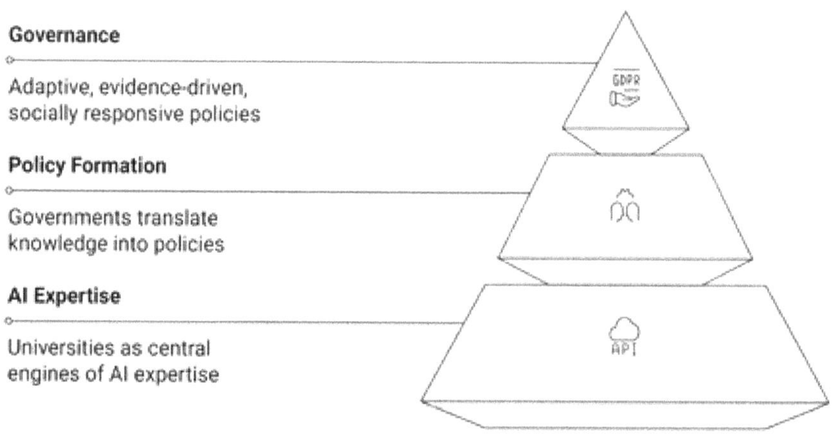

4.2 Interaction Dynamics of the University–Government Responsible AI Model

The dynamics of interaction between the university and government in the model of responsible AI indicate the multi-directionality of interactions to which ethical and responsible AI ecosystems are shaped. Such dynamics are implemented in form of organized partnerships including national AI councils, ethics oversight committees, policy innovation labs, and joint foresight. Universities can bring in knowledge on risk assessment, computational ethics, technical standards, and system assessment, whereas governments give regulatory frameworks, incentives as well as strategic priorities (Ayana et al., 2024). The communications do not only go through the formal channels but also through informal communications where there are collective conferences and open consultations that bring about understanding. Notably, these processes are defined by the existence of feedback, meaning that the decisions made by policymakers affect the research agendas, and at the same time, the findings of the scholars trigger a revision of the governance system. This cycle of rebuilding enhances the ability of both industries to react to new demands: some are algorithmic discrimination to generative AI misinformation (Agarwal & Nene, 2025). As it has been shown in the model, the responsible AI governance cannot be reached via individual efforts; it must be negotiated on a regular basis, with the exchange of knowledge, and the integration of scientific discovery and policy criteria. Table 1 Describes cooperation strategies which include advisory councils, policy laboratories, regulatory sandboxes, and collaborative research centers.

Table 1. Mechanisms of University-Government Collaboration in AI Governance

Mechanism	Description	Contribution to Governance
National AI Councils	Multi-stakeholder advisory bodies	Align research with policy priorities
Regulatory Sandboxes	Safe testing environments	Evaluate AI risks before deployment
Policy Innovation Labs	Collaborative design/testing of regulations	Enable iterative policymaking
Joint Research Hubs	Co-funded centers of excellence	Produce multidisciplinary insights

4.3 Governance Pathways for Ethical, Human-Centered AI

Ethical and human-centered AI governance routes include the forms, mechanisms, and legal tools that guide AI systems to be oriented to society and its foundational values and rights. Such pathways are risk-based regulation, algorithmic impact consideration, ethics-by-design, and continuous oversight, which are established by national AI strategies. The role of universities is significant as it provides interdisciplinary perspectives on equality, diversity, and openness hence to form the ethical grounds that are ingrained in policies. These insights are operationalised by governments in their governance structures including regulatory sandboxes, government AI guidelines and mandatory audit procedures. Several other pathways are also enhanced by multi-stakeholder consultations, the involvement of civil society, and human rights evaluations (Lase et al., 2025). The methodology recognizes that ethical AI goes beyond compliance and needs to be actively considered how it can affect society and ensure that human values are integrated through the AI lifecycle approach. These governance mechanisms enable the research-based ethics to be linked with the government-based regulation to make AI innovations reliable, socially positive, and responsible in their application in both the public and the private sector.

5. RESEARCH METHODOLOGY

The study approach to be used in this chapter is the synthesis of conceptual analysis, analysis of documents, and case-based research to investigate how universities and governments develop responsible AI ecosystems. Since AI governance is an interdisciplinary field, the approach is informed by the research of public policy, ethical AI literature, innovation theory, and the literature on collaboration in organizations. The chapter reviews the secondary sources of data such as national AI strategies, regulatory reports, scholarly articles and reports of international bodies such as OECD, UNESCO and the European Commission (Banozic-Tang & Taeihagh, 2022). It is a comparative case study approach applied to discuss recent examples of Europe, Asia, and North America that show the real-life implementation of university-government collaboration. The conceptual evaluation framework also uses the methodology to evaluate the role of co-creation processes in responsible AI governance like advisory committees, regulatory sandboxes and AI ethics centers. The multi-method approach allows to gain a holistic approach to the processes of institutional dynamics, challenges, and strategic directions to increase AI governance so that the conclusions will be based on both the empirical data and theoretical knowledge.

5.1 Analytical Approach and Scope of the Chapter

The analytical method is based on a qualitative prism, which is concerned with how universities and governments relate structurally and functionally to responsible AI. This method allows a thorough investigation of policy processes, flows of knowledge and governance structures as opposed to quantitative modeling. The chapter is deliberately wide in scope so as to include developments taking place around the globe to give a comparative context on how various regions would have conceptualized and applied responsible AI governance. The review involves the discussion of the country-level strategies, regulatory, interdisciplinary research, and partnership-based governance efforts. As a result of the synthesis of results between varied contexts, the chapter will help to uncover general tendencies, deviations, and new best practices (Paracha, 2023). The qualitative method also enables the interpretation of intricate socio-technical processes that can give an insight into the operationalization of the ethical principles and how the institutions can address to the changing AI risks. Finally, this methodology serves the purpose of the chapter, which is to describe the process of co-creation as a dynamic and iterative process between knowledge institutions and policymakers.

5.2 Data Sources: Policy Documents, Case Studies, and Scholarly Literature

The chapter utilizes a wide variety of secondary sources of data to create an in-depth view of responsible AI co-creation. Policy reports, such as national AI strategies, regulatory principles, and ethics frameworks, as well as governmental white papers, offer crucial information regarding the model of how states define and regulate AI. The case studies in other parts of the world include the AI Act initiatives in Europe, Model AI Governance Framework in Singapore and the public-sector AI guidelines in Canada, which provide practical examples of university-government collaboration. Peer-reviewed journals, academic conferences, and even think-tank reports provide scholarly literature that serves as theoretical and empirical basis of AI ethics, socio-technical systems, and governance models (A. K. Sharma & Sharma, 2025). The combination of these sources allows the triangulation of the analysis, as the analysis is based on the authoritative and multiple points of view. Including international datasets and cross-sector opinions, the chapter creates a comprehensive vision of responsible AI governance and pinpoints the mechanisms with the help of which joint knowledge production directly affects the policy making and ethical oversight frameworks.

5.3 Framework for Evaluating Responsible AI Co-Creation

The model of assessing responsible AI co-creation evaluates the level of effectiveness of universities and government cooperation in creating ethical, transparent, and socially aligned AI ecosystems. This model is made up of three essential dimensions which are: institutional collaboration, knowledge integration, and the influence of governance. The institutional collaboration is based on the structures, including national AI councils, advisory committees, joint research programs, policy innovation labs. Knowledge integration will analyse how much academic evidence on fairness, transparency and risk mitigation is integrated in the regulation design and national strategies. Examples of the outcomes that are gauged in governance include the empowerment of ethical principles, better transparency in regulations, and greater trust in the government (Pasupuleti, 2025a). The framework also takes into account those enabling factors such as financial assistance, cross-disciplinary experience, openness of the policy, and involvement of stakeholders. Using this evaluating framework in the context of several case studies, the chapter is able to find patterns and gaps in the existing models of collaboration and outline opportunities to enhance responsible AI governance by making co-creation processes more systematic and evidence-driven.

6. LITERATURE REVIEW

According to the literature on responsible Artificial Intelligence (AI), there has been a rise in the interdependence of universities and governments in establishing ethical, transparent, and accountable AI ecosystems. Scholars have highlighted that responsible AI is impossible to be accomplished by technology innovation alone, institutional cooperation is necessary, and interdisciplinary knowledge is necessary. The Triple Helix model is a concept that has been extensively studied in literature on innovation that can be used to describe the collective effect of knowledge-generating institutions and state actors in determining the direction of technological change (Crişan et al., 2025). Within the framework of AI governance, universities play a great role as they can produce some empirical knowledge and ethical principles, whereas governments are involved in organizing the environment and setting up the regulations, national policies, and control tools. Another aspect mentioned in the literature is the move to have hybrid governance infrastructures such as advisory bodies, working groups, and regulatory sandboxes, which allow iteration and evidence-based policymaking (Ismail & Ahmad, 2025). This part will provide a synthesis of the existing literature in these fields to demonstrate the role of knowledge creation and integration of policy as a responsive element towards the development of AI. Table 2 Lists the leading global AI ethics (EU, OECD, UNESCO, etc.), and their main principles.

Table 2. Key Global AI Governance Frameworks and Principles

Framework	Region/Organization	Core Ethical Principles
EU AI Act	European Union	Risk-based regulation, accountability, transparency
OECD AI Principles	OECD Countries	Inclusive growth, human-centered values
UNESCO AI Ethics	Global	Dignity, fairness, environment, sustainability
Singapore Model Framework	Asia	Explainability, human oversight, robustness

6.1 University Contributions: Research, Ethics, and Talent Development

Universities have a complex role to play in the development of responsible AI, and in the literature, three main contributions to the role were named: research, ethics, and talent development. The technical innovations of fairness algorithms, explainability techniques, privacy-preserving machine learning, and robustness tests focus on academic research. The findings of these studies are directly translated into the regulation guidelines and best practices embraced by policymakers (Sophia LI, 2025). University-based ethical scholarship broadens knowledge in AI regarding its societal consequences, supports the creation of normative approaches and methodologies of impact assessment. Interdisciplinary centers, which is a fusion of computer science, philosophy, law and social sciences, are often mentioned as a necessary part of the development of holistic and human-centered AI governance (Pasupuleti, 2025b). Another significant contribution is the cultivation of talents since universities prepare future researchers, policymakers, and AI practitioners with the skills that they need to have in responsible innovation. Literature also highlights that universities are neutral environments where people can argue about the harms of algorithm, risk to society, and ethical design devoid of commercial or political influence. Such a scholarly climate puts universities in a pivotal role as a contribution to the evidence-based policy process of AI development.

6.2 Government Roles: Regulation, Funding, and Strategic Guiding Policies

The responsible AI is a topic that is heavily researched in policy literature and governance research. The political control over AI involves governments that establish regulatory frameworks that regulate the implementation of AI, which can encompass risk-based classification systems, the need to be transparent, audit necessities, and limitations on the use of AI to cause harm (Arshad & Tripathi, 2025). Examples of states that regulate AI accountability via enforceable guidelines include the European Union AI Act, the Canada Directive on Automated Decision-Making and the Singapore Model AI Governance Framework. Another important role of a government is funding; national investments in AI research centers, ethics programs, and innovation hubs are the stimulating factor of responsible technologies, interdisciplinary expertise. The strategic guiding policies, which are available in national AI strategies that provide a description of ethical principles, institutional responsibilities, and national long-term priorities, are also considered important in the literature (Liu et al., 2025). Such strategies dictate the research agenda, affect curriculum and encourage engagement with knowledge institutions. All these policy tools combined make sure that the values, human rights, and welfare of the society are at the center of AI development. Table 3 Summarizes the unique and complementary role in responsible AI development that the university and the government have.

Table 3. Comparison of University and Government Roles in Responsible AI

Actor	Key Roles	Contribution to Responsible AI
Universities	Research, ethics scholarship, talent development	Provide evidence-based insights, fairness tools, and ethical frameworks
Governments	Regulation, funding, national AI strategies	Establish legal standards, support innovation, and enforce accountability
Joint Impact	Knowledge–policy integration	Produces robust, adaptive, and transparent AI governance models

6.3 Models of Joint Advisory Bodies, National Councils, and Regulatory Sandboxes

Recent research gives importance to the development of hybrid regimes of governance that enhance the cooperation between universities and governments. Such things as national AI ethics committees and expert working groups are examples of how scholarly knowledge can be used to inform regulatory design. Scholars, industry representatives and the actors of the civil society are frequently included in national AI councils to offer a multidisciplinary supervision (Goktas & Grzybowski, 2025). These organizations bring orderly evidence-based decision making and make sure that the regulations are in line with the current research findings. Another new governance tool that has been addressed in literature is regulatory sandboxes. These highly regulated experimental settings enable universities, start-ups, and government agencies to be able to test AI systems in a real-world setting without compromising ethics. Sandboxes facilitate learning, openness and repeated enhancement of the governance processes (Wang, 2025). Collectively, advisory committees, national councils and regulatory sandboxes are examples of how hybrid models apply co-creation, to allow scientific discovery and policy implementation to be constantly fed back. Such models have turned into the necessary elements of the worldwide trend to responsible AI.

7. CASE STUDIES

The history of responsible AI generation throughout the globe has been informed by individual partnerships between universities and governments, with each being informed by regional interests, regulatory practices, and institutional capabilities. Case studies are indispensable in giving information on how such partnerships are put into practice, outside the theoretical frameworks and policy dreams. Europe has become one of the world leaders in the formulation of AI ethics rules and regulations, with large part of it being due to a heated collaboration among academic researchers, policy organizations and supranational authorities. Conversely, Asian nations have prioritized the creation of policy-oriented AI research centers and national policies along with an innovation and digital sovereignty-driven approach to economic competitiveness, including ethical concerns (Cheng et al., 2019). An analysis of these cases shows that various governance philosophies, institutional forms and social values affect the process of co-creation. The cases combined show that sustainable responsible AI ecosystem is based on adaptable, multi-disciplinary, and repeated cooperation between knowledge institutions and the government. All these instances provide the insights into how to structure AI governance frameworks in the world in the future.

7.1 Europe: University–Government Collaboration in AI Ethics and Regulation

One of the most vivid examples of university-government cooperation in the formulation of AI ethics and regulation is in Europe. The High-Level Expert Group on AI (HLEG-AI) is an academic and policymaker-civil society-industry leader group that has been instrumental in providing guidance on ethics like the Ethics Guidelines on Trustworthy AI. Principles such as transparency, fairness, explainability, and human oversight were therefore developed by academic researchers in major institutions, including Oxford, TU Delft, KU Leuven and the University of Edinburgh (Mikhaylov et al., 2018). These recommendations had an impact on the future policy tools, the most notable of them being the EU AI Act that translates ethical concepts into legal binding mandates. European national governments (including Germany, France, and Finland) have set up AI ethics hubs and government testing platforms on which universities in collaboration with regulatory bodies are running algorithmic audits and impact evaluation. The adoption of regulatory sandboxes in such countries as Spain or the UK can offer a controlled setting of studying the risks of AI without violating cooperation and experimentation (Department of Science and Information Technology, 2025). This coherent ecosystem illustrates the fact that the governance strategy of Europe is grounded on multidisciplinary scholarly input, robust policy frameworks and regional pledge to human-focused AI. The figure 3 shows the chronological order of integrating the academic knowledge into the ethical principles, regulatory frameworks, and responsible AI institutional configurations in Europe.

Figure 3. European AI Ethics and Regulation Development

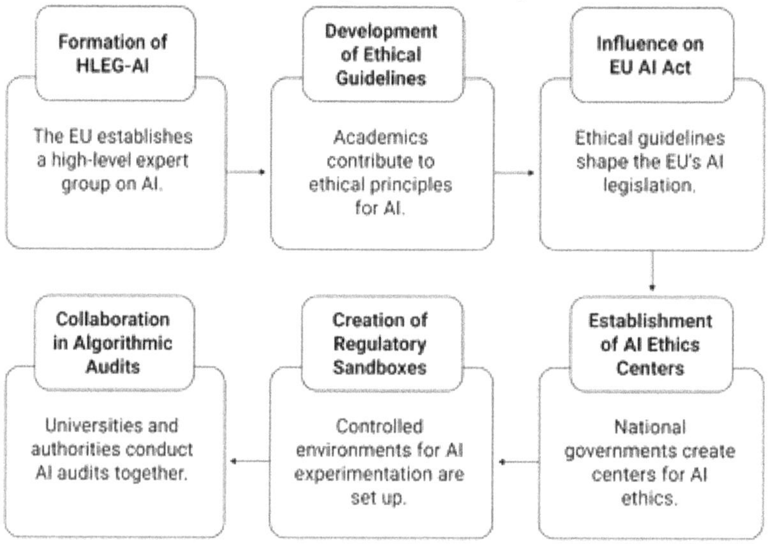

7.2 Asia: Policy-Driven AI Research Hubs and National AI Strategies

The strategy of responsible AI development in Asia is highly authoritative, which is accompanied by the widespread university-based research systems. Singapore, Japan, South Korea, and India are some of the countries that have introduced national AI plans, which make AI a core economic engine, digital transformation, and technological sovereignty. Singapore sets a bright example with its Model AI Governance Framework and AI Verify testing toolkit, both of which were created with the involvement of NUS, NTU and other research institutes in the country and abroad (Gianni et al., 2022). The Society 5.0 program in Japan incorporates research at the university level in deploying AI in the public sector with the focus on well-being and social resilience. With NITI Aayog in the lead, India has the National Programme on AI to develop ethical guidelines, datasets and public-sector AI projects with the collaboration of IITs, IISc and AI research centres. The AI Ethics Charter of South Korea was also co-designed with the involvement of academics and focused on the safety, inclusivity, and transparency. The governments are also making large investments in AI innovation hubs, supercomputing infrastructure, and cross-disciplinary research centers across Asia, so that the academic knowledge is reflected in national priorities (Chan, 2023). Although the strategies in the region are also innovation-based, moral aspects are becoming integrated with the help of joint research, pilot projects, and state AI norms developed with references to the scholarly experience. The figure 4 shows that the swift development of AI in Asia is influenced by the government leadership, ethical priorities, academic ecosystems, and infrastructure investments as a whole.

Figure 4. Asia's AI Development Landscape

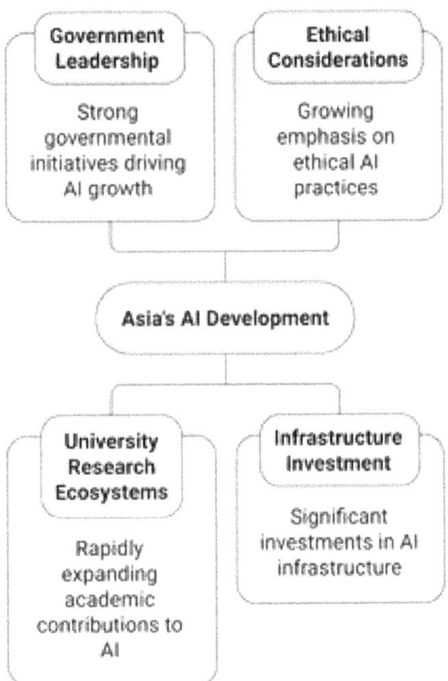

7.3 Cross-Case Synthesis: Lessons Learned and Emerging Global Trends

In Europe and Asia, multiple lessons are common in the area of effective university-government cooperation in the responsible AI governance. These two regions indicate that the most robust ethical AI schemes are those that are firmly based on multi-disciplinary academic research and are assisted by formal mechanisms of advice. Europe is characterized by the emphasis on regulatory rigor and standardization of ethics, and Asia is characterized by the emphasis on innovation ecosystems based on national development requirements. Nonetheless, both of them are dependent on universities to gain evidence-based knowledge, risk management, and capacity development (Kwon et al., 2012). One of the most important global trends is the emergence of hybrid forms of governance creating regulatory sandboxes, national councils, jointly funded research centers, etc. to support information learning and adaptation of policies. The other tendency is the growing expenditure on AI ethics education and talent development in order to make it long-term sustainable. The cases jointly indicate that the most effective approach to responsible AI governance is that in which scientific knowledge and the policy used by the government evolve together in ongoing structured cooperation. Table 4 A comparison between policy approaches, ethical priorities, and models of collaboration between Europe and Asia.

Table 4. Case Study Comparison: Europe vs Asia in Responsible AI Development

Region	Collaboration Approach	Policy Characteristics	Ethical Focus
Europe	Strong academic involvement	Formal regulations (EU AI Act)	Human-centered AI, rights protection
Asia	Policy-driven research hubs	National innovation strategies	Safety, economic growth, societal benefit
Shared Themes	Advisory bodies, national AI strategies	Knowledge–policy integration	Fairness, transparency

8. RESULTS/DISCUSSION

The findings of this research indicate that AI responsible governance would be best realized when universities and governments can put in place way-engineered, perpetual, and mutually sustaining mechanisms of cooperation. It has been shown that knowledge flows, i.e. the empirical research, ethics scholarship, technical assessment, and interdisciplinary knowledge flow, are decisive in forming the policies that are both responsive to society, as well as scientifically based. Through case studies, it has been found out that the co-creation processes can improve the development of policies by introducing transparency, accountability, and equity in the regulatory systems. Much of the theory-practice interplay comes in the form of collaborative initiatives (e.g. advisory councils and regulatory sandboxes) (Bearman et al., 2022). Nonetheless, the research also finds that there exists serious impediments that hinder a smooth cooperation. The existence of bureaucratic rigidity, the lack of technical skills in the work of state institutions, geopolitical tensions, and the fast development of AI technologies introduce a discrepancy between the results of research and the practical application of the policy (Walter, 2024). These conclusions highlight the fact that more adaptive governance models are required that will be able to evolve in line with new risks and technological changes. All the results imply that the most effective and enforceable AI governance can be achieved by reinforcing institutional synergy to implement ethical principles.

8.1 HowKnowledge Flows Shape Responsible AI Governance

The interchange of knowledge between universities and governments plays a great role in responsible AI governance, as it is important to make sure that policy-making is informed by evidence-based data, sound moral judgment, and technical aspects. Academic studies are providing input into the issues of algorithmic discrimination, lack of visibility, breach of privacy, and social impact, which policymakers might be unable to assess without professional advice. Such knowledge disseminations are arranged in the form of advisory reports, legislative consultations, co-research projects and dedicated ethics committees (Etzkowitz, 2003). These flows strengthen the quality of the regulations when well-integrated in order to assist the governments to forecast risk, and harmonize the governance mechanisms with the new trends in the technologies. Besides, interdisciplinary research in the university provides a variety of perspectives based on law, philosophy, sociology, and computer science, which enriches policy discussions and prevents technical parochialism. The research indicates that good knowledge flows lead to more holistic governance paradigms that consider the impacts in the society, rather than technological performance (Radu, 2021). These flows, in turn, are the depth and continuity of flows that determine the strength, validity, and flexibility of responsible AI governance.

8.2 IMpact of Co-Creation on Ethical Standards and Policy Innovation

Co-creation between governments and universities enhances ethical principles and facilitates policy creativity due to mutual experience and joint experimentation.

Ethical principles of fairness, accountability and human-centered design are ingrained in the regulatory framework when researchers and policymakers work together to formulate guidelines or be part of an advisory body. The policy innovation supported through the concept of co-creation assists governments in experimenting with policy tools, which include, but are not limited to: risk-based classification, algorithmic impact analysis and regulatory sandboxes based on academic expertise (Jelovac et al., 2022). Such partnerships also promote iterative learning, in which policy issues in the real world instigate new research questions and research results result in new governance mechanisms. The research reveals that the more advanced co-creation systems are in countries the more elaborate and progressive responsible AI policies are structured. It is also this synergy that increases the legitimacy and trust by the people since the policies are based on transparent and research driven processes. By co-creation, therefore, there is a gap bridging between the theoretical and practical governance to ensure that ethical principles are continuously developed with the growth of technology.

8.3 Barriers: Bureaucracy, Talent Gaps, Geopolitics, and Fast-Evolving AI Risks

Despite the benefits of collaboration, several challenges that inhibit successful co-creation between the government and the university in responsible AI exist. Bureaucratic processes which may be lengthy approval process and rigid organizational processes usually interfere with the incorporation of academic findings into policy frameworks. The absence of talent in the domain of public agencies, especially, the insufficiency of AI ethicists, data scientists, and technical auditors limit the capacity of the governments to learn about the unclear research results and apply them. Geopolitical dynamics are also a challenge to collaboration because there are issues of digital sovereignty, international competition, and international cross-border data flows that characterize the priorities of strategy (Li, 2024). The biggest problem is however the rapid pace of AI development which is significantly out of the old policy makers cycles, and leaves the regulatory blind spots. Emerging types of ethical risk, such as generative AI, autonomous systems, and live surveillance systems are in need of on-the-fly and proactive governing systems. The barriers highlight the significance of adaptive regulatory processes, capacity-building, and continued discussions in such a way that the accountable AI regulation will correspond to social requirements and technological realities. Table 5 The main challenges identified include bureaucracy, shortage of talent, geopolitics, and fast emerging risks of AI.

Table 5. Barriers to University–Government Co-Creation in Responsible AI

Barrier Category	Explanation	Impact on Governance
Bureaucratic Rigidity	Slow policy cycles, administrative delays	Hinders rapid adaptation
Talent Gaps	Lack of AI experts within government	Limits evidence-based decisions
Geopolitical Pressures	Digital sovereignty & global competition	Shapes strategic priorities
Rapid Innovation	Fast-evolving technologies	Creates regulatory blind spots

9. FUTURE RESEARCH

The problem of responsible AI governance should be confronted in the future by new challenges of complexity and the necessity of multidisciplinary and long-term research. Since AI systems are likely to have a greater impact on the functioning of the administration, the health sector, finances, and even national security, it is time to conduct long-term research, which would inspect the ways in which policies develop, evolve, and have specific effects on society. The idea of solving to integrate different stakeholders especially civil society, marginalized communities and non-technical experts into co creation processes is also an aspect that requires further investigation (Aarthi, Ravikumar, & Pardaev, 2025). The literature also shows that there has been an increasing issue regarding power imbalances, digital inequalities, and marginalization of vulnerable groups in governance discourse. The future studies ought to, therefore, explore the idea of inclusive models that guarantee fair participation and representation. Also, the new technologies, like generative AI, autonomous decision-making systems, biometric surveillance, and AI-enabled cyber operations, introduce unaddressed ethical and regulatory issues. The research of these areas will expand the knowledge of risk mitigation, the human supervision system, and the governance requirements in the long term. Altogether, the upcoming studies should be concerned with the development of resilient, evidence-based models that can keep up with technological and social changes.

9.1 Need for Longitudinal Studies on AI Policy Maturation

Longitudinal research is vital to the development of insights into how AI governance frameworks develop with time and how policy intervention influences outcomes in real world environments. The bulk of the literature is concerned with the development of the AI regulations but does not provide much information about the effectiveness of these policies in reality, their ability to respond to new challenges, and the impact on the behavior of the institutions. In the long-run, research will demonstrate the sustainability of governance systems: was it impact assessment, auditing or risk-based classification which will be effective as technologies evolve (Madan & Ashok, 2023). It is also able to monitor the development of the national strategies due to geopolitical pressure, technological advancements, and citizen demands. Using the policy patterns over long-term periods researchers can determine the success pattern, regulatory stagnation or unintended consequences. Longitudinal studies also offer evidence-based discussions that can be used to make changes in the designing of policies so that the governance is alwayss up-to-date and progressive. This kind of research is especially important in rapidly changing areas such as AI where preliminary regulations can soon become obsolete unless they are regularly reviewed and revised.

9.2 Integrating Civil Society and Marginalized Groups Into Co-Creation Models

The inclusion aspect of governance is becoming a crucial aspect of responsible AI, and future studies should examine how the civil society, community-focused, and marginalized groups can engage in the co-creation of policies actively. The dominant models tend to give more precedence to expert and institutional discourses at the expense of governance structures that do not take equity issues and lived experiences into consideration. The studies are necessary to locate the mechanisms that enhance various viewpoints including participatory design approaches, citizen assemblies, community advisory boards and community consultations. Learning about the ways marginalized populations suffer due to AI-based harms may help to formulate more just rules concerning privacy, algorithms, and algorithms-based decision-making (Meszaros et al., 2022). Research should also focus on power relations that impede inclusive participation such as digital inequalities, low awareness, and institutional barriers in the governance systems. Inclusion of these groups into co-creation models may contribute to the enhancement of policy design, enhanced legitimacy, and responsible AI principles to meet the needs of the society beyond technological performance. This line of research is critical towards achieving equity and fairness in AI ecosystem.

9.3 Research Gaps in Generative AI, Surveillance, and Autonomous Systems Governance

The recent development of generative artificial intelligence, surveillance systems, and autonomous systems is introducing novel governance issues that are poorly covered in existing literature. Generative AI is prone to misinformation, deepfakes, infringement of intellectual property, and authenticity of content, and as such, innovative regulatory and technical measures are necessary. Facial recognition, biometric tracking, and predictive analytics powered systems of surveillance should be questioned because of the likelihood of discrimination, privacy theft, and targeted profiling. Self-driving cars and other automatized systems of decisions bring up the issue of who is liable, who will manage those systems, and how safety will be guaranteed. Studies need to examine systems of governance that can be adaptive to these new risks; they should be based on adaptive regulation, technical audits, red-teaming methods, and ethical design specifications (Goracinova et al., 2017). Also, interdisciplinary research is required to investigate the consequences of the society such as trust, cultural reactions and democratic accountability. By filling these gaps, it will be possible to develop strong policy tools that will be in a position to curb the future developments of AI in a responsible manner.

10. MANAGERIAL IMPLICATIONS

The management implications of the present research indicate the practical measures that should be undertaken by the universities, governments, and collaborative ecosystems to make responsible AI governance stronger. In the case of the universities, the findings focus on the importance of developing interdisciplinary research interest, integrating ethics in technical programs, and developing alliances to enable academics to directly apply their knowledge to policy development. To governments, the implications emphasize the need to design adaptive regulatory frameworks that are based on evidence and investing in talent development and establishing governance environments that are free to academic cooperation (Masters et al., 2024). Sustainable infrastructures (such as AI ethics centers, regulatory sandboxes and long-term research funding programs) should be among the priorities of joint ecosystems, in which universities and governments collaborate. These processes are necessary to make sure that the flow of knowledge is not disrupted and that ethical principles are transferred into practice. Moreover, the managers should identify the obstacles: bureaucratic delays, lack of technical capacity and quickly changing risks, and take the initiative to come up with mitigative strategies. All of these implications are a roadmap towards making institutional collaboration stronger and enabling a better societal value of responsible AI.

10.1 For Universities: Building Multidisciplinary AI Ethics and Policy Capacity

Effective multidisciplinary abilities in the universities should be enhanced to be able to facilitate responsible AI governance. This deals with the incorporation of ethics, law, social science and public policy into traditional computer science and computer engineering courses. Considering that AI ethics and governance should be developed with the creation of special centers, a setting where researchers working in various fields collaborate to resolve multifaceted socio-technical issues can be established. The universities should also increase collaboration with governments via policy laboratories, advisory agreements and co-funded research projects to allow the academic findings to influence the policy-making process. Another important dimension is talent development: providing students and researchers with competencies of ethical reasoning, regulatory knowledge, and social analysis increases their chances of making a valuable contribution to the eco-responsible AI systems (Jose et al., 2016). Also, the transparency of data and open science practices, as well as the involvement of the population, should become the priority of universities in order to enhance trust and lead to inclusive governance. Through effective multidisciplinary capacity building, universities will be able to come out as the major players in the evidenced-based, technology-centered development of AI.

10.2 For Governments: Designing Adaptive and Evidence-Based AI Regulations

The governments need to embrace dynamic and evidence-based regulatory methods in order to stay in line with the fast changes in AI. This entails investment in technical knowhow, creation of agile policy frameworks and constant communication with institutions of learning. The governments must focus on risk-based regulatory frameworks, algorithmic impact evaluation and auditing frameworks capable of translating ethical principles into enforced mechanisms. The cooperation with universities in the form of advisory bodies and joint research programs will make sure that the regulations are scientifically based and conditioned on the new knowledge (Folorunso et al., 2024). The capacity-building in the field of AI ethics, data governance, and socio-technical risks is required in the sphere of policymakers training. Governments should also facilitate transparency, accountability and citizen involvement; they should come up with open consultation mechanisms and guidelines on responsible AI procurement. Governments can ensure they bring about regulatory environments that support innovation and use adaptive, research-based models of governance, which safeguard societal values.

10.3 For Joint Ecosystems: Creating Sustainable Responsible AI Infrastructures

The long-term responsible AI infrastructures are also developed through the university-government collaborative ecosystems. The advantage of these ecosystems is that common types of governance have national AI councils, ethics laboratories, government-run innovation hubs and protection sandboxes, which incorporate policy use and research. The sustainable cooperation involves predictability of financial sources and the long-term research relations and the internalized tradition to transfer knowledge. It is also significant that the public confidence in the joint ecosystems should be given priority and this by offering transparency, the publication of the appraisal outcome, incorporation of wider societal views. Continuous learning and adaptation should be enabled by practical infrastructures which may be common datasets, open-source governance tools, and institutional training programs (Naili et al., 2024). Strong frameworks that are capable of resisting the new threat and technological encroachment are such ecosystems that might be capable of these by means of a shared investment in the capacity-building, technical evaluation, and interdisciplinary research. Finally, to make sure that the values and ethics of humanity is at the forefront of the AI development, both within the industry and throughout the years, the sustainable responsible AI systems will be implemented. Table 6 Sums up the main strategic measures that every stakeholder group should take in order to make AI responsible.

Table 6. Managerial Implications for Universities, Governments, and Joint Ecosystems

Stakeholder	Key Actions	Expected Outcomes
Universities	Build interdisciplinary ethics capacity	Stronger evidence for policymaking
Governments	Implement adaptive, research-driven regulations	Trustworthy and future-ready AI systems
Joint Ecosystems	Invest in sandboxes, ethics centers, open data	Sustainable responsible AI infrastructure

11. CONCLUSION

Responsible Artificial Intelligence (AI) can be increasingly developed through well-established cooperation between the universities and the governments, as it is observed throughout this chapter. It can be seen in the analysis that the knowledge-policy integration is one of the pillars of ethical and responsible AI ecosystems. Universities bring the latest innovative research, interdisciplinary ethical models, and evidence-based evaluations to light to assist in clarifying the social impact of the new technologies. Governments, in their turn, translate these insights into regulatory frameworks, national AI strategies as well as governmental structures of governing the overall direction of AI deployment. This mutual interaction will ensure the AI systems are dynamic in society in the sense of transparency, equity, human rights, and trust among people.

Another point made in the chapter is that the responsible AI ecosystems that can be co-created with the support of policy labs, advisory councils, regulatory sandboxes, and ethics centers allow learning and responsive governance. Such cooperative systems play a significant role in overcoming obstacles to bureaucratic sluggishness, staffing deficits, geopolitical strains, and the blisteringly dynamic generative and autonomous companies AI. In the future, the road to the ethical, accountable and competitive AI futures involves reinforcing the inclusion by incorporating civil society, marginalized groups, and interdisciplinary knowledge into the governance frameworks. It also requires adaptive regulatory processes that can adjust to changes in technology and protect the values in the society. Through the long-term institutional collaboration, capacity-building and encouraging open and transparent, evidence-based policymaking, universities and governments can come up with AI ecosystems, which do not only embrace technological innovation but also embrace ethical competence and social responsibility. The model presented as co-creation provides a map of the path that countries should take to develop credible, stable, and internationally competitive AI systems that will support the current and future generations.

REFERENCES

Aarthi, S., Ravikumar, R. N., Khudayberganov, S., Ismailov, A., & Khujaniyozova, O. (2025). Using Intelligent Tutoring Systems to enhance student engagement. In *Advances in Computational Intelligence and Robotics* (pp. 155–188). IGI Global. https://doi.org/DOI: 10.4018/979-8-3373-1827-1.ch008

Aarthi, S., Ravikumar, R. N., & Pardaev, J. (2025). Synergizing multimodal generative AI and blockchain for the future of digital media. In *Advances in Computational Intelligence and Robotics* (pp. 1–34). IGI Global Scientific Publishing. https://doi.org/DOI: 10.4018/979-8-3373-1504-1.ch001

Agarwal, A., & Nene, M. J. (2025). A five-layer framework for AI governance: Integrating regulation, standards, and certification. *Transforming Government People Process and Policy*, *19*(3), 535–555. DOI: 10.1108/tg-03-2025-0065

Ahmed, F., Fattani, M. T., Ali, S. R., & Enam, R. N. (2022). Strengthening the bridge between academic and the industry through the academia-Industry Collaboration Plan design model. *Frontiers in Psychology*, *13*, 875940. DOI: 10.3389/fpsyg.2022.875940

Arshad, M. D., & Tripathi, C. K. (2025). Algorithmic accountability and ethical AI frameworks for regulatory governance in financial technologies. *International Journal of Science and Research Archive*, *16*(3), 796–799. DOI: 10.30574/ijsra.2025.16.3.2599

Atkinson-Toal, A., & Guo, C. (2024). Generative artificial intelligence (AI) education policies of UK universities. *Enhancing Teaching and Learning in Higher Education*, *2*, 70–94. DOI: 10.62512/etlhe.20

Ayana, G., Dese, K., Daba Nemomssa, H., Habtamu, B., Mellado, B., Badu, K., Yamba, E., Faye, S. L., Ondua, M., Nsagha, D., Nkweteyim, D., & Kong, J. D. (2024). Decolonizing global AI governance: Assessment of the state of decolonized AI governance in Sub-Saharan Africa. *Royal Society Open Science*, *11*(8), 231994. DOI: 10.1098/rsos.231994

Banozic-Tang, A., & Taeihagh, A. (2022). Perspective on research–policy interface as a partnership: The study of best practices in CREATE. *Science & Public Policy*, *49*(5), 801–805. DOI: 10.1093/scipol/scac028

Bearman, M., Ryan, J., & Ajjawi, R. (2022). Discourses of artificial intelligence in higher education: A critical literature review. *Higher Education*. Advance online publication. DOI: 10.1007/s10734-022-00937-2

Brereton, T. A., Malik, M. M., Lifson, M., Greenwood, J. D., Peterson, K. J., & Overgaard, S. M. (2023). The role of artificial intelligence model documentation in translational science: Scoping review. *Interactive Journal of Medical Research, 12*, e45903. DOI: 10.2196/45903

Chan, C. K. Y. (2023). A comprehensive AI policy education framework for university teaching and learning. *International Journal of Educational Technology in Higher Education, 20*(1). Advance online publication. DOI: 10.1186/s41239-023-00408-3

Cheng, Y., Liu, Y., Fan, W., Yan, Z., & Ye, X. (2019). Triple helix on globalization: A case study of the China International Nanotech Innovation Cluster. *Information Development, 35*(2), 272–289. DOI: 10.1177/0266666917743050

Chintoh, G. A., Segun-Falade, O. D., Odionu, C. S., & Ekeh, A. H. (2024). Legal and ethical challenges in AI governance: A conceptual approach to developing ethical compliance models in the U.s. *International Journal of Social Science Exceptional Research, 3*(1), 103–109. DOI: 10.54660/ijsser.2024.3.1.103-109

Crişan, G.-A., Suciu, A.-A., Domenteanu, A., & Popescu, M. E. (2025). Digitalization and the innovation of Artificial Intelligence: A systematic review. *Proceedings of the International Conference on Business Excellence, 19*(1), 2740–2754. https://doi.org/DOI: 10.2478/picbe-2025-0211

Department of Computer Science and Information Technology Pune Maharashtra 412201 India, M. I. T. A. D. and T. U., Pathan, M. S., Patare, S., & Department of Computer Science and Information Technology Pune Maharashtra 412201 India, M. I. T. A. D. and T. U. (2025). The socioeconomic impact of artificial Intelligence: Profit-driven growth and the struggle for control. *Journal of Collective Sciences and Sustainability, 1*(1), 1–8. https://doi.org/DOI: 10.64189/css.25402

Edler, J., & Fagerberg, J. (2017). Innovation policy: What, why, and how. *Oxford Review of Economic Policy, 33*(1), 2–23. DOI: 10.1093/oxrep/grx001

Etzkowitz, H. (2003). Innovation in innovation: The Triple Helix of university-industry-government relations. *Social Sciences Information. Information Sur les Sciences Sociales, 42*(3), 293–337. DOI: 10.1177/05390184030423002

Farinha, L., Ferreira, J., & Gouveia, B. (2016). Networks of innovation and competitiveness: A triple helix case study. *Journal of the Knowledge Economy, 7*(1), 259–275. DOI: 10.1007/s13132-014-0218-3

Folorunso, A., Olanipekun, K., Adewumi, T., & Samuel, B. (2024). A policy framework on AI usage in developing countries and its impact. *Global Journal of Engineering and Technology Advances, 21*(1), 154–166. DOI: 10.30574/gjeta.2024.21.1.0192

Gianni, R., Lehtinen, S., & Nieminen, M. (2022). Governance of responsible AI: From ethical guidelines to cooperative policies. *Frontiers of Computer Science*, *4*(873437). Advance online publication. DOI: 10.3389/fcomp.2022.873437

Goktas, P., & Grzybowski, A. (2025). Shaping the future of healthcare: Ethical clinical challenges and pathways to trustworthy AI. *Journal of Clinical Medicine*, *14*(5), 1605. DOI: 10.3390/jcm14051605

Goracinova, E., Warrian, P., & Wolfe, D. A. (2017). Challenges of coordination: Automotive innovation in the Ontario supply chain in comparative context. *Canadian Public Policy*, *43*(S1), S90–S102. DOI: 10.3138/cpp.2016-024

Ismail, O., & Ahmad, N. (2025). Ethical and governance frameworks for artificial intelligence: A systematic literature review. [IJIM]. *International Journal of Interactive Mobile Technologies*, *19*(14), 121–136. DOI: 10.3991/ijim.v19i14.56981

Jelovac, D., Ljubojević, Č., & Ljubojević, L. (2022). HPC in business: The impact of corporate digital responsibility on building digital trust and responsible corporate digital governance. *Digital Policy Regulation and Governance*, *24*(6), 485–497. DOI: 10.1108/dprg-11-2020-0164

Jobin, A., Ienca, M., & Vayena, E. (2019). The global landscape of AI ethics guidelines. *Nature Machine Intelligence*, *1*(9), 389–399. DOI: 10.1038/s42256-019-0088-2

Jose, K., Venn, A., Jarman, L., Seal, J., Teale, B., Scott, J., & Sanderson, K. (2016). Partnering Healthy@Work: An Australian university—government partnership facilitating policy-relevant research. *Health Promotion International*, daw033. Advance online publication. DOI: 10.1093/heapro/daw033

Kwon, K.-S., Park, H. W., So, M., & Leydesdorff, L. (2012). Has globalization strengthened South Korea's national research system? National and international dynamics of the Triple Helix of scientific. *Scientometrics*, *90*(1), 163–176. DOI: 10.1007/s11192-011-0512-9

Lase, D., Waruwu, E., Zai, A. Y., & Waruwu, R. M. P. (2025). Should the government regulate Artificial Intelligence and its dangers in society? *Tuhenori: Jurnal Ilmiah Multidisiplin*, *3*(4), 260–282. DOI: 10.62138/tuhenori.v3i4.161

Li, Z. (2024). AI ethics and transparency in operations management: How governance mechanisms can reduce data bias and privacy risks. *Journal of Applied Economics and Policy Studies*, *13*(1), 89–93. DOI: 10.54254/2977-5701/13/2024130

Liu, X., Fang, Y., & Lan, X. (2025). Regulations, technology policies and universities' attitudes to artificial intelligence in China. *Higher Education Quarterly*, *79*(4). Advance online publication. DOI: 10.1111/hequ.70055

Madan, R., & Ashok, M. (2023). AI adoption and diffusion in public administration: A systematic literature review and future research agenda. *Government Information Quarterly*, *40*(1), 101774. DOI: 10.1016/j.giq.2022.101774

Masters in Criminal Justice Lamar University Beaumont Texas USA, C. of A. and S., Talukder, K. A., Shompa, T. F., & Advocate Dhaka Bangladesh, D. J. C. (2024). Artificial intelligence in criminal justice management: A systematic literature review. *Non Human Journal*, *1*(01), 63–82. DOI: 10.70008/jmldeds.v1i01.42

Meszaros, J., Minari, J., & Huys, I. (2022). The future regulation of artificial intelligence systems in healthcare services and medical research in the European Union. *Frontiers in Genetics*, *13*, 927721. DOI: 10.3389/fgene.2022.927721

Mikhaylov, S. J., Esteve, M., & Campion, A. (2018). Artificial intelligence for the public sector: Opportunities and challenges of cross-sector collaboration. *Philosophical Transactions. Series A, Mathematical, Physical, and Engineering Sciences*, *376*(2128), 20170357. DOI: 10.1098/rsta.2017.0357

Naili, Y. T., Simanjuntak, E. L., & Kostruba, A. (2024). The role of AI in health research: A policy review of higher education foundations. *Journal of Advanced Health Informatics Research*, *2*(2), 102–108. DOI: 10.59247/jahir.v2i2.295

(OECD), O. for E. C.-O. and D. (2021). State of implementation of the OECD AI Principles. In *OECD Digital Economy Papers*. https://doi.org/DOI: 10.1787/1cd40c44-en

(OECD), O. for E. C.-O. and D. (2023). The state of implementation of the OECD AI Principles four years on. In *OECD Artificial Intelligence Papers*. https://doi.org/DOI: 10.1787/835641c9-en

Paracha, A. (2023). Analyzing the difficulties and possibilities of combining responsible and ethical technological advancement with innovation. *Indus Journal of Law and Social Sciences*, *II*(II), 15–22. DOI: 10.70540/ijlss.2023(ii-ii).03

Pasupuleti, M. K. (2025a). Governance Frameworks for ethical AI deployment in Public Sector services. [IJAIRI]. *International Journal of Academic and Industrial Research Innovations*, *05*(05), 561–573. DOI: 10.62311/nesx/rphcr17

Pasupuleti, M. K. (2025b). *Securing AI: Combating deepfakes, misinformation, and bias with Trustworthy Systems*. National Education Services., DOI: 10.62311/nesx/97891

Radu, R. (2021). Steering the governance of artificial intelligence: National strategies in perspective. *Policy and Society*, *40*(2), 178–193. DOI: 10.1080/14494035.2021.1929728

Ravikumar, R. N., Aarthi, S., Ruzimova, F., & Mamadiyarov, Z. (2025). Training and development in AI-driven education scaling solutions. In *Advances in Computational Intelligence and Robotics* (pp. 267–298). IGI Global Scientific Publishing. https://doi.org/DOI: 10.4018/979-8-3373-2185-1.ch010

Sharma, A. K., & Sharma, R. (2025). Governance in the age of artificial intelligence: A comparative analysis of policy framework in BRICS nations. *AI Magazine*, *46*(2). Advance online publication. DOI: 10.1002/aaai.70010

Sharma, S. (2024). The role of government in regulating Ai for economic benefit. *ShodhKosh: Journal of Visual and Performing Arts*, *5*(1). Advance online publication. DOI: 10.29121/shodhkosh.v5.i1.2024.1659

Sigfrids, A., Leikas, J., Salo-Pöntinen, H., & Koskimies, E. (2023). Human-centricity in AI governance: A systemic approach. *Frontiers in Artificial Intelligence*, *6*, 976887. DOI: 10.3389/frai.2023.976887

Sophia, L. I. (2025). The social harms of AI-generated fake news: Addressing deepfake and AI political manipulation. *Digital Society & Virtual Governance*, *1*(1), 72–88. DOI: 10.6914/dsvg.010105

Walter, Y. (2024). Managing the race to the moon: Global policy and governance in Artificial Intelligence regulation—A contemporary overview and an analysis of socioeconomic consequences. *Discover Artificial Intelligence*, *4*(1). Advance online publication. DOI: 10.1007/s44163-024-00109-4

Wang, S. (2025). The application and challenges of artificial intelligence in personalized learning for higher education. *Lecture Notes in Education Psychology and Public Media*, *106*(1), 164–170. DOI: 10.54254/2753-7048/2025.cb25753

Zhang, B., Anderljung, M., Kahn, L., Dreksler, N., Horowitz, M. C., & Dafoe, A. (2021). Ethics and governance of artificial intelligence: Evidence from a survey of machine learning researchers. *Journal of Artificial Intelligence Research*, *71*. Advance online publication. DOI: 10.1613/jair.1.12895

KEY TERMS AND DEFINITIONS

Accountability: Ensuring that developers, organizations, or institutions are responsible for AI outcomes and decisions.

AI Ethics Center: A university or institutional unit that studies ethical issues related to AI and supports policy development.

AI Governance: Rules, policies, and frameworks that guide how AI technologies are created, used, and monitored.

Algorithmic Fairness: Ensuring AI systems treat individuals and groups equally without bias or discrimination.

Co-Creation: Joint collaboration between universities, governments, and other stakeholders to design responsible AI solutions.

Ethical Framework: A set of principles guiding the responsible design and deployment of AI systems.

Human-Centered AI: AI systems designed to enhance human well-being, protect rights, and support ethical values.

Interdisciplinary Research: Collaboration across multiple fields such as computer science, law, ethics, and social sciences to address AI challenges.

Knowledge–Policy Integration: The process of using academic research and scientific evidence to inform government decisions and regulations.

National AI Strategy: A government plan outlining goals, policies, and investments for AI development and ethical use.

Policy Lab: A space where researchers and policymakers work together to design, test, and evaluate new regulations.

Regulatory Sandbox: A controlled environment where new AI systems can be tested safely under government supervision.

Responsible AI: Designing and deploying AI systems that are safe, fair, transparent, and aligned with human values.

Transparency: Making AI systems understandable, including how they work and why they make certain decisions.

Triple Helix Model: A collaboration framework involving universities, governments, and industry to drive innovation.

Chapter 6
Consent as Creative Labor:
Ethical AI Governance Through University-Government-Industry Collaboration in the Creative Sector

Azalia Primadita Muchransyah
https://orcid.org/0000-0002-3737-4837
Bina Nusantara University, Indonesia

ABSTRACT

The emergence of generative artificial intelligence (AI) has redefined authorship, creativity, and ownership in the digital economy, raising complex ethical and regulatory challenges. This chapter examines how university-government-industry collaboration, as outlined in the Triple Helix model, can strengthen ethical AI governance by redefining consent and creative labor. Using Indonesia as a focal point, the analysis examines how national and regional frameworks, particularly those of ASEAN, seek to align innovation with cultural and ethical accountability. By exploring case studies in education, policy, and creative industries, this chapter highlights how universities can operationalize ethical AI literacy and contribute to participatory governance. Ultimately, it argues that integrating creative consent into institutional collaboration provides a foundation for sustainable and inclusive AI ecosystems in Southeast Asia.

DOI: 10.4018/979-8-3373-7620-2.ch006

INTRODUCTION

The rapid integration of artificial intelligence (AI) into creative industries has intensified long-standing debates about authorship, ownership, and ethical responsibility. In sectors such as film, media, and digital content production, AI systems increasingly participate in processes of ideation, generation, editing, and distribution. These developments challenge conventional legal and cultural frameworks that assume creativity to be the product of identifiable human agents and stable intellectual property regimes. As governments, universities, and industry actors accelerate AI adoption, questions of consent, data provenance, and creative labor have moved from peripheral ethical concerns to central governance issues (Variety Intelligence Platform, 2024a; Zirpoli, 2025).

This chapter examines these issues through the lens of consent as creative labor, arguing that consent should not be understood merely as a legal formality or contractual checkbox, but as an ongoing, value-producing practice embedded in creative workflows. In AI-mediated environments, creative workers' decisions about whether, how, and under what conditions their data, performances, or stylistic signatures are used become forms of labor that sustain AI systems economically and culturally. Nevertheless, these contributions are often rendered invisible within prevailing AI governance frameworks, which tend to prioritize innovation, scalability, and efficiency over creative agency and accountability (UNCTAD, 2024; OECD, 2023).

The urgency of these questions is particularly evident in Southeast Asia, where governments actively promote AI-driven growth while simultaneously grappling with regulatory uncertainty. Indonesia and ASEAN member states have articulated ambitious national and regional AI strategies that emphasize ethical principles, talent development, and public–private collaboration (Association of Southeast Asian Nations, 2024, 2025; Government of Singapore, 2023). At the same time, legal debates surrounding AI and intellectual property remain unsettled, with policymakers acknowledging gaps in existing frameworks related to authorship, liability, and consent (Mahardika & Priancha, 2021; Siregar, 2024). These tensions create a governance landscape in which AI systems increasingly mobilize creative labor without precise mechanisms for recognition, protection, or redress.

To address this complexity, the chapter adopts the Triple Helix model of university–government–industry relations as its primary analytical framework. Originally developed to explain innovation dynamics in knowledge-based economies, the Triple Helix highlights how universities, governments, and industries co-evolve through overlapping roles and collaborative mechanisms (Etzkowitz & Leydesdorff, 2000). In AI governance, this model offers a way to move beyond siloed accounts of regulation or market behavior by examining how ethical norms, technical infrastructures, and institutional policies are co-produced across sectors.

Building on later extensions that acknowledge cultural and societal dimensions of innovation (Carayannis & Campbell, 2009), the chapter situates creative consent within a broader ecosystem of policy-making, educational practice, and industrial deployment.

Empirically, the chapter draws on policy documents, institutional initiatives, and industry-university collaborations in Indonesia and the ASEAN region. Examples include national AI strategies, higher education guidelines on generative AI, legislative debates on AI regulation, and partnerships between universities and technology firms aimed at AI research and talent development (Direktorat Jenderal Pendidikan Tinggi, 2024; Antara News, 2025; Tokopedia–UI AI Center of Excellence, 2024). These cases are not presented as exhaustive or representative, but as illustrative sites through which the dynamics of consent, governance, and creative labor can be analyzed in context.

The chapter makes three core contributions. First, it reframes consent as a form of creative labor that sustains AI systems and creative economies, rather than as a peripheral ethical safeguard. Second, it demonstrates how Triple Helix interactions concretely shape ethical AI governance through policy design, institutional norms, and industry practices. Third, it highlights the unevenness of AI governance across cultural and infrastructural contexts, cautioning against universal models that obscure local conditions and creative precarity (UNESCO, 2025; Prilliadi, 2024).

By foregrounding consent, authorship, and governance within AI-enabled creative production, the chapter seeks to bridge ethical theory and institutional practice. Rather than proposing a prescriptive regulatory model, it offers an analytically grounded framework for understanding how ethical outcomes emerge—or fail to emerge—through collaborative governance arrangements. In doing so, it positions creative consent not as a constraint on innovation but as a critical site for the meaningful enactment of ethical AI governance.

CONCEPTUAL FRAMEWORK

This chapter develops a conceptual framework that brings together teaching with machines and consent as creative labor in order to analyze ethical AI governance within university–government–industry collaboration. Positioned early in the chapter for theoretical clarity, the framework establishes how creative practice, education, and governance intersect in AI-mediated environments. Rather than treating AI as a neutral technology or governance as a purely regulatory domain, the framework emphasizes relational, interpretive, and institutional processes through which ethical outcomes are produced.

The framework rests on two linked propositions. First, AI systems mediate creative and educational practice through ongoing human–machine relations rather than discrete acts of automation. Second, consent operates within these relations not merely as a legal authorization, but as a form of creative labor that sustains AI systems culturally, pedagogically, and economically. Together, these propositions enable an analysis of how ethical AI governance emerges—or fails to emerge—across institutional settings in Indonesia and the ASEAN region.

Human–AI Relational Pedagogy

Teaching with machines refers to an educational condition in which AI systems participate in learning environments as mediating actors rather than autonomous authorities or neutral tools. In higher education and creative disciplines, AI increasingly supports content generation, feedback, and simulation, shaping how knowledge is produced and evaluated (Direktorat Jenderal Pendidikan Tinggi, 2024). Importantly, these systems do not replace human judgment but reconfigure pedagogical relations by redistributing agency between educators, students, and computational systems.

This relational understanding aligns with regional and international AI governance frameworks that emphasize human oversight, accountability, and contextual use rather than full automation (Association of Southeast Asian Nations, 2024; OECD, 2023). Teaching with machines thus foregrounds interaction, interpretation, and decision-making as core pedagogical activities, highlighting that ethical and educational responsibility remains situated in human institutions rather than delegated to algorithms.

Creative Authorship and Mediation

In creative education and industry-linked training, AI systems actively mediate authorship by participating in ideation, stylistic reproduction, and content generation. These processes complicate conventional distinctions between original and derivative work, particularly in film, media, and digital content production. National and regional debates on AI and intellectual property acknowledge that existing legal frameworks struggle to account for hybrid human-AI authorship (Mahardika & Priancha, 2021; Zirpoli, 2025).

Within teaching contexts, this mediation becomes pedagogically significant. Universities engaged in AI research and industry collaboration increasingly encounter questions about attribution, responsibility, and creative ownership, primarily when students and practitioners work with generative systems trained on large, often opaque datasets (Tokopedia–UI AI Center of Excellence, 2024). Teaching with machines, therefore, requires not only technical literacy but also interpretive frameworks that help learners account for how authorship is distributed across human and algorithmic processes.

Consent as Ongoing, Not Transactional

Crucially, teaching with machines reframes consent as an ongoing process rather than a one-time authorization. Educational guidelines and policy documents increasingly emphasize responsible AI use, yet often operationalize consent through initial disclosure or platform terms of service (Kementerian Komunikasi dan Informatika, 2023; Direktorat Jenderal Pendidikan Tinggi, 2024). In practice, however, AI-mediated learning involves repeated moments of decision-making about data use, content generation, and attribution.

This ongoing nature of consent becomes evident in creative and practice-based settings, where students and educators continuously negotiate how machine-generated outputs are incorporated, evaluated, and circulated. Consent, in this sense, is embedded within pedagogical practice itself, shaping how learning unfolds and how creative responsibility is understood.

Distinguishing Consent from Legal and Technical Categories

This chapter advances the concept of consent as creative labor to distinguish it from narrower understandings of consent as a legal checkbox, a question of intellectual property ownership, or a matter of data rights alone. Legal consent typically focuses on compliance with statutory requirements, while IP frameworks emphasize ownership and economic rights (Paralegals Indonesia, 2024; Ver, 2024). Data rights approaches, meanwhile, prioritize control over personal or creative data within AI training pipelines (UNCTAD, 2024).

While these dimensions are important, they do not fully capture how consent functions in creative AI ecosystems. Consent often operates in contexts where legal clarity is absent, enforcement is weak, or cultural norms shape expectations more strongly than formal regulation (Siregar, 2024). Reducing consent to legal authorization risks obscuring the human work required to interpret, negotiate, and sustain ethical boundaries in practice.

Consent as Interpretive, Ethical, and Cultural Work

Positioning consent as creative labor foregrounds the interpretive and ethical work performed by creators, educators, and institutions. This labor includes evaluating how one's creative output may be transformed by AI systems, anticipating cultural and reputational consequences, and negotiating acceptable uses within institutional or collaborative settings. Such work generates value by enabling AI systems to function, yet it often remains unrecognized within governance frameworks that privilege technical innovation and scalability (OECD, 2021; Prilliadi, 2024).

In educational contexts, consent as creative labor also takes pedagogical form. Educators guide students in reflecting on how AI-generated content is produced, whose contributions are embedded within it, and how responsibility should be attributed. These practices align with UNESCO's emphasis on ethical AI readiness that integrates policy, education, and cultural awareness rather than relying solely on regulation (UNESCO, 2025).

Linkage to AI-Generated Content and Creative Practice

The relevance of consent as creative labor becomes particularly clear in AI-generated content within the creative sector. Industry reports on generative AI, digital replicas, and training data practices reveal growing concern over the use of creative works without meaningful consent or attribution (Variety Intelligence Platform, 2024a, 2024b). In many cases, consent is obtained through broad or opaque agreements that shift ethical risk onto creators while maximizing data extraction.

By contrast, framing consent as creative labor highlights the need for governance mechanisms that recognize and support ongoing ethical negotiation. Within Triple Helix collaborations, universities, governments, and industry actors each shape how such negotiation is enabled or constrained—through policy guidelines, institutional norms, and platform design. Consent, therefore, becomes a central site where ethical AI governance is enacted, contested, and made visible within creative practice.

TRIPLE HELIX GOVERNANCE OF AI IN THE CREATIVE SECTOR

This section positions the Triple Helix not as a descriptive model of innovation ecosystems, but as an analytical framework for examining how ethical AI governance is produced through interaction among universities, government, and industry. In the context of the creative sector, where AI systems rely heavily on cultural data, creative labor, and educational pipelines, governance outcomes cannot be attributed to any single actor. Instead, they emerge through coordinated—and sometimes contested—relations among institutional domains that shape how consent, authorship, and accountability are defined and operationalized.

By reframing the Triple Helix as a governance mechanism rather than an innovation metaphor, this chapter examines how ethical AI practices are enacted through collaboration, negotiation, and institutional alignment. Consent as creative labor becomes the connective tissue linking the three helices, enabling ethical outcomes to materialize across policy, education, and industry practice.

The Triple Helix Model and AI Governance

The Triple Helix model conceptualizes innovation as a dynamic interaction among universities, industry, and government, where each sphere partially assumes the roles of the others (Etzkowitz & Leydesdorff, 2000). Rather than operating in isolation, these actors co-evolve through overlapping functions: universities engage in applied research and industry partnerships, governments facilitate innovation through regulation and funding, and industries contribute to knowledge production and skills development.

This model is particularly well-suited to AI governance in the creative sector for three reasons. First, AI systems are knowledge-intensive and depend on continuous flows of data, expertise, and labor, much of which originates in universities and creative education ecosystems (Direktorat Jenderal Pendidikan Tinggi, 2024; Tokopedia–UI AI Center of Excellence, 2024). Second, the creative sector is highly regulated by intellectual property, cultural policy, and labor norms, placing government actors at the center of ethical and legal mediation (Dewan Perwakilan Rakyat Republik Indonesia, 2025; Kementerian Komunikasi dan Informatika, 2023). Third, industry actors drive AI deployment and commercialization, shaping how consent and creative contribution are operationalized in practice (Variety Intelligence Platform, 2024a).

In Southeast Asia, and particularly in Indonesia, AI governance is explicitly framed as a collaborative endeavor. National AI strategies, ethical guidelines, and readiness assessments emphasize cross-sector coordination rather than unilateral regulation (Association of Southeast Asian Nations, 2024, 2025; UNESCO, 2025). This aligns with the Triple Helix logic, where governance emerges through interaction rather than top-down control. Table 1 maps the current configuration of university-government-industry coordination in Indonesia's AI ecosystem, highlighting how governance, capacity-building, and innovation responsibilities are distributed across institutional actors.

Table 1. Triple Helix coordination in Indonesia's AI ecosystem

Sector	Key Roles	Illustrative Activities	Expected Outcomes
Government	Policy formulation, regulation, and funding	National AI strategy, public–private task forces, talent-factory initiatives	Ethical compliance, infrastructure support
Universities	Research, curriculum development, community engagement	AI curriculum integration, ethics training, collaborative R&D	Human-capital development, knowledge transfer
Industry	Innovation, commercialization, and upskilling	AI labs, corporate–academic partnerships, and responsible IP practices	Scalable innovation, digital-economy growth

Source: Author, based on Badan Pengkajian dan Penerapan Teknologi. (2020), Direktorat Jenderal Pendidikan Tinggi (2024), and Ermaningtiastuti (2024).

However, while the Triple Helix model explains where governance happens, it does not automatically explain how ethical outcomes are produced. This chapter argues that consent—understood as creative labor—provides the missing analytical link between collaboration and governance effectiveness.

Mapping Consent as Creative Labor Across the Triple Helix

The conceptual Table 2 maps how consent as creative labor is produced, mediated, and governed across the three helices. Rather than treating consent as a static legal requirement, the table illustrates how it functions as an ongoing institutional practice shaped by distinct roles, interaction mechanisms, and governance consequences.

Table 2. Triple helix mapping of consent as creative labor in AI governance for the creative sector

Helix Actor	Primary Institutional Role	Consent as Creative Labor: Key Functions	Interaction Mechanisms	Governance Implications
University	Knowledge production, education, and ethical mediation	Interprets consent as an ongoing pedagogical and cultural practice rather than a one-time legal agreement	• Cultivates reflexive authorship, ethical literacy, and critical awareness of AI-mediated creation • Makes visible the hidden labor of consent in creative and educational contexts • Research ethics review and academic discourse • Training creative practitioners and AI developers • Shapes future professionals' understanding of responsibility, authorship, and accountability • Acts as an ethical intermediary between policy and practice	• Curriculum design and assessment practices • Translates abstract ethical principles into situated practices
Government	Regulation, policy-making, public accountability	Formalizes consent through legal and regulatory frameworks	• Defines minimum standards for data use, intellectual property, and AI deployment • Frames consent as a rights-based and public-interest concern • Ethical guidelines and regulatory instruments • Oversight of education and creative industries • Legitimizes consent as a governance requirement • Balances innovation with protection of cultural and creative labor	• National AI strategies and roadmaps • Establishes enforceable boundaries for AI use

continued on following page

Table 2. Continued

Helix Actor	Primary Institutional Role	Consent as Creative Labor: Key Functions	Interaction Mechanisms	Governance Implications
Industry	Technology development, platform operation, and commercialization	Operationalizes consent through platform design, data pipelines, and user agreements	• Often minimizes or obscures consent-related labor in favor of efficiency and scalability • Shapes how consent is experienced in practice by creators and users • AI system design and training practices • Industry–university and industry–government partnerships • Influences norms of authorship, attribution, and creative ownership • Can reinforce or challenge extractive data practices	• Platform governance and terms of service • Determines practical conditions under which consent is granted, negotiated, or bypassed

Source: Author's conceptual synthesis based on Etzkowitz and Leydesdorff (2000), ASEAN (2024, 2025), and UNESCO (2025).

Unlike purely regulatory approaches to artificial intelligence governance, which locate ethical responsibility primarily within state-led compliance frameworks, the Triple Helix model emphasizes governance as a co-produced and dynamic process. Regulatory-only models tend to frame AI ethics in terms of legal thresholds, risk mitigation, and post hoc enforcement, often treating consent, authorship, and data protection as formal requirements to be satisfied after systems are deployed. While such mechanisms are necessary, they are insufficient for addressing the situated, processual, and relational dimensions of creative labor in AI-mediated environments. In contrast, a Triple Helix approach foregrounds ongoing coordination among universities, government bodies, and industry actors, thereby enabling ethical considerations—such as consent, accountability, and creative agency—to be embedded earlier and more reflexively in AI development, education, and deployment processes (Etzkowitz & Leydesdorff, 2000).

As illustrated in Table 2, the governance of consent as creative labor emerges not from any single institutional actor, but from the interactional dynamics among the three helices. Universities contribute pedagogical frameworks and critical reflexivity, shaping how future creators, developers, and policymakers understand authorship, ethical responsibility, and AI mediation. Government actors establish normative boundaries through national strategies, ethical guidelines, and emerging legal instruments, providing legitimacy and public accountability. Industry actors, meanwhile, operationalize AI systems at scale, translating ethical principles into platform design choices, data practices, and contractual arrangements. The table makes explicit that ethical outcomes are not the automatic result of regulation or innovation alone, but of negotiated alignment across these domains.

These interactions are neither linear nor frictionless. Feedback loops play a crucial role in shaping governance outcomes. Educational institutions respond to policy directives and industry practices by adapting curricula, assessment models, and research agendas, while also generating critique that can feed back into policy debates. Governments, in turn, adjust regulatory approaches based on institutional capacity, industry innovation cycles, and international norms. Industry actors selectively interpret both policy and academic discourse, often prioritizing scalability and competitiveness, which can create tensions with pedagogical or ethical commitments. Table 2 highlights these feedback loops by showing how consent practices are continuously redefined as they circulate across educational, regulatory, and commercial contexts.

At the same time, misalignment and negotiation are intrinsic to Triple Helix governance. Universities may emphasize pedagogical care and creative agency in ways that exceed or challenge existing legal frameworks. Governments may promote ethical AI principles without fully addressing the technical and labor conditions under which consent is operationalized. Industry platforms may comply with formal requirements while externalizing interpretive and ethical labor onto users and creators. Rather than viewing these tensions as governance failures, this chapter treats them as sites where consent as creative labor becomes visible—where ethical responsibility is negotiated, contested, and unevenly distributed.

By explicitly mapping these dynamics, Table 2 demonstrates how collaborative governance can produce more context-sensitive and ethically robust outcomes than regulation alone. However, it also reveals the conditions under which ethical aspirations may break down, particularly when power asymmetries limit meaningful negotiation. In this sense, the Triple Helix functions not as a harmonious model of consensus but as an analytical lens for tracing how ethical AI governance in the creative sector is continuously co-produced through interaction, conflict, and care.

Building on the interactional dynamics outlined above, Figure 1 conceptualizes a Collaborative Consent Infrastructure (CCI) as an emergent governance arrangement in which ethical AI practices are co-produced across the Triple Helix. Rather than locating responsibility within a single institutional domain, the CCI model visualizes how consent, authorship, and accountability are sustained through coordinated yet uneven contributions from government, universities, and industry actors.

Within this model, government institutions establish regulatory boundaries, policy direction, and transparency mechanisms that define the normative conditions under which AI systems may operate (Kementerian Komunikasi dan Informatika, 2023). Universities function as sites of pedagogical design and knowledge production, embedding AI literacy, research integrity, and ethical reflexivity into creative education and training (Direktorat Jenderal Pendidikan Tinggi, 2024). Industry actors, including platforms and technology firms, operationalize ethical commitments through data governance practices, attribution standards, and emerging remuneration or licensing schemes for creative labor (Ermaningtiastuti, 2024; Tokopedia–UI AI Center of Excellence, 2024).

By visualizing these interdependencies, Figure 1 complements Table X by shifting from role-based mapping to processual coordination. It illustrates how consent functions not as a one-time legal authorization but as an infrastructural and relational achievement, continuously negotiated across institutional boundaries. The figure also foregrounds points of fragility, where misalignment or power asymmetries can externalize ethical labor onto creators and educators, reinforcing the need for sustained cross-sectoral engagement.

Figure 1. Collaborative Consent Infrastructure (CCI) model integrating policy, education, and industry ethics

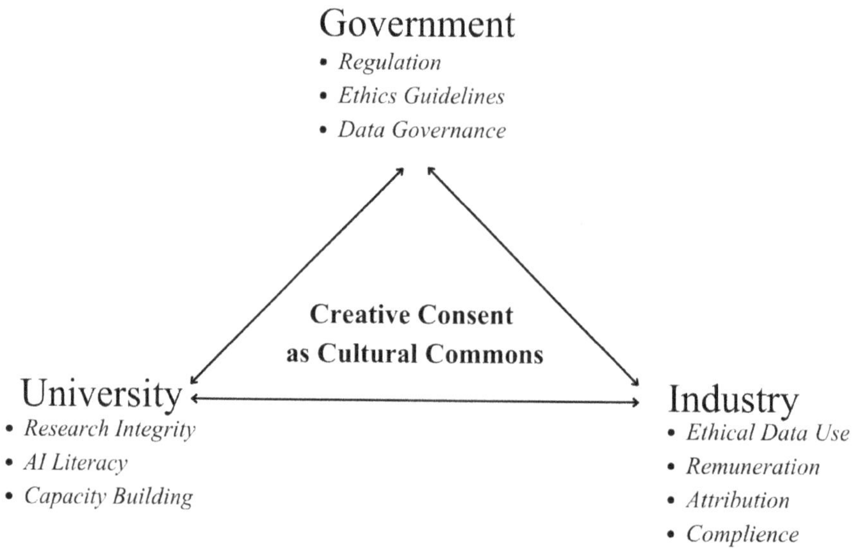

Source: Author, based on Kementerian Komunikasi dan Informatika (2023); Direktorat Jenderal Pendidikan Tinggi (2024); Ermaningtiastuti (2024); Tokopedia-UI AI Center of Excellence (2024); Association of Southeast Asian Nations (2025)

Distinct Roles Across the Helices

Universities play a central role in cultivating consent as interpretive and ethical labor. Through education, research ethics protocols, and industry collaboration, universities shape how creators and students understand authorship, data use, and responsibility in AI-mediated creative work (Direktorat Jenderal Pendidikan Tinggi, 2024; Hendra, 2024). They function as sites where consent is articulated, debated, and pedagogically enacted.

Government actors define the normative and regulatory boundaries within which consent operates. Through AI ethics guidelines, digital economy strategies, and emerging legislation, governments formalize expectations around accountability, transparency, and cultural protection (Kementerian Komunikasi dan Informatika, 2023; Association of Southeast Asian Nations, 2025; Dewan Perwakilan Rakyat Republik Indonesia, 2025). These frameworks legitimize consent as a governance concern rather than a purely contractual issue.

Industry actors operationalize consent within AI systems and creative platforms. Decisions about data sourcing, model training, licensing, and user agreements determine how consent is implemented—or bypassed—in practice (Variety Intelligence Platform, 2024b; UNCTAD, 2024). Industry thus transforms ethical principles into technical and contractual infrastructures.

Interaction Mechanisms

Ethical outcomes emerge not from isolated roles but from interaction mechanisms among the helices. University–industry partnerships shape how creative data is shared and used, influencing whether consent is negotiated meaningfully or subsumed under standard agreements (Ermaningtiastuti, 2024). Government-university collaboration translates policy principles into educational guidelines and research governance (UNESCO, 2025). Government-industry interaction determines enforcement, compliance incentives, and accountability mechanisms.

These interactions create feedback loops. For example, educational practices inform policy revisions, while regulatory pressure reshapes industry standards. Consent as creative labor circulates through these loops, gaining or losing institutional recognition depending on the strength of coordination.

Governance Consequences and Causal Pathways

Table 2 makes explicit the causal pathways through which Triple Helix collaboration produces ethical AI governance. When universities articulate consent as a pedagogical and creative practice, governments codify it within ethical and legal frameworks, and industries embed it into system design, ethical outcomes such as transparency, accountability, and cultural respect become structurally supported.

Conversely, when one helix dominates—such as industry prioritizing scalability without institutional oversight—consent is reduced to a formal or symbolic gesture, weakening governance outcomes (OECD, 2021; Siregar, 2024). Ethical AI governance in the creative sector, therefore, depends not on ethical principles alone but on the alignment and co-evolution of institutional practices across the Triple Helix.

By mapping consent as creative labor across universities, government, and industry, this section demonstrates how ethical AI governance is actively produced rather than passively enforced. The Triple Helix framework thus provides a means to analyze not only collaboration but also the conditions under which collaboration generates ethically robust outcomes.

METHODOLOGICAL AND CASE-STUDY APPROACH

This chapter adopts a qualitative, interpretive approach to examine how ethical AI governance—specifically consent as creative labor—emerges through interactions among universities, government, and industry in the creative sector. Rather than testing causal hypotheses or producing generalizable metrics, the analysis is designed to clarify relationships, governance mechanisms, and institutional practices that shape how consent is articulated, negotiated, and operationalized across different domains. The methodological orientation is therefore exploratory and illustrative, allowing the chapter to surface patterns, tensions, and governance logics that are often obscured in purely technical or regulatory accounts of AI systems.

Analytical Approach

The chapter employs an exploratory and illustrative case-based analysis. The cases are not intended to be exhaustive, representative, or comparative in a statistical sense. Instead, they are selected to illuminate how consent functions as creative, ethical, and institutional labor within distinct yet interconnected domains of the Triple Helix. This approach allows the chapter to trace governance dynamics across education, policy, and industry without collapsing their differences or imposing a singular evaluative framework.

Analytically, the chapter combines policy analysis, institutional document review, and interpretive reading of public-facing initiatives, guidelines, and collaborations related to AI development and deployment. These materials are examined through the conceptual lenses developed earlier—teaching with machines, creative consent, and Triple Helix governance—to identify how consent is framed, operationalized, and contested in practice. The analysis prioritizes how consent is enacted rather than whether it meets predefined legal or technical standards.

The scope of the analysis is intentionally bounded. The chapter does not evaluate the technical performance of AI systems, audit compliance with specific regulations, or measure the effectiveness of individual programs. Instead, it focuses on governance logics and relational processes, acknowledging that ethical outcomes in AI systems are shaped as much by institutional coordination and cultural norms as by formal rules. This bounded approach supports conceptual clarity while avoiding overgeneralization.

Case Contexts

The chapter examines three interconnected case contexts corresponding to the core actors of the Triple Helix: universities, government institutions, and creative industry platforms. Each context highlights a distinct dimension of consent as creative labor while demonstrating how ethical AI governance depends on their interaction.

1. Universities are examined as sites where AI is integrated into creative and media education, research, and skills development. The analysis focuses on how higher education institutions frame consent in relation to authorship, student labor, data use, and creative responsibility. University guidelines, curricular initiatives, and industry-linked AI programs are treated as spaces where ethical norms are taught, negotiated, and institutionalized, positioning consent as an ongoing pedagogical and creative practice rather than a one-time agreement.
2. Government institutions are analyzed through national and regional AI strategies, ethical guidelines, and emerging regulatory frameworks. The chapter examines how consent is articulated within governance documents addressing data governance, intellectual property, and responsible AI deployment. Rather than treating policy as a top-down solution, the analysis highlights how governmental frameworks create enabling—or constraining—conditions for ethical practice across education and industry, shaping how consent is defined, enforced, and interpreted.
3. Industry actors, including creative platforms and AI developers, are examined as sites where consent becomes operational and contested. The analysis focuses on how industry practices related to data sourcing, model training, content generation, and contractual arrangements translate ethical principles into commercial workflows. Industry cases illustrate how consent is negotiated at scale, often revealing tensions between creative labor, economic incentives, and governance expectations.

Together, these case contexts demonstrate that ethical AI governance in the creative sector does not reside within any single institution. Instead, it emerges through the coordination, misalignment, and negotiation among universities, government bodies, and industry actors. By examining these domains in relation rather than isolation, the chapter advances an understanding of consent as creative labor embedded within a broader Triple Helix governance ecology.

CASE ANALYSIS

This section examines how consent as creative labor is operationalized across the three institutional domains of the Triple Helix: universities, government, and industry. Rather than treating consent as a singular legal act or policy requirement, the analysis traces how consent is enacted, negotiated, and redistributed through pedagogical practices, regulatory frameworks, and platform infrastructures. By organizing the analysis along helix-specific interactions, the section makes visible how ethical AI governance emerges unevenly through institutional roles, power relations, and forms of labor that are often obscured in formal governance models.

Universities: Pedagogical Consent and Creative Agency

Within universities, consent emerges most clearly as a pedagogical and creative practice rather than a contractual one. In film, media, and creative technology programs, AI systems are increasingly embedded in teaching, research, and production workflows. Students and educators engage with generative tools for scripting, visualization, editing, and research assistance, making consent inseparable from questions of authorship, creative agency, and learning accountability.

Pedagogical consent in this context operates through instructional design and assessment practices. Educators are required to make decisions about when AI use is permissible, how it should be disclosed, and how machine involvement reshapes evaluative criteria. These decisions demand interpretive labor: instructors must translate abstract ethical guidelines into situated classroom practices that acknowledge AI's mediating role without displacing student responsibility. Consent is therefore enacted through syllabus design, assignment framing, and reflective documentation rather than formal consent forms alone.

Authorship further complicates consent in educational settings. AI-generated content destabilizes individualistic models of originality by producing hybrid outputs that combine students' intentions, institutional expectations, and machine inference. Universities often respond by emphasizing transparency and reflexivity, asking students to account for how AI tools inform their creative choices. In doing so, consent becomes a shared responsibility: students consent to participate in AI-mediated learning environments, while educators consent to evaluate work shaped by algorithmic mediation. This mutual consent is sustained through ongoing dialogue rather than discrete authorization.

Importantly, this labor is unevenly distributed. Educators absorb much of the ethical and pedagogical burden, mediating between institutional policies, technological affordances, and student experimentation. Consent here functions less as compliance and more as a form of creative and pedagogical care—an ongoing effort to align learning outcomes, ethical responsibility, and creative freedom in AI-augmented classrooms.

Within universities, the operationalization of consent as creative labor is most visibly negotiated through assessment practices, where tensions emerge between evaluative accountability, creative experimentation, and AI-assisted production. While institutional guidelines increasingly permit or regulate the use of generative AI in coursework, assessment frameworks often remain anchored in assumptions of individual authorship, traceable process, and demonstrable skill acquisition. This creates friction for both students and educators, as AI tools simultaneously support ideation, drafting, and technical execution while obscuring the boundaries of contribution. In practice, students engage in substantial interpretive labor—deciding when AI assistance enhances creative exploration versus when it risks undermining originality or academic integrity—yet this labor is rarely formally acknowledged. Educators, in turn, must navigate the dual role of encouraging reflective AI use while enforcing assessment standards that were not designed for probabilistic or co-creative systems. As a result, consent operates less as a formal permission to use AI and more as an ongoing pedagogical negotiation, embedded in feedback processes, self-reflection statements, and informal classroom norms. This situated negotiation highlights how creative consent in educational contexts is sustained through relational trust and interpretive judgment rather than solely through institutional policy (Direktorat Jenderal Pendidikan Tinggi, 2024).

Government: Policy Frameworks and Ethical Mandates

At the governmental level, consent is articulated through national AI strategies, ethical guidelines, and emerging regulatory frameworks. These documents position consent as a cornerstone of trustworthy AI, often linking it to data protection, intellectual property, and accountability. However, policy-level consent tends to operate at a high level of abstraction, emphasizing principles rather than implementation.

Government frameworks play a crucial coordinating role by establishing normative expectations for AI use across sectors. Ethical mandates related to transparency, fairness, and accountability create the conditions under which universities and industry actors are expected to operate. However, these mandates rarely specify how consent should be enacted in creative or educational contexts where authorship, data reuse, and collaborative production are central. As a result, consent becomes a boundary object—recognized as essential but interpreted differently across institutional domains.

The analysis reveals that governmental approaches to consent often rely on downstream actors to perform the labor of interpretation and application. Universities translate policy principles into pedagogical norms, while industry actors operationalize them through platform governance and contractual mechanisms. This delegation produces gaps between ethical aspiration and practical enforcement, particularly in fast-moving creative AI contexts where regulatory clarity lags behind technological adoption.

Governmental consent frameworks also interact with intellectual property regimes, where existing legal categories struggle to accommodate AI-generated content. While policy documents emphasize protection and accountability, they often leave unresolved questions about collective authorship, derivative works, and data provenance. Consequently, consent functions less as a settled legal condition and more as an evolving governance problem that requires coordination across the Triple Helix.

At the level of government, ethical AI governance frameworks articulate ambitious commitments to transparency, accountability, and human-centered design, yet significant gaps persist between normative guidelines and enforcement capacity. Indonesian and ASEAN policy documents emphasize principles such as informed consent, data protection, and respect for intellectual property, particularly in relation to generative AI systems (Association of Southeast Asian Nations, 2024; Kementerian Komunikasi dan Informatika, 2023). However, these frameworks often rely on soft-law instruments, voluntary compliance, or sectoral self-regulation, limiting their effectiveness in rapidly evolving creative and platform-based industries. In practice, regulatory agencies face constraints related to technical expertise, cross-border platform governance, and the opacity of proprietary AI models, which complicate oversight of data sourcing and model training practices. As a result, ethical responsibility is frequently displaced downward—onto universities, creators, and users—who must interpret and operationalize abstract policy principles without clear mechanisms for redress or accountability. This misalignment underscores how consent, while rhetorically central to AI governance, remains unevenly institutionalized, revealing a structural tension between ethical aspiration and regulatory capacity within the Triple Helix arrangement.

Industry: Platforms, Data Pipelines, and Hidden Consent Labor

In industry contexts, consent is most heavily mediated by platforms, contracts, and technical infrastructures. Creative AI platforms operationalize consent primarily through terms of service, licensing agreements, and user policies that govern data use, content generation, and model training. While these mechanisms satisfy formal legal requirements, they often obscure the extent and consequences of consent for creative workers.

Platform-based consent is typically asymmetrical. Users are required to accept standardized terms that permit the use of uploaded content, interaction data, or creative outputs for system improvement and model training. This form of consent is transactional rather than deliberative, shifting ethical responsibility onto users while limiting their ability to negotiate terms meaningfully. The labor of understanding, managing, and accepting these conditions is essentially invisible, even though it directly supports the development of AI systems.

Training data practices further complicate consent. Creative works—images, scripts, performances, and texts—are often incorporated into large-scale datasets with minimal transparency regarding sourcing or authorization. Creative labor thus becomes a substrate for AI systems without corresponding recognition or control. Consent, in this context, is displaced from creators to platforms, where it is absorbed into technical pipelines and governance abstractions.

Power asymmetries are central to this dynamic. Industry actors possess the technical, legal, and economic capacity to define how consent is operationalized, while individual creators and institutions operate within constrained choices. The result is a redistribution of creative consent labor: platforms externalize ethical complexity while universities and governments grapple with its consequences in educational and regulatory settings.

TENSIONS, LIMITS, AND UNEVEN POWER RELATIONS

While the Triple Helix framework highlights the potential of collaboration among universities, government, and industry, the preceding analysis demonstrates that ethical AI governance in the creative sector is shaped as much by tension and asymmetry as by alignment. Consent as creative labor does not circulate evenly across the helix. Instead, it is frequently fragmented, deferred, or absorbed by actors with limited power to shape structural conditions. This section synthesizes key tensions that emerge when ethical aspirations encounter institutional constraints, market logics, and global technological infrastructures.

Innovation Versus Protection

A central tension lies between the drive for rapid innovation and the imperative to protect creative labor, cultural expression, and individual rights. Government policies and industry initiatives often frame AI development as a strategic priority tied to competitiveness, economic growth, and technological leadership. Within this framing, consent is acknowledged rhetorically but operationalized minimally, treated as a prerequisite to be cleared rather than a practice to be sustained.

Universities and creative workers are frequently positioned as sites of experimentation, where AI tools can be tested and refined under the banner of innovation. However, the risks associated with data reuse, authorship ambiguity, and cultural misrepresentation are disproportionately borne by students, educators, and creators. Protection mechanisms—such as ethical review processes, pedagogical safeguards, or cultural consultation—tend to lag behind deployment, rendering consent reactive rather than anticipatory. In these conditions, consent becomes a compensatory labor performed after innovation has already advanced.

Scalability Versus Care

Another structural tension emerges between scalability and pedagogical or cultural care. Industry platforms and national AI strategies prioritize solutions that can be scaled across populations, institutions, and markets. Standardization enables efficiency, but it also flattens contextual differences. Consent mechanisms designed for scale—click-through agreements, generalized disclosures, or uniform policy language—struggle to accommodate the relational and situated nature of creative work.

Universities, particularly in creative and media education, attempt to reintroduce care through reflective practices, dialogue, and contextual evaluation. However, these care-oriented approaches are labor-intensive and difficult to scale. Educators and institutional actors must continually interpret, mediate, and explain ethical expectations, absorbing the emotional and intellectual labor that automated systems displace. As a result, care becomes localized and precarious, sustained by individual commitment rather than institutional infrastructure.

Global Platforms and Local Cultures

Consent further fractures along global-local lines. Many AI systems used in creative production and education are developed by transnational platforms whose governance models reflect global market priorities and dominant cultural norms. These systems circulate across diverse linguistic, legal, and cultural contexts, often without meaningful adaptation.

Local creative cultures, pedagogical traditions, and regulatory environments must therefore negotiate consent within infrastructures they did not design. Cultural specificity—such as collective authorship traditions, Indigenous knowledge systems, or locally embedded creative practices—may be poorly represented or inadequately protected. Consent in these contexts requires additional interpretive labor: translating platform logics into culturally meaningful terms and compensating for systemic blind spots. This labor is rarely acknowledged by platform governance structures, reinforcing asymmetries between global technological power and local cultural responsibility.

Where Consent Breaks Down

Across the helix, consent tends to break down at points where responsibility becomes diffuse. When creative content flows from educational settings into industry platforms, or when policy principles are delegated to institutional implementation, accountability becomes fragmented. No single actor is clearly responsible for ensuring that consent remains informed, ongoing, and ethically meaningful.

These breakdowns are especially evident in data pipelines, where creative outputs are repurposed for training or optimization without transparent feedback loops. Consent is often secured once but enacted many times, detached from subsequent uses and consequences. In such cases, consent functions more as a legal artifact than as an ethical practice, undermining its legitimacy as a foundation for creative governance.

Invisible and Uneven Labor

Ultimately, the labor of consent is unevenly distributed. Educators, students, and creative workers perform much of the interpretive, emotional, and ethical work required to make AI systems usable and defensible. They explain limitations, mitigate harms, and reconcile institutional demands with personal and cultural values. Industry actors benefit from this labor while maintaining structural control over platforms and data. Governments, meanwhile, rely on downstream actors to realize ethical commitments articulated at the policy level.

Recognizing these asymmetries is essential to avoiding overly optimistic accounts of Triple Helix collaboration. Consent as creative labor exposes not only the possibilities of ethical AI governance but also its limits. Ethical outcomes do not emerge automatically from collaboration; they depend on how labor, power, and responsibility are distributed across institutional boundaries.

Invisible Labor and Affective Work in AI-Mediated Creativity

A critical tension in the operationalization of consent as creative labor lies in the invisibility of the work required to sustain ethical engagement with AI systems. Beyond formal compliance with policies or platform terms, educators, students, and creative workers perform ongoing affective and interpretive labor to manage uncertainty, responsibility, and risk. This includes the emotional effort of navigating ambiguous authorship boundaries, the cognitive labor of evaluating AI-generated outputs, and the ethical work of deciding when and how machine assistance aligns with creative or pedagogical values. Such labor is rarely recognized within institutional metrics of productivity, assessment, or innovation, yet it is essential to preventing harm, misrepresentation, and erosion of trust. In university settings, educators absorb much of this burden through informal mentoring, additional feedback, and ethical scaffolding that exceeds formal workload models (Direktorat Jenderal Pendidikan Tinggi, 2024). In industry contexts, creators similarly shoulder the affective cost of monitoring platform use of their work, contesting opaque decisions, and adapting to shifting terms of service (Variety Intelligence Platform, 2024b). Framing consent as creative labor makes these hidden forms of work visible, highlighting how ethical AI governance depends not only on institutional structures but also on sustained, often uncompensated human effort.

Global South Asymmetries and Platform Power

These tensions are further intensified by structural asymmetries between Global South creative ecosystems and globally dominant AI platforms. While national and regional frameworks in Southeast Asia emphasize inclusive development, cultural protection, and ethical AI adoption, many generative systems operating in these contexts are developed, governed, and monetized elsewhere (Association of Southeast Asian Nations, 2025; Prilliadi, 2024). This creates a misalignment between local policy objectives and the operational realities of platform governance, in which consent mechanisms are standardized, contractual, and poorly attuned to local legal or cultural norms. Creative workers and educational institutions in Indonesia and the broader ASEAN region often engage with AI systems as downstream users rather than co-designers, limiting their ability to influence how data is sourced, labeled, or valued. As a result, consent becomes unevenly distributed: global platforms externalize ethical risk while local actors absorb the consequences of data extraction, cultural misrepresentation, and limited recourse. Within the Triple Helix framework, this imbalance challenges assumptions of symmetrical collaboration and highlights the need for governance arrangements that account for transnational power differentials. Recognizing these asymmetries reinforces the chapter's argument that ethical AI governance cannot rely solely on universal principles but must be grounded in situated negotiations that address infrastructural, economic, and cultural inequalities.

TRANSFERABILITY AND LIMITATIONS

The analytical framework developed in this chapter is grounded in Indonesia and the broader ASEAN context, where AI governance, creative industries, and higher education intersect within uneven regulatory, infrastructural, and cultural conditions. While the specific cases and policy configurations discussed are context-dependent, several conceptual insights travel beyond this setting. Table 3 situates the AI governance approach within ASEAN (Indonesia, Singapore, and Thailand) policy frameworks and selected regional comparator cases (Japan and South Korea) to illuminate areas of alignment, divergence, and constraint in the cross-context transfer of ethical AI and consent-based governance models.

Table 3. AI Governance in ASEAN and Selected Regional Comparator Frameworks

Sector	Key Policy Document	Primary Focus Areas	Implementation Challenges
Indonesia	Badan Pengkajian dan Penerapan Teknologi (2020); Kementerian Komunikasi dan Informatika (2023)	Ethics, education, and creative-industry innovation	Fragmented coordination, limited IP protection
Singapore	Government of Singapore (2023)	Governance, global partnerships, digital trust	High cost of compliance for SMEs
Thailand	Organisation for Economic Co-operation and Development (2025b)	Transparency, risk assessment, social impact	Enforcement and institutional capacity
Japan	Organisation for Economic Co-operation and Development (2025a)	Accountability, safety, human oversight	Cross-sector implementation
South Korea	Organisation for Economic Co-operation and Development (2025c)	Data interoperability, R&D investment	Market concentration, talent imbalance

Source: Author, based on Association of Southeast Asian Nations (2024, 2025); Badan Pengkajian dan Penerapan Teknologi (2020); Kementerian Komunikasi dan Informatika (2023); Government of Singapore (2023); Organisation for Economic Co-operation and Development (2021, 2025a, 2025b, 2025c).

While the framework of consent as creative labor and its governance through Triple Helix collaboration are developed in Indonesian and ASEAN contexts, their analytical value lies in their capacity to illuminate dynamics rather than prescribe a universally applicable model. The chapter does not claim that institutional arrangements, policy instruments, or industry practices described here can be directly replicated across regions. Instead, it offers a relational lens for examining how ethical AI governance emerges through negotiated interactions among universities, governments, and industry actors under specific cultural, legal, and infrastructural conditions.

One key limitation to transferability lies in legal incompatibilities across jurisdictions. Intellectual property regimes, data protection laws, and definitions of consent vary significantly between regions, shaping how creative labor and data rights are recognized and enforced (Lucchi, 2025; Zirpoli, 2025). Models developed within ASEAN's consensus-oriented regulatory environment may encounter friction in jurisdictions characterized by adversarial legal systems or market-driven governance. Similarly, language and data inequities constrain the applicability of consent mechanisms embedded in AI systems primarily trained on English-language and Global North datasets. These asymmetries not only affect representational outcomes but also determine whose cultural labor is rendered legible, compensable, or governable within AI pipelines (United Nations Conference on Trade and Development, 2024).

Institutional capacity also shapes what can travel. The effectiveness of collaborative consent governance depends on the presence of functioning regulatory bodies, research infrastructures, and educational institutions capable of sustaining dialogue across helices. In contexts where such capacities are uneven or fragmented, the burden of ethical mediation may fall disproportionately on individual educators or creators rather than institutional actors. Acknowledging these limits reinforces the chapter's central claim: ethical AI governance is not a portable technical solution but a situated practice, contingent on local histories, power relations, and institutional arrangements.

What Travels Beyond Indonesia and ASEAN

The framing of consent as creative labor offers a transferable analytical lens for examining AI-mediated creative practice in other regions. Across diverse contexts, AI systems increasingly rely on human interpretation, negotiation, and ethical judgment that exceed formal legal consent. The emphasis on consent as an ongoing, relational process—rather than a one-time contractual act—resonates with global debates on authorship, data ethics, and cultural representation in creative AI.

Similarly, the use of the Triple Helix model as an analytical device, rather than a prescriptive governance solution, can be applied to other national or regional contexts. Mapping interactions among universities, government, and industry helps surface where ethical responsibility is concentrated, deferred, or obscured, particularly in sectors where creative labor intersects with platform economies.

Cultural, Legal, and Infrastructural Constraints

At the same time, the applicability of the model is shaped by local conditions. Legal frameworks governing intellectual property, data protection, and AI accountability vary significantly across jurisdictions. In contexts with stronger enforcement mechanisms or more mature regulatory regimes, consent may be formalized differently, potentially reducing—but not eliminating—the burden of informal ethical labor borne by educators and creators.

Cultural norms surrounding authorship, collaboration, and creative ownership also affect how consent is understood and practiced. Collective or community-based creative traditions, for instance, challenge individualistic consent models embedded in many AI platforms. Infrastructural disparities—including access to computational resources, institutional support, and digital literacy—further shape who can meaningfully negotiate AI-mediated creative work.

When the Model May Not Apply

The framework is least applicable in settings where creative production is entirely subsumed under proprietary AI systems with minimal human agency, or where education and industry operate in isolation rather than interaction. In highly centralized or opaque AI ecosystems, opportunities for pedagogical or ethical intervention may be severely constrained.

Moreover, the chapter does not claim that collaborative governance alone can resolve structural inequalities embedded in global AI markets. Where power asymmetries are extreme, consent as creative labor risks becoming symbolic rather than transformative.

By acknowledging these limits, the chapter positions its contribution not as a universal blueprint, but as a situated analytical approach. Its value lies in making visible the often-unrecognized labor that sustains ethical AI practices in creative and educational contexts—and in clarifying the conditions under which such labor can, and cannot, meaningfully shape governance outcomes.

POLICY AND PEDAGOGICAL IMPLICATIONS

The analysis presented in this chapter suggests that effective AI governance in creative and educational contexts depends less on expanding compliance mechanisms than on recognizing and supporting consent as an ongoing practice. Treating consent as creative labor reframes governance challenges across universities, public institutions, and creative industries, shifting attention from formal authorization toward everyday interpretive and ethical work.

Implications for University Governance

For universities, the findings underscore the need to move beyond policy statements that focus narrowly on acceptable AI use or academic integrity enforcement. Institutional governance should instead support pedagogical structures that make consent visible within creative and scholarly practice. This includes assessment frameworks that value reflexivity, documentation of human–AI interaction, and ethical reasoning alongside technical or creative outcomes.

At the governance level, universities play a mediating role between regulatory expectations and industry practices. Recognizing consent as pedagogical work implies allocating institutional support—such as professional development, curriculum flexibility, and shared guidelines—to reduce the burden on individual educators to negotiate AI ethics in isolation.

Implications for Public Policy

For policymakers, the chapter highlights the limits of AI governance frameworks that treat consent primarily as a legal or procedural requirement. While regulatory instruments related to data protection, intellectual property, and AI accountability remain essential, they do not capture the situated negotiations that occur in creative and educational settings.

Public policy can more effectively support ethical AI by enabling participatory and adaptive governance mechanisms that acknowledge the role of universities and creative practitioners as sites of interpretation and experimentation. Rather than prescribing uniform standards of AI use, policy frameworks should allow space for contextualized practices of consent that respond to cultural norms, creative traditions, and institutional capacities.

Implications for Creative Industry Standards

Within creative industries and platform-based ecosystems, the analysis points to the need for standards that recognize the hidden labor involved in consent and attribution. Industry practices that rely on broad terms of service or opaque data pipelines risk externalizing ethical responsibility onto creators and educators, while maintaining asymmetrical control over data and outputs.

Reframing consent as a practice suggests the value of more precise disclosure mechanisms, negotiated uses of creative data, and collaborative standard-setting involving educational institutions and creative communities. Such approaches do not eliminate power imbalances but can make ethical responsibilities more explicit and contestable.

Across these domains, the central implication is that ethical AI governance cannot be achieved through compliance alone. By foregrounding consent as an active, interpretive, and relational practice, this chapter argues for governance and pedagogical approaches that sustain human agency, creative accountability, and ethical responsibility in AI-mediated environments.

CONCLUSION

This chapter has argued that ethical AI governance in the creative sector cannot be adequately understood through legal compliance, technical safeguards, or institutional policy alone. By conceptualizing consent as creative labor, this approach advances a theoretical shift in how AI ethics is framed: from a static condition secured in advance to an ongoing, relational practice embedded in creative, educational, and institutional work. This reframing makes visible the interpretive, cultural, and pedagogical labor that sustains ethical engagement with AI but is often rendered invisible by dominant governance models.

Repositioning consent in this way contributes to ongoing debates on AI governance and creative labor by challenging the assumption that ethical responsibility can be fully delegated to regulatory instruments or platform design. Instead, the chapter demonstrates that consent is continually produced through human judgment—by educators guiding learning processes, by policymakers translating abstract principles into institutional mandates, and by creative practitioners navigating authorship, attribution, and data use in AI-mediated environments.

Within this framework, the Triple Helix model is rearticulated not merely as an innovation ecosystem but as a mode of ethical co-production. Universities, government bodies, and industry actors do not simply occupy functional roles; they actively shape how ethical norms are interpreted, operationalized, and contested. Ethical outcomes emerge not from any single helix, but from their interaction—where pedagogical practice, regulatory frameworks, and platform logics intersect, align, or come into conflict. Recognizing this dynamic clarifies why ethical AI governance is uneven, context-dependent, and shaped by power relations rather than universally standardized.

By foregrounding Indonesia and the ASEAN region, the chapter also underscores the importance of contextual governance. Ethical AI practices are shaped by cultural norms, institutional capacities, and regional policy environments, limiting the effectiveness of governance models that assume global uniformity. At the same time, the conceptual framing offered here—consent as creative labor within a Triple Helix of ethical co-production—provides an analytical lens that can be adapted to other contexts, rather than a prescriptive model to be replicated.

Future research can build on this framework by examining how consent is operationalized—or resisted—within specific AI systems, contractual arrangements, and pedagogical designs. Comparative studies across regions, creative sectors, or governance regimes would further illuminate how ethical labor is distributed and whose work remains unrecognized. Rather than seeking definitive solutions, such inquiries can deepen understanding of ethical AI governance as an evolving practice—one sustained not by automation, but by continuous human negotiation, care, and creative responsibility.

Beyond its empirical and policy-oriented insights, this chapter contributes to Triple Helix scholarship by repositioning ethical AI governance as a form of co-produced cultural labor rather than a downstream regulatory outcome. While traditional Triple Helix models emphasize innovation, commercialization, and knowledge transfer, this chapter extends the framework to account for ethical coordination—showing how consent, authorship, and accountability are actively negotiated through the interactions of universities, government agencies, and industry platforms. In doing so, it demonstrates that ethical governance is not external to innovation systems but constitutive of them, especially in creative sectors where value, meaning, and legitimacy are continuously produced.

Crucially, the chapter argues that consent in AI-mediated creative practice cannot be reduced to contractual authorization or formal compliance. Consent functions as an ongoing practice involving interpretation, negotiation, and care across pedagogical, institutional, and infrastructural contexts. Treating consent as a checkbox mechanism obscures the distributed labor required to sustain ethical AI systems and displaces responsibility onto individuals least able to bear it. By framing consent as creative labor, the chapter foregrounds the invisible work of educators, policymakers, and creators who mediate between technical systems and cultural values.

This reframing invites a shift in how AI governance is evaluated: not by the presence of policies alone, but by the quality of institutional practices that enable ethical judgment, reflexivity, and shared responsibility to emerge over time.

OPEN DATA STATEMENT

No new empirical data were generated for this study. All referenced materials are publicly available through institutional, governmental, and organizational sources as cited in the References section.

OPEN CONTRIBUTORSHIP STATEMENT

This chapter was conceptualized, researched, and written solely by the author. All analytical interpretations and conclusions are the author's own.

ACKNOWLEDGMENT

This research received no specific grant from any funding agency in the public, commercial, or not-for-profit sectors. The author acknowledges using ChatGPT (OpenAI, GPT-5) and Grammarly as digital writing and editing aids to refine language and maintain stylistic consistency. No generative tools were used to produce or analyze data; all interpretations and syntheses reflect the author's original scholarly work.

REFERENCES

Antara News. (2025). *Indonesia scales AI talent factory to boost government programs.* https://en.antaranews.com/news/381061/indonesia-scales-ai-talent-factory-to-boost-government-programs

Association of Southeast Asian Nations. (2024). *ASEAN guide on AI governance and ethics.* https://asean.org/wp-content/uploads/2024/02/ASEAN-Guide-on-AI-Governance-and-Ethics_beautified_201223_v2.pdf

Association of Southeast Asian Nations. (2025). *Expanded ASEAN guide on AI governance and ethics – Generative AI.* https://asean.org/wp-content/uploads/2025/01/Expanded-ASEAN-Guide-on-AI-Governance-and-Ethics-Generative-AI.pdf

Badan Pengkajian dan Penerapan Teknologi. (2020). *Strategi nasional untuk kecerdasan artifisial: Indonesia 2020-2045.* https://oecd-ai.case-api.buddyweb.fr/storage//policy-initiatives/Jul2025/fu_4fi5jmh3ywepzcb.pdf

Carayannis, E. G., & Campbell, D. F. J. (2009). "Mode 3" and "Quadruple Helix": Toward a 21st-century fractal innovation ecosystem. *International Journal of Technology Management*, *46*(3–4), 201–234. DOI: 10.1504/IJTM.2009.023374

Dewan Perwakilan Rakyat Republik Indonesia. (2025). *Info Singkat: Rancangan Undang-Undang tentang Kecerdasan Buatan (AI Bill).* https://berkas.dpr.go.id/pusaka/files/info_singkat/Info%20Singkat-XVII-9-I-P3DI-Mei-2025-2417-EN.pdf

Direktorat, J. P. T. (2024). *Buku panduan penggunaan generative artificial intelligence pada pembelajaran di perguruan tinggi.* Ministry of Education, Culture, Research, and Technology., https://lldikti3.kemdikbud.go.id/wp-content/uploads/2024/11/Buku-Panduan-_-Penggunaan-Generative-AI-pada-Pembelajaran-di-Perguruan-Tinggi-cetak.pdf

Ermaningtiastuti, C. (2024). *Anabatic Technologies and BINUS University demonstrate a commitment to filling the gap between industry and education.* https://www.anabatic.com/blogs/anabatic-technologies-and-binus-university-show-commitment-to-fill-the-gap-between-industry-and-education-sectors/

Etzkowitz, H., & Leydesdorff, L. (2000). The dynamics of innovation: From National Systems and "Mode 2" to a Triple Helix of university–industry–government relations. *Research Policy, 29*(2), 109–123. DOI: 10.1016/S0048-7333(99)00055-4

Government of Singapore. (2023). *National AI strategy 2023.* https://www.smartnation.gov.sg/initiatives/national-ai-strategy/

Hendra, D. (2024). *BINUS University bangun riset AI pertama di Indonesia.* https://swa.co.id/read/173219/binus-university-bangun-riset-ai-pertama-di-indonesia

Indonesia, P. (2024). *AI vs. kekayaan intelektual (KI): Apakah hukum Indonesia siap menghadapi era AI generatif?* https://cms.paralegals.id/uploads/Salinan_dari_AI_vs_Kekayaan_Intelektual_KI_Apakah_Hukum_Indonesia_Siap_Menghadapi_Era_AI_Generatif_100be2823d.pdf

Kementerian Komunikasi dan Informatika. (2023). *Surat edaran Menteri Komunikasi dan Informatika nomor 9 tahun 2023 tentang etika kecerdasan artifisial.* https://jdih.komdigi.go.id/produk_hukum/view/id/883/t/surat+edaran+menteri+komunikasi+dan+informatika+nomor+9+tahun+2023

Lucchi, N. (2025). *Artificial intelligence act: A comparative analysis of the EU and international AI governance frameworks.* https://www.europarl.europa.eu/RegData/etudes/STUD/2025/774095/IUST_STU(2025)774095_EN.pdf

Mahardika, Z. P., & Priancha, A. (2021). *Pengaturan hukum artificial intelligence Indonesia saat ini.* https://www.hukumonline.com/berita/a/pengaturan-hukum-artifical-intelligence-indonesia-saat-ini-lt608b740fb22b7/

Monash University Indonesia. (2024). *Ministry of Communication and Digital Affairs and Monash University Indonesia initiate AI collaboration for research and public protection.* https://www.monash.edu/indonesia/news/ministry-of-communication-and-digital-affairs-and-monash-university-indonesia-initiate-ai-collaboration-for-research-and-public-protection

Organisation for Economic Co-operation and Development. (2021). *State of Implementation of The OECD AI Principles: Insights from National AI Policies.* https://www.oecd.org/content/dam/oecd/en/publications/reports/2021/06/state-of-implementation-of-the-oecd-ai-principles_38a4a286/1cd40c44-en.pdf

Organisation for Economic Co-operation and Development. (2023). *The state of implementation of the OECD AI Principles four years on.* OECD Artificial Intelligence Papers. https://oecd-ai.case-api.buddyweb.fr/storage/policy-initiatives/Jul2025/fu_s2cdv9y6354q9jt.pdf

Organisation for Economic Co-operation and Development. (2025a). *Japan's national AI strategy and principles for trustworthy AI.* https://oecd-ai.case-api.buddyweb.fr/storage//policy-initiatives/Jul2025/fu_an8s59prsbi4ivz.pdf

Organisation for Economic Co-operation and Development. (2025b). *Thailand's national AI strategy for inclusive digital transformation.* https://oecd-ai.case-api.buddyweb.fr/storage//policy-initiatives/Jul2025/fu_wtw4h5f5zfv7hqk.pdf

Organisation for Economic Co-operation and Development. (2025c). *Republic of Korea's AI innovation strategy for global competitiveness.* https://oecd-ai.case-api.buddyweb.fr/storage//policy-initiatives/Jul2025/fu_2ej83gnpgww3tcm.pdf

Prilliadi, H. (2024). *Harnessing AI for ASEAN's future.* https://www.eria.org/uploads/Harnessing-AI-for-ASEAN%E2%80%99s-Future.pdf

Siregar, P. D. (2024). *Problem payung hukum dalam penggunaan artificial intelligence.* https://www.hukumonline.com/berita/a/problem-payung-hukum-dalam-penggunaan-artificial-intelligence-lt66d4b01adeaf2/

Tokopedia-UI AI Center of Excellence. (2024). *AI and data innovation booklet.* Tokopedia-Universitas Indonesia. https://tokopedia-ai.cs.ui.ac.id/booklet/

UNESCO. (2025). *Artificial intelligence readiness in Indonesia: Progress, policy, and potential.* https://unesdoc.unesco.org/ark:/48223/pf0000392317

United Nations Conference on Trade and Development. (2024). *Digital economy report 2024: The role of AI in trade and development.* https://unctad.org/system/files/official-document/ditctsce2024d2_en.pdf

Variety Intelligence Platform. (2024a). *Generative AI, celebrity deepfakes, and digital replicas: Special report.* https://variety.com/vip-special-reports/generative-ai-celebrity-deepfakes-digital-replicas-special-report-1236218083/

Variety Intelligence Platform. (2024b). *Creative consent and data ethics in AI model training: AI training – consent & content report.* https://read-vip.variety.com/html5/reader/production/default.aspx?pubname=&edid=f72ee533-d63a-40af-969f-8b05af56de44

Ver. (2024). *Kecerdasan buatan (AI) sebagai objek hukum vs subjek hukum dalam pelindungan kekayaan intelektual.* https://www.dgip.go.id/index.php/artikel/detail-artikel-berita/kecerdasan-buatan-ai-sebagai-objek-hukum-vs-subjek-hukum-dalam-pelindungan-kekayaan-intelektual?kategori=liputan-humas

Zirpoli, C. T. (2025). *Artificial intelligence and intellectual property rights: Emerging policy challenges* (CRS Legal Sidebar No. LSB10922). https://www.congress.gov/crs-product/LSB10922

ADDITIONAL READING

Barassi, V. (2020). *Child data citizen: How tech companies are profiling us from before birth.* MIT Press., DOI: 10.7551/mitpress/12415.001.0001

Checketts, L., Boyles, R. J., Chan, B. S. B., Gan, Z.-R., Hongladarom, S., Kimura, T., Robertson, R. S., Son, W.-C., Wong, P.-H., Yeung, L. K. C., & Gonzalez-Ferrer Garcia, A. (2025). Ethical and social concerns of artificial intelligence in Asia. *NanoEthics, 19*(2), 12. DOI: 10.1007/s11569-025-00472-1

Clarke, M., & Joffe, M. (2025). Beyond replacement or augmentation: How creative workers reconfigure division of labour with generative AI. *Proceedings of the ACM on Human-Computer Interaction.* https://arxiv.org/abs/2505.18938

Kyi, L., Mahuli, A., Silberman, M. S., Binns, R., Zhao, J., & Biega, A. J. (2025). *Governance of generative AI in creative work: Consent, credit, compensation, and beyond.* arXiv. https://doi.org//arXiv.2501.11457DOI: 10.48550

Pasquinelli, M., & Joler, V. (2020). The Nooscope manifested: AI as instrument of knowledge extractivism. *AI & Society, 36*, 1267–1280. DOI: 10.1007/s00146-020-01197-6 PMID: 33250587

Putra, B. A. (2024). Governing AI in Southeast Asia: ASEAN's way forward. *Frontiers in Artificial Intelligence.* Advance online publication. DOI: 10.3389/frai.2024.1411838 PMID: 39282475

Tay, P. C., Sadik, S., & Chan, K. (2025, July 24). *Shaping the future of work in South-East Asia: Augmenting intelligence.* Tony Blair Institute for Global Change. https://institute.global/insights/tech-and-digitalisation/augmenting-intelligence-shaping-the-future-of-work-in-south-east-asia

White, A. R., Darodjat, T. A., & Maryano, M. (2025). Artificial intelligence and the future of work in Southeast Asia: A desktop study of opportunities, challenges, and workforce readiness. *PENANOMICS: International Journal of Economics*, *4*(2). Advance online publication. DOI: 10.56107/penanomics.v4i2.224

Xu, J., Lee, T., & Goggin, G. (2024). AI governance in Asia: Policies, praxis and approaches. *Communication Research and Practice*, *10*(2), 145–162. DOI: 10.1080/22041451.2024.2391204

Zylinska, J. (2020). *AI art: Machine visions and warped dreams*. Open Humanities Press.

KEY TERMS AND DEFINITIONS

Artificial Intelligence (AI): A field of computer science focused on creating systems that can perform tasks requiring human-like intelligence, such as reasoning, learning, and creativity.

ASEAN Policy: Regional guidelines and cooperative frameworks established by the Association of Southeast Asian Nations to promote responsible, ethical, and inclusive AI governance among member states.

Authorship: The recognition of human creative contribution in the production of works, including those generated or assisted by AI systems.

Consent: The act of granting permission for the use of creative data in AI training and production, reframed in this chapter as a continuous and collective form of creative labor.

Creative Industries: Economic sectors based on individual creativity and cultural expression, including film, design, animation, and digital media.

Cultural Inclusion: The principle of ensuring that technological and creative innovations respect and represent diverse cultural identities and perspectives.

Data Provenance: The documentation and traceability of data sources used in AI development, ensuring accountability, transparency, and respect for intellectual property.

Digital Governance: The creation and enforcement of policies and regulations that guide the ethical use of digital technologies, including AI, within national and regional frameworks.

Ethical Innovation: The process of developing technology that aligns with social values, human rights, and public accountability, rather than focusing solely on efficiency or profit.

Triple Helix Collaboration: A model of innovation emphasizing interaction among universities, industry, and government to drive technological progress while maintaining ethical and cultural balance.

Chapter 7
Strategic AI Governance in Saudi Higher Education:
A Triple Helix Model for University–Government–Industry Integration

Mossab Saud Alholiby
https://orcid.org/0000-0002-8899-8770
King Faisal University, Saudi Arabia

ABSTRACT

This chapter examines AI governance in Saudi higher education through a Triple Helix model of university–government–industry integration, grounded in Saudi Vision 2030 and the National Strategy for Data and Artificial Intelligence (NSDAI). It analyzes how national strategy, regulatory requirements for data protection and cybersecurity, and institutional governance practices shape AI adoption across universities. Building on helix-based innovation theory and qualitative policy analysis, the chapter proposes a Strategic Governance Framework for Artificial Intelligence (SGF-AI) that integrates strategic alignment, ethical and legal oversight, operational coordination, and multidimensional impact evaluation. The framework is illustrated through a case study from the Applied College at King Faisal University and extended with Quadruple and Quintuple Helix perspectives to incorporate societal engagement and sustainability, concluding with a phased roadmap for 2025–2035.

DOI: 10.4018/979-8-3373-7620-2.ch007

1. INTRODUCTION

Artificial intelligence (AI) has become a transformative force in higher education, reshaping teaching and learning practices, administrative governance, research management, and institutional decision-making. Universities increasingly deploy AI-enabled systems to support student advising, automate workflows, enhance learning analytics, optimize resource allocation, and inform strategic planning. These developments promise substantial gains in efficiency, personalization, and innovation. At the same time, they introduce complex governance challenges related to transparency, accountability, data protection, cybersecurity, and societal trust.

As AI systems become embedded within core academic and administrative functions, governance arrangements originally designed for incremental digital transformation are proving insufficient. Unlike conventional information systems, AI technologies rely on opaque algorithmic processes, large-scale data extraction, and automated decision-making, often with limited explainability. Consequently, higher-education institutions face heightened risks related to algorithmic bias, erosion of academic autonomy, and loss of public confidence if AI systems are deployed without robust and institutionally embedded governance frameworks (Floridi, 2021; UNESCO, 2021).

Recent scholarship increasingly conceptualizes AI adoption in higher education not merely as a technical or pedagogical issue, but as a governance challenge that requires coordinated institutional, regulatory, and societal responses. AI systems are developed, regulated, and implemented across interconnected domains involving public policy, market dynamics, and normative values. Fragmented or institutionally isolated governance approaches risk amplifying ethical and operational vulnerabilities, while undermining legitimacy and accountability (OECD, 2021; Carayannis & Campbell, 2009).

Within this context, Saudi Arabia presents a particularly instructive case. Under Vision 2030, artificial intelligence and data-driven innovation are positioned as strategic enablers of economic diversification, human-capital development, and global competitiveness. The National Strategy for Data and Artificial Intelligence (NSDAI) further institutionalizes this ambition by identifying education as a foundational pillar for AI talent development, applied research, and ecosystem building. Saudi universities are therefore expected not only to adopt AI technologies, but also to govern them responsibly in alignment with national legislation, cybersecurity standards, and ethical principles.

This chapter argues that the Triple Helix model—conceptualizing innovation and governance as the outcome of structured interaction among universities, government, and industry—offers a robust architecture for addressing these challenges. When extended through Quadruple Helix and Quintuple Helix perspectives, the model provides a comprehensive lens for institutionalizing AI governance in higher education in a manner that is strategically coherent, socially legitimate, and environmentally responsible. By integrating theory, policy, and institutional practice, the chapter advances a governance framework capable of supporting responsible and sustainable AI adoption in policy-driven higher-education systems.

2. BACKGROUND AND PROBLEM STATEMENT

The accelerated adoption of artificial intelligence in higher education has generated substantial scholarly attention concerning its pedagogical, organizational, and ethical implications. Universities worldwide employ AI-driven analytics to monitor student progression, automated systems to support assessment, and machine-learning tools to enhance research productivity and institutional planning. While these applications offer opportunities for efficiency, personalization, and data-informed decision-making, they simultaneously introduce governance risks associated with algorithmic bias, limited transparency, and the management of sensitive personal data (Borenstein et al., 2022; OECD, 2021).

These risks are particularly pronounced in public higher-education systems, where institutions operate under heightened expectations of accountability, equity, and social responsibility. Governance failures in AI deployment may compromise academic integrity, infringe privacy rights, and erode public trust in educational institutions. Contemporary research therefore emphasizes the necessity of embedding ethical oversight, legal compliance, and continuous evaluation within institutional AI strategies, rather than treating governance considerations as external constraints or post hoc safeguards (Floridi, 2021; UNESCO, 2023).

In Saudi Arabia, the governance challenge is intensified by the pace and scale of national digital transformation. Vision 2030 and the National Strategy for Data and Artificial Intelligence (NSDAI) articulate a clear strategic vision for AI-driven development across economic and social sectors. Higher education is positioned as a central pillar within this vision, expected to supply skilled human capital, advance applied research, and support innovation ecosystems. However, the translation of these national ambitions into coherent and institutionally embedded AI governance practices remains uneven across the higher-education sector.

AI initiatives within Saudi universities are frequently implemented as localized projects, pilot programs, or technology-driven solutions responding to immediate operational needs. While such initiatives may generate short-term efficiency gains, their fragmented nature limits universities' ability to manage ethical risks systematically, ensure consistent regulatory compliance, and coordinate effectively with governmental and industrial partners. The absence of overarching governance frameworks also exacerbates disparities in institutional readiness, as universities differ in digital infrastructure, governance capacity, and human expertise.

Moreover, the complexity of the regulatory environment—encompassing data protection, cybersecurity, and public-sector accountability—places additional demands on institutional governance structures. Without centralized coordination mechanisms, universities may struggle to operationalize legal requirements, monitor compliance across units, and respond effectively to emerging risks associated with AI systems.

2.1 Problem Statement

Despite the existence of comprehensive national strategies and regulatory frameworks, there is currently no unified, institutionally embedded AI governance framework that effectively aligns higher-education practices in Saudi Arabia with national policy objectives, legal requirements, and cross-sector collaboration mechanisms. This governance gap increases the risk of inconsistent implementation, weak ethical oversight, and fragmented coordination, thereby constraining the sustainable and responsible integration of artificial intelligence within Saudi higher education.

3. THEORETICAL FOUNDATIONS: HELIX-BASED MODELS AND AI GOVERNANCE

3.1 The Triple Helix Model: From Innovation to Governance

The Triple Helix model, originally articulated by Etzkowitz and Leydesdorff (1995), conceptualizes innovation as the outcome of structured interaction among universities, government, and industry. While the model was initially developed to explain knowledge-based economic development, subsequent scholarship has extended its analytical scope to encompass governance challenges associated with complex and transformative technologies. In contemporary analyses, the Triple Helix is increasingly understood not merely as an innovation framework, but as a governance architecture capable of coordinating actors, managing uncertainty, and aligning technological development with public objectives (Etzkowitz & Leydesdorff, 2021).

Within higher education, the Triple Helix reframes universities as active governance actors rather than passive recipients of regulation or technology. Universities contribute scientific knowledge, human-capital development, and institutional implementation capacity; governments provide strategic vision, regulatory authority, and coordination mechanisms; and industry actors supply technological infrastructure, applied expertise, and pathways for innovation deployment. This interdependence is particularly critical in the context of artificial intelligence, where fragmented governance may exacerbate ethical risks, legal ambiguity, and operational inefficiencies.

Empirical research indicates that higher-education systems characterized by strong Triple Helix coordination demonstrate higher levels of policy coherence, institutional readiness, and innovation effectiveness in digital transformation initiatives (Ranga & Etzkowitz, 2013; Ivančić et al., 2022). In policy-driven environments such as Saudi Arabia, where AI development is guided by centralized national strategies, the Triple Helix offers a structured mechanism for translating policy intent into coordinated institutional practice while preserving differentiated roles and accountability.

3.2 The Quadruple Helix: Societal Engagement and Governance Legitimacy

The Quadruple Helix model extends the traditional Triple Helix by incorporating **civil society** as a fourth dimension of innovation and governance systems (Carayannis & Campbell, 2009). This extension reflects growing recognition that technological innovation must be socially embedded to achieve legitimacy, trust, and long-term sustainability. In the domain of artificial intelligence, societal acceptance is particularly salient due to concerns surrounding surveillance, bias, transparency, and the consequences of automated decision-making.

In higher education, societal actors include students, faculty members, professional associations, employers, and the broader public. Universities, as public-interest institutions, bear a distinct responsibility to ensure that AI systems deployed in educational contexts respect academic values, equity, and human dignity. Research consistently shows that stakeholder engagement, transparency mechanisms, and participatory governance arrangements reduce resistance to AI adoption and strengthen institutional legitimacy (OECD, 2021; UNESCO, 2023).

Within Saudi Arabia, societal engagement is closely linked to national priorities related to workforce readiness, social cohesion, and public-sector accountability. The Quadruple Helix perspective therefore complements the Triple Helix by emphasizing that effective AI governance in higher education must extend beyond institutional and regulatory domains to include communication, consultation, and capacity-building mechanisms that foster societal trust and shared ownership of digital transformation.

3.3 The Quintuple Helix: Sustainability-Oriented AI Governance

The Quintuple Helix model introduces the **environmental dimension** into innovation and governance systems, highlighting the interdependence between knowledge production, societal development, and ecological sustainability (Carayannis & Barth, 2021). Although artificial intelligence applications in higher education are often perceived as environmentally neutral, their cumulative energy consumption, reliance on digital infrastructure, and contribution to data-centre expansion raise sustainability concerns that warrant governance attention.

Sustainability-oriented AI governance in universities involves adopting energy-efficient computing practices, encouraging research on environmentally responsible AI applications, and integrating sustainability indicators into institutional decision-making. International frameworks, including the United Nations Sustainable Development Goals (SDGs), emphasize the responsibility of educational institutions to align technological innovation with environmental stewardship and long-term societal well-being (UNESCO, 2021).

In the Saudi context, the Quintuple Helix aligns closely with sustainability objectives embedded within Vision 2030. Integrating environmental considerations into AI governance ensures that digital transformation in higher education contributes to balanced and sustainable development rather than short-term technological gains.

3.4 Helix-Based Role Differentiation in AI Governance

To clarify the governance logic underpinning helix-based AI adoption, it is essential to distinguish the differentiated yet interdependent roles of governance actors across helix dimensions. Table 1 summarizes these roles as they relate specifically to artificial intelligence governance in higher education.

Table 1. Differentiated yet interdependent roles of governance actors across Triple/Quadruple/Quintuple Helix dimensions

Helix Dimension	*Governance Actor*	*Core Roles and Responsibilities in AI Governance within Higher Education*
Triple Helix	***Universities***	*Development and delivery of AI-related academic programs; institutional AI strategy formulation; ethical oversight of AI deployment; capacity building for students, faculty, and administrative staff; operational implementation of AI systems in teaching, research, and administration.*
	Government	*Formulation of national AI strategies and digital transformation agendas; establishment of legal and regulatory frameworks (data protection, cybersecurity, ethics); policy coordination across sectors; monitoring compliance and ensuring alignment with national priorities such as Vision 2030 and NSDAI.*
	Industry	*Provision of technological platforms and AI solutions; applied expertise and innovation capabilities; collaboration with universities on curriculum relevance, applied research, and skills development; facilitation of technology transfer and workforce integration.*
Quadruple Helix	***Civil Society and Stakeholders***	*Enhancement of governance legitimacy and public trust; stakeholder engagement (students, faculty, employers, professional bodies); participation in consultation and feedback mechanisms; promotion of transparency, inclusiveness, and social acceptance of AI systems in education.*
Quintuple Helix	***Environmental Dimension***	*Integration of sustainability considerations into AI governance; promotion of energy-efficient computing and responsible digital infrastructure; alignment of AI adoption with environmental stewardship and long-term sustainable development goals.*

The distribution of roles outlined in Table 1 demonstrates that effective AI governance does not depend on centralized control by a single actor, but on structured coordination among complementary institutions. The Triple Helix provides the foundational governance architecture, while Quadruple and Quintuple Helix extensions ensure that societal legitimacy and sustainability considerations are embedded within decision-making processes.

3.5 Strategic Relevance of Helix-Based Governance for AI in Higher Education

Compared to alternative governance models—such as purely regulatory, network-based, or platform-centric approaches—the helix-based framework offers a strategically integrated perspective capable of addressing the complexity of AI adoption in higher education. It enables vertical alignment between national policy and institutional practice while facilitating horizontal collaboration among innovation actors.

For Saudi higher education, this integration is particularly significant. Government entities establish strategic direction and regulatory baselines; universities operationalize AI through academic, administrative, and research functions; and industry partners provide applied expertise and innovation pathways. By embedding these interactions within a helix-based governance framework, higher-education institutions can mitigate ethical and operational risks while enhancing innovation capacity and public accountability.

4. LITERATURE REVIEW: ARTIFICIAL INTELLIGENCE GOVERNANCE IN HIGHER EDUCATION

4.1 Global Trends in AI Adoption in Higher Education

The adoption of artificial intelligence in higher education has accelerated significantly over the past decade, driven by advances in machine learning, learning analytics, and digital infrastructure. Universities across diverse regions increasingly deploy AI-enabled systems to personalize learning pathways, automate administrative processes, enhance research analytics, and support institutional planning. These applications are progressively embedded within learning management systems, student information systems, and research platforms, positioning AI as a core component of contemporary university operations (Middlehurst, 2020; OECD, 2023).

Despite the rapid diffusion of AI technologies, the literature consistently highlights a growing gap between technological adoption and governance readiness. AI initiatives frequently emerge as technology-driven responses to efficiency pressures rather than as strategically governed interventions aligned with institutional missions and public responsibilities. As a result, governance mechanisms often lag behind implementation, creating vulnerabilities related to accountability, oversight, and long-term sustainability (Cotton et al., 2023).

Comparative studies suggest that institutions with explicit AI governance strategies—integrating ethical guidelines, legal compliance mechanisms, and cross-functional coordination—are better positioned to realize the benefits of AI while mitigating associated risks. Conversely, ad hoc adoption patterns tend to exacerbate institutional fragmentation and increase exposure to ethical, legal, and reputational challenges (OECD, 2021).

4.2 Ethical Challenges and Normative Governance Frameworks

Ethical considerations occupy a central position in scholarly debates on artificial intelligence in higher education. Core concerns include algorithmic bias, opacity in automated decision-making, reduced human oversight, and the potential erosion of academic values. These risks are particularly salient when AI systems influence high-stakes processes such as admissions, assessment, progression monitoring, and student support (Borenstein et al., 2022).

Floridi (2021) argues that effective AI governance requires an *ethics-by-design* approach, whereby normative principles are embedded throughout the AI lifecycle—from system design and data selection to deployment and post-implementation evaluation. This approach moves beyond compliance-oriented ethics toward proactive governance arrangements that anticipate and mitigate harm before it materializes.

International organizations have reinforced this orientation through principle-based governance frameworks. UNESCO's *Recommendation on the Ethics of Artificial Intelligence* emphasizes human dignity, fairness, transparency, and accountability as foundational values guiding AI adoption in education and research (UNESCO, 2021). Similarly, the OECD's AI principles advocate human-centered design, robustness, and responsible innovation across public-sector applications, including higher education (OECD, 2019). The literature increasingly converges on the view that ethical principles must be operationalized through institutional governance mechanisms rather than remaining abstract normative commitments.

4.3 Legal and Regulatory Dimensions of AI Governance

Alongside ethical considerations, legal and regulatory compliance constitutes a critical dimension of AI governance in higher education. Universities manage extensive datasets containing sensitive personal, academic, and behavioural information, rendering them subject to stringent data-protection and privacy obligations. Legal scholars emphasize that AI systems amplify existing data-protection risks by increasing the scale, speed, and opacity of data processing (Brkan, 2021).

Comparative legal analyses indicate that institutions operating within robust regulatory environments demonstrate higher levels of legitimacy and public confidence. However, the literature also emphasizes that compliance alone is insufficient to ensure effective governance. Regulatory frameworks typically establish minimum standards, leaving institutions responsible for translating legal requirements into operational practices supported by governance structures, staff training, and continuous monitoring (OECD, 2021).

In the higher-education context, this translation challenge underscores the importance of institutional governance capacity. Without clear internal accountability mechanisms and centralized coordination, universities may struggle to operationalize complex legal requirements, particularly as AI technologies evolve more rapidly than regulatory instruments.

4.4 Governance Gaps Identified in the Literature

Despite the proliferation of ethical guidelines, legal frameworks, and national AI strategies, the literature identifies persistent governance gaps in higher education. These include weak integration between institutional AI initiatives and national policy frameworks, limited cross-sector collaboration, and the absence of standardized metrics for evaluating ethical, social, and environmental impact (OECD, 2021; UNESCO, 2023).

A recurring theme across studies is the fragmentation of governance responsibilities within universities. AI initiatives are often distributed across departments, research centres, or administrative units without centralized oversight. This fragmentation complicates ethical review, undermines compliance consistency, and limits strategic alignment with national objectives (Middlehurst, 2020).

Scholars increasingly argue that addressing these gaps requires governance models capable of coordinating multiple actors and aligning institutional practice with broader policy and societal expectations. Helix-based governance frameworks respond directly to this need by conceptualizing AI governance as a collaborative, multi-actor process rather than a purely institutional or regulatory function.

4.5 Implications for Helix-Based AI Governance

The literature reviewed in this section supports the argument that effective AI governance in higher education requires integrated frameworks capable of bridging ethics, law, institutional strategy, and cross-sector collaboration. While ethical guidelines and regulatory instruments establish essential normative baselines, their practical impact depends on institutional capacity and governance coherence.

Helix-based governance models offer a structured response to these challenges by aligning universities, government, and industry within a shared governance architecture. When extended through Quadruple and Quintuple Helix perspectives, these models further integrate societal legitimacy and sustainability considerations, addressing governance dimensions frequently overlooked in technology-driven adoption.

5. METHODOLOGICAL DESIGN AND ANALYTICAL STRATEGY

5.1 Research Design and Analytical Orientation

This chapter adopts a **qualitative, interpretive research design** to examine artificial intelligence governance in Saudi higher education through the lens of helix-based governance models. Qualitative approaches are particularly appropriate for investigating governance phenomena that involve institutional roles, policy coordination, ethical considerations, and organizational dynamics that cannot be meaningfully reduced to quantitative indicators alone (Creswell & Poth, 2018).

Rather than testing causal hypotheses or measuring isolated variables, the study seeks to develop an analytically grounded understanding of how governance structures shape the adoption, oversight, and institutionalization of AI within higher-education systems. This orientation aligns with the chapter's theory-informed and policy-oriented objectives, which emphasize conceptual integration, contextual analysis, and institutional practice over statistical generalization.

The research design is therefore exploratory and explanatory in nature, aiming to illuminate governance logics, coordination mechanisms, and institutional responses to AI adoption within a nationally driven transformation context.

5.2 Rationale for a Governance-Oriented Analytical Framework

Artificial intelligence governance in higher education operates at the intersection of public policy, institutional strategy, technological innovation, and societal values. As such, it requires an analytical framework capable of capturing multi-actor interaction, layered decision-making, and evolving accountability arrangements.

Helix-based governance models—particularly the Triple Helix and its Quadruple and Quintuple extensions—provide an appropriate conceptual foundation for this purpose. These models enable systematic examination of how universities, government entities, industry partners, and societal actors interact in shaping AI governance arrangements across strategic, operational, and normative dimensions.

In this chapter, helix theory is employed as an organizing analytical lens rather than as a deterministic explanatory model. This allows for sensitivity to institutional diversity, policy context, and governance maturity, while maintaining conceptual coherence. Such an approach is consistent with contemporary governance scholarship emphasizing relational analysis, institutional embeddedness, and adaptive governance capacity (Pierre & Peters, 2020).

5.3 Data Sources and Document Analysis

The empirical basis of the chapter is derived primarily from systematic document analysis. Core sources include national policy documents, regulatory frameworks, strategic plans, and institutional materials relevant to AI governance in Saudi Arabia. These include, but are not limited to, Saudi Vision 2030, the National Strategy for Data and Artificial Intelligence (NSDAI), the Personal Data Protection Law (PDPL), national cybersecurity frameworks, and higher-education policy guidelines issued by relevant authorities.

Document analysis enables examination of both formal governance arrangements and the underlying policy rationales shaping AI adoption in higher education. By triangulating across multiple authoritative sources, the study enhances analytical rigor and reduces the risk of selective interpretation. This method is well established in governance and policy research, particularly in contexts where access to primary empirical data may be constrained (Bowen, 2009).

The documents were analysed with attention to governance objectives, role allocation, compliance requirements, coordination mechanisms, and implicit assumptions regarding institutional responsibility and accountability.

5.4 Analytical Case Study Strategy

To complement the policy-level analysis, the chapter employs an analytical case study focusing on the Applied College at King Faisal University. The case was selected due to its relevance to national digital transformation priorities, its professionally oriented academic model, and its active engagement with AI-related academic programs and institutional governance initiatives.

The case selection was theoretically informed, aiming to illustrate governance dynamics rather than to claim statistical representativeness. The case study serves as an empirical illustration of how helix-based governance principles are operationalized at the institutional level, including governance structures, curriculum design, collaboration mechanisms, and capacity-building initiatives.

This analytical use of the case supports theory refinement by linking abstract governance concepts to concrete institutional practices, consistent with established case-study methodology in governance research (Yin, 2018).

5.5 Analytical Procedure

The analysis proceeded through three iterative and interconnected stages. First, policy and regulatory documents were reviewed to identify governance objectives, role allocations, and compliance requirements related to artificial intelligence in higher education. Second, these findings were mapped onto helix-based governance dimensions to examine patterns of coordination, interaction, and responsibility among key actors.

Third, insights from the institutional case study were used to assess how governance principles are translated into practice and to identify areas of alignment and tension between national strategy and institutional implementation. This iterative analytical procedure supports depth and coherence by enabling continuous movement between theory, policy, and practice.

Such an approach facilitates identification of governance gaps, best practices, and institutional lessons relevant to higher-education systems undergoing rapid digital transformation.

5.6 Research Rigor and Trustworthiness

To enhance methodological rigor, the study adheres to established qualitative research criteria, including credibility, transparency, and analytical coherence. Credibility is supported through triangulation of authoritative policy sources and alignment with established governance theories. Transparency is ensured by explicitly documenting data sources, analytical steps, and conceptual assumptions.

Analytical coherence is maintained through consistent application of helix-based frameworks across all sections of the chapter. While the study does not employ primary empirical data collection, its methodology is appropriate to the conceptual and policy-oriented objectives of the research.

The analytical strategy emphasizes transferability rather than generalizability, allowing insights to inform governance discussions in comparable higher-education contexts characterized by strong state coordination and rapid technological change.

5.7 Methodological Limitations

As with any qualitative and document-based study, certain limitations must be acknowledged. The analysis relies on publicly available policy and institutional documents, which may not fully capture informal governance practices or internal decision-making dynamics. In addition, the single-case design limits claims of representativeness across the entire Saudi higher-education system.

These limitations do not undermine the analytical contribution of the chapter. Instead, they highlight opportunities for future empirical research employing interviews, surveys, or comparative case studies to build upon the governance framework advanced in this study.

6. NATIONAL CONTEXT: AI GOVERNANCE AND HIGHER EDUCATION IN SAUDI ARABIA

6.1 Vision 2030 and the Strategic Repositioning of Universities

Saudi Arabia's approach to artificial intelligence is embedded within a comprehensive national transformation agenda articulated through Vision 2030. The vision positions digital technologies—and artificial intelligence in particular—as strategic enablers of economic diversification, productivity growth, and human-capital development. Within this framework, higher education is assigned a central role in preparing a digitally skilled workforce, advancing applied research, and supporting innovation-driven development (Vision 2030, 2016).

This strategic repositioning has profound governance implications for universities. Higher-education institutions are no longer viewed solely as providers of academic credentials; rather, they are expected to function as active contributors to national development priorities. Consequently, universities must align academic programs, research agendas, and institutional governance structures with national digital strategies while preserving academic integrity, regulatory compliance, and public accountability.

The emphasis on artificial intelligence within Vision 2030 intensifies these expectations. Universities are required not only to adopt AI-enabled systems, but also to govern them responsibly in accordance with national values, legal frameworks, and societal expectations. This dual mandate—innovation acceleration alongside accountability—underscores the need for governance models capable of coordinating institutional autonomy with centralized strategic direction.

6.2 The National Strategy for Data and Artificial Intelligence (NSDAI)

The National Strategy for Data and Artificial Intelligence (NSDAI) constitutes the principal policy framework guiding AI development in Saudi Arabia. Led by the Saudi Data and AI Authority (SDAIA), the strategy articulates national objectives related to data governance, AI talent development, research excellence, and global competitiveness. Education is identified as a foundational pillar, reflecting recognition that sustainable AI ecosystems depend on robust, future-oriented human-capital pipelines (SDAIA, 2022).

For higher-education institutions, NSDAI establishes expectations across multiple dimensions. Universities are encouraged to expand AI-related academic offerings, strengthen applied research capacity, and engage in structured collaboration with government and industry partners. At the same time, institutions are required to comply with national standards governing data protection, cybersecurity, and ethical AI deployment.

From a governance perspective, NSDAI functions both as a strategic roadmap and as a coordination mechanism linking institutional practices with national policy objectives. Importantly, the strategy reflects a shift toward networked and collaborative governance consistent with Triple Helix principles. Rather than relying exclusively on hierarchical regulation, NSDAI promotes coordinated engagement among universities, government agencies, and industry actors to accelerate AI adoption while mitigating associated risks.

6.3 Legal and Regulatory Foundations of AI Governance

Artificial intelligence governance in Saudi higher education operates within a comprehensive legal and regulatory environment designed to protect personal data, ensure cybersecurity, and safeguard public interests. The Personal Data Protection Law (PDPL) establishes binding requirements governing the collection, processing, storage, and sharing of personal data. As public institutions managing extensive student and staff datasets, universities are subject to heightened compliance obligations under this law (SDAIA, 2023).

In parallel, the Essential Cybersecurity Controls (ECC) issued by the National Cybersecurity Authority define baseline cybersecurity requirements for public-sector entities, including higher-education institutions. These controls are particularly relevant for AI systems that rely on large-scale data processing, interconnected platforms, and cloud-based infrastructure (NCA, 2018). Compliance with ECC standards constitutes a core element of institutional risk management and accountability.

While these regulatory instruments provide a robust compliance baseline, international research emphasizes that legal adherence alone is insufficient for effective AI governance. Universities must translate regulatory requirements into operational practices supported by trained personnel, clear decision-making structures, and continuous oversight mechanisms. Without such institutionalization, compliance risks becoming procedural rather than substantive, offering limited protection against ethical and operational failure (Brkan, 2021; OECD, 2021).

6.4 Institutional Governance Challenges in Saudi Universities

Despite the clarity of national strategies and regulatory frameworks, Saudi universities face several challenges in operationalizing AI governance. One recurring issue is institutional fragmentation, whereby AI initiatives are developed at departmental or project levels without centralized coordination. This fragmentation can lead to inconsistent ethical practices, uneven regulatory compliance, and duplication of effort.

A second challenge concerns variations in institutional capacity. While some universities possess advanced digital infrastructure and specialized expertise, others face constraints related to staffing, funding, or organizational readiness. These disparities highlight the need for governance frameworks that support competency development and facilitate knowledge sharing across the higher-education system.

A further challenge relates to role clarity within collaborative arrangements. As universities engage more extensively with governmental and industrial partners, boundaries between academic, regulatory, and commercial interests may become blurred. Without explicit governance mechanisms, such interactions risk generating conflicts of interest or undermining academic independence. Helix-based governance models address this challenge by enabling formalized partnership mechanisms while preserving accountability boundaries and role differentiation.

6.5 The Triple Helix as a Governance Architecture in Saudi Arabia

Within the Saudi higher-education context, the Triple Helix model provides a coherent governance architecture for coordinating AI adoption. Government entities—including SDAIA, the Ministry of Education, and the National Cybersecurity Authority—establish strategic direction and regulatory standards. Universities operationalize these standards through academic programs, research initiatives, and institutional governance mechanisms. Industry partners contribute applied expertise, technological platforms, and innovation pathways.

This configuration supports a distributed yet coordinated governance system in which responsibilities are shared but clearly differentiated. Empirical studies indicate that such arrangements enhance policy coherence and reduce implementation gaps in technologically complex domains (Ranga & Etzkowitz, 2013; Ivančić et al., 2022).

The Saudi case illustrates how centralized strategic vision can coexist with institutional autonomy when governance structures support alignment, coordination, and accountability. By embedding AI governance within a Triple Helix architecture, higher-education institutions are better positioned to balance innovation imperatives with ethical responsibility and public trust.

7. STRATEGIC GOVERNANCE FRAMEWORK FOR ARTIFICIAL INTELLIGENCE (SGF-AI)

7.1 Rationale and Conceptual Orientation

The preceding analysis demonstrates that artificial intelligence governance in higher education cannot rely on isolated institutional policies, ad hoc initiatives, or compliance-driven controls alone. In environments characterized by rapid technological change, regulatory complexity, and heightened societal sensitivity, AI governance must be approached as a systemic and strategic institutional function embedded within decision-making structures at multiple levels.

Although Saudi Arabia's national strategies—particularly Vision 2030 and the National Strategy for Data and Artificial Intelligence (NSDAI)—provide a strong policy foundation, universities require an integrated governance framework capable of translating strategic intent into coherent, accountable, and operational practice. Without such a framework, AI initiatives risk remaining fragmented, inconsistently governed, or weakly aligned with national objectives and ethical expectations.

The Strategic Governance Framework for Artificial Intelligence (SGF-AI) proposed in this chapter responds to this need by conceptualizing AI governance as a multi-level architecture that connects institutional strategy, regulatory compliance, operational coordination, and impact assessment. Grounded in the Triple Helix model and extended through Quadruple and Quintuple Helix perspectives, the framework aligns university governance with national policy objectives, industry collaboration, societal legitimacy, and sustainability considerations.

Rather than prescribing a rigid organizational structure, SGF-AI offers a flexible governance logic adaptable to institutional context while maintaining alignment with national legal and ethical standards. This flexibility is particularly important in higher-education systems characterized by institutional diversity, differentiated missions, and uneven digital maturity.

Conceptually, the helix models in this chapter function as the **system-level governance logic**: they specify *which actors matter* (university, government, industry, society, and the environment) and *why their interaction is necessary* for legitimate and resilient AI governance. By contrast, the SGF-AI functions as the **institution-level operating framework**: it translates helix principles into executable governance domains—strategic alignment, ethical and legal oversight, operational coordination, and multidimensional impact evaluation—through which universities can implement, monitor, and improve AI adoption in practice. In this way, SGF-AI operationalizes helix-based collaboration by converting actor interdependence into actionable institutional responsibilities and performance expectations.

7.2 Core Governance Domains of the SGF-AI

The SGF-AI is structured around **four interdependent governance domains** that collectively shape how artificial intelligence is adopted, managed, and evaluated within higher-education institutions. These domains are analytically distinct yet operationally interconnected, ensuring that AI governance is embedded throughout the institutional lifecycle rather than confined to isolated oversight mechanisms.

7.2.1 Strategic Alignment

Strategic alignment ensures that institutional AI initiatives are explicitly linked to national development priorities and regulatory frameworks. In the Saudi context, this involves aligning university AI strategies with Vision 2030 objectives, NSDAI priorities, and Ministry of Education directives. Strategic alignment reduces policy fragmentation and reinforces coherence between institutional autonomy and centralized national transformation agendas (Ranga & Etzkowitz, 2013).

At the institutional level, strategic alignment requires universities to articulate explicit AI governance objectives within strategic plans, digital transformation roadmaps, and quality-assurance frameworks. AI adoption is thus framed not as a technical upgrade but as a strategic institutional commitment subject to leadership oversight and performance evaluation.

7.2.2 Ethical and Legal Oversight

Ethical and legal oversight forms the normative foundation of the SGF-AI. This domain integrates ethical principles—fairness, transparency, accountability, and respect for human dignity—with legally binding requirements derived from the Personal Data Protection Law (PDPL) and national cybersecurity regulations.

The framework embeds ethical and legal considerations throughout the AI lifecycle, encompassing system design, procurement, deployment, monitoring, and post-implementation review. This approach reflects international best practices advocating ethics-by-design and governance-by-design, ensuring that ethical safeguards are proactive rather than reactive (Floridi, 2021; UNESCO, 2021).

Operationally, this domain requires the establishment of institutional review mechanisms, data-governance policies, and human-oversight protocols capable of addressing algorithmic bias, data misuse, and accountability gaps. By integrating legal compliance with ethical reasoning, SGF-AI strengthens institutional legitimacy and public trust.

7.2.3 Operational Coordination

Operational coordination addresses the organizational mechanisms required to manage AI initiatives across academic, administrative, and research units. This includes the establishment of institutional AI governance bodies, AI and data offices, and cross-functional committees responsible for ensuring consistency, accountability, and effective communication.

Coordinated governance mitigates risks associated with institutional silos and uneven implementation, which are frequently identified challenges in higher-education digital transformation (Middlehurst, 2020). Within the SGF-AI, operational coordination serves as the connective tissue linking strategic intent with day-to-day institutional practice.

Effective coordination also enables universities to engage productively with governmental and industrial partners, ensuring that collaborative initiatives are governed through clear accountability structures rather than informal or ad hoc arrangements.

7.2.4 Multidimensional Impact Evaluation

Impact evaluation emphasizes continuous assessment of the academic, social, economic, and environmental outcomes of AI adoption. Moving beyond efficiency-focused metrics, this domain adopts a multidimensional evaluation approach aligned with Quadruple and Quintuple Helix principles.

Regular monitoring enables institutions to identify unintended consequences, refine governance practices, and ensure that AI systems contribute positively to educational quality, equity, workforce relevance, and sustainability (Carayannis & Barth, 2021). Impact evaluation thus functions as a feedback mechanism supporting adaptive governance and institutional learning.

7.3 Governance Actors and Role Differentiation

A central strength of the SGF-AI lies in its clear differentiation of roles among governance actors. Universities retain responsibility for institutional implementation, academic integrity, and organizational upskilling. Government entities—such as SDAIA, the Ministry of Education, and the National Cybersecurity Authority—provide strategic direction, regulatory oversight, and coordination mechanisms. Industry partners contribute applied expertise, technological platforms, and innovation pathways connecting academic outputs to real-world applications.

This differentiation does not imply separation. Instead, the framework emphasizes structured interaction through formal coordination mechanisms, joint advisory structures, and collaborative platforms that facilitate knowledge exchange while preserving accountability boundaries. Governance research consistently demonstrates that systems characterized by well-defined yet interconnected roles are more resilient in managing complex and rapidly evolving technologies (Ivančić et al., 2022).

7.4 Integration of Quadruple and Quintuple Helix Dimensions

Beyond the core Triple Helix configuration, SGF-AI integrates Quadruple and Quintuple Helix dimensions to enhance legitimacy and long-term sustainability. The Quadruple Helix dimension emphasizes engagement with societal stakeholders, including students, faculty members, professional bodies, employers, and the broader public.

In practical terms, this engagement involves transparency initiatives, consultation processes, and AI literacy programs that enable stakeholders to understand, question, and shape the use of AI within educational settings. Such engagement strengthens governance legitimacy and aligns AI adoption with societal expectations and public values.

The Quintuple Helix dimension introduces environmental considerations into AI governance. Although AI applications in higher education are often perceived as low-impact, their cumulative energy consumption and reliance on digital infrastructure raise sustainability concerns. SGF-AI therefore encourages universities to adopt energy-efficient computing practices, support environmentally responsible AI research, and incorporate sustainability indicators into institutional decision-making, reinforcing alignment with Vision 2030 sustainability objectives.

7.5 Institutionalization and Scalability

For the SGF-AI to function effectively, it must be institutionalized rather than treated as a temporary initiative. Institutionalization involves embedding governance principles into university statutes, strategic plans, quality-assurance systems, and staff-development programs. This process ensures continuity, accountability, and adaptability in the face of leadership changes and technological evolution.

Scalability constitutes a further strength of the framework. While institutional capacity varies across the Saudi higher-education system, the SGF-AI's core domains are adaptable to different organizational contexts. By providing a shared governance language and structure, the framework supports inter-institutional coordination and contributes to the development of a coherent national AI ecosystem, as synthesized in Table 3.

Table 3. Strategic Governance Framework for Artificial Intelligence (SGF-AI)

Governance Domain	Core Components	Operational Implications for Higher Education
Strategic Alignment	Vision 2030; NSDAI; institutional AI strategies	Ensures coherence between national priorities and university AI initiatives; reduces policy fragmentation
Ethical & Legal Oversight	PDPL compliance; ethics-by-design; cybersecurity governance; human oversight	Embeds safeguards across the AI lifecycle; strengthens accountability and transparency
Operational Coordination	AI and Data Offices; governance committees; collaborations/partnerships	Mitigates institutional silos; standardizes AI decision-making
Impact Evaluation	Academic quality; social equity; economic relevance; environmental sustainability	Enables adaptive governance and continuous improvement

8. CASE STUDY: THE APPLIED COLLEGE AT KING FAISAL UNIVERSITY

8.1 Institutional Context and Strategic Orientation

The Applied College at King Faisal University (KFU) represents a particularly relevant institutional context for examining the operationalization of helix-based AI governance within Saudi higher education. Established to strengthen alignment between academic provision and labour-market needs, the college is strategically oriented toward professionally focused diploma programs emphasizing applied learning, digital competencies, and workforce readiness.

This mission situates the Applied College at the intersection of education policy, economic development, and national digital transformation priorities articulated under Vision 2030. Unlike traditional academic colleges, its governance logic is inherently practice-oriented, requiring sustained coordination with governmental and industry actors while maintaining compliance with national regulatory, quality-assurance, and accreditation frameworks.

Within the broader governance structure of King Faisal University, the Applied College has assumed an increasingly active role in digital transformation initiatives, including AI-enabled curriculum design, data-informed administrative processes, and institutional capacity-building programs. These initiatives position the college as an implementation node within the national AI ecosystem, translating high-level policy objectives into operational educational outcomes consistent with the Strategic Governance Framework for Artificial Intelligence (SGF-AI).

8.2 AI-Related Academic Programs and Human-Capital Governance

A central dimension of the Applied College's contribution to AI governance lies in its portfolio of officially accredited diploma programs in computing and digital technologies. These include:

- Web Application Programming Diploma
- Artificial Intelligence and Data Science Diploma
- Information Systems Diploma
- Computer Networks and Systems Administration Diploma
- Cybersecurity Diploma

These programs are explicitly designed to support national priorities related to digital skills development, data-driven decision-making, and cybersecurity readiness. Curricula emphasize applied competencies through project-based learning, laboratory instruction, and graduation projects addressing real-world organizational and technical challenges.

From a governance perspective, these academic programs function as human-capital governance instruments, operationalizing national AI and data strategies through structured educational pathways. Rather than treating skills development as a downstream outcome, the Applied College embeds workforce alignment directly into curriculum governance processes, including program approval, review, and continuous enhancement.

International evidence underscores the strategic importance of applied and vocationally oriented programs in strengthening AI talent pipelines and reducing skills mismatches in rapidly transforming economies (OECD, 2021; OECD, 2023). The Applied College case illustrates how curriculum governance can serve as a mechanism for aligning educational outputs with national AI ecosystems while preserving academic standards and institutional accountability.

8.3 Institutional AI Governance Structures and Coordination

To support coherent AI adoption, the Applied College has established a dedicated Artificial Intelligence and Data Office, which serves as a centralized coordination mechanism overseeing AI-related initiatives across academic and administrative domains. This unit supports data-informed decision-making, facilitates compliance with university policies and national regulations, and reduces fragmentation by providing a clear locus of governance responsibility.

The existence of such a unit aligns closely with the operational coordination domain of the SGF-AI. Governance research consistently highlights centralized coordination bodies as critical enablers of effective digital transformation in higher education, particularly in contexts characterized by regulatory complexity and cross-functional AI deployment (Middlehurst, 2020).

Complementing this structure, the college operates a Training Unit responsible for continuous professional development in artificial intelligence, digital competencies, and responsible technology use. Training programs target students, faculty members, and administrative staff, fostering institution-wide AI literacy and ethical awareness. These initiatives support the capacity-building function of AI governance, ensuring that institutional readiness evolves alongside technological adoption.

8.4 University–Government–Industry Collaborations

The Applied College maintains extensive collaborations and partnerships with governmental and industry actors, including Cisco, Tuwaiq Academy, the National Cybersecurity Authority, the Ministry of Education, Saudi Aramco, Monsha'at, and the NITI Institute. These collaborations support curriculum relevance, applied training opportunities, student engagement, and exposure to real-world innovation environments.

From a Triple Helix governance perspective, these partnerships illustrate structured interaction rather than informal cooperation. Government actors contribute strategic alignment and regulatory guidance; industry partners provide applied expertise, technological platforms, and innovation pathways; and the university retains authority over academic governance, assessment, and quality assurance.

Empirical studies demonstrate that such structured university–government–industry collaboration enhances governance effectiveness, reduces implementation gaps, and accelerates innovation diffusion in complex technological domains (Etzkowitz & Leydesdorff, 2021; Ranga & Etzkowitz, 2013). In the Applied College case, partnerships are embedded within institutional governance arrangements, reinforcing accountability and role clarity.

8.5 Student Engagement, Innovation, and Applied Outcomes

Student engagement constitutes a core component of the Applied College's AI ecosystem. As part of their academic progression, students complete AI-enabled and digitally oriented graduation projects addressing institutional, industrial, and societal challenges. These projects strengthen applied problem-solving skills and reinforce the link between academic learning and practical outcomes.

The college actively encourages student participation in institutional and national hackathons. Notably, a student team from the Applied College received the Best Industrial Impact Award at a Saudi Aramco Hackathon, demonstrating the capacity of applied diploma programs to generate innovation with tangible industrial relevance.

In addition, students contribute to the development of digital applications and AI-supported media products used for institutional communication and service delivery. These activities embed experiential learning within governance frameworks emphasizing accountability, quality assurance, and ethical technology use, reinforcing the Quadruple Helix dimension of societal engagement.

8.6 Digital Infrastructure and Learning Technologies

The Applied College's AI initiatives are supported by a robust digital infrastructure, including advanced computer laboratories, specialized technical facilities, learning-management systems, and AI-enabled educational platforms. The college delivers eighteen diploma programs through distance and blended-learning modalities, utilizing platforms such as Blackboard and immersive instructional technologies.

This infrastructure enables scalable digital education while maintaining compliance with quality-assurance and cybersecurity standards. From a governance perspective, digital infrastructure functions as an enabling condition rather than a substitute for oversight. International research confirms that effective AI adoption in higher education depends on the alignment of technological infrastructure with governance capacity, regulatory compliance, and institutional strategy (OECD, 2023).

8.7 Analytical Synthesis and Governance Alignment

The Applied College at King Faisal University provides a concrete illustration of how helix-based governance principles can be operationalized within a professionally oriented higher-education institution. Dedicated governance units enhance coherence and accountability; applied curricula align human-capital development with national priorities; structured collaborations strengthen policy alignment; and continuous training and student engagement reinforce innovation capacity while mitigating ethical and operational risks.

Collectively, these elements demonstrate alignment with all four governance domains of the Strategic Governance Framework for Artificial Intelligence (SGF-AI). The case confirms that effective AI governance in higher education emerges not from isolated technological initiatives, but from institutionalized, collaborative, and capacity-driven governance arrangements.

9. GOVERNANCE IMPLICATIONS AND INSTITUTIONAL LESSONS FROM THE SAUDI CASE

9.1 Institutional Governance and Strategic Coherence

The case of the Applied College at King Faisal University underscores the centrality of strategic coherence in the governance of artificial intelligence within higher education. One of the most significant governance implications concerns the role of centralized coordination structures in mitigating fragmentation and ensuring alignment between academic programs, administrative processes, and national regulatory requirements.

The establishment of a dedicated Artificial Intelligence and Data Office illustrates how universities can institutionalize AI governance as a permanent organizational function rather than treating AI initiatives as isolated or experimental projects. Such governance units act as intermediary structures that translate national strategies—most notably Vision 2030 and the National Strategy for Data and Artificial Intelligence—into operational institutional practices while preserving academic autonomy.

This finding aligns with governance scholarship emphasizing that complex digital transformations require clearly defined loci of responsibility supported by formal authority, procedural clarity, and cross-functional coordination (Middlehurst, 2020; Pierre & Peters, 2020). In the absence of such structures, AI governance risks becoming dispersed across departments, resulting in inconsistent ethical practices, uneven compliance, and limited strategic oversight.

9.2 Curriculum Governance and Workforce Alignment

A second major governance lesson relates to the strategic role of curriculum governance in national AI ecosystems. The Applied College's professionally oriented diploma programs in artificial intelligence, data science, cybersecurity, and information systems function not only as educational offerings but also as governance instruments that operationalize workforce-development priorities embedded within national policy frameworks.

By embedding applied competencies, project-based learning, and industry-relevant content into formally accredited programs, the college aligns academic governance processes—such as program approval, periodic review, and quality assurance—with labour-market needs and national digital strategies. This alignment demonstrates how curriculum design becomes a site of negotiated governance where academic standards, regulatory expectations, and industry requirements intersect.

From a Triple Helix perspective, curriculum governance serves as a strategic interface linking universities, government objectives, and industry demand. The

Saudi case demonstrates that such alignment can be achieved without compromising academic integrity, provided that governance mechanisms ensure transparency, accreditation rigor, and accountability.

9.3 Partnership Governance and Role Differentiation

The Applied College's collaborations and partnerships with governmental and industry actors provide important lessons regarding role differentiation within helix-based governance arrangements. Effective collaboration in the Saudi case was characterized by clarity of institutional roles rather than blurred boundaries between academic, regulatory, and commercial interests.

Government entities contributed strategic direction, regulatory guidance, and alignment with national priorities; industry partners provided applied expertise, technological platforms, and innovation pathways; and the university retained authority over academic content, assessment, and quality assurance. This configuration supports governance research emphasizing that successful Triple Helix systems depend on structured collaboration underpinned by accountability rather than informal or ad hoc interaction (Etzkowitz & Leydesdorff, 2021).

The case further illustrates that partnership governance mechanisms—when institutionally embedded—can enhance innovation capacity while safeguarding public-interest obligations and academic independence. This finding is particularly relevant in AI governance contexts, where commercial incentives and public responsibilities must be carefully balanced.

9.4 Capacity Building and Organizational Learning

Another critical governance implication concerns the role of continuous capacity building as a foundation for sustainable AI governance. The Applied College's investment in training initiatives targeting students, faculty members, and administrative staff contributes to shared institutional understanding of AI tools, ethical considerations, and regulatory responsibilities.

These initiatives reinforce organizational learning and reduce reliance on isolated technical expertise. Governance research consistently indicates that AI governance effectiveness depends not only on formal policies but also on institutional culture, competence, and adaptability (OECD, 2023). Capacity-building mechanisms enable universities to update governance practices in response to technological evolution, emerging ethical risks, and changing regulatory expectations.

From a Quadruple Helix perspective, organizational upskilling also strengthens societal legitimacy by enhancing transparency and stakeholder understanding of AI systems deployed within educational contexts.

9.5 Transferability within the Saudi Higher-Education System

While the Applied College represents a specific institutional context, its governance lessons exhibit a significant degree of transferability across the Saudi higher-education system, particularly for applied colleges and professionally oriented programs. Governance mechanisms such as centralized coordination units, applied curricula aligned with national priorities, structured partnerships, and continuous training are not inherently institution specific.

However, the case also underscores the importance of contextual adaptation. Variations in institutional size, mission, and digital maturity necessitate flexible implementation of helix-based governance principles rather than uniform replication. This insight aligns with the SGF-AI's emphasis on scalability and institutional responsiveness.

9.6 Advancing Helix-Based AI Governance Theory

Analytically, the Saudi case contributes to helix-based governance theory by demonstrating how Triple Helix arrangements in higher education can evolve toward Quadruple and Quintuple Helix configurations. Societal engagement—through student participation, transparency practices, and public-facing digital initiatives—enhances governance legitimacy, while emerging sustainability considerations signal the relevance of environmental dimensions even in educational AI contexts.

These findings reinforce the theoretical proposition that AI governance in higher education is most effective when conceptualized as an adaptive, multi-actor system rather than a static regulatory framework. The Applied College case thus provides empirical grounding for extending helix-based models beyond innovation logic toward comprehensive governance architectures.

9.7 Summary of Institutional Lessons

In synthesis, the Saudi case identifies several institutional lessons critical for effective AI governance in higher education:

- Centralized governance structures are essential for strategic coherence and regulatory alignment.
- Curriculum governance functions as a key mechanism for aligning AI education with national workforce priorities.
- Structured partnerships require clear role differentiation to preserve accountability and academic integrity.

- Continuous competency development underpins ethical awareness, compliance, and institutional adaptability.
- Societal engagement and sustainability considerations enhance legitimacy and long-term governance effectiveness.

These lessons collectively inform the policy roadmap and discussion presented in subsequent sections.

10. POLICY ROADMAP FOR AI GOVERNANCE IN SAUDI HIGHER EDUCATION (2025–2035)

The institutionalization of artificial intelligence governance in Saudi higher education requires a phased, time-bound, and capacity-sensitive policy roadmap that translates national strategic ambitions into sustainable institutional practice. While Vision 2030 and the National Strategy for Data and Artificial Intelligence (NSDAI) provide a comprehensive macro-level direction, universities require an operational roadmap that accounts for institutional diversity, governance maturity, and resource availability.

Building on the Strategic Governance Framework for Artificial Intelligence (SGF-AI), this section proposes a four-phase policy roadmap (2025–2035) designed to guide Saudi higher-education institutions toward coherent, ethical, and sustainable AI governance. The roadmap reflects helix-based governance principles by aligning institutional development with governmental coordination, industry engagement, societal legitimacy, and environmental sustainability.

10.1 Phase I: Institutional Foundations (2025–2026)

The first phase focuses on establishing the foundational governance infrastructure required for responsible AI adoption. During this period, AI governance must transition from ad hoc or project-based initiatives to a formally recognized institutional function embedded within university governance systems.

Key priorities include the creation or formalization of AI governance structures such as AI and data offices, institutional AI committees, or cross-functional governance bodies with clearly defined mandates. These entities should be responsible for overseeing AI strategy, ensuring compliance with the Personal Data Protection Law (PDPL) and national cybersecurity controls, and coordinating AI initiatives across academic and administrative units.

Equally important during this phase is competency development. Universities should invest in structured AI literacy programs targeting senior leadership, faculty members, and administrative staff. These programs should address not only technical competencies but also ethical principles, regulatory obligations, and governance responsibilities. Without a shared understanding of AI governance fundamentals, subsequent phases risk remaining symbolic rather than operational.

From a Triple Helix perspective, Phase I establishes the institutional interface through which universities can engage coherently with government agencies and industry partners.

Illustrative success indicators for Phase I include: (i) establishment of an AI governance office or equivalent central unit; (ii) adoption of institution-wide AI governance policies aligned with PDPL and national cybersecurity controls; and (iii) documented completion of baseline AI governance training for senior leadership and relevant operational units.

10.2 Phase II: Integration and Operationalization (2026–2028)

The second phase emphasizes the integration of AI governance principles into core institutional functions. Rather than operating as parallel structures, AI governance mechanisms should be embedded within academic program design, administrative workflows, and research-management systems.

During this phase, ethical review processes, data-governance protocols, and cybersecurity assessments become routine components of AI system deployment. Universities standardize documentation, risk assessment, and audit procedures to ensure consistency across units and projects. This operationalization reduces governance fragmentation and enhances institutional accountability.

Formalized partnership mechanisms with government and industry are expanded through coordination protocols aligned with Triple Helix principles. These mechanisms support joint curriculum development, applied research initiatives, and innovation partnerships while preserving institutional autonomy and compliance integrity.

Illustrative success indicators for Phase II include: (i) standardized AI risk assessment and documentation adopted across units; (ii) routine ethical review and cybersecurity assessment integrated into AI procurement and deployment; and (iii) completion of internal compliance audits for priority AI systems used in academic and administrative decision-making.

10.3 Phase III: Ecosystem Expansion and Innovation Scaling (2028–2032)

Phase III shifts the focus from internal consolidation toward ecosystem-level expansion and innovation scaling. As institutional governance capacity matures, universities are positioned to deepen cross-institutional collaboration, share AI platforms and best practices, and participate more actively in national and regional innovation ecosystems.

Societal engagement—consistent with Quadruple Helix principles—becomes increasingly prominent during this phase. Universities strengthen transparency mechanisms, stakeholder consultation processes, and AI literacy initiatives targeting students and the broader public. Multidimensional impact evaluation frameworks are institutionalized, enabling systematic assessment of academic quality, social equity, economic relevance, and ethical outcomes.

This phase also supports national objectives related to innovation diffusion and talent mobility by facilitating collaboration among universities, research centres, and industry partners across regions and disciplines.

Illustrative success indicators for Phase III include: (i) formalized partnership mechanisms for joint curriculum and applied research with government and industry; (ii) operational stakeholder engagement processes (e.g., consultation and transparency reporting) for AI-enabled services; and (iii) deployment of multidimensional impact evaluation metrics covering academic quality, equity, and societal outcomes.

10.4 Phase IV: Sustainability and Helix Consolidation (2032–2035)

The final phase consolidates Quadruple and Quintuple Helix integration, embedding sustainability and long-term evaluation into AI governance frameworks. Universities adopt sustainability indicators for AI systems, including energy efficiency, infrastructure optimization, and environmentally responsible computing practices.

Longitudinal evaluations assess the cumulative ethical, social, and environmental impacts of AI adoption in higher education. Governance mechanisms are refined based on empirical evidence, ensuring adaptability in response to technological evolution and emerging societal expectations.

By the conclusion of this phase, AI governance is fully institutionalized as a continuous, adaptive function aligned with national development priorities and global best practices.

Illustrative success indicators for Phase IV include: (i) adoption of sustainability-oriented AI indicators (e.g., energy efficiency criteria for compute-intensive systems); (ii) longitudinal evaluation reports documenting ethical, social, and environmental impacts; and (iii) evidence-based updating of governance mechanisms in response to technological and regulatory change.

Table 2. Phased Policy Roadmap for AI Governance in Saudi Higher Education

Phase	Period	Key Governance Priorities
Phase I	2025–2026	Institutional governance structures, compliance readiness, AI literacy
Phase II	2026–2028	Integration of AI governance into academic and administrative operations
Phase III	2028–2032	Ecosystem collaboration, innovation scaling, multidimensional impact evaluation
Phase IV	2032–2035	Sustainability integration, long-term governance consolidation

10.5 Strategic Significance of the Roadmap

The proposed roadmap operationalizes the SGF-AI by sequencing governance development in a manner responsive to institutional capacity and national priorities. It reinforces the principle that effective AI governance is not a one-time regulatory exercise but a progressive institutional learning process. By aligning governance maturity with helix-based collaboration, the roadmap supports Saudi higher education in balancing innovation acceleration with ethical responsibility and societal trust.

11. DISCUSSION: INTEGRATING THEORY, POLICY, AND INSTITUTIONAL PRACTICE

This chapter has examined artificial intelligence governance in higher education through a helix-based analytical lens, integrating theoretical models, national policy frameworks, and institutional practice. The preceding sections demonstrate that effective AI adoption in higher education is not primarily a technological challenge, but a governance challenge requiring strategic coordination, ethical oversight, and sustained institutional capacity.

The Saudi higher-education context offers a particularly instructive case. Under Vision 2030 and the National Strategy for Data and Artificial Intelligence (NSDAI), universities are positioned as central actors in national transformation agendas. However, the success of these ambitions depends on the extent to which governance arrangements can reconcile innovation acceleration with accountability, legitimacy, and long-term sustainability. The findings of this chapter underscore that such reconciliation cannot be achieved through isolated institutional initiatives or compliance-driven approaches alone.

11.1 Reframing the Triple Helix: From Innovation Logic to Governance Architecture

A central contribution of this chapter lies in reframing the Triple Helix model from an innovation-centric framework into a governance architecture suitable for artificial intelligence in higher education. Classical Triple Helix theory emphasizes knowledge production, commercialization, and economic development. While these dimensions remain relevant, the governance of AI introduces additional layers of ethical responsibility, regulatory complexity, and societal scrutiny.

In the Saudi case, government entities articulate strategic direction and regulatory baselines; universities operationalize AI through academic programs, research, and institutional systems; and industry actors contribute applied expertise and technological infrastructure. When these roles are clearly differentiated yet institutionally aligned, governance systems exhibit greater resilience to policy fragmentation and technological uncertainty.

This reframing extends the analytical utility of the Triple Helix model by positioning universities not merely as innovation engines, but as active governance actors responsible for ethical stewardship, compliance assurance, and the cultivation of public trust.

11.2 Governance Trade-Offs and Structural Tensions

Despite its strengths, helix-based AI governance entails inherent trade-offs. One persistent tension concerns the balance between institutional autonomy and centralized coordination. Strong national strategies enhance coherence and reduce duplication; however, excessive centralization may constrain institutional experimentation and responsiveness.

The Saudi experience suggests that governance effectiveness depends on preserving institutional agency within a clearly articulated strategic framework. Universities require flexibility to tailor AI governance mechanisms to their mission, capacity, and stakeholder environment, while remaining aligned with national objectives and regulatory requirements.

A second tension relates to innovation speed versus ethical assurance. Rapid AI deployment may generate efficiency gains but risks outpacing ethical and legal safeguards. The Strategic Governance Framework for Artificial Intelligence (SGF-AI) addresses this challenge by embedding ethical and legal oversight throughout the AI lifecycle, consistent with international calls for ethics-by-design and governance-by-design.

11.3 Institutional Readiness and Differential Capacity

The analysis highlights significant variation in institutional readiness across higher-education systems. Differences in digital infrastructure, governance maturity, leadership commitment, and organizational culture shape universities' ability to adopt and govern AI responsibly.

The Applied College at King Faisal University illustrates how professionally oriented institutions can leverage applied curricula, centralized coordination units, and structured partnerships to accelerate AI integration while maintaining accountability. This finding reinforces the importance of scalable governance frameworks capable of accommodating institutional diversity without sacrificing coherence.

Rather than prescribing uniform governance structures, helix-based models support context-sensitive implementation, enabling institutions to adopt governance mechanisms proportionate to their capacity and strategic role.

11.4 Societal Legitimacy and the Quadruple Helix Dimension

The integration of the Quadruple Helix dimension underscores the centrality of societal legitimacy in AI governance. In higher education, AI systems influence decisions related to admissions, assessment, student support, and institutional planning—domains closely linked to fairness, transparency, and public trust.

The findings indicate that governance legitimacy is strengthened through stakeholder engagement, transparency mechanisms, and AI literacy initiatives targeting students, faculty members, and administrative staff. These practices not only mitigate resistance but also enhance institutional learning and accountability.

In the Saudi context, societal trust is further reinforced by aligning AI governance with public-sector accountability norms and national values, positioning universities as responsible stewards of digital transformation rather than opaque technology adopters.

11.5 Sustainability and the Quintuple Helix Perspective

The incorporation of the Quintuple Helix perspective extends AI governance beyond immediate institutional concerns to include environmental sustainability. Although AI applications in higher education are often perceived as low-impact, their cumulative energy consumption, reliance on digital infrastructure, and contribution to data-centre expansion warrant governance attention.

Embedding sustainability indicators into AI governance frameworks ensures alignment with national sustainability objectives and global commitments, including the United Nations Sustainable Development Goals. This perspective reinforces the argument that responsible AI governance must account for long-term societal and environmental consequences, not solely short-term efficiency gains.

11.6 Synthesis: Conditions for Effective AI Governance in Higher Education

Synthesizing theory, policy, and institutional practice, the discussion identifies several conditions essential for effective AI governance in higher education:

- Strategic alignment between national policy objectives and institutional governance structures.
- Clear role differentiation among universities, government, and industry within helix-based collaboration.
- Institutionalized ethical and legal oversight embedded throughout the AI lifecycle.
- Continuous capacity building to support organizational learning and adaptability.
- **Societal engagement and sustainability integration** to enhance legitimacy and long-term impact.

These conditions collectively support a governance approach capable of balancing innovation with responsibility, autonomy with coordination, and efficiency with public trust.

12. CONCLUSION AND IMPLICATIONS

Artificial intelligence is reshaping higher education by transforming teaching and learning processes, administrative governance, research management, and institutional decision-making. In policy-driven national contexts such as Saudi Arabia—where AI is positioned as a strategic enabler of economic diversification, human-capital development, and global competitiveness under Vision 2030—universities are expected to function not only as sites of technological adoption, but as strategic governance actors responsible for ethical stewardship, regulatory compliance, and societal trust.

This chapter has demonstrated that the integration of artificial intelligence into higher education is fundamentally a governance challenge rather than a purely technical one. Fragmented, project-based, or compliance-only approaches are insufficient to manage the ethical, legal, organizational, and societal complexities associated with AI systems embedded in core academic and administrative functions. Instead, effective AI adoption requires coordinated, multi-actor governance arrangements capable of aligning innovation with accountability and long-term sustainability.

12.1 Summary of Key Findings

The analysis confirms that the Triple Helix model, when reconceptualized as a governance architecture rather than solely an innovation framework, provides a robust foundation for coordinating AI adoption in higher education. By structuring interaction among universities, government, and industry, the model enables alignment between national strategy, institutional implementation, and technological capability.

The Saudi case illustrates how centralized strategic vision—articulated through Vision 2030 and the National Strategy for Data and Artificial Intelligence (NS-DAI)—can coexist with institutional autonomy when governance mechanisms support coordination, accountability, and competency development. Universities emerge as operational anchors translating national policy into educational practice, while government entities provide strategic direction and regulatory baselines, and industry partners contribute applied expertise and innovation pathways.

The empirical illustration drawn from the Applied College at King Faisal University further demonstrates how helix-based governance principles can be operationalized within professionally oriented higher-education settings. Through applied diploma programs, centralized AI coordination structures, protocol-driven engagements, and continuous capacity building, the case shows that responsible AI governance is achievable even in rapidly transforming institutional environments.

12.2 Contributions to Theory

From a theoretical perspective, this chapter advances helix-based governance scholarship by proposing the Strategic Governance Framework for Artificial Intelligence (SGF-AI) tailored specifically to higher education. The framework integrates four interdependent governance domains—strategic alignment, ethical and legal oversight, operational coordination, and multidimensional impact evaluation—within a single, scalable architecture.

By extending the analysis through Quadruple and Quintuple Helix perspectives, the chapter demonstrates how societal engagement and sustainability considerations can be systematically embedded within AI governance. This contribution responds directly to growing calls in the literature to move beyond innovation-centric models toward governance frameworks capable of addressing ethical legitimacy, public trust, and long-term societal impact.

The chapter thus contributes to the evolution of helix theory by illustrating its applicability not only to innovation systems, but also to complex governance challenges arising from transformative digital technologies.

12.3 Policy Implications

The findings carry several important implications for policymakers overseeing AI-driven transformation in higher education. First, national AI strategies should be complemented by explicit expectations regarding institutional governance capacity, including the establishment of AI governance units, ethical review mechanisms, and compliance structures within universities.

Second, coherence across data-protection, cybersecurity, and education regulation is essential to reduce fragmentation and implementation risk. While legal frameworks such as the Personal Data Protection Law and national cybersecurity controls provide a necessary compliance baseline, their effectiveness depends on universities' ability to institutionalize governance processes rather than treating regulation as a procedural requirement.

Third, helix-based collaboration mechanisms should be formalized to ensure sustained coordination among universities, government entities, and industry partners. Informal or ad hoc collaboration is insufficient in technologically complex domains such as artificial intelligence, where governance failures may have far-reaching ethical and societal consequences.

For Saudi Arabia, these implications reinforce the importance of aligning higher-education governance reforms with Vision 2030 objectives while preserving institutional flexibility to innovate responsibly. The phased policy roadmap proposed earlier in this chapter offers a practical mechanism for operationalizing these principles over the coming decade.

12.4 Implications for University Leadership and Practice

University leadership plays a decisive role in translating national AI strategies into institutional action. The chapter's findings suggest that leadership commitment to governance coherence, ethical responsibility, and continuous organizational upskilling is essential for sustainable AI adoption.

Establishing dedicated governance structures, investing in staff development, and embedding ethical considerations into decision-making processes enhance institutional readiness and resilience. For applied and professionally oriented institutions—such as the Applied College at King Faisal University—helix-based governance offers a pathway for aligning academic programs with labour-market needs while maintaining public accountability.

These institutions can function as innovation intermediaries, bridging policy objectives and industry demand through applied education, structured collaboration, and responsible technology deployment. Such a role strengthens both institutional relevance and societal trust.

12.5 Implications for Future Research

The chapter also identifies several directions for future research. Empirical studies employing interviews, surveys, or comparative case analyses could deepen understanding of how AI governance mechanisms operate across diverse institutional contexts. Comparative research examining helix-based governance models in different national systems would further elucidate the conditions under which such frameworks enhance effectiveness and legitimacy.

In addition, future scholarship should explore the long-term sustainability implications of AI adoption in higher education, including environmental impact, energy consumption, and evolving ethical norms. As generative AI technologies continue to advance, governance research must remain attentive to new forms of risk, responsibility, and institutional adaptation.

12.6 Concluding Remarks

In conclusion, artificial intelligence presents higher education with unprecedented opportunities alongside complex governance challenges. The Saudi experience demonstrates that ambitious national strategies can catalyse innovation, but their success ultimately depends on universities' capacity to govern AI responsibly, coherently, and transparently.

By integrating helix-based governance models with ethical oversight, societal engagement, and sustainability considerations, higher-education systems can navigate digital transformation in a manner that balances innovation with public trust. The Strategic Governance Framework for Artificial Intelligence (SGF-AI) advanced in this chapter offers a transferable model for policy-driven and emerging economies seeking to harness AI for educational advancement while safeguarding ethical and societal values.

As higher education continues to evolve in the age of artificial intelligence, governance will remain the defining factor shaping its contribution to inclusive, legitimate, and sustainable development.

REFERENCES

Borenstein, J., Howard, A., & Howard, D. (2022). Ethical governance of artificial intelligence in education. *AI & Society, 37*(4), 1465–1478. DOI: 10.1007/s00146-021-01258-9

Bowen, G. A. (2009). Document analysis as a qualitative research method. *Qualitative Research Journal, 9*(2), 27–40. DOI: 10.3316/QRJ0902027

Brkan, M. (2021). Artificial intelligence and data protection: A legal perspective. *Common Market Law Review, 58*(5), 1337–1370.

Carayannis, E. G., & Barth, T. D. (2021). The Quintuple Helix innovation model: Global warming as a challenge and driver for innovation. *Journal of Innovation and Entrepreneurship, 10*(1), 1–12. DOI: 10.1186/s13731-021-00162-x

Carayannis, E. G., & Campbell, D. F. J. (2009). "Mode 3" and Quadruple Helix innovation systems: Twenty-first-century democratic innovation. *International Journal of Technology Management, 46*(3–4), 201–234. DOI: 10.1504/IJTM.2009.023374

Cotton, D. R. E., Cotton, P. A., & Shipway, J. R. (2023). Educators' perspectives on artificial intelligence in higher education. *Computers & Education, 197*, 104763. DOI: 10.1016/j.compedu.2023.104763

Creswell, J. W., & Poth, C. N. (2018). *Qualitative inquiry and research design: Choosing among five approaches* (4th ed.). Sage Publications.

Etzkowitz, H., & Leydesdorff, L. (1995). The Triple Helix of university–industry–government relations. *Research Policy, 24*(2), 197–210. DOI: 10.1016/0048-7333(94)00744-6

Etzkowitz, H., & Leydesdorff, L. (2021). The Triple Helix: A twenty-five-year retrospective. *Science & Public Policy, 48*(2), 145–157. DOI: 10.1093/scipol/scaa038

Floridi, L. (2021). The ethics of artificial intelligence: Principles, challenges, and opportunities. *Philosophy & Technology, 34*(4), 1377–1394. DOI: 10.1007/s13347-020-00402-y

Ivančić, L., Vuksanović Herceg, I., & Dabić, M. (2022). Triple Helix and digital transformation: A systematic literature review. *Technological Forecasting and Social Change, 174*, 121204. DOI: 10.1016/j.techfore.2021.121204

Middlehurst, R. (2020). Governing higher education in a digital age. *Higher Education Policy, 33*(4), 695–713. DOI: 10.1057/s41307-020-00186-1

Organisation for Economic Co-operation and Development (OECD). (2019). *Recommendation of the Council on Artificial Intelligence*. OECD Publishing. https://legalinstruments.oecd.org/en/instruments/OECD-LEGAL-0449

Organisation for Economic Co-operation and Development (OECD). (2021). *AI and data governance in education*. OECD Publishing., DOI: 10.1787/50c98cbd-

Organisation for Economic Co-operation and Development (OECD). (2023). *OECD digital education outlook 2023: Pushing the frontiers with AI*. OECD Publishing., DOI: 10.1787/c74f03de-

Saudi Data and AI Authority (SDAIA). (2022). *National strategy for data and artificial intelligence*. https://www.sdaia.gov.sa

Saudi Data and AI Authority (SDAIA). (2023). *Personal data protection law*. https://www.sdaia.gov.sa

UNESCO. (2021). *Recommendation on the ethics of artificial intelligence*. UNESCO Publishing. https://www.unesco.org/en/artificial-intelligence/ethics

UNESCO. (2023). *Guidance for generative AI in education and research*. UNESCO Publishing. https://www.unesco.org/en/articles/guidance-generative-ai-education-and-research

Vision 2030. (2016). *Saudi Vision 2030*. https://www.vision2030.gov.sa

Chapter 8

Governing Intelligent Futures Through AI-Ready Education Ecosystems in the Triple Helix Model:

Extended Helix Regimes of Educational Management

Ashraf Alam
https://orcid.org/0000-0001-6178-1187
Alliance University, Bengaluru, India

ABSTRACT

This chapter theorises AI-ready education ecosystems as complex, multi-scalar infrastructures for governing intelligent futures. Integrating National Innovation Systems, Triple and extended Helix models, socio-technical transition theory, capability-oriented justice frames, and learning-sciences metatheory, it reconceptualises education as a strategic regime that co-produces AI competencies, normative orientations, and civic agency. Through ideal-typical AI strategy regimes, multilevel talent pipelines, industry-university-government partnership modalities, and reflexive governance architectures, the chapter assembles a conceptual matrix linking actor constellations, knowledge flows, and regulatory instruments. It advances a design vocabulary centred on human-AI co-flourishing, epistemic and data justice, ecological responsibility, and experimentalist public-value governance, and sketches a research agenda for academics, policymakers, and digital learning technologists.

DOI: 10.4018/979-8-3373-7620-2.ch008

1. INTRODUCTION

1.1 AI as a General-Purpose Technology and Epistemic Inflection in Education

Artificial intelligence functions as a *general-purpose technology* that reorganises not only industrial production and public administration but also the deep grammar of knowledge creation, circulation, and recognition. In education, AI systems reconfigure what counts as expertise, how problems are framed, and which cognitive tasks remain distinctly human. Large scale models and data intensive infrastructures compress the time between discovery, dissemination, and uptake of knowledge, while adaptive platforms and algorithmic tutors modulate learning trajectories in real time (Barry et al., 2025; Byrne et al., 2025; AlMalki & Durugbo, 2024; Pitan, 2023). Credentialing architectures begin to incorporate AI mediated portfolios, simulations, and performance analytics that track latent competences rather than only discrete course completions. This constellation marks an inflection in the epistemic order of education in which human learners increasingly co construct understanding with *non-human cognitive agents*. AI readiness therefore cannot be reduced to technical skill acquisition and instead requires a systemic reorientation of educational ecosystems toward hybrid human machine intelligence.

1.2 Triple Helix Lens and the Reconceptualisation of Education as Strategic Regime

The *Triple Helix* model interprets universities, governments, and industry as intertwined helices that jointly generate innovation capacity, each helix partially assuming functions traditionally associated with the others. Within AI intensive societies, this configuration renders education a strategic regime rather than a peripheral human capital pipeline. Universities become loci for AI knowledge production, ethical deliberation, and talent formation. Governments architect regulatory and funding environments that privilege certain AI applications, indirectly shaping curricular priorities and institutional strategies (Arman & Al-Qudsi, 2024; González-Aleu et al., 2024; Moldashev et al., 2025). Industry influences the semantics of AI competence through competency frameworks, vendor certifications, and proprietary platforms. Education is therefore simultaneously an object of AI innovation, a medium through which AI norms and skills are reproduced, and a critical arena where societal visions of intelligent futures are legitimised or contested. An AI-ready education ecosystem must be understood as an emergent property of these coupled helices rather than as an isolated sectoral subsystem.

1.3 Systemic Problematisation of AI Education and Coordination Failures Across Helices

The rapid insertion of AI into economic and civic life exposes structural incoherences that cannot be addressed through incremental curriculum tweaks or isolated policy reforms. AI policy often evolves within digital economy or industrial competitiveness frames, while higher education strategies follow separate logics anchored in legacy disciplines, fiscal constraints, and massification pressures. The result is a misalignment between AI curricula and labour market structures, fragmented responsibilities for AI ethics, and uneven distribution of AI learning opportunities across regions and social groups. These pathologies signify coordination failures across helices, driven by incompatible temporal horizons, divergent accountability regimes, and asymmetries of information and power (Yessimova et al., 2024; Figueiredo et al., 2023; Giannini et al., 2025). Without an explicit conceptual architecture that links innovation theory, education theory, and governance theory, interventions risk amplifying inequities, entrenching proprietary dependencies, and undermining democratic oversight. A robust narrative review therefore must reframe AI education as a complex governance challenge rather than a technocratic curriculum problem.

1.4 Guiding Questions, Conceptual Boundaries, and Core Constructs of AI-Ready Ecosystems

This chapter investigates how AI-ready education ecosystems can be theorised as multi-level, multi-actor formations that mediate the translation of AI capabilities into socially legitimate and ethically defensible practices. Guiding questions centre on how Triple Helix configurations structure AI talent pipelines, how governance architectures orchestrate or destabilise collaboration in AI education, and how extended helix models that include civil society and ecological systems can support justice oriented AI learning. The conceptual terrain is delimited to higher, vocational, and professional education while recognising their articulation with schools, corporate training, and lifelong learning circuits. Core constructs include the *AI talent pipeline* understood as a sequence of formal and informal learning spaces, the *education governance node* as a locus of decision making and norm setting, and the *normative orientation* that encodes priorities such as competitiveness, public value, or justice. These constructs anchor the subsequent theoretical elaborations.

1.5 Argumentative Architecture and Anticipated Contributions for Global Stakeholders

The chapter unfolds through a sequenced architecture that moves from abstract theoretical integration to governance-oriented synthesis. The second section develops an integrated foundation that interweaves innovation systems theory, Triple Helix logics, socio-technical transition perspectives, and educational theory in order to conceptualise AI-ready ecosystems as complex adaptive systems. The third section examines national and regional AI strategies and policy architectures, elucidating how differing strategic imaginaries position education within AI agendas. The fourth section reconceptualises universities and education systems as AI innovation infrastructures that span curricula, pedagogies, and lifelong learning pathways. The fifth section analyses industry, startups, and innovation ecosystems as co designers and co users of AI education architectures. The sixth section advances governance and ethics frameworks that extend beyond the Triple Helix to Quadruple and Quintuple configurations. The concluding section distils normative design principles and a conceptual research agenda for academics, policy makers, workforce strategists, and digital learning technologists across diverse global contexts.

2. THEORETICAL FOUNDATIONS FOR INNOVATION ORIENTED AI EDUCATION ECOSYSTEMS

2.1 Classical and Contemporary Innovation Metatheories for AI Intensive Societies

Innovation metatheories such as *National Innovation Systems*, *Regional Innovation Systems*, and *Sectoral Innovation Systems* conceptualise economic transformation as the emergent outcome of structured interactions among firms, universities, regulatory agencies, and financial intermediaries embedded in specific institutional architectures. Within these lenses, education is a distributed cognitive infrastructure that generates absorptive capacity, problem framing repertoires, and boundary spanning competences rather than a passive reservoir of generic labour (Chatterjee & Roy, 2025; Planck et al., 2025; Alam & Mohanty, 2024). Contemporary constructs such as *open innovation*, *mission-oriented innovation policy*, and *transformative innovation policy* foreground transdisciplinary collaboration, challenge driven coalitions, and experimental policy mixes in which educational organisations become strategic nodes of innovation regimes. When AI is introduced into these architectures, AI readiness is variably framed as narrow technical proficiency, systemic socio technical reflexivity, or capability expansion. These divergent emphases are rendered commensurable in Table 1, which consolidates key ontological assumptions, educational roles, AI configurations, and design implications into a single comparative matrix that underpins the remainder of this chapter.

2.2 Triple Helix Logics, Hybrid Institutional Configurations, and Educational Regimes

The *Triple Helix* construct interprets universities, governments, and industry as interpenetrating institutional helices whose roles partially overlap and recursively co evolve through boundary spanning interactions. In AI intensive environments, this configuration yields hybrid formations such as university-based AI accelerators that host public sector pilots, state supported AI institutes with embedded teaching mandates, and corporate academies that emulate university like curricula and credentialing architectures (Mêgnigbêto, 2025; Agbebi et al., 2024; Haryadi et al., 2025). Education becomes a strategic regime where academic logics of epistemic authenticity, bureaucratic logics of procedural accountability, market logics of competitiveness, and civic logics of public value are simultaneously enacted and periodically recalibrated. These dynamics generate joint AI curricula, shared data infrastructures, multi stakeholder advisory bodies, and cross appointed practitioner scholars who mediate tensions among helices. When the Triple Helix lens is read against the metatheoretical patterns summarised in Table 1, AI education appears as a power saturated field in which institutional logics, partnership modalities, and governance arrangements co determine whose AI capabilities are cultivated, recognised, and legitimised across the ecosystem.

2.3 Socio Technical Transition Perspectives and Governance Architectures for AI Ecosystems

Socio technical transition constructs such as the *Multi-Level Perspective* and *socio-technical systems theory* conceptualise AI as part of nested dynamics that involve macro level landscape trends, meso level regime structures, and micro level niches where alternative configurations are incubated. Within this schema, education is both a regime stabiliser that reproduces dominant AI imaginaries through standardised curricula and credentialing, and a niche incubator that nurtures exploratory human machine assemblages in experimental programmes, living labs, and interdisciplinary studios (Ezeuduji et al., 2023; Morrar & Arman, 2024; Qu & Kim, 2025). Governance constructs such as *network governance*, *meta-governance*, and *public value governance* emphasise coordination through negotiated interdependence, reflexive steering, and iterative learning among distributed actors, rather than centralised command. To navigate AI intensive transitions coherently, stakeholders require a consolidated view of how these metatheories conceptualise institutions, learning, and technological agency, which is precisely what the comparative matrix in Table 1 provides.

Table 1. Comparative Metatheoretical Matrix for AI Ready Education Ecosystems

Metatheoretical Lens	Core Ontological Assumptions	View of Education Assemblages	Configuration of AI Logics	Implications for Ecosystem Design
National Innovation Systems	Co-evolving institutions, technologies, and markets within territorially bounded development complexes	Human capital and organisational learning reservoir that amplifies absorptive capacity and productivity	General purpose enabling technology aligned with industrial upgrading and techno economic competitiveness trajectories	Prioritise STEM intensive pipelines, research intensive universities, and cluster-based AI skills formation architectures
Triple Helix Configurations	Interpenetrating institutional spheres with recursive role hybridisation and boundary spanning actor networks	Strategic regime for talent formation, normative orientation, and cross sector brokerage among helices	Co-produced capability distributed across universities, firms, and states through joint infrastructures and platforms	Engineer joint AI curricula, co funded laboratories, and coordinated talent governance with embedded ethical safeguards
Multi-Level Socio Technical Transitions	Nested landscape, regime, and niche dynamics with path dependence, lock in, and emergent tipping points	Arena that stabilises dominant regimes while nurturing experimental learning niches and alternative imaginaries	Regime stabiliser and disruptor shaped by transition pressures, protective spaces, and reflexive learning loops	Embed protected AI learning niches, adaptive monitoring, and phased scaling trajectories for pedagogical and organisational innovations
Capability Oriented Justice Frames	Individuals and collectives as capability bearing agents situated within unequal structural and data ecosystems	Mechanism for expanding substantive freedoms, voice, and epistemic recognition for diverse learner constituencies	Socio-technical assemblage with distributive, procedural, and recognition effects on capability sets	Hard wire equity, data justice, and participatory co design into AI curricula, credentialing architectures, and governance regimes
Learning Sciences and Design Metatheory	Learning as situated, socially mediated, and tool configured activity within complex adaptive systems	Complex arrangement of learners, artefacts, tasks, and institutions that co-produce expertise and identities	Mediating artefact that reshapes cognition, collaboration, feedback ecologies, and assessment configurations	Design iterative, analytics informed, universally designed AI pedagogies with strong metacognitive and self-regulatory scaffolding

Table 1 shows that each metatheoretical lens encodes distinctive ontologies of institutions, epistemologies of learning, and normative horizons for AI deployment, which generate divergent yet partially compatible design heuristics for AI ready education ecosystems. National innovation views foreground territorial competitiveness and industrial upgrading, Triple Helix configurations emphasise organisational choreography and hybridisation, socio technical transition perspectives highlight temporal dynamics and niche experimentation, capability-oriented frames prioritise distributional and recognition justice, while learning sciences metatheory centres micro level learning processes in complex adaptive systems. When integrated, these lenses invite decision makers to treat AI education reforms as coordinated interventions in a complex ecosystem, where infrastructural investment, curriculum architecture, partnership modalities, and regulatory instruments must be synchronised and continually recalibrated rather than adjusted in isolation.

2.4 Critical, Decolonial, and Justice Oriented Lenses for AI Education Ecosystem Design

Critical and decolonial constructs interpret AI infrastructures as deeply entangled with long histories of extraction, racialisation, and epistemic domination, which shape how AI ready education ecosystems allocate risks, opportunities, and recognition. Within this register, ostensibly neutral programmes that promote AI literacy can become sites where certain languages, ontologies, and knowledge traditions are centred, while others are marginalised through dataset composition, canonical examples, and assessment standards (Yang & Park, 2025; Otarola et al., 2025; Mayho et al., 2024). Concepts such as *data colonialism*, *algorithmic discrimination*, and *epistemic injustice* foreground how AI mediated classification, prediction, and recommendation can reproduce structural asymmetries if not subjected to robust scrutiny and democratic oversight. The *Capability Approach* reframes evaluation of AI education away from narrow metrics such as enrolment counts or short-term employment, toward expansion of real freedoms, including the capacity to understand, challenge, and redesign the AI systems that structure social reproduction. Read together with the metatheories in Table 1, these lenses redirect design attention toward collective data sovereignty, linguistic and epistemic plurality, and alignment of AI learning infrastructures with planetary boundaries and intergenerational responsibility.

2.5 Educational Metatheories and Integrated Frames for AI Ready Learning Architectures

Educational metatheories such as *socio-constructivism*, *communities of practice*, *activity theory*, *transformative learning*, *connectivism*, and *Universal Design for Learning* conceptualise learning as distributed across people, artefacts, and environments, with identity formation and power relations woven into everyday pedagogical practice. Within this ensemble, AI systems operate as mediating artefacts that configure participation structures, feedback regimes, and representations of knowledge, which can either amplify or constrain learner agency depending on design and governance choices (Chfadi et al., 2025; Senthil et al., 2025; Guo et al., 2025). Learning analytics frameworks and *design-based research* approaches provide methodological scaffolds for iteratively engineering AI intensive learning environments that are adaptive yet transparent, personalised yet non-discriminatory, and data rich yet privacy preserving. Competency based architectures recast curricula as orchestrated progressions of demonstrable capabilities, within which AI systems can support simulation-based practice, granular formative assessment, and personalised pathways without eroding academic integrity (Mulyadi et al., 2024; Thomas et al., 2025; Pinedo-López et al., 2025). Interpreted through the integrative lens provided by Table 1, these educational constructs imply that AI ready learning architectures must align micro level pedagogy, meso level institutional culture, and macro level innovation and governance regimes in a coherent manner, so that learners develop technical fluency, ethical discernment, socio political awareness, and collaborative problem solving dispositions within a single, deliberately orchestrated ecosystem.

3. NATIONAL AND REGIONAL AI STRATEGIES AND POLICY ARCHITECTURES FOR EDUCATION-CENTRIC TRIPLE HELIX

3.1 Ideal-Typical AI Strategy Regimes and the Positioning of Education

National and regional AI strategies crystallise distinct *governance regimes* that encode implicit theories of growth, security, democracy, and justice, and these regimes position education in very different ways. Competitiveness oriented regimes treat AI as a general-purpose productivity engine and configure education as a skills pipeline that feeds high value sectors (Panta & Thapaliya, 2025; Nasir et al., 2025; Alam & Mohanty, 2023). Security oriented regimes interpret AI as a strategic asset for defence, cyber resilience, and strategic autonomy, and mandate education systems that produce technically elite but tightly vetted cohorts. Public-value oriented regimes frame AI as a lever for social innovation and welfare optimisation, while justice-oriented regimes foreground redistribution, recognition, and ecological responsibility in AI design (Lulaj & Brajković, 2025; Bonenberg & Angoneze-Grela, 2023; Jumiyati, 2024). Hybrid regimes seek to combine these imperatives but often produce internal contradictions. These variations can be formalised as an ideal-typical typology, summarised in Table 2, which links strategy regimes to discursive frames, educational roles, instrument choices, and characteristic Triple Helix configurations.

3.2 Policy Instruments, Institutional Architectures, and Strategy-Education Coupling

Policy architectures operationalise AI strategy regimes through specific *instrument mixes* and institutional arrangements that couple or decouple education from AI objectives. Instruments include competitive grants for AI centres, tax credits for workforce upskilling, performance-linked funding for universities, accreditation standards for AI programmes, regulatory sandboxes for AI in education, and public procurement schemes that favour AI infused solutions (Park, 2024; Liu et al., 2025; Carayannis & Morawska, 2023). These instruments are enacted through ministries, funding councils, innovation agencies, quality assurance bodies, and regional authorities whose mandates may align or conflict. Table 2 provides a compact matrix that juxtaposes AI strategy regimes with dominant discourses, educational framings, instrument repertoires, and typical Triple Helix constellations, thereby revealing how instrument choices stabilise certain educational roles while marginalising others.

Table 2. Ideal-Typical AI Strategy Regimes and Educational Roles

AI Strategy Regime	Dominant Policy Discourse and Imaginary	Positioning of Education within the Regime	Characteristic Policy Instrument Repertoires	Typical Triple Helix and Extended Helix Configuration
Competitiveness-Driven Regime	Innovation race, productivity frontier expansion, global value chain upgrading	Skills pipeline and research engine for high-tech export sectors	R and D tax credits, excellence grants, STEM expansion funding, performance-based contracts	Strong industry university alliances, state as enabler, limited civil society involvement
Security-Driven Regime	Strategic autonomy, cyber sovereignty, critical infrastructure resilience	Elite technical cadre formation and sensitive domain vetting	Classified research funds, security clearance-based fellowships, restricted data sandboxes	Tight state steering, specialised universities, security agencies as latent fourth helix
Public-Value-Driven Regime	Inclusive innovation, welfare optimisation, data-informed public services	Civic infrastructure for AI literacies and public sector innovation capacity	Challenge prizes, mission-oriented labs, public sector AI academies, open data mandates	Balanced university state industry triads, strong public sector anchor, consultative forums
Justice-Oriented Regime	Data justice, redistribution, recognition, ecological and intergenerational responsibility	Capability-expanding institution for marginalised groups and critical AI stewardship	Equity-weighted funding, community AI fellowships, participatory design grants, audit mandates	Quadruple and Quintuple Helix with strong civil society, community, and environmental actors
Hybrid-Regime Configuration	Mixed signals of growth, security, welfare, and rights, often rhetorically harmonised	Fragmented assemblage combining skills pipeline, elite training, and pockets of inclusion	Layered incentive schemes, overlapping strategies, ad hoc pilots, fragmented regulatory tools	Complex, contested Triple Helix plus episodic civil society engagement and platform influence

The typology in Table 2 shows that AI strategy regimes are not merely rhetorical postures but structuring devices that allocate resources, authority, and legitimacy across the education system. Competitiveness-driven regimes channel investment into research-intensive universities and STEM-heavy programmes, often privileging metropolitan hubs and deepening regional stratification. Security-driven regimes produce highly specialised institutions and programmes that may be insulated from broader pedagogical innovation and public scrutiny. Public-value-driven regimes foster strong linkages between universities and public administrations, creating AI labs and academies that incubate data-informed social policies. Justice-oriented regimes attempt to reconfigure curricula, credentials, and governance to expand the capabilities of historically marginalised communities and address ecological constraints. Hybrid regimes, which are prevalent in practice, generate tensions between growth imperatives and justice commitments, requiring sophisticated policy coordination to avoid symbolic inclusion and substantive exclusion.

3.3 Regional Asymmetries, Peripheral Contexts, and Transnational Reconfigurations

The effects of AI strategy regimes are refracted through regional development patterns, producing starkly different AI education ecologies in metropolitan cores, secondary cities, and peripheral territories. Agglomeration dynamics concentrate AI research institutes, high-end computing resources, and flagship programmes in global and national hubs, while peripheral regions rely on satellite campuses, distance provision, or imported training services. Concepts such as *brain drain*, *brain circulation*, and *talent pipelines* become salient as learners and professionals migrate in response to scholarships, wage differentials, and prestige hierarchies (Daliri, 2024; Ferdinands et al., 2024; Samperio Sánchez, 2023). Transnational education arrangements, including joint degrees, cross-border campuses, and global MOOCs, reconfigure spatialities of AI learning by decoupling place of instruction from place of accreditation and employment. Regional alliances and supranational bodies add another layer by issuing AI capacity-building frameworks and funding cross-border initiatives that may either mitigate or exacerbate existing asymmetries (Viale & Cucchiarini, 2025; Kowch, 2025; Thomas et al., 2024). Within each AI strategy regime in Table 2, these spatial dynamics determine whether education systems function as centripetal forces that concentrate AI capabilities or as centrifugal mechanisms that redistribute knowledge and opportunity.

3.4 Policy Narratives, Discursive Frames, and Legitimation of AI Education

AI strategies are sustained by *policy narratives* and *sociotechnical imaginaries* that render particular constellations of actors and instruments legitimate. Narratives of skills gaps and innovation races support competitiveness-driven regimes, while storylines of existential cyber threats and strategic dependence energise security-driven regimes (Alam & Mohanty, 2022; Zhao Yi et al., 2025; Weidenfeld & Anusik, 2025). Public-value-driven regimes draw on imaginaries of data-responsive welfare states and evidence-informed service delivery, whereas justice-oriented regimes invoke frames of digital rights, climate responsibility, and decolonial reparations. These narratives circulate through white papers, speeches, media coverage, and consultation documents, shaping how education stakeholders understand their obligations and opportunities (Zhuang & Zhou, 2023; Cervini, 2025; Kumar et al., 2024). The regimes catalogued in Table 2 can thus be interpreted not only as clusters of instruments but as discursive formations that organise expectations about who should be educated in AI, for what purposes, and under whose authority. Discursive choices influence whether AI education is framed as a technocratic fix, a democratic project, or a site of structural contestation, and they condition the willingness of learners, educators, and communities to participate in AI-related reforms.

3.5 Conceptual Tensions, Design Dilemmas, and Coordination Challenges in AI Policy

The architecture of AI strategies aimed at education-centric Triple Helix configurations is traversed by persistent conceptual tensions and design dilemmas. Centralisation can enable coherent strategic direction, shared infrastructures, and uniform quality standards, but may stifle local experimentation and ignore contextual specificities (Zhuang et al., 2024; Suminar et al., 2025; Zhuang et al., 2025). Decentralisation can empower regions and institutions but may fragment standards, data regimes, and investment flows. Market oriented approaches promise responsiveness and innovation but risk overproducing short-cycle credentials and underproviding foundational and critical capacities. Rights-based and justice-oriented approaches prioritise equity and participation but may face resource constraints and political contestation (Van Dijk, 2025; Bruno et al., 2025; Kim et al., 2025). Temporal tensions also arise between short-term employability goals and long-term capacity for critical inquiry, creativity, and civic stewardship. The hybrid regimes described in Table 2 often amplify these contradictions, especially when growth, security, welfare, and justice objectives coexist without clear prioritisation or coordination mechanisms. Effective design therefore requires meta-governance capacities that can orchestrate policy mixes, reconcile competing logics, and iteratively recalibrate AI education strategies in response to societal feedback and technological evolution.

4. UNIVERSITIES AND EDUCATION SYSTEMS AS AI INNOVATION INFRASTRUCTURES

4.1 Universities as Entrepreneurial-Civic-Platform Institutions in AI Ecosystems

Universities in AI intensive societies operate as *entrepreneurial-civic-platform institutions* that simultaneously generate knowledge, cultivate talent, mediate public reasoning, and orchestrate digital infrastructures. As entrepreneurial entities they host spinout ventures, joint laboratories, and patent portfolios that feed AI intensive value chains. As civic institutions they anchor democratic deliberation about algorithmic systems, facilitate public engagement with complex socio-technical controversies, and train professionals for public-sector transformation (Cooke, 2025; de Oliveira et al., 2024; Carayannis et al., 2025). As platform institutions they integrate cloud services, data repositories, and learning analytics environments that reconfigure how teaching, research, and administration are performed. These layered roles position universities as central nodes in AI innovation ecosystems, yet also expose them to platform dependency, reputational risk, and ethical liability (Thorpe et al., 2025; Rossoni et al., 2024; da Rocha et al., 2024). Within this configuration, universities must align their internal governance, data architectures, and partnership strategies with broader national and regional AI regimes, while also articulating how different educational levels contribute to AI talent pipelines as synthesised later in Table 3.

4.2 Formal AI Curricula and Programmatic Architectures as Innovation Engines

Formal AI curricula constitute the structured backbone of AI talent formation, embedding *competency-based architectures* within degree programmes, minors, and interdisciplinary tracks. These architectures must reconcile deep disciplinary expertise in machine learning, data science, and algorithmic design with transversal capacities such as systems thinking, ethical reasoning, and socio-political analysis of AI deployment (Phiri, 2024; Liu & Jiang, 2025; binti Saaidun et al., 2025). Curriculum design involves sequencing foundational mathematics, statistical reasoning, and computational thinking with advanced topics in representation learning, optimisation, and human-computer interaction, while maintaining porous interfaces with law, humanities, and domain sciences. Modularisation and micro-credential layering allow programmes to adapt to rapidly evolving AI toolchains without sacrificing conceptual depth (Flechas et al., 2023; Ma & Yang, 2024; Alam, 2023c). Accreditation criteria, internal quality assurance, and external advisory boards become powerful steering devices that can either entrench narrow technicalism or foster reflexive, justice-oriented orientations. The distribution of these formal provisions across schooling, undergraduate, postgraduate, and professional levels, and their relational positioning within innovation ecosystems, is captured conceptually in Table 3.

4.3 Non-Formal, Informal, and Lifelong AI Learning Pathways as Distributed Infrastructures

Non-formal and lifelong AI learning pathways complement formal curricula by providing flexible, modular, and context-specific opportunities for learners at different life stages and in diverse institutional settings. These pathways include corporate academies, professional-development institutes, bootcamps, online platforms, community technology centres, and maker spaces that deliver AI-related knowledge through short courses, workshops, micro-credentials, and practice communities (Arya et al., 2025; Rosienkiewicz et al., 2024; Subrahmanyam, 2025). Such environments frequently operate at the interface of multiple helices, where firms seek rapid reskilling, governments pursue digital inclusion, and civil society organisations address localised problems with AI mediated methods. Recognition, portability, and stackability of learning outcomes become central design concerns, especially when learners attempt to reinsert non-formal achievements into formal qualification frameworks (Bhatia & Kaur, 2024; Petrenko et al., 2025; Holguín Rengifo et al., 2023). The variegated landscape of AI learning opportunities across education levels and institutional forms, and their alignment with different innovation functions, can be read through the design matrix presented in Table 3.

Table 3. Multilevel AI Talent Pipelines across Systems

Education Level or Modality	Core AI-Related Competences	Dominant Pedagogical Paradigms	Lead Triple Helix and Extended Helix Partners	Primary Innovation and Capacity Functions
Upper-Secondary and Schooling	Computational thinking, data literacy, ethical awareness	Inquiry-based learning, project-based learning, design tasks	Schools, education ministries, youth organisations	Early socialisation into AI logics, widening of participation base
Undergraduate and First-Cycle Programmes	Foundational AI theory, programming, modelling, abstraction	Studio-based learning, problem-based learning, lab practica	Universities, industry consortia, standards bodies	Formation of generalist AI workforce, seeding of innovation culture
Postgraduate and Advanced Programmes	Specialised AI methods, research design, socio-technical analysis	Research-based learning, thesis work, interdisciplinary studios	Research universities, public agencies, mission labs	Production of advanced expertise, policy-relevant knowledge creation
Continuing Professional Development	Domain-specific AI application, governance literacy	Work-integrated learning, simulation-based learning, coaching	Employers, professional associations, regulatory authorities	Organisational capability upgrading, diffusion of best practices
Community, Non-Formal, and Civic Learning	Basic AI literacy, critical data skills, civic oversight capacities	Community-of-practice learning, peer-led workshops, experiential projects	Civil society organisations, municipalities, social enterprises	Inclusion of marginalised groups, co-creation of context-sensitive AI uses

Table 3 portrays AI talent development as a multilevel, multi-actor system rather than a unidirectional pipeline, with each level and modality contributing distinct competences, pedagogical logics, and innovation functions. Upper-secondary environments build the cognitive and ethical foundations that enable later specialisation and critical engagement, while undergraduate programmes stabilise a broad AI-capable workforce and inculcate collaborative problem-solving habits. Postgraduate programmes concentrate advanced research and design capabilities that feed both scientific innovation and public-policy experimentation. Continuing professional development regimes ensure that existing workforces adapt to evolving AI assemblages and governance norms, and community-based learning ecologies widen participation, surface local knowledges, and foster democratic oversight. For policy makers and institutional leaders, the table underscores the need to align resourcing, recognition, and quality assurance across these layers so that AI learning opportunities are cumulative, interoperable, and socially responsive rather than fragmented and exclusionary.

4.4 Pedagogical Paradigms and AI-Mediated Learning Designs as Cognitive Infrastructures

Pedagogical paradigms in AI education operate as *cognitive infrastructures* that shape how learners encounter complex abstractions, engage with uncertainty, and internalise ethical commitments. Project-based, problem-based, and challenge-based learning architectures situate AI concepts within authentic socio-technical problems, enabling learners to grapple with messy data, competing objectives, and multi-stakeholder constraints (Gong et al., 2025; Hakeem et al., 2023; Loggers et al., 2025). Studio pedagogy and design thinking frameworks emphasise iterative prototyping, critique, and reflection, which are crucial for responsible AI system design and evaluation. AI-mediated tools such as intelligent tutoring systems, code-generation assistants, and adaptive simulators can scaffold learning by tailoring feedback, modelling solution strategies, and visualising complex model behaviour, provided they remain transparent, contestable, and aligned with human-centred learning objectives (Pereira et al., 2023; Lessa et al., 2023; Fang et al., 2023). When these paradigms are mapped onto the levels distinguished in Table 3, they reveal the importance of calibrating cognitive load, autonomy, and collaboration differently across schooling, higher education, and professional settings, while maintaining a coherent trajectory of deepening conceptual understanding and socio-ethical sophistication.

4.5 Faculty Development, Academic Identities, and System-Level Learning Dynamics

Faculty members and academic-support professionals constitute a critical *meso-level substrate* for AI innovation in education systems, since their identities, capabilities, and networks mediate how strategies and technologies are translated into everyday practice. Faculty development must therefore move beyond ad hoc technical workshops toward sustained communities of practice, cross-disciplinary fellowships, and joint appointments that integrate AI expertise with pedagogy, ethics, and domain knowledge (Alam, 2023b; Tagliazucchi et al., 2024; Shin et al., 2023). Organisational learning constructs highlight the importance of feedback loops through which local experiments in AI-enabled teaching are documented, evaluated, and diffused within and across institutions. At system level, consortia, disciplinary societies, and quality-assurance bodies can function as carriers of AI pedagogical innovation, curating exemplars and articulating norms for responsible AI use in teaching and assessment (Sadykova et al., 2025; Wu et al., 2025; Xia et al., 2025). When faculty trajectories are positioned within the multilevel ecosystem depicted in Table 3, they appear as dynamic connectors who link education levels, sectors, and regions, and whose professional agency can either accelerate inclusive AI readiness or entrench narrow, exclusionary models of AI expertise.

5. INDUSTRY, STARTUPS, AND INNOVATION ECOSYSTEMS IN AI EDUCATION

5.1 Industry as Co-Designer, Co-Funder, and Co-User of AI Education Architectures

Industry actors function as powerful co-designers, co-funders, and intensive co-users of AI education architectures, since their competency frameworks, technology roadmaps, and organisational imaginaries shape what counts as legitimate AI expertise. Through advisory boards, curriculum taskforces, joint steering committees, and informal epistemic communities, firms articulate granular skill taxonomies for data engineering, *machine-learning operations*, AI product management, and *algorithmic governance* (Kunwar & Ulak, 2024; Yazıcı, 2023; Han et al., 2024). These specifications can enrich curricular design by embedding real-world problem structures, toolchains, and workflow logics, yet they can also narrow education to short-term employability targets and vendor-specific stacks. In many jurisdictions, industrial federations and platform corporations participate in multi-actor councils that orchestrate AI workforce strategies, making industry an integral helix in the governance of AI talent pipelines (Nwaichi et al., 2024; Ideland & Serder, 2023; Nzeyimana et al., 2025). The partnership configurations that arise from these interactions, and their distinct educational orientations, are systematically compared in Table 4, which maps leading partnership modalities to theoretical framings, governance mechanisms, and the benefits and risks they generate for AI education ecosystems.

5.2 Work-Integrated Learning and Experiential Regimes in AI-Intensive Domains

Work-integrated learning regimes embed learners within live AI-intensive production environments, thereby fusing disciplinary instruction with situated practice and tacit socialisation. Internships, apprenticeships, cooperative education programmes, dual-study arrangements, and industry-embedded capstone projects position students as legitimate peripheral participants within data science teams, AI research groups, and digital-transformation units (Kunwar & Ulak, 2023; Rubén Cukierman, 2025; Bhimavarapu, 2025). Drawing on constructs such as *experiential learning*, *situated learning*, and *practice theory*, these regimes enable learners to engage with noisy datasets, governance constraints, organisational politics, and multi-stakeholder trade-offs that are difficult to simulate in purely academic settings. At the same time, work-integrated designs raise concerns about unpaid or underpaid labour, exclusion of learners lacking social capital, and instrumentalisation of education for routinised production tasks (Esangbedo et al., 2024; Zhou & Wang, 2023; Sam, 2025). As highlighted later in Table 4, partnership modalities that organise work-integrated learning differ markedly in their balance of pedagogical control, contractual protection, and innovation orientation for students, employers, and universities within AI ecosystems.

5.3 Corporate Platforms, Vendor Credentials, and AI Learning Infrastructures

Corporate AI platforms and vendor-credential ecosystems operate as de facto AI learning infrastructures that permeate or sometimes bypass formal education systems. Large platform providers curate extensive catalogues of online modules, hands-on laboratories, and certification examinations that encode preferred architectures, toolchains, and governance philosophies (Hossen et al., 2025; Alam, 2023a; Schebesch et al., 2024). Universities, training providers, and public agencies frequently integrate these assets into programmes, motivated by access to up-to-date tools, strong labour-market signalling power, and subsidised licences. In this context, platform firms become quasi-regulatory actors that define curricular content, assessment thresholds, and legitimacy markers for AI capabilities. Table 4 positions this modality alongside curriculum committees, joint laboratories, and startup incubators, allowing comparative scrutiny of how corporate platform integration reconfigures educational sovereignty, standard-setting power, and long-term intellectual diversity in AI learning.

Table 4. Typology of Partnership Modalities for AI Education Ecosystems

Partnership Modality	Primary Educational Orientation	Dominant Theoretical Framing	Governance and Coordination Mechanisms	Key Benefits and Latent Risks
Curriculum Co-Design Committees	Alignment of programme outcomes with evolving AI competency architectures	*Co-creation, stakeholder theory, institutional logics*	Formal curriculum boards, memoranda-of-understanding, periodic review cycles	Rich labour-market relevance, risk of curricular capture and attenuation of critical inquiry
Work-Integrated Learning Schemes	Embedding learners in AI-intensive workplaces for situated competence	*Experiential learning, situated learning, practice theory*	Tripartite agreements, learning contracts, structured supervisory triads	Deep practical insight, risk of exploitation, inequitable access, and blurred learner-worker roles
Joint Laboratories and Endowed AI Chairs	Long-horizon knowledge production and translational research training	*Open innovation, Triple Helix, knowledge co-production*	Shared governance councils, cost-sharing formulas, joint intellectual-property norms	Advanced research ecosystems, risk of dependency, IP conflicts, and opaque priority setting
Corporate Platform and Credential Integration	Rapid diffusion of vendor-specific AI tools and procedural proficiencies	*Platform governance, network effects, standard-setting*	Licence agreements, curriculum-embedding templates, shared analytics dashboards	Immediate tool access and recognition, risk of lock-in, monoculture, and data extractivism
Startup Incubators and Social-Innovation Hubs	Entrepreneurial, mission-driven experimentation with AI for public value	*Entrepreneurial ecosystem, mission-oriented innovation, social innovation*	Incubation cohorts, seed-funding schemes, mentorship networks, impact-evaluation frames	High creative intensity and local problem-solving, risk of precarity and uneven scaling

Table 4 illustrate how AI education is increasingly organised through dense contractual and relational infrastructures rather than isolated institutional offerings. Curriculum co-design committees can generate nuanced mappings between academic modules and industrial roles, yet they may marginalise non-market values if civic and ecological perspectives are underrepresented. Work-integrated schemes can deepen learning and employability, while hardening social stratification if entry channels remain informal or exclusionary. Joint laboratories and endowed chairs produce high-end knowledge and symbolic capital but can redirect university agendas toward partner priorities and proprietary horizons. Corporate platform integration accelerates diffusion of cutting-edge tools but compresses curricular diversity and institutional autonomy through subtle standard-setting effects. Startup incubators and social-innovation hubs incubate context-sensitive AI applications and entrepreneurial mindsets, yet they often rely on precarious funding cycles and uneven mentoring ecologies, which can concentrate benefits among already advantaged groups unless explicitly counterbalanced.

5.4 Startups, Entrepreneurial Ecosystems, and Mission-Driven Ventures in AI Education

Startups and entrepreneurial ecosystems constitute dynamic arenas where AI education, innovation, and venture formation are tightly intertwined. University-linked incubators, accelerators, and living labs provide spaces where students, researchers, and practitioners co-produce AI solutions while simultaneously acquiring entrepreneurial literacies such as opportunity recognition, lean experimentation, and impact metrics design (Wang et al., 2025; Liao & Lai, 2023; Wawak et al., 2024). Mission-driven ventures dedicated to inclusive AI literacy, educational diagnostics, and AI-for-social-good embed pedagogical agendas within sustainable business models or hybrid organisational forms. Constructs such as *entrepreneurial ecosystems*, *regional innovation clusters*, and *social entrepreneurship* clarify how dense networks of mentors, investors, service providers, and public agencies determine which AI ideas are nurtured, which communities are engaged, and which learning trajectories are valorised (Fasi, 2024; Daradkah et al., 2023; Navarro et al., 2024). Read together with Table 4, these constructs show that incubators and hubs are not mere infrastructural add-ons but formative environments that can democratise AI capability-building or reinforce elite enclaves, depending on how admission criteria, governance arrangements, and support structures are configured.

5.5 Structural Constraints, Systemic Risks, and Normative Dilemmas in AI Education Partnerships

The proliferation of university–industry–government partnerships in AI education generates structural constraints, systemic risks, and normative dilemmas that demand explicit ethical and regulatory design. Information asymmetries enable dominant firms to steer curricula toward proprietary ecosystems and data infrastructures that maximise their own network effects (Espuny et al., 2025; Liu & Zhu, 2023; Zhao et al., 2024). Resource differentials allow well-funded institutions to secure preferential partnerships and cutting-edge AI infrastructures, leaving less-resourced institutions dependent on generic or outdated offerings. Critical-political-economy constructs highlight how education can be commodified when students become quasi-workers, teachers become platform intermediaries, and universities function as talent pipelines for precarious AI labour markets. *Labour-process theory* points to intensification of surveillance and metric-driven control when AI tools are deployed for learning analytics, productivity monitoring, or automated scoring without robust safeguards (Nwaichi et al., 2025; Addy et al., 2025; Luong, 2023). Environmental and social-justice lenses query the externalities of energy-intensive AI infrastructures and extractive data practices underpinning many modalities summarised in Table 4. Addressing these dilemmas requires governance arrangements grounded in *public-value governance* and *reflexive regulation*, ensuring that AI education partnerships are evaluated against criteria of transparency, accountability, equity, and ecological responsibility, rather than narrow indices of throughput or short-run competitiveness.

6. GOVERNANCE, ETHICS, AND EXTENDED HELIX FRAMEWORKS FOR AI-READY EDUCATION ECOSYSTEMS

6.1 Multi-Level and Networked Governance Architectures for AI Education

Governance of AI-ready education ecosystems unfolds across multiple scales, from institutional boards to transnational standard-setting bodies, and is structured through intricate *multi-level governance* and *network-governance* configurations. At institutional level, senates, councils, and ethics committees negotiate how AI tools, curricula, and data infrastructures are adopted, while sectoral consortia coordinate accreditation norms and professional expectations (Xiong et al., 2025; Cheng et al., 2024; Zhu & Park, 2025). Nationally, ministries, funding councils, and regulatory agencies define strategy regimes, allocate resources, and set compliance thresholds for AI-related programmes. Transnationally, epistemic communities, standards organisations, and platform consortia shape interoperability protocols and soft-law expectations (Xin et al., 2025; Lin et al., 2025; Shyiramunda & van den Bersselaar, 2024). These layers are not hierarchical in a simple sense but are characterised by overlapping jurisdictions, reciprocal dependencies, and contested authority. Table 5 later distils these scalar and helix-based patterns into an integrated governance matrix, linking actor constellations, normative orientations, instrument types, and reflexive capacities that together determine how AI education is steered under conditions of uncertainty, inequality, and rapid technological change.

6.2 Ethical, Legal, and Societal Dimensions of AI Education Governance

Ethical, legal, and societal considerations are not add-ons but constitutive dimensions of AI education governance, since decisions about data, algorithms, and pedagogical uses of AI directly affect rights, opportunities, and social trust. Constructs such as *fairness*, *accountability*, *transparency*, and *contestability* provide normative anchors for evaluating AI-mediated teaching, assessment, and advising, while data-protection regimes and academic-freedom guarantees delineate the legal perimeter within which institutions operate (Kasirye, 2025; Alam, 2022; Wang et al., 2024). When AI systems are deployed for learning analytics, proctoring, or automated feedback, they create new modalities of surveillance, nudging, and behavioural modulation that must be scrutinised through *human-rights* and *public-value* lenses. System-level governance must therefore ensure that impact assessments, ethical review, and stakeholder consultation are embedded in decision processes rather than treated as ex post compliance rituals. The actor arrangements and normative orientations summarised in Table 5 clarify which governance scales and helix configurations are best positioned to safeguard these ethical and legal commitments across diverse AI education settings.

6.3 Extended Helix Configurations and Coordinated Governance of AI Education

Extended helix models, particularly the *Quadruple Helix* and *Quintuple Helix* constructs, expand the traditional university–industry–government triangle by incorporating civil society, cultural institutions, and ecological systems as co-constitutive actors. In AI education, this means that learners, parents, unions, NGOs, local communities, and environmental advocates participate alongside universities, firms, and state agencies in shaping curricula, tools, and governance instruments (Nwaichi et al., 2024; Said & Abdullah, 2024; Hailu, 2024). Coordination across these helices must be scaled to institutional, sectoral, national, and transnational arenas, requiring architectures that tolerate plural values while maintaining system coherence. Table 5 synthesises these configurations into a single integrated matrix, showing how helix combinations at different scales embody distinct actor constellations, normative orientations, and governance logics, and how they distribute reflexive capacities for learning, oversight, and course correction.

Table 5. Integrated Governance for AI-Ready Education Ecosystems

Governance Scale and Helix Configuration	Key Actor Constellations	Dominant Normative Orientation	Governing Instruments for AI Education	Reflexive Capacities and Latent Risks
Institutional Triple-Helix Node	University leadership, faculties, student bodies, local firms, municipal agencies	Quality enhancement, competitiveness, academic integrity	Institutional AI policies, ethics codes, curriculum-approval protocols, data charters	High granularity learning and rapid adaptation, risk of insularity and unequal intra-system capacities
Sectoral Quadruple-Helix Arena	Professional bodies, sectoral firms, unions, NGOs, specialised universities	Public value, safety, professional responsibility	Sectoral accreditation norms, competency frameworks, joint training standards	Strong domain alignment and co-production, risk of path dependence and exclusion of lay perspectives
National Triple-Helix Regime	Ministries, funding councils, peak industry bodies, national university networks	Growth, security, inclusion rhetoric	Strategy documents, funding formulas, regulatory sandboxes, audit and reporting schemes	Macro-coordination and resource mobilisation, risk of politicisation and one-size-fits-all templates
Transnational Quadruple-Helix Network	Standards organisations, platform consortia, regional alliances, advocacy coalitions	Interoperability, reciprocity, soft-law norm convergence	Guidelines, reference frameworks, cross-border projects, voluntary compliance regimes	Norm diffusion and shared benchmarks, risk of normative hegemony and weak local accountability
Quintuple-Helix Sustainability Configuration	Universities, governments, industry, civil society, environmental and community actors	Justice, ecological responsibility, intergenerational stewardship	Participatory foresight, green-AI criteria, impact assessments, co-governed data infrastructures	Deep reflexivity and holistic metrics, risk of slow decision cycles and implementation fatigue

The integrated view in Table 5 demonstrates that governance choices are always mediated by scale and helix composition, which together shape whose interests are foregrounded and which learning loops are activated. Institutional nodes can experiment quickly with AI teaching models and data policies, but their influence on national platforms and international standards is limited. Sectoral arenas can internalise domain-specific ethics and safety norms, though they may become path-dependent and resistant to disruptive innovation. National regimes excel at mobilising resources and signalling priorities, yet they can crowd out local experimentation and minority perspectives. Transnational networks diffuse benchmarks and reference models that lower coordination costs, but they risk entrenching the preferences of powerful states and corporations. Quintuple-Helix configurations bring environmental and community interests into decision processes, enhancing legitimacy and long-term resilience, while also increasing complexity and the need for robust facilitation and conflict-resolution mechanisms.

6.4 Justice-Oriented and Decolonial Perspectives in AI Education Governance

Justice-oriented and decolonial perspectives interrogate how AI education governance may reproduce, or disrupt, entrenched hierarchies of race, class, gender, language, and geography. Constructs such as *epistemic justice*, *data colonialism*, and *intersectionality* highlight the ways curriculum content, training datasets, and institutional priorities can privilege certain knowledge traditions and social groups while rendering others invisible or disposable (Edo & Nwonkwo, 2025; Androniceanu & Colesca, 2025; Fu & Ji, 2024). In many contexts, AI policy discourses emphasise global competitiveness and digital leadership, while neglecting structural under-investment in marginalised communities, linguistic diversity, and local knowledge systems. A justice-oriented governance stance requires power-sharing arrangements in which communities affected by AI deployments participate in agenda-setting, curriculum design, and oversight bodies, mirroring the Quintuple-Helix configurations in Table 5. Decolonial approaches call for rebalancing epistemic authority, including the integration of indigenous, Southern, and subaltern perspectives on technology and development, and for reconfiguring metrics of success away from narrow productivity indicators toward expanded capabilities, cultural survival, and environmental regeneration.

6.5 Reflexive Governance Instruments and Integrated Frameworks for AI-Ready Ecosystems

Reflexive governance instruments are essential for steering AI-ready education ecosystems in ways that acknowledge radical uncertainty, contested values, and evolving evidence. Constructs such as *experimentalist governance*, *adaptive regulation*, and *reflexive law* emphasise iterative cycles of rule-making, monitoring, feedback, and revision, rather than static compliance checklists. In AI education this translates into algorithmic-impact assessments for teaching and assessment tools, dynamic accreditation standards for AI programmes, public registers of AI systems used in educational contexts, and participatory oversight bodies that include students, educators, and community representatives. These instruments must be configured differently at each scale and helix composition identified in Table 5, yet they should collectively form an integrated framework in which institutional experimentation informs national strategies, sectoral standards align with justice commitments, and transnational guidelines remain open to local adaptation. In such a framework, AI education governance becomes a continuous learning process, where normative commitments to human flourishing, democratic accountability, and ecological sustainability are repeatedly tested and recalibrated in light of new technological developments and social feedback.

7. CONCLUSION

7.1 Synthesis of the Conceptual Ensemble and Systemic Insights

The preceding sections have conceptualised AI-ready education ecosystems as complex, multi-scalar formations in which innovation logics, pedagogical architectures, and governance regimes are tightly coupled. By interweaving *National Innovation Systems*, *Triple Helix* and extended-helix configurations, *Multi Level Perspective* transition theory, the *Capability Approach*, and learning-sciences metatheory, the chapter has reframed AI education from a narrow skills discourse into a systemic, socio-technical, and justice-inflected project. Education systems emerge as distributed infrastructures for cultivating AI-related capabilities, critical reflexivity, and civic agency, rather than as passive pipelines for labour markets. Tables 1 to 5 have shown how metatheoretical lenses, strategy regimes, multilevel talent architectures, partnership modalities, and governance scales jointly shape who is able to learn with AI, who is authorised to design and regulate AI, and which futures of intelligent agency become probable or precluded. The central insight is that AI education cannot be governed as a technical subsystem, but must be treated as a core regime within broader innovation and democratic ecosystems.

7.2 Normative Design Commitments for AI-Ready Education Ecosystems

From this conceptual scaffolding, a set of normative design commitments for AI-ready education ecosystems becomes unavoidable. First, a human-centred and capability-expanding orientation requires that AI curricula and credentials systematically strengthen learners' abilities to interrogate, contest, and reconfigure algorithmic systems, rather than only operate them. Second, *epistemic justice* and decolonial commitments imply that linguistic plurality, local knowledges, and subaltern perspectives must be integral to AI content, datasets, and assessment logics, not peripheral add-ons. Third, *public value governance* and *reflexive regulation* demand that AI-related decisions in education are transparent, participatory, and revisable, with clear responsibilities across institutional, sectoral, national, and transnational arenas as mapped in Table 5. Fourth, ecological responsibility, as encoded in *Quintuple Helix* thinking, obliges designers to treat energy use, material infrastructures, and planetary limits as core parameters of AI-learning design. Together, these commitments convert AI education from a narrow competitiveness agenda into a project of socially robust, ecologically sane, and democratically legitimate intelligent futures.

7.3 Conceptual Research Programmes and Reflections

The chapter also delineates a rich conceptual research programme that can guide future empirical, comparative, and design-based inquiry. One line of work concerns comparative mapping of AI education regimes across the ideal-typical strategy configurations in Table 2, examining how different policy mixes and discourses translate into concrete arrangements of curricula, partnerships, and participation. A second line invites multi-site and multi-level analyses of AI talent architectures, using the multilevel matrix in Table 3 to investigate how learning opportunities accumulate or fracture across schooling, higher education, professional development, and community learning. A third line focuses on the political economy and ethics of partnership modalities in Table 4, probing how power, value extraction, and resistance operate within joint laboratories, platform integrations, and mission-driven hubs. Finally, longitudinal and action-oriented studies of the governance constellations in Table 5 can test how *experimentalist governance* and *extended helix* configurations affect resilience, inclusion, and ecological performance. In aggregate, these research trajectories can help transform AI-ready education ecosystems from aspirational rhetoric into rigorously designed, critically monitored, and continuously renewed infrastructures for governing intelligent futures.

REFERENCES

Addy, E., Adabor, E. S., & Badu, Y. A. (2025). Promoting sustainable innovations in technical universities: Critical success factors of the triple helix model. *Industry and Higher Education*, *39*(4), 453–471.

Agbebi, M., Song, J., Mamman, A., & Baydoun, N. (2024). Afrocentric triple helix: A communal perspective on addressing Africa's economic and social challenges. *Africa Journal of Management*, *10*(3), 351–382.

Alam, A. (2022). Impact of university's human resources practices on professors' occupational performance: empirical evidence from India's higher education sector. In *Inclusive businesses in developing economies: Converging people, profit, and corporate citizenship* (pp. 107–131). Springer International Publishing.

Alam, A. (2023a). Media multitasking with M-learning technology in real-time classroom learning: Analysing the dynamics in formal educational settings for the future of E-learning in India. In *2023 2nd International Conference on Smart Technologies and Systems for Next Generation Computing (ICSTSN)* (pp. 1-6). IEEE.

Alam, A. (2023b). The secret sauce of student success: Cracking the code by navigating the path to personalized learning with educational data mining. In *2023 2nd International Conference on Smart Technologies and Systems for Next Generation Computing (ICSTSN)* (pp. 1-8). IEEE.

Alam, A. (2023c). Intelligence unleashed: An argument for AI-enabled learning ecologies with real world examples of today and a peek into the future. In *International Conference on Innovations in Computer Science, Electronics & Electrical Engineering*-2022 (Vol. 2717, No. 1, p. 030001). AIP Publishing LLC.

Alam, A., & Mohanty, A. (2022, December). Facial analytics or virtual avatars: competencies and design considerations for student-teacher interaction in AI-powered online education for effective classroom engagement. In *International Conference on Communication, Networks and Computing* (pp. 252-265). Cham: Springer Nature Switzerland.

Alam, A., & Mohanty, A. (2023, January). Learning on the move: a pedagogical framework for state-of-the-art mobile learning. In *International Conference on Data Management, Analytics & Innovation* (pp. 735-748). Singapore: Springer Nature Singapore.

Alam, A., & Mohanty, A. (2024). Integrated constructive robotics in education (ICRE) model: A paradigmatic framework for transformative learning in educational ecosystem. *Cogent Education*, *11*(1), 2324487.

AlMalki, H. A., & Durugbo, C. M. (2024). Institutionalising Industry 4.0: A Delphi study of institutional change readiness for the fourth industrial revolution in an emerging economy. *Production Planning and Control, 35*(14), 1741–1759.

Androniceanu, A., & Colesca, S. E. (2025). Triple Helix Model and Artificial Intelligence in Public Administration. *Central European Public Administration Review, 23*(2), 63–91.

Arman, H., & Al-Qudsi, S. (2024). A strategic framework to analyse the East Asian miracle within triple helix model–lessons for Kuwait. *Journal of Science and Technology Policy Management, 15*(2), 244–267.

Arya, V., Saraf, A., Chichkanov, N., Papa, A., & Romano, M. (2025). AI-enhanced competency transfer hubs: A conceptual framework for university-industry engagement and knowledge sharing. *The Journal of Technology Transfer*, 1–31.

Barry, G., Hashim, S., Zain, A. A. M., & Lah, N. H. C. (2025). Digital Literacy among Bakery Industry Entrepreneurs: A Review based on the Triple Helix Model. [TENIAT]. *International Journal of Creative Future and Heritage, 13*(2), 108–122.

Bhatia, R., & Kaur, J. (2024). Collaborating Academia, Industry, and Government: Enhancing Business Practices Through Innovative Pedagogies. In *Fostering Industry-Academia Partnerships for Innovation-Driven Trade* (pp. 40-53). IGI Global.

Bhimavarapu, U. (2025). AI in Technology Transfer Developing Sustainable Models Through University-Industry Collaboration. In *Bridging Technology and Development for Sustainable Innovation and Geopolitical Dynamics* (pp. 67-86). IGI Global Scientific Publishing.

binti Saaidun, N. S. N., bin Ariffin, A. S., bin Jamil, A. I., & binti Nor, N. F. (2025). Fostering Sustainable Partnership in the Halal Sector: A Triple Helix Model for Enhanced Food Security and Graduate Employability. *KnE Social Sciences, 10*(24), 25-35.

Bonenberg, A., & Angoneze-Grela, E. (2023). University–municipality–business (Triple Helix) cooperation model in practice–ecological district of innovation and technology in Poznan (EDIT Poznań). *Przestrzeń i Forma*, (56), 199–218.

Bruno, A. I., Shafiq, M., & Jalil, F. (2025). Impact of STI Policy on Innovation Creation by HEIs In Pakistan: Exploring from the Triple Helix Model (THM) Perspective. *Qlantic Journal of Social Sciences, 6*(2), 104–118.

Byrne, M. F., Rittscher, J., & East, J. E. (2025). Synergies Among Clinicians, Academia, and Industry in the Age of Artificial Intelligence. *Gastroenterology, 169*(3), 531–544.

Carayannis, E. G., Draper, J., & Erokhin, V. (2025). Highlighting Paradigms Relevant to PIT-AI-Fusion Co-development: The Quintuple Helix. In *Democracy, Environment, and Technology: The Cases of AI and Fusion Energy* (pp. 23–46). Springer Nature Switzerland.

Carayannis, E. G., & Morawska, J. (2023). University and education 5.0 for emerging trends, policies and practices in the concept of industry 5.0 and society 5.0. In *Industry 5.0: Creative and Innovative Organizations* (pp. 1–25). Springer International Publishing.

Cervini, E. M. L. F. (2025). Harmony in the Helix: Navigating the "AI Race" through Collaborative Geopolitics. In *The Routledge Handbook of Artificial Intelligence and International Relations* (pp. 92-111). Routledge.

Chatterjee, R., & Roy, I. (2025). Role of Absorptive Capacity and Science and Technology Parks in Regional Innovation: A Triple Helix Perspective From India. *Journal of Public Affairs*, *25*(2), e70029.

Cheng, C., Cheng, S., & Feng, C. (2024). The Triple Helix Model for Industry-Education City Integration in China: A Development Approach. *SAGE Open*, *14*(2), 21582440241250111.

Chfadi, T., Abdulkader, B., & Chirinda, N. (2025). From syllabi to startups: Lessons from eight African case studies on university-industry collaboration and agri-entrepreneurship education. *Frontiers in Sustainable Food Systems*, *9*, 1572898.

Cooke, P. (2025). Triple helix selection in the regional innovation systems field. In memoriam: Loet Leydesdorff. *Scientometrics*, •••, 1–10.

da Rocha, A. B. T., Espuny, M., Kandsamy, J., & Oliveira, O. (2024). Advancing sustainability in the steel industry: The key role of the triple helix sectors. *Environmental Science and Pollution Research International*, *31*(31), 43591–43615.

Daliri, H. (2024). AI Revolution and the Triple Helix Dynamics in Economy. *Journal of Science and Technology Policy*, *17*(4), 53–70.

Daradkah, A. M., Alotaibi, T. K., Mahmoud, A. M. A., Awais, B. E., Al-Qudah, M. A., & Shannaq, R. M. A., ... & Mahmoud10, S. S. M. (2023). A Proposed Model for Integration and Cooperation between University, Industry, and Government in Arab countries: Innovation Triple Helix Model. *Applied Mathematics & Information Sciences*, *17*(6), 1109–1144.

de Oliveira, O. J., da Rocha, A. B. T., Costa, A. C. F., & Espuny, M. (2024). Technical-Scientific Scenario Based on the Triple Helix: Innovative Approach Beyond Bibliometrics. In *Bibliometrics-An Essential Methodological Tool for Research Projects*. IntechOpen.

Edo, B. L., & Nwonkwo, S. (2025). Triple Helix Partnership in Educational Administration and Planning in Tertiary Institutions in Nigeria. *International Journal of Educational Management, Rivers State University., 1*(2), 325-338.

Esangbedo, C. O., Zhang, J., Esangbedo, M. O., Kone, S. D., & Xu, L. (2024). The role of industry-academia collaboration in enhancing educational opportunities and outcomes under the digital driven Industry 4.0. *Journal of Infrastructure. Policy and Development, 8*(1), 2569.

Espuny, M., Reis, J. S. D. M., Giupponi, E. C. B., Rocha, A. B. T., Costa, A. C. F., Poltronieri, C. F., & Oliveira, O. J. D. (2025). The role of the triple helix model in promoting the circular economy: Government-led integration strategies and practical application. *Recycling, 10*(2), 50.

Ezeuduji, I. O., Nzama, A. T., Nkosi, G. S., Kheswa, T. P., & Shokane, A. L. (2023). Stakeholder perceptions of university-industry collaboration on tourism and business students' employability in two continents. *Journal of Teaching in Travel & Tourism, 23*(3), 330–353.

Fang, B., Zhang, P., & Kim, S. (2023). National human resource development in China: Government–industry–university relations and roles. *European Journal of Training and Development, 47*(1/2), 183–202.

Fasi, M. A. (2024). Triple helix collaboration: Uncovering research opportunities among industry, academia, and researchers—A case study of Saudi Aramco's patent portfolio analysis. *Journal of the Knowledge Economy, 15*(3), 14486–14520.

Ferdinands, R., Azam, S. F., & Khatibi, A. (2024). The work in progress of a developing nation's triple helix and its impact on patent commercialization. The case of Sri Lanka. *Journal of Science and Technology Policy Management, 15*(4), 839–862.

Figueiredo, R., Soliman, M., Al-Alawi, A. N., & Fatnassi, T. (2023). Could the 'Spinner Innovation' and 'Triple Helix' Models Improve System Innovation? *Applied System Innovation, 6*(2), 42.

Flechas, X. A., Kazunari Takahashi, C., & Bastos de Figueiredo, J. C. (2023). The triple helix and the quality of the startup ecosystem: A global view. *Revista de Gestao, 30*(3), 238–252.

Fu, T., & Ji, Y. (2024). Government-university relationship in China's AI talent development: A triple helix perspective. *SAGE Open*, *14*(2), 21582440241259012.

Giannini, R., Fernández Martínez, J. L., Irigaray García de Serrana, J., & Tomás–Pérez, C. (2025). Fostering Innovation Ecosystems Through Academia: A Strategic Approach to Business Entrepreneurship and Knowledge Transfer. In *Business Entrepreneurship and Innovation: The Advocacy for a Tech-Corporate Ecosystem* (pp. 1–26). Springer Nature Switzerland.

Gong, Y., Singh, R., & Mi, J. (2025). Collaborative governance based on Triple Helix strategy for disaster risk reduction digitalization: Experience from China. *Disaster Prevention and Management: An International Journal*, *34*(3), 385–397.

González-Aleu, F., Francisco Suarez Barraza, M., Garza-Reyes, J. A., & Antony, J. (2024). Guest editorial: Quality 4.0 and Kaizen during disruptive times: addressing the triple helix actors' COVID-19 pandemic challenges. *The TQM Journal*, *36*(6), 1397–1401.

Guo, T., He, A., Zhai, L., & Yan, S. (2025). Can Interactive Platform of University Science Parks Enhance the Quality of University Research Outcomes? Evidence from a Differencein-Differences Model. *Frontiers in Physics*, *13*, 1642172.

Hailu, A. T. (2024). The role of university–industry linkages in promoting technology transfer: Implementation of triple helix model relations. *Journal of Innovation and Entrepreneurship*, *13*(1), 25.

Hakeem, M. M., & Goi, H. C., Frendy, & Ito, H. (2023). Regional sustainable development using a Quadruple Helix approach in Japan. *Regional Studies, Regional Science*, *10*(1), 119–138.

Han, C., Li, F., Wang, M., Zhou, C., Liu, Z., & Yang, C. (2024, September). Framework of a PBL tutor system based on the triple helix model in environmental science. In *Proceedings of the 2024 the 16th International Conference on Education Technology and Computers* (pp. 511-517).

Haryadi, A., Sulistyadi, E., & Asmoro, N. (2025). Driving Innovation in the Defense Sector: Unlocking the Power of Industry, Academia, and Government Collaboration. *Formosa Journal of Multidisciplinary Research*, *4*(2), 991–1002.

Holguín Rengifo, Y. X., Herrera Vargas, J. F., & Valencia-Arias, A. (2023). Proposal for a Comprehensive Tool to Measure Smart Cities under the Triple-Helix Model: Capacities Learning, Research, and Development. *Sustainability*, *15*(18), 13549.

Hossen, M. A., Misbauddin, S. M., Molla, C., Nabi, M. N. U., & Sakib, M. N. (2025). Decoding university–industry collaboration: A SEM-ANN quadruple helix approach. *Future Business Journal, 11*(1), 236.

Ideland, M., & Serder, M. (2023). Edu-business within the Triple Helix. Value production through assetization of educational research. *Education Inquiry, 14*(3), 336–351.

Jumiyati, S. (2024). Development of climate smart agriculture based on empowering farmers around forests through triple-helix collaboration. *Interaction, Community Engagement, and Social Environment, 2*(1), 75–91.

Kasirye, F. (2025). The Evolution of University Industry Relations: Fostering Innovation and Economic Development in Georgia through the Triple Helix Model. *Journal of Effective Teaching and Learning Practices, 2*(2), 97–109.

Kim, G. Y., Lee, W. J., Choi, B., & Lew, Y. K. (2025). Fostering collaborative opportunities for AI start-ups: The case of a hybrid business incubator in Seoul. *The Journal of Technology Transfer, 50*(2), 552–581.

Kowch, E. G. (2025). An innovation policy analysis of G10 nations' strategic plans for future AI leaders and researchers in higher education. In *Navigating Generative AI in Higher Education* (pp. 211–234). Edward Elgar Publishing.

Kumar, V., Verma, P., Mittal, A., Gupta, P., Raj, R., & Kaswan, M. S. (2024). Addressing the Kaizen business operations: The role of triple helix actors during COVID-19 outbreak. *The TQM Journal, 36*(6), 1665–1694.

Kunwar, R. R., & Ulak, N. (2023). Understanding the Triple Helix Model and capitalization of knowledge. *Journal of APF Command and Staff College, 6*(01), 1–34.

Kunwar, R. R., & Ulak, N. (2024). Extension of the triple helix to quadruple to quintuple helix model. *Journal of APF Command and Staff College, 7*(1), 241–280.

Lessa, L. S., de Oliveira, M. M., & Canciglieri, O., Junior. (2023, July). Innovative Development in a University Environment Based on the Triple Helix Concepts: A Systematic Literature Review. In *IFIP International Conference on Product Lifecycle Management* (pp. 181-190). Cham: Springer Nature Switzerland.

Liao, F., & Lai, H. (2023). A Collaborative Training Mechanism for Accounting Digital Intelligence Talents Based on the Triple Helix Theory. *Journal of Intelligence and Knowledge Engineering (ISSN: 2959-0620), 1*(3), 1.

Lin, Y., Lin, Y., Liu, J., Tan, Z., & Han, W. (2025). Triple Helix Synergy Model in China's new technology diplomacy: Perspectives from AI startups. *Telecommunications Policy*, •••, 103079.

Liu, D., & Zhu, Y. P. (2023). Evolution of knowledge structure in an emerging field based on a triple helix model: The case of smart factory. *Journal of the Knowledge Economy*, *14*(4), 4583–4607.

Liu, J., & Jiang, M. (2025). The Impact of Industry-University-Research Institute Cooperation on the Innovation Capability of Chinese University Faculty. *Higher Education Studies*, *15*(4), 298–311.

Liu, J., Wang, X., Miao, W., & Wang, X. (2025). What factors enable sustainable university-industry collaboration communities? Evidence from a symbiosis theory perspective. *Sustainable Futures : An Applied Journal of Technology, Environment and Society*, *10*, 101166.

Loggers, J. C. J., Reinders, M. E. J., van Gelder, T., van der Horst, V. M., Bischoff, K. M. S. L., & Guchelaar, H. J. (2025). Academic–industry collaboration in biomedical innovation: A multi-model review of barriers and facilitators. *Drug Discovery Today*, •••, 104560.

Lulaj, E., & Brajković, M. (2025). The Moderating Role of Finance, Accounting, and Digital Disruption in ESG, Financial Reporting, and Auditing: A Triple-Helix Perspective. *Journal of Risk and Financial Management*, *18*(5), 245.

Luong, A. N. (2023). Aligning the Quintuple Helix model of innovation with Vietnams context: evidence from artificial intelligence innovation dialogues. In *The Elgar Companion to Digital Transformation, Artificial Intelligence and Innovation in the Economy, Society and Democracy* (pp. 254-275). Edward Elgar Publishing.

Ma, J., & Yang, D. (2024). Research on the mechanism of government-industry-university-research collaboration for cultivating innovative talent based on game theory. *Heliyon*, *10*(3).

Mayho, S., Mumford, D., Ellis, L., Lloyd, D. C., Redmond, E. C., & Clifton, N. (2024). The evolution of regional triple helix food sector SME interventions: A longitudinal study, Wales, UK. *European Planning Studies*, *32*(9), 2046–2069.

Mêgnigbêto, E. (2025). Convexity of the triplc helix of innovation game. *International Journal of Innovation Science*, *17*(3), 563–580.

Moldashev, K., Sahimbekov, B., & Kozhakhmet, S. (2025). The institutional logics of research commercialisation: Reform, misalignment, and hybridisation. *Social Sciences & Humanities Open*, *12*, 102000.

Morrar, R., & Arman, H. (2024). The transformational role of a third actor within the Triple Helix Model–the case of Palestine. *Innovation (Abingdon)*, *37*(2), 340–360.

Mulyadi, E., Valeriani, D., & Fitriyanti, E. (2024). Implementation of the Triple Helix Model in Increasing Economic Opportunities for Waste Management in Pangkalpinang City. *Equity: Jurnal Ekonomi*, *12*(1), 39–47.

Nasir, N., Azhar, S. M., Ishaq, M. I., & Shafqat, I. (2025). A study on the dynamics of government-university-industry knowledge transfer in emerging knowledge-based economies. *Science & Public Policy*, •••, scaf038.

Navarro, J., Solé-Beteta, X., Carreras-Coch, A., Caballero, V., Pappa, L., Tyrovolas, M., & Zaballos, A. (2024). Bridging academia and industry in the era of Industry 4.0 by means of the triple helix: The PLANET4 initiative. *Journal of Infrastructure. Policy and Development*, *8*(9), 1–35.

Nwaichi, E. O., Egbe, T. I., & Halilu, A. (2024, October). Democratizing Innovation: The 10: 10: 10: 10 Vision of Triple Helix Nigeria. In *Triple Helix Nigeria SciBiz Annual Conference* (pp. 71-93). Cham: Springer Nature Switzerland.

Nwaichi, P. I., Olayiwola, A., Egbe, T. I., Agi, A., Halilu, A., & Nwaichi, E. O. (2024, October). Future of Triple Helix in Nigeria: Emerging Trends and Opportunities in University-Industry-Government Collaboration. In *Triple Helix Nigeria SciBiz Annual Conference* (pp. 3-25). Cham: Springer Nature Switzerland.

Nwaichi, P. I., Olayiwola, A., Egbe, T. I., Agi, A., Halilu, A., & Nwaichi, E. O. (2025, March). Future of Triple Helix in Nigeria: Emerging Trends and Opportunities. In *Triple Helix Nigeria SciBiz Annual Conference 2024: THN SciBiz* (p. 2). Springer Nature.

Nzeyimana, B. S., Gandhi, J., Tiwari, S., Santos, T. F., Nair, S. S. G., & Santos, C. M. (2025). Bridging gaps in sustainability: HEI-industry collaborations for accelerating SDGs. *Journal of Cleaner Production*, *529*, 146768.

Otarola, M. C., Rodríguez, Y. V., Albornoz, J. J., Palomo, J. M., Vera, J. R., & Badilla, J. R. (2025). Innovation systems in Chile: The four helix model of Chilean universities. *Technology in Society*, •••, 103013.

Panta, S., & Thapaliya, S. (2025). The Future of Doctoral Education: The Role of Professional Doctorates in Bridging Academia and Industry. *Journal of Integrative Education Studies*, *1*(2), 18–28.

Park, H. W. (2024). measuring innovation and collaboration system using big data: A case study about Ho Chi Minh city. *Triple Helix (Heidelberg)*, *10*(2), 205–214.

Pereira, D., Leitao, J., Oliveira, T., & Peirone, D. (2023). Proposing a holistic research framework for university strategic alliances in sustainable entrepreneurship. *Heliyon*, *9*(5).

Petrenko, E. S., Panshin, I. V., Sozinova, A. A., & Fedorkova, A. V. (2025). Collaboration of Universities and Business in Industry 4.0: International Experience of Reducing the Divide Between the University Education Market and the Job Market. In *Bridging the Gap Between the Higher Education and Labor Markets: Relevance of the Fourth Industrial Revolution* (pp. 159–166). Springer Nature Singapore.

Phiri, J. (2024). Performance reporting for innovation partnerships–the case of the triple helix in Zambia. *Cogent Business & Management*, *11*(1), 2411447.

Pinedo-López, J., Baena-Navarro, R., & Torres-Hoyos, F. (2025). Science, Technology and Innovation in Colombia: Impact of the Relationships Between Enterprises, Government and Universities. *Science, Technology & Society*, *30*(2), 363–385.

Pitan, O. S. (2023). Leveraging the triple helix system for effective employability delivery in Nigerian universities. In *Handbook of research on sustainable career ecosystems for university students and graduates* (pp. 77–96). IGI Global.

Planck, S., Tomasi, S., Maisch, B., Henry, C., Gabriel, B., Singer, S., & Stoeckmann, C. (2025). Introduction. A New Social Contract for Higher Education Institutions: Exploring the Role of HEIs in European Innovation Ecosystems. *Triple Helix (Heidelberg)*, *11*(3), 245–257.

Qu, C., & Kim, E. (2025). Artificial-Intelligence-Enabled Innovation Ecosystems: A Novel Triple-Layer Framework for Micro, Small, and Medium-Sized Enterprises in the Chinese Apparel-Manufacturing Industry. *Sustainability*, *17*(11), 5019.

Rosienkiewicz, M., Helman, J., Cholewa, M., Molasy, M., Górecka, A., Kohen-Vacs, D., & Benis, A. (2024). Enhancing technology-focused entrepreneurship in higher education institutions ecosystem: Implementing innovation models in international projects. *Education Sciences*, *14*(7), 797.

Rossoni, A. L., de Vasconcellos, E. P. G., & de Castilho Rossoni, R. L. (2024). Barriers and facilitators of university-industry collaboration for research, development and innovation: A systematic review. *Management Review Quarterly*, *74*(3), 1841–1877.

Rubén Cukierman, U. (2025). The Triple Helix of Knowledge: Synergies and Potentialities among Engineering, Art, and Education. *International Journal of Engineering Pedagogy*, *15*(5).

Sadykova, A., Berikkhanova, A., Atabekova, B., Sholpankulova, G., & Abdykhalykova, Z. (2025, February). Social partnerships among academia, industry, and government in education: A bibliometric analysis. [). Frontiers Media SA.]. *Frontiers in Education*, *10*, 1516358.

Said, N. A., & Abdullah, Z. (2024). The Triple Helix of Innovation: A Case Study of the Role and Social Relations of Universities, Industry and Government. *Akademika*, *94*(3), 283–299.

Sam, M. (2025). Optimizing Data Governance via Triple Helix Model: A Systematic Review and Bibliometric Analysis. *Public Governance Practices in the Age of AI*, 327-354.

Samperio Sánchez, F. (2023). The Gestation of a Triple Helix in Queretaro, Its Contribution to the Formation of the Global Value Chain of the Aerospace Industry and the Type of Upgrading That Powers. In *Global Value Chains in Latin America: Experiences of Transformations* (pp. 251–285). Springer Nature Switzerland.

Schebesch, K. B., Soim, H. F., & Blaga, R. L. (2024). The triple-helix model as foundation of innovative entrepreneurial ecosystems. *Journal of Ethics in Entrepreneurship and Technology*, *4*(2), 104–129.

Senthil, B. A., Prema, R. K., & Sharif, L. S. (2025). Industry-Academia Partnerships: Bridging the Gap for R&D Success. In *Evolving Landscapes of Research and Development: Trends, Challenges, and Opportunities* (pp. 191-208). IGI Global Scientific Publishing.

Shin, B., Rask, M., & Kahma, N. (2023). Measuring the Quadruple Helix in social media: A case study of university–industry collaboration. *Technological Forecasting and Social Change*, *194*, 122711.

Shyiramunda, T., & van den Bersselaar, D. (2024). Local community development and higher education institutions: Moving from the triple helix to the quadruple helix model. *International Review of Education*, *70*(1), 51–85.

Subrahmanyam, S. (2025). Strategic Collaboration and Partnerships in R&D for Innovation. In *Research and Development Practices in Innovation* (pp. 283–314). IGI Global Scientific Publishing.

Suminar, T., Sutarto, J., Raharjo, T. J., Kisworo, B., Cahyani, A. D., & Raharjo, S. R. (2025). Development of a Triple Helix-Based Course and Training Management Model to Accelerate the Transformation of Work Competencies in the Era of Disruption. *TEM Journal*, *14*(3), 2537.

Tagliazucchi, G., Della Santa, S., & Gherardini, F. (2024). Design of a living lab for autonomous driving: An investigation under the lens of the triple helix model. *The Journal of Technology Transfer*, *49*(3), 876–899.

Thomas, D. O., Nwaichi, E. O., & Umunna, A. O. (2024, October). Enhancing Workplace Safety Through Innovation and Human Factors Engineering: A Collaborative Approach Among Academia, Industry, and Government. In *Triple Helix Nigeria SciBiz Annual Conference* (pp. 117-139). Cham: Springer Nature Switzerland.

Thomas, D. O., Nwaichi, E. O., & Umunna, A. O. (2025, March). Enhancing Workplace Safety Through. In *Triple Helix Nigeria SciBiz Annual Conference 2024: THN SciBiz* (p. 117). Springer Nature.

Thorpe, M., Healy, C., & Olsen, D. (2025). Bridging workforce skills gaps in rural America amid 'the great resignation'by leveraging a triple helix collaboration. *Industry and Higher Education*, *39*(2), 198–211.

Van Dijk, M. P. (2025). Triple Helix approach to innovation in Rwanda's agriculture resulted in a partnership between educational institutions and a private firm producing clean seed potatoes. *Journal of Agribusiness in Developing and Emerging Economies*, *15*(4), 832–848.

Viale, R., & Cucchiarini, V. (2025). Behavioral Triple Helix for Innovation. Triple Helix, 1(aop), 1-23.

Wang, L., Ni, Y., Zhao, Y., & Chen, Y. (2024). The triple helix collaboration: Lessons from a Chinese provincial innovation ecosystem. *Chinese Management Studies*, *18*(4), 1276–1289.

Wang, T., Suo, B., Jiang, J., & Jia, W. (2025). A triple helix model analysis of China's regional industry-university-research collaborative innovation in low-carbon technologies. *International Journal of Climate Change Strategies and Management*, *17*(1), 846–866.

Wawak, S., Teixeira Domingues, J. P., & Sampaio, P. (2024). Quality 4.0 in higher education: Reinventing academic-industry-government collaboration during disruptive times. *The TQM Journal*, *36*(6), 1569–1590.

Weidenfeld, A., & Anusik, J. (2025). Exploring the systemic qualities and institutions of a Triple Helix municipal knowledge network. *European Planning Studies*, *33*(12), 2184–2206.

Wu, X., Zheng, Y., & Wang, X. (2025). Government–Industry–Academia Collaboration for Sustainable Autonomous Vehicle Development: A Qualitative Case Study in Suzhou, China. *Sustainability*, *17*(12), 5348.

Xia, S., Zhou, Y., Wang, Z., He, Q., & Parry, G. (2025). Enhancing green innovation through university–industry collaboration and artificial intelligence: Insights from regional innovation systems in China. *The Journal of Technology Transfer*, •••, 1–29.

Xin, P., Arshad, N. I., Mohamad, U. H., Huang, Y., & Su, S. J. (2025). Reframing the Triple Helix for Sustainability: A Mechanism-Based Framework for University–Industry–Government Collaboration in Global Innovation Systems. *European Journal of Education*, *60*(4), e70361.

Xiong, W., Song, Y., & Fu, H. Z. (2025). The diversity and Triple Helix interactions among universities, industries and governments: Case of climate change field. *Scientometrics*, •••, 1–26.

Yang, B. B., & Park, S. D. (2025). Evolving Innovation Ecosystems: Longitudinal Insights into the Triple Helix Model and Enterprise Innovation in China. *SAGE Open*, *15*(4), 21582440251393200.

Yazıcı, A. M. (2023). The quintuple helix, industrial 5.0, and society 5.0. In *Digitalization, Sustainable Development, and Industry 5.0: An Organizational Model for Twin Transitions* (pp. 317-336). Emerald Publishing Limited.

Yessimova, S., Rakhymzhanov, Y., Spanova, B., Baizhanova, S., Seidakhmetov, M., Yessenova, A., & Altynbassov, B. (2024). Strengthening the Nexus: Policy and Legislative Reforms for University-Industry Collaboration in Kazakhstan. *Theoretical and Practical Research in Economic Fields*, *15*(1), 136–144.

Zhao, X., Wang, L., & Chen, L. (2024, February). Industry and Education Integration for Chinese University of Applied Science and Technology, Based on the Triple Helix Theory. In *3rd International Conference on Education, Language and Art (ICELA 2023)* (pp. 316-328). Atlantis Press.

Zhao Yi, Z. Y., Guo Qian, G. Q., & Fu Rao, F. R. (2025). University-Industry Collaborative Innovation for County-Level Prosperity-Driven Industries: Dynamic Mechanisms and Implementation Pathways. *University-Industry Collaborative Innovation for County-Level Prosperity-Driven Industries. Dynamic Mechanisms and Implementation Pathways*, *2*(11), 172–177.

Zhou, J., & Wang, M. (2023). The role of government-industry-academia partnership in business incubation: Evidence from new R&D institutions in China. *Technology in Society*, *72*, 102194.

Zhu, Y. P., & Park, H. W. (2025). Publication, collaboration, citation performance, and triple helix innovation gene of artificial intelligence research in the communication field: Comparing Asia to the rest of the world. *Journal of the Knowledge Economy*, *16*(2), 10308–10328.

Zhuang, T., Oh, M., & Kimura, K. (2025). Modernizing higher education with industrial forces in Asia: A comparative study of discourse of university-industry collaboration in China, Japan and Singapore. *Asia Pacific Education Review*, *26*(1), 195–210.

Zhuang, T., & Zhou, H. (2023). Developing a synergistic approach to engineering education: China's national policies on university–industry educational collaboration. *Asia Pacific Education Review*, *24*(1), 145–165.

Zhuang, T., Zhou, H., & Sun, Q. (2024). Ushering in industrial forces for teaching-focused university-industry collaboration in China: A resource-dependence perspective. *Studies in Higher Education*, *49*(12), 2357–2375.

Compilation of References

Aarthi, S., Ravikumar, R. N., & Pardaev, J. (2025). Synergizing multimodal generative AI and blockchain for the future of digital media. In *Advances in Computational Intelligence and Robotics* (pp. 1–34). IGI Global Scientific Publishing. https://doi .org/DOI: 10.4018/979-8-3373-1504-1.ch001

Aarthi, S., Ravikumar, R. N., Khudayberganov, S., Ismailov, A., & Khujaniyozova, O. (2025). Using Intelligent Tutoring Systems to enhance student engagement. In *Advances in Computational Intelligence and Robotics* (pp. 155–188). IGI Global. https://doi.org/DOI: 10.4018/979-8-3373-1827-1.ch008

Addy, E., Adabor, E. S., & Badu, Y. A. (2025). Promoting sustainable innovations in technical universities: Critical success factors of the triple helix model. *Industry and Higher Education*, *39*(4), 453–471.

Agarwal, A., & Nene, M. J. (2025). A five-layer framework for AI governance: Integrating regulation, standards, and certification. *Transforming Government People Process and Policy*, *19*(3), 535–555. DOI: 10.1108/tg-03-2025-0065

Agbebi, M., Song, J., Mamman, A., & Baydoun, N. (2024). Afrocentric triple helix: A communal perspective on addressing Africa's economic and social challenges. *Africa Journal of Management*, *10*(3), 351–382.

Ahmad, W., Khan, S., Mazhar, T., Shahzad, T., Jiang, W., & Hamam, H. (2025). Industry 4.0 for smart transport systems: Foundations and applications. *Telematics and Informatics Reports*, *20*, 100255. DOI: 10.1016/j.teler.2025.100255

Ahmed, F., Fattani, M. T., Ali, S. R., & Enam, R. N. (2022). Strengthening the bridge between academic and the industry through the academia-Industry Collaboration Plan design model. *Frontiers in Psychology*, *13*, 875940. DOI: 10.3389/ fpsyg.2022.875940

Alam, A. (2023a). Media multitasking with M-learning technology in real-time classroom learning: Analysing the dynamics in formal educational settings for the future of E-learning in India. In *2023 2nd International Conference on Smart Technologies and Systems for Next Generation Computing (ICSTSN)* (pp. 1-6). IEEE.

Alam, A. (2023b). The secret sauce of student success: Cracking the code by navigating the path to personalized learning with educational data mining. In *2023 2nd International Conference on Smart Technologies and Systems for Next Generation Computing (ICSTSN)* (pp. 1-8). IEEE.

Alam, A., & Mohanty, A. (2022, December). Facial analytics or virtual avatars: competencies and design considerations for student-teacher interaction in AI-powered online education for effective classroom engagement. In *International Conference on Communication, Networks and Computing* (pp. 252-265). Cham: Springer Nature Switzerland.

Alam, A., & Mohanty, A. (2023, January). Learning on the move: a pedagogical framework for state-of-the-art mobile learning. In *International Conference on Data Management, Analytics & Innovation* (pp. 735-748). Singapore: Springer Nature Singapore.

Alam, A. (2022). Impact of university's human resources practices on professors' occupational performance: empirical evidence from India's higher education sector. In *Inclusive businesses in developing economies: Converging people, profit, and corporate citizenship* (pp. 107–131). Springer International Publishing.

Alam, A. (2023c). Intelligence unleashed: An argument for AI-enabled learning ecologies with real world examples of today and a peek into the future. In *International Conference on Innovations in Computer Science, Electronics & Electrical Engineering*-2022 (Vol. 2717, No. 1, p. 030001). AIP Publishing LLC.

Alam, A., & Mohanty, A. (2024). Integrated constructive robotics in education (ICRE) model: A paradigmatic framework for transformative learning in educational ecosystem. *Cogent Education, 11*(1), 2324487.

Ali, A. (2025). Ethical Implications of Artificial Intelligence: Ensuring Patient Data Security. In *Transforming Healthcare Sector through Artificial Intelligence and Environmental Sustainability* (pp. 149-164). Singapore: Springer Nature Singapore. https://doi.org/DOI: 10.1007/978-981-97-9555-0_8

Ali, Z. A., Hasan, R., Alsanad, A., Alhogail, A., & Gumaei, A. H. (2025). Multiple knowledge depiction of digital twin-driven circular economy: Concepts, integrated advanced technologies, triple bottom line of smart construction, and exploratory case studies. In *Journal of Engineering Research*. Elsevier B.V., DOI: 10.1016/j.jer.2025.08.018

AlMalki, H. A., & Durugbo, C. M. (2024). Institutionalising Industry 4.0: A Delphi study of institutional change readiness for the fourth industrial revolution in an emerging economy. *Production Planning and Control*, *35*(14), 1741–1759.

Almeida, F., & Deutsch, N. (2025). Urban living labs as catalysts for innovation: Advancing urban ecosystems within the quintuple helix model. *Urban Governance*, *5*(2), 133–141. DOI: 10.1016/j.ugj.2025.05.005

Androniceanu, A., & Colesca, S. E. (2025). Triple Helix Model and Artificial Intelligence in Public Administration. *Central European Public Administration Review*, *23*(2), 63–91.

Ansari, A. I., Singh, A., Pattanaik, S., Patnaik, R., & Suryawanshi, U. (2024). Exploring the Role of AI-Powered Virtual Assistants in Optimizing Self-Service Experiences for Customers Within the Service Sector. In Nadda, V., Tyagi, P., Singh, A., & Singh, V. (Eds.), *Integrating AI-Driven Technologies Into Service Marketing* (pp. 225–238). IGI Global., DOI: 10.4018/979-8-3693-7122-0.ch013

Ansell, C., & Gash, A. (2008). Collaborative governance in theory and practice. *Journal of Public Administration Research and Theory: J-PART*, *18*(4), 543–571. DOI: 10.1093/jopart/mum032

Antara News. (2025). *Indonesia scales AI talent factory to boost government programs*. https://en.antaranews.com/news/381061/indonesia-scales-ai-talent-factory-to-boost-government-programs

Arman, H., & Al-Qudsi, S. (2024). A strategic framework to analyse the East Asian miracle within triple helix model–lessons for Kuwait. *Journal of Science and Technology Policy Management*, *15*(2), 244–267.

Arora, A. S., Saboia, L., Arora, A., & McIntyre, J. R. (2025). Human-centric versus state-driven. *International Journal of Intelligent Information Technologies*, *21*(1), 1–13. DOI: 10.4018/ijiit.367471

Arshad, M. D., & Tripathi, C. K. (2025). Algorithmic accountability and ethical AI frameworks for regulatory governance in financial technologies. *International Journal of Science and Research Archive*, *16*(3), 796–799. DOI: 10.30574/ijsra.2025.16.3.2599

Artyukhov, A., Krmela, J., Krmelova, V., & Volk, I. (2021). Quality of scientific activity, technology transfer and research integrity: Case of Ukrainian university. *Business Ethics and Leadership*, *5*(4), 101–109. DOI: 10.21272/bel.5(4).101-109.2021

Arya, V., Saraf, A., Chichkanov, N., Papa, A., & Romano, M. (2025). AI-enhanced competency transfer hubs: A conceptual framework for university-industry engagement and knowledge sharing. *The Journal of Technology Transfer*, 1–31.

Aschhoff, B., & Grimpe, C. (2014). Contemporaneous peer effects, career age and the industry involvement of academics in biotechnology. *Research Policy*, *43*(2), 367–381. DOI: 10.1016/j.respol.2013.11.002

Association of Southeast Asian Nations. (2024). *ASEAN guide on AI governance and ethics*. https://asean.org/wp-content/uploads/2024/02/ASEAN-Guide-on-AI-Governance-and-Ethics_beautified_201223_v2.pdf

Association of Southeast Asian Nations. (2025). *Expanded ASEAN guide on AI governance and ethics – Generative AI*. https://asean.org/wp-content/uploads/2025/01/Expanded-ASEAN-Guide-on-AI-Governance-and-Ethics-Generative-AI.pdf

Atkinson-Toal, A., & Guo, C. (2024). Generative artificial intelligence (AI) education policies of UK universities. *Enhancing Teaching and Learning in Higher Education*, *2*, 70–94. DOI: 10.62512/etlhe.20

Ayana, G., Dese, K., Daba Nemomssa, H., Habtamu, B., Mellado, B., Badu, K., Yamba, E., Faye, S. L., Ondua, M., Nsagha, D., Nkweteyim, D., & Kong, J. D. (2024). Decolonizing global AI governance: Assessment of the state of decolonized AI governance in Sub-Saharan Africa. *Royal Society Open Science*, *11*(8), 231994. DOI: 10.1098/rsos.231994

Badan Pengkajian dan Penerapan Teknologi. (2020). *Strategi nasional untuk kecerdasan artifisial: Indonesia 2020-2045*. https://oecd-ai.case-api.buddyweb.fr/storage//policy-initiatives/Jul2025/fu_4fi5jmh3ywepzcb.pdf

Balasubramaniam, N., Kauppinen, M., Hiekkanen, K., & Kujala, S. (2022, March). Transparency and explainability of AI systems: ethical guidelines in practice. In *International working conference on requirements engineering: foundation for software quality* (pp. 3-18). Cham: Springer International Publishing. https://doi.org/DOI: 10.1007/978-3-030-98464-9_1

Balsalobre-Lorente, D., Shah, S. A. R., & Huseynova, R. (2024). Do circular economy, public-private Partnership and carbon policy manage the environmental stress? Developed countries' situation under the Prism of COP27. *Heliyon*, *10*(13). Advance online publication. DOI: 10.1016/j.heliyon.2024.e33532

Banad, Y. M., Sharif, S. S., & Rezaei, Z. (2025). Artificial intelligence and machine learning for smart grids: from foundational paradigms to emerging technologies with digital twin and large language model-driven intelligence. In *Energy Conversion and Management: X* (Vol. 28). Elsevier Ltd., DOI: 10.1016/j.ecmx.2025.101329

Banifatemi, A. (2025). Human Agency and AI. In *AI for Community* (pp. 122–158). Chapman and Hall/CRC.

Banozic-Tang, A., & Taeihagh, A. (2022). Perspective on research–policy interface as a partnership: The study of best practices in CREATE. *Science & Public Policy*, *49*(5), 801–805. DOI: 10.1093/scipol/scac028

Barry, G., Hashim, S., Zain, A. A. M., & Lah, N. H. C. (2025). Digital Literacy among Bakery Industry Entrepreneurs: A Review based on the Triple Helix Model. [TENIAT]. *International Journal of Creative Future and Heritage*, *13*(2), 108–122.

Bearman, M., Ryan, J., & Ajjawi, R. (2022). Discourses of artificial intelligence in higher education: A critical literature review. *Higher Education*. Advance online publication. DOI: 10.1007/s10734-022-00937-2

Bengoa, A., Maseda, A., Iturralde, T., & Aparicio, G. (2021). A bibliometric review of the technology transfer literature. *The Journal of Technology Transfer*, *46*(5), 1514–1550. DOI: 10.1007/s10961-019-09774-5

Bhalla, A., Singh, P., & Singh, A. (2023). Technological Advancement and Mechanization of the Hotel Industry. In Tailor, R. (Ed.), *Application and Adoption of Robotic Process Automation for Smart Cities* (pp. 57–76). IGI Global., DOI: 10.4018/978-1-6684-7193-7.ch004

Bhatia, R., & Kaur, J. (2024). Collaborating Academia, Industry, and Government: Enhancing Business Practices Through Innovative Pedagogies. In *Fostering Industry-Academia Partnerships for Innovation-Driven Trade* (pp. 40-53). IGI Global.

Bhimavarapu, U. (2025). AI in Technology Transfer Developing Sustainable Models Through University-Industry Collaboration. In *Bridging Technology and Development for Sustainable Innovation and Geopolitical Dynamics* (pp. 67-86). IGI Global Scientific Publishing.

Bhushan, S. (2025). The Rise of India's Start-up Ecosystem: Transforming into an Entrepreneurial Powerhouse. *The Indian Journal of Public Administration*, *71*(3), 463–479. DOI: 10.1177/00195561251368730

Biju, P. R., & Gayathri, O. (2024). The Indian approach to Artificial Intelligence: An analysis of policy discussions, constitutional values, and regulation. *AI & Society*, *39*(5), 2321–2335. DOI: 10.1007/s00146-023-01685-2 binti Saaidun, N. S. N., bin Ariffin, A. S., bin Jamil, A. I., & binti Nor, N. F. (2025). Fostering Sustainable Partnership in the Halal Sector: A Triple Helix Model for Enhanced Food Security and Graduate Employability. *KnE Social Sciences, 10*(24), 25-35.

Blankesteijn, M. L., & Ghorbani, A. (2025). Embracing the Digital Horizon: Future Scenarios for the Dutch Higher Education System. *Futures*, •••, 103702.

Bonenberg, A., & Angoneze-Grela, E. (2023). University–municipality–business (Triple Helix) cooperation model in practice–ecological district of innovation and technology in Poznan (EDIT Poznań). *Przestrzeń i Forma*, (56), 199–218.

Borenstein, J., Howard, A., & Howard, D. (2022). Ethical governance of artificial intelligence in education. *AI & Society*, *37*(4), 1465–1478. DOI: 10.1007/s00146-021-01258-9

Bowen, G. A. (2009). Document analysis as a qualitative research method. *Qualitative Research Journal*, *9*(2), 27–40. DOI: 10.3316/QRJ0902027

Bozhikin, I., Macke, J., & Miri, D. (2024). Mapping creative territories with actors, partnerships, innovations, and regulatory mechanisms based on literature review. *Cleaner and Responsible Consumption*, *12*. Advance online publication. DOI: 10.1016/j.clrc.2024.100186

Brereton, T. A., Malik, M. M., Lifson, M., Greenwood, J. D., Peterson, K. J., & Overgaard, S. M. (2023). The role of artificial intelligence model documentation in translational science: Scoping review. *Interactive Journal of Medical Research*, *12*, e45903. DOI: 10.2196/45903

Brkan, M. (2021). Artificial intelligence and data protection: A legal perspective. *Common Market Law Review*, *58*(5), 1337–1370.

Brodny, J., & Tutak, M. (2025). Towards a sixfold helix model for green smart cities? A conceptual exploration of stakeholder collaboration, interaction mechanisms, and role allocation. *Journal of Open Innovation*, *11*(4). Advance online publication. DOI: 10.1016/j.joitmc.2025.100681

Bruno, A. I., Shafiq, M., & Jalil, F. (2025). Impact of STI Policy on Innovation Creation by HEIs In Pakistan: Exploring from the Triple Helix Model (THM) Perspective. *Qlantic Journal of Social Sciences*, *6*(2), 104–118.

Byrne, M. F., Rittscher, J., & East, J. E. (2025). Synergies Among Clinicians, Academia, and Industry in the Age of Artificial Intelligence. *Gastroenterology*, *169*(3), 531–544.

Cabrera, B. M., Luiz, L. E., & Teixeira, J. P. (2025). The Artificial Intelligence Act: Insights regarding its application and implications. *Procedia Computer Science, 256*, 230–237. DOI: 10.1016/j.procs.2025.02.116

Camilleri, M. A. (2024). Artificial intelligence governance: Ethical considerations and implications for social responsibility. *Expert Systems: International Journal of Knowledge Engineering and Neural Networks, 41*(7), e13406. DOI: 10.1111/exsy.13406

Campbell, E. G., Powers, J. B., Blumenthal, D., & Biles, B. (2004). Inside the triple helix: Technology transfer and commercialization in the life sciences. *Health Affairs (Project Hope), 23*(1), 64–76. DOI: 10.1377/hlthaff.23.1.64

Carayannis, E. G., & Barth, T. D. (2021). The Quintuple Helix innovation model: Global warming as a challenge and driver for innovation. *Journal of Innovation and Entrepreneurship, 10*(1), 1–12. DOI: 10.1186/s13731-021-00162-x

Carayannis, E. G., & Campbell, D. F. J. (2009). "Mode 3" and "Quadruple Helix": Toward a 21st century fractal innovation ecosystem. [International Journal of Technology Management]. *Journal International de La Gestion Technologique, 46*(3/4), 201. DOI: 10.1504/ijtm.2009.023374

Carayannis, E. G., & Campbell, D. F. J. (2009). "Mode 3" and "Quadruple Helix": Toward a 21st-century fractal innovation ecosystem. *International Journal of Technology Management, 46*(3–4), 201–234. DOI: 10.1504/IJTM.2009.023374

Carayannis, E. G., Campbell, D. F., & Grigoroudis, E. (2022). Helix trilogy: The triple, quadruple, and quintuple innovation helices from a theory, policy, and practice set of perspectives. *Journal of the Knowledge Economy, 13*(3), 2272–2301. DOI: 10.1007/s13132-021-00813-x

Carayannis, E. G., Draper, J., & Erokhin, V. (2025). Highlighting Paradigms Relevant to PIT-AI-Fusion Co-development: The Quintuple Helix. In *Democracy, Environment, and Technology: The Cases of AI and Fusion Energy* (pp. 23–46). Springer Nature Switzerland.

Carayannis, E. G., & Morawska, J. (2023). University and education 5.0 for emerging trends, policies and practices in the concept of industry 5.0 and society 5.0. In *Industry 5.0: Creative and Innovative Organizations* (pp. 1–25). Springer International Publishing.

Cervini, E. M. L. F. (2025). Harmony in the Helix: Navigating the "AI Race" through Collaborative Geopolitics. In *The Routledge Handbook of Artificial Intelligence and International Relations* (pp. 92-111). Routledge.

Chan, C. K. Y. (2023). A comprehensive AI policy education framework for university teaching and learning. *International Journal of Educational Technology in Higher Education, 20*(1). Advance online publication. DOI: 10.1186/s41239-023-00408-3

Chatterjee, R., & Roy, I. (2025). Role of Absorptive Capacity and Science and Technology Parks in Regional Innovation: A Triple Helix Perspective From India. *Journal of Public Affairs*, *25*(2), e70029.

Chekanov, A. (2022). The Triple Helix in transition economies and Skolkovo: A Russian innovation ecosystem case. *Journal of Evolutionary Studies in Business*, *7*(2), 160–183. DOI: 10.1344/jesb2022.2.j110

Cheng, C., Cheng, S., & Feng, C. (2024). The Triple Helix Model for Industry-Education City Integration in China: A Development Approach. *SAGE Open*, *14*(2), 21582440241250111.

Cheng, Y., Liu, Y., Fan, W., Yan, Z., & Ye, X. (2019). Triple helix on globalization: A case study of the China International Nanotech Innovation Cluster. *Information Development*, *35*(2), 272–289. DOI: 10.1177/0266666917743050

Chen, H., Zeng, Y., & Cai, D. (2025). Deep learning for cardiovascular management: Optimizing pathways and cost control under diagnosis-related group models. *Frontiers in Artificial Intelligence*, *8*(1580445), 1580445. DOI: 10.3389/frai.2025.1580445

Chen, Z., Little, V. J., & Thuan, N. H. (2025). The evolving role of technology transfer offices in the entrepreneurial university: Go-betweens or playmakers? *The Journal of Technology Transfer*, *50*(3), 1060–1079. DOI: 10.1007/s10961-024-10123-4

Chfadi, T., Abdulkader, B., & Chirinda, N. (2025). From syllabi to startups: Lessons from eight African case studies on university-industry collaboration and agri-entrepreneurship education. *Frontiers in Sustainable Food Systems*, *9*, 1572898.

Chinen, M. (2025). International Governance of AI. In *Handbook of Human-Centered Artificial Intelligence* (pp. 1–37). Springer Nature Singapore., DOI: 10.1007/978-981-97-8440-0_83-1

Chintoh, G. A., Segun-Falade, O. D., Odionu, C. S., & Ekeh, A. H. (2024). Legal and ethical challenges in AI governance: A conceptual approach to developing ethical compliance models in the U.s. *International Journal of Social Science Exceptional Research*, *3*(1), 103–109. DOI: 10.54660/ijsser.2024.3.1.103-109

Chowdhury, P. P., Khan, M. M. A., Sayem, A., Asif, M. A. R., & Roy, A. (2025). Assessment of organizations' maturity towards circular economy practice in manufacturing industries: Evidence from a developing economy. *Cleaner Logistics and Supply Chain*, *17*, 100286. DOI: 10.1016/j.clscn.2025.100286

Conruyt, N., Sébastien, V., Sébastien, O., Sébastien, D., & Grosser, D. (2014, September). Sign management for the future of e-education: examples of collaborative e-services in a Living Lab. In *IFIP International Workshop on Artificial Intelligence for Knowledge Management* (pp. 1-20). Cham: Springer International Publishing.

Cooke, P. (2025). Triple helix selection in the regional innovation systems field. In memoriam: Loet Leydesdorff. *Scientometrics*, •••, 1–10.

Cotton, D. R. E., Cotton, P. A., & Shipway, J. R. (2023). Educators' perspectives on artificial intelligence in higher education. *Computers & Education, 197*, 104763. DOI: 10.1016/j.compedu.2023.104763

Creswell, J. W., & Poth, C. N. (2018). *Qualitative inquiry and research design: Choosing among five approaches* (4th ed.). Sage Publications.

Crişan, G.-A., Suciu, A.-A., Domenteanu, A., & Popescu, M. E. (2025). Digitalization and the innovation of Artificial Intelligence: A systematic review. *Proceedings of the International Conference on Business Excellence, 19*(1), 2740–2754. https://doi.org/DOI: 10.2478/picbe-2025-0211

da Rocha, A. B. T., Espuny, M., Kandsamy, J., & Oliveira, O. (2024). Advancing sustainability in the steel industry: The key role of the triple helix sectors. *Environmental Science and Pollution Research International, 31*(31), 43591–43615.

Dadhich, A., & Bansal, Y. (2025). Implementing Responsible and Ethical Artificial Intelligence in India: Balancing Innovation and Regulation for Sustainable AI Development. In *AI Ethics in Practice: Navigating Academic Insight, Managerial Expertise, and Philosophical Inquiry* (pp. 23-40). Cham: Springer Nature Switzerland. https://doi.org/DOI: 10.1007/978-3-031-87023-1_3

Daliri, H. (2024). AI Revolution and the Triple Helix Dynamics in Economy. *Journal of Science and Technology Policy, 17*(4), 53–70.

Daradkah, A. M., Alotaibi, T. K., Mahmoud, A. M. A., Awais, B. E., Al-Qudah, M. A., & Shannaq, R. M. A., ... & Mahmoud10, S. S. M. (2023). A Proposed Model for Integration and Cooperation between University, Industry, and Government in Arab countries: Innovation Triple Helix Model. *Applied Mathematics & Information Sciences, 17*(6), 1109–1144.

de Lima Figueiredo, N., Fernandes, C. I., & Abrantes, J. L. (2023). Triple helix model: Cooperation in knowledge creation. *Journal of the Knowledge Economy, 14*(2), 854–878. DOI: 10.1007/s13132-022-00930-1 de Oliveira, O. J., da Rocha, A. B. T., Costa, A. C. F., & Espuny, M. (2024). Technical-Scientific Scenario Based on the Triple Helix: Innovative Approach Beyond Bibliometrics. In *Bibliometrics-An Essential Methodological Tool for Research Projects*. IntechOpen.

Department of Computer Science and Information Technology Pune Maharashtra 412201 India, M. I. T. A. D. and T. U., Pathan, M. S., Patare, S., & Department of Computer Science and Information Technology Pune Maharashtra 412201 India, M. I. T. A. D. and T. U. (2025). The socioeconomic impact of artificial Intelligence: Profit-driven growth and the struggle for control. *Journal of Collective Sciences and Sustainability, 1*(1), 1–8. https://doi.org/DOI: 10.64189/css.25402

Deri, M. N., Zaazie, P., & Singh, A. (2024). Digital Future of the Hospitality Industry and Hospitality Education Globally. In Sharma, A. (Ed.), *International Handbook of Skill, Education, Learning, and Research Development in Tourism and Hospitality. Springer International Handbooks of Education*. Springer., DOI: 10.1007/978-981-97-4318-6_14

Dewan Perwakilan Rakyat Republik Indonesia. (2025). *Info Singkat: Rancangan Undang-Undang tentang Kecerdasan Buatan (AI Bill)*. https://berkas.dpr.go.id/pusaka/files/info_singkat/Info%20Singkat-XVII-9-I-P3DI-Mei-2025-2417-EN.pdf

Direktorat, J. P. T. (2024). *Buku panduan penggunaan generative artificial intelligence pada pembelajaran di perguruan tinggi*. Ministry of Education, Culture, Research, and Technology., https://lldikti3.kemdikbud.go.id/wp-content/uploads/2024/11/Buku-Panduan-_-Penggunaan-Generative-AI-pada-Pembelajaran-di-Perguruan-Tinggi-cetak.pdf

Dooley, L., & Kirk, D. (2007). University-industry collaboration. *European Journal of Innovation Management, 10*(3), 316–332. DOI: 10.1108/14601060710776734

Dunleavy, P., & Margetts, H. (2025). Data science, artificial intelligence and the third wave of digital era governance. *Public Policy and Administration, 40*(2), 185–214. DOI: 10.1177/09520767231198737

Edler, J., & Fagerberg, J. (2017). Innovation policy: What, why, and how. *Oxford Review of Economic Policy, 33*(1), 2–23. DOI: 10.1093/oxrep/grx001

Edmunds, L. D., Gluderer, S., Ovseiko, P. V., Kamerling, R., Ton, J., Vis, L., Jenni, M., Tutton, G., Lawton-Smith, H., Nadabán, M. V., Rab, M., Rees, J., Anson, J., Rushforth, A. D., Allen, M., Buchan, A. M., Vendrell, M., Casta, A., Mehes, G., & Hassan, A. B. (2019). New indicators and indexes for benchmarking university-industry-government innovation in medical and life science clusters: Results from the European FP7 Regions of Knowledge HealthTIES project. *Health Research Policy and Systems*, *17*(1), 10. DOI: 10.1186/s12961-019-0414-5

Edo, B. L., & Nwonkwo, S. (2025). Triple Helix Partnership in Educational Administration and Planning in Tertiary Institutions in Nigeria. *International Journal of Educational Management, Rivers State University.*, *1*(2), 325-338.

Ermaningtiastuti, C. (2024). *Anabatic Technologies and BINUS University demonstrate a commitment to filling the gap between industry and education.* https://www.anabatic.com/blogs/anabatic-technologies-and-binus-university-show-commitment-to-fill-the-gap-between-industry-and-education-sectors/

Esangbedo, C. O., Zhang, J., Esangbedo, M. O., Kone, S. D., & Xu, L. (2024). The role of industry-academia collaboration in enhancing educational opportunities and outcomes under the digital driven Industry 4.0. *Journal of Infrastructure. Policy and Development*, *8*(1), 2569.

Escobar, S., & Sciortino, D. (2022). *Artificial intelligence in Canada. International perspectives on artificial intelligence, 13*. Anthem Press.

Espuny, M., Reis, J. S. D. M., Giupponi, E. C. B., Rocha, A. B. T., Costa, A. C. F., Poltronieri, C. F., & Oliveira, O. J. D. (2025). The role of the triple helix model in promoting the circular economy: Government-led integration strategies and practical application. *Recycling*, *10*(2), 50.

Etzkowitz, H. (2003). Innovation in innovation: The Triple Helix of university-industry-government relations. *Social Sciences Information. Information Sur les Sciences Sociales*, *42*(3), 293–337. DOI: 10.1177/05390184030423002

Etzkowitz, H., & Klofsten, M. (2005). The innovating region: Toward a theory of knowledge-based regional development. *R & D Management*, *35*(3), 243–255. DOI: 10.1111/j.1467-9310.2005.00387.x

Etzkowitz, H., & Leydesdorff, L. (1995). The Triple Helix of university–industry–government relations. *Research Policy*, *24*(2), 197–210. DOI: 10.1016/0048-7333(94)00744-6

Etzkowitz, H., & Leydesdorff, L. (2000). The dynamics of innovation: From National Systems and "Mode 2" to a Triple Helix of university–industry–government relations. *Research Policy*, *29*(2), 109–123. DOI: 10.1016/S0048-7333(99)00055-4

Etzkowitz, H., & Leydesdorff, L. (2021). The Triple Helix: A twenty-five-year retrospective. *Science & Public Policy*, *48*(2), 145–157. DOI: 10.1093/scipol/scaa038

Evjemo, L. D., Gjerstad, T., Grøtli, E. I., & Sziebig, G. (2020). Trends in smart manufacturing: Role of humans and industrial robots in smart factories. *Current Robotics Reports*, *1*(2), 35–41. DOI: 10.1007/s43154-020-00006-5

Ezeuduji, I. O., Nzama, A. T., Nkosi, G. S., Kheswa, T. P., & Shokane, A. L. (2023). Stakeholder perceptions of university-industry collaboration on tourism and business students' employability in two continents. *Journal of Teaching in Travel & Tourism*, *23*(3), 330–353.

Fang, B., Zhang, P., & Kim, S. (2023). National human resource development in China: Government–industry–university relations and roles. *European Journal of Training and Development*, *47*(1/2), 183–202.

Farinha, L., Ferreira, J., & Gouveia, B. (2016). Networks of innovation and competitiveness: A triple helix case study. *Journal of the Knowledge Economy*, *7*(1), 259–275. DOI: 10.1007/s13132-014-0218-3

Fasi, M. A. (2024). Triple helix collaboration: Uncovering research opportunities among industry, academia, and researchers—A case study of Saudi Aramco's patent portfolio analysis. *Journal of the Knowledge Economy*, *15*(3), 14486–14520.

Ferdinands, R., Azam, S. F., & Khatibi, A. (2024). The work in progress of a developing nation's triple helix and its impact on patent commercialization. The case of Sri Lanka. *Journal of Science and Technology Policy Management*, *15*(4), 839–862.

Fernandes, E. B., Wegner, D., & Möllering, G. (2023). Governance of interorganizational projects: A process-based approach applied to a Latin American–European case. *Project Management Journal*, *54*(3), 219–234. DOI: 10.1177/87569728221145927

Figueiredo, R., Soliman, M., Al-Alawi, A. N., & Fatnassi, T. (2023). Could the 'Spinner Innovation' and 'Triple Helix' Models Improve System Innovation? *Applied System Innovation*, *6*(2), 42.

Fisk, R., Fuessel, A., Laszlo, C., Struebi, P., Valera, A., & Weiss, C. (2019). Systemic social innovation: Co-creating a future where humans and all life thrive. *Humanistic Management Journal*, *4*(2), 191–214.

Flechas, X. A., Kazunari Takahashi, C., & Bastos de Figueiredo, J. C. (2023). The triple helix and the quality of the startup ecosystem: A global view. *Revista de Gestao*, *30*(3), 238–252.

Floridi, L. (2021). The ethics of artificial intelligence: Principles, challenges, and opportunities. *Philosophy & Technology*, *34*(4), 1377–1394. DOI: 10.1007/s13347-020-00402-y

Folorunso, A., Olanipekun, K., Adewumi, T., & Samuel, B. (2024). A policy framework on AI usage in developing countries and its impact. *Global Journal of Engineering and Technology Advances*, *21*(1), 154–166. DOI: 10.30574/gjeta.2024.21.1.0192

Fujii, T., Guo, T., & Kamoshida, A. (2018, August). A consideration of service strategy of Japanese electric manufacturers to realize super smart society (Society 5.0). In *International Conference on Knowledge Management in Organizations* (pp. 634-645). Cham: Springer International Publishing.

Fu, T., & Ji, Y. (2024). Government-university relationship in China's AI talent development: A triple helix perspective. *SAGE Open*, *14*(2), 21582440241259012.

Garg, A., Singh, A., & Yanan, J. (2024). Exploring the Impact of Digital Detoxification on Higher Education Students' Learning. In Grima, S., Chaudhary, S., Sood, K., & Kumar, S. (Eds.), *Business Drivers in Promoting Digital Detoxification* (pp. 111–126). IGI Global Scientific Publishing., DOI: 10.4018/979-8-3693-1107-3.ch008

George, A. J., & Tarr, J. A. (2024). A case study in innovation policymaking: Standard contracts as a tool to improve university–industry collaboration. *Journal of Science and Technology Policy Management*, *15*(5), 1085–1109. DOI: 10.1108/JSTPM-11-2021-0175

Georgiou, O., Maksymenko, M., & Russo, S. (2025). Responsible Research and Innovation. In *R&D Management and Technology Commercialization: Practical Concepts, Innovation, and Case Studies* (pp. 247-255). Cham: Springer Nature Switzerland. https://doi.org/DOI: 10.1007/978-3-031-86789-7_15

Giannini, R., Fernández Martínez, J. L., Irigaray García de Serrana, J., & Tomás–Pérez, C. (2025). Fostering Innovation Ecosystems Through Academia: A Strategic Approach to Business Entrepreneurship and Knowledge Transfer. In *Business Entrepreneurship and Innovation: The Advocacy for a Tech-Corporate Ecosystem* (pp. 1–26). Springer Nature Switzerland.

Gianni, R., Lehtinen, S., & Nieminen, M. (2022). Governance of responsible AI: From ethical guidelines to cooperative policies. *Frontiers of Computer Science, 4*(873437). Advance online publication. DOI: 10.3389/fcomp.2022.873437

Global, N., & Kazanskaia, A. N. (2025). *Machine learning models and algorithms: Approaches, applications, and best practices*. NEYA Global Journal of Non-Profit Studies., DOI: 10.64357/neya-gjnps-ai-mch-lr-04

Goktas, P., & Grzybowski, A. (2025). Shaping the future of healthcare: Ethical clinical challenges and pathways to trustworthy AI. *Journal of Clinical Medicine, 14*(5), 1605. DOI: 10.3390/jcm14051605

Golec, M., Hatay, E. S., Gill, S. S., & Buyya, R. (2025). Artificial Intelligence (AI): Foundations, trends and future directions. *Telematics and Informatics Reports, 20*. Advance online publication. DOI: 10.1016/j.teler.2025.100265

Gong, Y., Singh, R., & Mi, J. (2025). Collaborative governance based on Triple Helix strategy for disaster risk reduction digitalization: Experience from China. *Disaster Prevention and Management: An International Journal, 34*(3), 385–397.

González-Aleu, F., Francisco Suarez Barraza, M., Garza-Reyes, J. A., & Antony, J. (2024). Guest editorial: Quality 4.0 and Kaizen during disruptive times: addressing the triple helix actors' COVID-19 pandemic challenges. *The TQM Journal, 36*(6), 1397–1401.

Goracinova, E., Warrian, P., & Wolfe, D. A. (2017). Challenges of coordination: Automotive innovation in the Ontario supply chain in comparative context. *Canadian Public Policy, 43*(S1), S90–S102. DOI: 10.3138/cpp.2016-024

Government of Singapore. (2023). *National AI strategy 2023*. https://www.smartnation.gov.sg/initiatives/national-ai-strategy/

Guevara, K. M., Martínez-Valenzuela, G., Sánchez-Vásquez, V., Guerrero-Ruiz, K., & Fiallos-Cárdenas, M. (2025). Trends and perspectives on bacterial nanocellulose: A comprehensive analysis from the three helixes of innovation. In *Materials Today Sustainability* (Vol. 30). Elsevier Ltd., DOI: 10.1016/j.mtsust.2025.101090

Güneş, A., & Kaban, A. L. (2025). A Delphi study on ethical challenges and ensuring academic integrity regarding AI research in higher education. *Higher Education Quarterly, 79*(4). Advance online publication. DOI: 10.1111/hequ.70057

Guo, T., He, A., Zhai, L., & Yan, S. (2025). Can Interactive Platform of University Science Parks Enhance the Quality of University Research Outcomes? Evidence from a Differencein-Differences Model. *Frontiers in Physics, 13*, 1642172.

Gupta, C., & Pandey, P. (2025). Catalysing sustainable development: the role of DST in attaining SDGs in India and the way forward. *Proceedings of the Indian National Science Academy*, 1-14. https://doi.org/DOI: 10.1007/s43538-025-00398-y

Hailu, A. T. (2024). The role of university–industry linkages in promoting technology transfer: Implementation of triple helix model relations. *Journal of Innovation and Entrepreneurship, 13*(1), 25.

Hakeem, M. M., & Goi, H. C., Frendy, & Ito, H. (2023). Regional sustainable development using a Quadruple Helix approach in Japan. *Regional Studies, Regional Science, 10*(1), 119–138.

Han, C., Li, F., Wang, M., Zhou, C., Liu, Z., & Yang, C. (2024, September). Framework of a PBL tutor system based on the triple helix model in environmental science. In *Proceedings of the 2024 the 16th International Conference on Education Technology and Computers* (pp. 511-517).

Haryadi, A., Sulistyadi, E., & Asmoro, N. (2025). Driving Innovation in the Defense Sector: Unlocking the Power of Industry, Academia, and Government Collaboration. *Formosa Journal of Multidisciplinary Research, 4*(2), 991–1002.

Hendra, D. (2024). *BINUS University bangun riset AI pertama di Indonesia*. https://swa.co.id/read/173219/binus-university-bangun-riset-ai-pertama-di-indonesia

Hoareau, K. (2025). Knowledge, power and the blue economy: Breaking down barriers. *Marine Policy, 182*. Advance online publication. DOI: 10.1016/j.marpol.2025.106883

Holguín Rengifo, Y. X., Herrera Vargas, J. F., & Valencia-Arias, A. (2023). Proposal for a Comprehensive Tool to Measure Smart Cities under the Triple-Helix Model: Capacities Learning, Research, and Development. *Sustainability, 15*(18), 13549.

Hosseini Tabaghdehi, S. A., & Ayaz, Ö. (2025). AI ethics in action: A circular model for transparency, accountability and inclusivity. *Journal of Managerial Psychology*. Advance online publication. DOI: 10.1108/JMP-03-2024-0177

Hossen, M. A., Misbauddin, S. M., Molla, C., Nabi, M. N. U., & Sakib, M. N. (2025). Decoding university–industry collaboration: A SEM-ANN quadruple helix approach. *Future Business Journal, 11*(1), 236.

Hsu, S. C. J., Hsu, H. M., & Hwang, S. Y. (2020). Co-creating future of Artificial Intelligence of Things (AIoT) through ecosystem partnership: a case study of Advantech Co., Ltd. In *Business Innovation with New ICT in the Asia-Pacific: Case Studies* (pp. 111–132). Springer Nature Singapore.

Huang, J., Xu, Y., Wang, Q., & Wang, Q. (Cheems), Liang, X., Wang, F., Zhang, Z., Wei, W., Zhang, B., Huang, L., Chang, J., Ma, L., Ma, T., Liang, Y., Zhang, J., Guo, J., Jiang, X., Fan, X., An, Z., … Fei, A. (2025). Foundation models and intelligent decision-making: Progress, challenges, and perspectives. In *Innovation* (Vol. 6, Issue 6). Cell Press. https://doi.org/DOI: 10.1016/j.xinn.2025.100948

Huang, X., & Zhou, Q. (2025). Knowledge management model in the integration of open innovation and circular economy driven by digital intelligence: A comparative multi-case study. *Journal of Innovation and Knowledge*, *10*(6). Advance online publication. DOI: 10.1016/j.jik.2025.100839

Ideland, M., & Serder, M. (2023). Edu-business within the Triple Helix. Value production through assetization of educational research. *Education Inquiry*, *14*(3), 336–351.

Inampudi, S., & Gaurav, A. K. (2024). Transforming Institutions for Inclusive and Sustainable Governance: An Empirical Analysis of NITI Aayog's Role in India. In *Governance and Sustainable Development in South Asia: Bridging the Gap* (pp. 177-195). Cham: Springer Nature Switzerland. https://doi.org/DOI: 10.1007/978-3-031-67616-1_10

Indonesia, P. (2024). *AI vs. kekayaan intelektual (KI): Apakah hukum Indonesia siap menghadapi era AI generatif?* https://cms.paralegals.id/uploads/Salinan_dari_AI_vs_Kekayaan_Intelektual_KI_Apakah_Hukum_Indonesia_Siap_Menghadapi_Era_AI_Generatif_100be2823d.pdf

Ismail, O., & Ahmad, N. (2025). Ethical and governance frameworks for artificial intelligence: A systematic literature review. [IJIM]. *International Journal of Interactive Mobile Technologies*, *19*(14), 121–136. DOI: 10.3991/ijim.v19i14.56981

Ivančić, L., Vuksanović Herceg, I., & Dabić, M. (2022). Triple Helix and digital transformation: A systematic literature review. *Technological Forecasting and Social Change*, *174*, 121204. DOI: 10.1016/j.techfore.2021.121204

Jelovac, D., Ljubojević, Č., & Ljubojević, L. (2022). HPC in business: The impact of corporate digital responsibility on building digital trust and responsible corporate digital governance. *Digital Policy Regulation and Governance*, *24*(6), 485–497. DOI: 10.1108/dprg-11-2020-0164

Jobin, A., Ienca, M., & Vayena, E. (2019). The global landscape of AI ethics guidelines. *Nature Machine Intelligence*, *1*(9), 389–399. DOI: 10.1038/s42256-019-0088-2

Jose, K., Venn, A., Jarman, L., Seal, J., Teale, B., Scott, J., & Sanderson, K. (2016). Partnering Healthy@Work: An Australian university—government partnership facilitating policy-relevant research. *Health Promotion International*, daw033. Advance online publication. DOI: 10.1093/heapro/daw033

Joy, Z. H., Master of Science in Business Analytics Michigan USA, T. U., Rahman, M. M., Uzzaman, A. U., Maraj, M. A. A., Master of Computer and Information Science Arkansas USA, S. A. U., Graduate Researcher College of Business Lamar University Beaumont Texas USA, M. I. S., & Graduate Researcher College of Business Lamar University Beaumont Texas USA, M. I. S. (2024). Integrating machine learning and big data analytics for real-time disease detection in smart healthcare systems. *Global Mainstream Journal*, *1*(3), 16–27. DOI: 10.62304/ijhm.v1i3.162

Jumiyati, S. (2024). Development of climate smart agriculture based on empowering farmers around forests through triple-helix collaboration. *Interaction, Community Engagement, and Social Environment*, *2*(1), 75–91.

Kasirye, F. (2025). The Evolution of University Industry Relations: Fostering Innovation and Economic Development in Georgia through the Triple Helix Model. *Journal of Effective Teaching and Learning Practices*, *2*(2), 97–109.

Kaur, S. (2024). Advancements in artificial Intelligence: Machine Learning techniques and their real-world applications. *Journal of Sustainable Solutions*, *1*(4), 138–144. DOI: 10.36676/j.sust.sol.v1.i4.45

Keith, A. J. (2024). Governance of artificial intelligence in Southeast Asia. *Global Policy*, *15*(5), 937–954. DOI: 10.1111/1758-5899.13458

Kementerian Komunikasi dan Informatika. (2023). *Surat edaran Menteri Komunikasi dan Informatika nomor 9 tahun 2023 tentang etika kecerdasan artifisial.* https://jdih.komdigi.go.id/produk_hukum/view/id/883/t/surat+edaran+menteri+komunikasi+dan+informatika+nomor+9+tahun+2023

Kim, G. Y., Lee, W. J., Choi, B., & Lew, Y. K. (2025). Fostering collaborative opportunities for AI start-ups: The case of a hybrid business incubator in Seoul. *The Journal of Technology Transfer*, *50*(2), 552–581.

Konno, N., & Schillaci, C. E. (2021). Intellectual capital in Society 5.0 by the lens of the knowledge creation theory. *Journal of Intellectual Capital*, *22*(3), 478–505.

Kowch, E. G. (2025). An innovation policy analysis of G10 nations' strategic plans for future AI leaders and researchers in higher education. In *Navigating Generative AI in Higher Education* (pp. 211–234). Edward Elgar Publishing.

Kumar, V., Verma, P., Mittal, A., Gupta, P., Raj, R., & Kaswan, M. S. (2024). Addressing the Kaizen business operations: The role of triple helix actors during COVID-19 outbreak. *The TQM Journal*, *36*(6), 1665–1694.

Kunwar, R. R., & Ulak, N. (2023). Understanding the Triple Helix Model and capitalization of knowledge. *Journal of APF Command and Staff College*, *6*(01), 1–34.

Kunwar, R. R., & Ulak, N. (2024). Extension of the triple helix to quadruple to quintuple helix model. *Journal of APF Command and Staff College*, *7*(1), 241–280.

Kwon, K.-S., Park, H. W., So, M., & Leydesdorff, L. (2012). Has globalization strengthened South Korea's national research system? National and international dynamics of the Triple Helix of scientific. *Scientometrics*, *90*(1), 163–176. DOI: 10.1007/s11192-011-0512-9

Laï, M.-C., Brian, M., & Mamzer, M.-F. (2020). Perceptions of artificial intelligence in healthcare: Findings from a qualitative survey study among actors in France. *Journal of Translational Medicine*, *18*(1), 14. DOI: 10.1186/s12967-019-02204-y

Larson, D. B., Magnus, D. C., Lungren, M. P., Shah, N. H., & Langlotz, C. P. (2020). Ethics of using and sharing clinical imaging data for artificial intelligence: A proposed framework. *Radiology*, *295*(3), 675–682. DOI: 10.1148/radiol.2020192536

Lase, D., Waruwu, E., Zai, A. Y., & Waruwu, R. M. P. (2025). Should the government regulate Artificial Intelligence and its dangers in society? *Tuhenori: Jurnal Ilmiah Multidisiplin*, *3*(4), 260–282. DOI: 10.62138/tuhenori.v3i4.161

Lau, P. L. (2025). The AI Act and Data Protection: The Interplay Between Artificial Intelligence and Data: The AI Act and the GDPR. In *The European Artificial Intelligence Act: Promises and Perils?* (pp. 289-313). Cham: Springer Nature Switzerland. https://doi.org/DOI: 10.1007/978-3-031-98406-8_12

Law, T., & McCall, L. (2024). Artificial intelligence policymaking: An agenda for sociological research. *Socius: Sociological Research for a Dynamic World*, *10*, 23780231241261596. DOI: 10.1177/23780231241261596

Lee, C., & Ma, L. (2020). The role of policy labs in policy experiment and knowledge transfer: A comparison across the UK, Denmark, and Singapore. *Journal of Comparative Policy Analysis*, *22*(4), 281–297.

Lessa, L. S., de Oliveira, M. M., & Canciglieri, O., Junior. (2023, July). Innovative Development in a University Environment Based on the Triple Helix Concepts: A Systematic Literature Review. In *IFIP International Conference on Product Lifecycle Management* (pp. 181-190). Cham: Springer Nature Switzerland.

Leung, R., & Loo, P. T. (2022). Co-creating interactive dining experiences via interconnected and interoperable smart technology. *Asian Journal of Technology Innovation*, *30*(1), 45–67.

Leydesdorff, L. (2012). The triple helix, quadruple helix, …, and an N-tuple of helices: Explanatory models for analyzing the knowledge-based economy? *Journal of the Knowledge Economy*, *3*(1), 25–35. DOI: 10.1007/s13132-011-0049-4

Leydesdorff, L. (2021). Evolutionary and institutional triple helix models. In *The Evolutionary Dynamics of Discursive Knowledge: Communication-Theoretical Perspectives on an Empirical Philosophy of Science* (pp. 89–113). Springer International Publishing., DOI: 10.1007/978-3-030-59951-5_5

Liao, F., & Lai, H. (2023). A Collaborative Training Mechanism for Accounting Digital Intelligence Talents Based on the Triple Helix Theory. *Journal of Intelligence and Knowledge Engineering (ISSN: 2959-0620)*, *1*(3), 1.

Liao, H. T., Pan, C. L., & Wu, Z. (2024). Digital transformation and innovation and business ecosystems: A bibliometric analysis for conceptual insights and collaborative practices for ecosystem innovation. *International Journal of Innovation Studies*, *8*(4), 406–431. DOI: 10.1016/j.ijis.2024.04.003

Lim, W. M. (2026). Theory and theory development: Guidelines for establishing theoretical gaps, foundations, contributions, and implications. *Journal of Business Research*, *202*. Advance online publication. DOI: 10.1016/j.jbusres.2025.115745

Lin, Y., Lin, Y., Liu, J., Tan, Z., & Han, W. (2025). Triple Helix Synergy Model in China's new technology diplomacy: Perspectives from AI startups. *Telecommunications Policy*, •••, 103079.

Liu, D., & Zhu, Y. P. (2023). Evolution of knowledge structure in an emerging field based on a triple helix model: The case of smart factory. *Journal of the Knowledge Economy*, *14*(4), 4583–4607.

Liu, J., & Jiang, M. (2025). The Impact of Industry-University-Research Institute Cooperation on the Innovation Capability of Chinese University Faculty. *Higher Education Studies*, *15*(4), 298–311.

Liu, J., Wang, X., Miao, W., & Wang, X. (2025). What factors enable sustainable university-industry collaboration communities? Evidence from a symbiosis theory perspective. *Sustainable Futures : An Applied Journal of Technology, Environment and Society*, *10*, 101166.

Liu, X., Fang, Y., & Lan, X. (2025). Regulations, technology policies and universities' attitudes to artificial intelligence in China. *Higher Education Quarterly*, *79*(4). Advance online publication. DOI: 10.1111/hequ.70055

Li, Z. (2024). AI ethics and transparency in operations management: How governance mechanisms can reduce data bias and privacy risks. *Journal of Applied Economics and Policy Studies*, *13*(1), 89–93. DOI: 10.54254/2977-5701/13/2024130

Loggers, J. C. J., Reinders, M. E. J., van Gelder, T., van der Horst, V. M., Bischoff, K. M. S. L., & Guchelaar, H. J. (2025). Academic–industry collaboration in biomedical innovation: A multi-model review of barriers and facilitators. *Drug Discovery Today*, •••, 104560.

Lubaba, M., Hassan, S., Sultana, M., Morshed, S. M., & Bari, A. B. M. M. (2025). Assessment of the challenges to implementing green manufacturing in the food and beverage industry: An emerging economy perspective. *Waste Management Bulletin*, *3*(3). Advance online publication. DOI: 10.1016/j.wmb.2025.100225

Lucchi, N. (2025). *Artificial intelligence act: A comparative analysis of the EU and international AI governance frameworks*. https://www.europarl.europa.eu/RegData/etudes/STUD/2025/774095/IUST_STU(2025)774095_EN.pdf

Lulaj, E., & Brajković, M. (2025). The Moderating Role of Finance, Accounting, and Digital Disruption in ESG, Financial Reporting, and Auditing: A Triple-Helix Perspective. *Journal of Risk and Financial Management*, *18*(5), 245.

Luo, H. (2020). An emergency management system for government data security based on artificial intelligence. *Ingénierie Des Systèmes d Information*, *25*(2), 207–213. DOI: 10.18280/isi.250208

Luong, A. N. (2023). Aligning the Quintuple Helix model of innovation with Vietnams context: evidence from artificial intelligence innovation dialogues. In *The Elgar Companion to Digital Transformation, Artificial Intelligence and Innovation in the Economy, Society and Democracy* (pp. 254-275). Edward Elgar Publishing.

Lu, Q., Zhao, D., Liu, Y., Zhang, H., Zhu, L., Xu, X., Shi, A., Tan, T., & Kazman, R. (2026). AgentArcEval: An architecture evaluation method for foundation model based agents. *Journal of Systems and Software*, *232*, 112656. DOI: 10.1016/j.jss.2025.112656

Lu, Q., Zhu, L., Xu, X., & Whittle, J. (2023). Responsible-AI-by-design: A pattern collection for designing responsible AI systems. *IEEE Software*, •••, 1–7. DOI: 10.1109/ms.2022.3233582

Madan, R., & Ashok, M. (2023). AI adoption and diffusion in public administration: A systematic literature review and future research agenda. *Government Information Quarterly*, *40*(1), 101774. DOI: 10.1016/j.giq.2022.101774

Mahardika, Z. P., & Priancha, A. (2021). *Pengaturan hukum artificial intelligence Indonesia saat ini.* https://www.hukumonline.com/berita/a/pengaturan-hukum-artifical-intelligence-indonesia-saat-ini-lt608b740fb22b7/

Mahetaji, K., Zogheib, C., & Spencer, R. (2025). Intersections between government data and AI strategies: A case study of technology policies in Canada's federal service. *Proceedings of the Association for Information Science and Technology*, *62*(1), 1024–1029. DOI: 10.1002/pra2.1333

Ma, J., & Yang, D. (2024). Research on the mechanism of government-industry-university-research collaboration for cultivating innovative talent based on game theory. *Heliyon*, *10*(3).

Malhotra, C., & Malhotra, U. (2024). Putting interests of digital nagriks first: Digital personal data protection (dpdp) act 2023 of India. *The Indian Journal of Public Administration*, *70*(3), 516–531. DOI: 10.1177/00195561241271575

Mamès, M., Donner, M., & de Vries, H. (2025). Partnerships for sustainable food and bioeconomy systems in Europe: Exploring the role of intermediaries. *Sustainable Futures : An Applied Journal of Technology, Environment and Society*, *10*. Advance online publication. DOI: 10.1016/j.sftr.2025.101361

Mao, Z., Wu, J., & Liu, M. (2023). A CIO-centric local government data-sharing leadership ecosystem in China. *Information Development*, *39*(4), 798–810. DOI: 10.1177/02666669211054176

Masters in Criminal Justice Lamar University Beaumont Texas USA, C. of A. and S., Talukder, K. A., Shompa, T. F., & Advocate Dhaka Bangladesh, D. J. C. (2024). Artificial intelligence in criminal justice management: A systematic literature review. *Non Human Journal*, *1*(01), 63–82. DOI: 10.70008/jmldeds.v1i01.42

Matovu, B., Mim, T. A., & Lutalo, B. (2025). Where and how can Africa and India leverage the blue economy opportunities of the Indian Ocean region as a driver for sustainable development and partnerships? In *Sustainable Futures* (Vol. 10). Elsevier Ltd., DOI: 10.1016/j.sftr.2025.101218

Mayho, S., Mumford, D., Ellis, L., Lloyd, D. C., Redmond, E. C., & Clifton, N. (2024). The evolution of regional triple helix food sector SME interventions: A longitudinal study, Wales, UK. *European Planning Studies*, *32*(9), 2046–2069.

McCradden, M. D., Baba, A., Saha, A., Ahmad, S., Boparai, K., Fadaiefard, P., & Cusimano, M. D. (2020). Ethical concerns around use of artificial intelligence in health care research from the perspective of patients with meningioma, caregivers and health care providers: A qualitative study. *CMAJ Open*, *8*(1), E90–E95. DOI: 10.9778/cmajo.20190151

McCradden, M. D., Sarker, T., & Paprica, P. A. (2020). Conditionally positive: A qualitative study of public perceptions about using health data for artificial intelligence research. *BMJ Open*, *10*(10), e039798. DOI: 10.1136/bmjopen-2020-039798

Mêgnigbêto, E. (2025). Convexity of the triple helix of innovation game. *International Journal of Innovation Science*, *17*(3), 563–580.

Meszaros, J., Minari, J., & Huys, I. (2022). The future regulation of artificial intelligence systems in healthcare services and medical research in the European Union. *Frontiers in Genetics*, *13*, 927721. DOI: 10.3389/fgene.2022.927721

Miah, M. T., Aiupova, N., Erdei-Gally, S., & Fekete-Farkas, M. (2025). Digital entrepreneurship ecosystems: Then vs. now-a future perspectives. *Digital Business*, *5*(1). Advance online publication. DOI: 10.1016/j.digbus.2025.100110

Middlehurst, R. (2020). Governing higher education in a digital age. *Higher Education Policy*, *33*(4), 695–713. DOI: 10.1057/s41307-020-00186-1

Mikhaylov, S. J., Esteve, M., & Campion, A. (2018). Artificial intelligence for the public sector: Opportunities and challenges of cross-sector collaboration. *Philosophical Transactions. Series A, Mathematical, Physical, and Engineering Sciences*, *376*(2128), 20170357. DOI: 10.1098/rsta.2017.0357

Miller, K., McAdam, M., & McAdam, R. (2014). The changing university business model: A stakeholder perspective. *R & D Management*, *44*(3), 265–287. DOI: 10.1111/radm.12064

Moldashev, K., Sahimbekov, B., & Kozhakhmet, S. (2025). The institutional logics of research commercialisation: Reform, misalignment, and hybridisation. *Social Sciences & Humanities Open*, *12*. Advance online publication. DOI: 10.1016/j.ssaho.2025.102000

Monash University Indonesia. (2024). *Ministry of Communication and Digital Affairs and Monash University Indonesia initiate AI collaboration for research and public protection.* https://www.monash.edu/indonesia/news/ministry-of-communication-and-digital-affairs-and-monash-university-indonesia-initiate-ai-collaboration-for-research-and-public-protection

Morrar, R., & Arman, H. (2024). The transformational role of a third actor within the Triple Helix Model–the case of Palestine. *Innovation (Abingdon)*, *37*(2), 340–360.

Ms. Lolakshi, P. K., Satwik, K. D., Rai, S. R., Patgar, S. M., & Poojary, S. R. (2024). A review on A study of impact of technological advancement of intellectual property and research methodologies. International Journal of Advanced Research in Science. *Tongxin Jishu*, *389–393*. Advance online publication. DOI: 10.48175/ijarsct-19259

Mulyadi, E., Valeriani, D., & Fitriyanti, E. (2024). Implementation of the Triple Helix Model in Increasing Economic Opportunities for Waste Management in Pangkalpinang City. *Equity: Jurnal Ekonomi*, *12*(1), 39–47.

Naili, Y. T., Simanjuntak, E. L., & Kostruba, A. (2024). The role of AI in health research: A policy review of higher education foundations. *Journal of Advanced Health Informatics Research*, *2*(2), 102–108. DOI: 10.59247/jahir.v2i2.295

Nasir, N., Azhar, S. M., Ishaq, M. I., & Shafqat, I. (2025). A study on the dynamics of government-university-industry knowledge transfer in emerging knowledge-based economies. *Science & Public Policy*, •••, scaf038.

Navarro, J., Solé-Beteta, X., Carreras-Coch, A., Caballero, V., Pappa, L., Tyrovolas, M., & Zaballos, A. (2024). Bridging academia and industry in the era of Industry 4.0 by means of the triple helix: The PLANET4 initiative. *Journal of Infrastructure. Policy and Development*, *8*(9), 1–35.

Nicoletti, B., & Appolloni, A. (2025). The Impact of AI Foundation models on the future of digital engineering for logistics and supply Chain. *Digital Engineering*, *7*, 100058. DOI: 10.1016/j.dte.2025.100058

Nikolinakos, N. T. (2023). Ethical principles for trustworthy AI. In *EU policy and legal framework for artificial intelligence, robotics and related technologies-the AI Act* (pp. 101–166). Springer International Publishing., DOI: 10.1007/978-3-031-27953-9_3

Nilsson, J., Javed, S., Albertsson, K., Delsing, J., Liwicki, M., & Sandin, F. (2024). Ai concepts for system of systems dynamic interoperability. *Sensors (Basel)*, *24*(9), 2921. DOI: 10.3390/s24092921

Novelli, C., Taddeo, M., & Floridi, L. (2024). Accountability in artificial intelligence: What it is and how it works. *AI & Society*, *39*(4), 1871–1882. DOI: 10.1007/s00146-023-01635-y

Noya, S., Taneo, S. Y. M., Melany, M., & Widyaningrum, S. (2024). Collaboration with Triple Helix: The mediating effect of mass media in expanding SMEs' information access. *Quality Innovation Prosperity*, *28*(1), 67–87. DOI: 10.12776/qip.v28i1.1940

Nuong Deri, M., Singh, A., Zaazie, P., & Anandene, D. (2024). Leveraging Artificial Intelligence in Higher Educational Institutions: A Comprehensive Overview. *Education and Law Review*, (30). Advance online publication. DOI: 10.1344/REYD2024.30.45777

Nwaichi, E. O., Egbe, T. I., & Halilu, A. (2024, October). Democratizing Innovation: The 10: 10: 10: 10 Vision of Triple Helix Nigeria. In *Triple Helix Nigeria SciBiz Annual Conference* (pp. 71-93). Cham: Springer Nature Switzerland.

Nwaichi, P. I., Olayiwola, A., Egbe, T. I., Agi, A., Halilu, A., & Nwaichi, E. O. (2024, October). Future of Triple Helix in Nigeria: Emerging Trends and Opportunities in University-Industry-Government Collaboration. In *Triple Helix Nigeria SciBiz Annual Conference* (pp. 3-25). Cham: Springer Nature Switzerland.

Nwaichi, P. I., Olayiwola, A., Egbe, T. I., Agi, A., Halilu, A., & Nwaichi, E. O. (2025, March). Future of Triple Helix in Nigeria: Emerging Trends and Opportunities. In *Triple Helix Nigeria SciBiz Annual Conference 2024: THN SciBiz* (p. 2). Springer Nature.

Nzeyimana, B. S., Gandhi, J., Tiwari, S., Santos, T. F., Nair, S. S. G., & Santos, C. M. (2025). Bridging gaps in sustainability: HEI-industry collaborations for accelerating SDGs. *Journal of Cleaner Production*, *529*, 146768.

Ojo, A., Porwol, L., Waqar, M., Stasiewicz, A., Osagie, E., Hogan, M., Harney, O., & Zeleti, F. A. (2016). Realizing the innovation potentials from open data: Stakeholders' perspectives on the desired affordances of open data environment. In Collaboration in a Hyperconnected World (pp. 48–59). Springer International Publishing. https://doi.org/DOI: 10.1007/978-3-319-45390-3_5

Olayinka, A. (2023). Synergistic integration of Artificial Intelligence and machine learning in smart manufacturing (Industry 4.0). *World Journal of Advanced Engineering Technology and Sciences*, *10*(1), 255–263. DOI: 10.30574/wjaets.2023.10.1.0264

Oliveira, T., Alves, H., & Leitão, J. (2024). Co-creation and innovation in higher education institutions: A systematic literature review and research agenda. *International Journal of Educational Management*, *38*(3), 839–872.

Organisation for Economic Co-operation and Development (OECD). (2019). *Recommendation of the Council on Artificial Intelligence*. OECD Publishing. https://legalinstruments.oecd.org/en/instruments/OECD-LEGAL-0449

Organisation for Economic Co-operation and Development (OECD). (2021). *AI and data governance in education*. OECD Publishing., DOI: 10.1787/50c98cbd-

Organisation for Economic Co-operation and Development (OECD). (2023). *OECD digital education outlook 2023: Pushing the frontiers with AI.* OECD Publishing., DOI: 10.1787/c74f03de-

Organisation for Economic Co-operation and Development. (2021). *State of Implementation of The OECD AI Principles: Insights from National AI Policies.* https://www.oecd.org/content/dam/oecd/en/publications/reports/2021/06/state-of-implementation-of-the-oecd-ai-principles_38a4a286/1cd40c44-en.pdf

Organisation for Economic Co-operation and Development. (2023). *The state of implementation of the OECD AI Principles four years on.* OECD Artificial Intelligence Papers. https://oecd-ai.case-api.buddyweb.fr/storage/policy-initiatives/Jul2025/fu_s2cdv9y6354q9jt.pdf

Organisation for Economic Co-operation and Development. (2025a). *Japan's national AI strategy and principles for trustworthy AI.* https://oecd-ai.case-api.buddyweb.fr/storage//policy-initiatives/Jul2025/fu_an8s59prsbi4ivz.pdf

Organisation for Economic Co-operation and Development. (2025b). *Thailand's national AI strategy for inclusive digital transformation.* https://oecd-ai.case-api.buddyweb.fr/storage//policy-initiatives/Jul2025/fu_wtw4h5f5zfv7hqk.pdf

Organisation for Economic Co-operation and Development. (2025c). *Republic of Korea's AI innovation strategy for global competitiveness.* https://oecd-ai.case-api.buddyweb.fr/storage//policy-initiatives/Jul2025/fu_2ej83gnpgww3tcm.pdf

Otarola, M. C., Rodríguez, Y. V., Albornoz, J. J., Palomo, J. M., Vera, J. R., & Badilla, J. R. (2025). Innovation systems in Chile: The four helix model of Chilean universities. *Technology in Society*, •••, 103013.

Pallett, H., Price, C., Chilvers, J., & Burall, S. (2024). Just public algorithms: Mapping public engagement with the use of algorithms in UK public services. *Big Data & Society*, *11*(1), 20539517241235867. DOI: 10.1177/20539517241235867

Pandey, P. (2025). Digital Sovereignty and AI: Developing India's National AI Stack for Strategic Autonomy. *Procedia Computer Science*, *254*, 250–259. DOI: 10.1016/j.procs.2025.02.084

Pan, J., & Guo, J. (2022). Innovative collaboration and acceleration: An integrated framework based on knowledge transfer and triple helix. *Journal of the Knowledge Economy*, *13*(4), 3223–3247. DOI: 10.1007/s13132-021-00852-4

Panta, S., & Thapaliya, S. (2025). The Future of Doctoral Education: The Role of Professional Doctorates in Bridging Academia and Industry. *Journal of Integrative Education Studies*, *1*(2), 18–28.

Paracha, A. (2023). Analyzing the difficulties and possibilities of combining responsible and ethical technological advancement with innovation. *Indus Journal of Law and Social Sciences*, *II*(II), 15–22. DOI: 10.70540/ijlss.2023(ii-ii).03

Parekh, P. (2024). Analytics for Public Governance: A Case of Aspirational Districts Program of NITI Aayog. In *Integrating Advancements in Education, and Society for Achieving Sustainability* (pp. 57-64). Routledge.

Park, H. W. (2024). measuring innovation and collaboration system using big data: A case study about Ho Chi Minh city. *Triple Helix (Heidelberg)*, *10*(2), 205–214.

Pasupuleti, M. K. (2025a). Governance Frameworks for ethical AI deployment in Public Sector services. [IJAIRI]. *International Journal of Academic and Industrial Research Innovations*, *05*(05), 561–573. DOI: 10.62311/nesx/rphcr17

Pasupuleti, M. K. (2025b). *Securing AI: Combating deepfakes, misinformation, and bias with Trustworthy Systems*. National Education Services., DOI: 10.62311/nesx/97891

Pearce, T., Maple, M., Shakeshaft, A., Wayland, S., & McKay, K. (2020). What is the co-creation of new knowledge? A content analysis and proposed definition for health interventions. *International Journal of Environmental Research and Public Health*, *17*(7), 2229. DOI: 10.3390/ijerph17072229

Peddinti, S. R. (2025). AI and Federated Learning for cross-industry data collaboration: Applications in finance, E-commerce, and medical tech. *Journal of Information Systems Engineering & Management*, *10*(30s), 78–82. DOI: 10.52783/jisem.v10i30s.4777

Pereira, D., Leitao, J., Oliveira, T., & Peirone, D. (2023). Proposing a holistic research framework for university strategic alliances in sustainable entrepreneurship. *Heliyon*, *9*(5).

Petrenko, E. S., Panshin, I. V., Sozinova, A. A., & Fedorkova, A. V. (2025). Collaboration of Universities and Business in Industry 4.0: International Experience of Reducing the Divide Between the University Education Market and the Job Market. In *Bridging the Gap Between the Higher Education and Labor Markets: Relevance of the Fourth Industrial Revolution* (pp. 159–166). Springer Nature Singapore.

Phiri, J. (2024). Performance reporting for innovation partnerships–the case of the triple helix in Zambia. *Cogent Business & Management*, *11*(1), 2411447.

Pinedo-López, J., Baena-Navarro, R., & Torres-Hoyos, F. (2025). Science, Technology and Innovation in Colombia: Impact of the Relationships Between Enterprises, Government and Universities. *Science, Technology & Society*, *30*(2), 363–385.

Pinedo-López, J., Baena-Navarro, R., & Torres-Hoyos, F. (2025). Science, technology and innovation in Colombia: Impact of the relationships between enterprises, government and universities. *Science, Technology & Society*, *30*(2), 363–385. DOI: 10.1177/09717218251326826

Pique, J. M., Berbegal-Mirabent, J., & Etzkowitz, H. (2018). Triple Helix and the evolution of ecosystems of innovation: The case of Silicon Valley. *Triple Helix (Heidelberg)*, *5*(1). Advance online publication. DOI: 10.1186/s40604-018-0060-x

Pislaru, M., Vlad, C. S., Ivascu, L., & Mircea, I. I. (2024). Citizen-centric governance: Enhancing citizen engagement through artificial intelligence tools. *Sustainability*, *16*(7), 2686. DOI: 10.3390/su16072686

Pitan, O. S. (2023). Leveraging the triple helix system for effective employability delivery in Nigerian universities. In *Handbook of research on sustainable career ecosystems for university students and graduates* (pp. 77–96). IGI Global.

Planck, S., Tomasi, S., Maisch, B., Henry, C., Gabriel, B., Singer, S., & Stoeckmann, C. (2025). Introduction. A New Social Contract for Higher Education Institutions: Exploring the Role of HEIs in European Innovation Ecosystems. *Triple Helix (Heidelberg)*, *11*(3), 245–257.

Poddar, A., & Rao, S. R. (2024). Evolving intellectual property landscape for AI-driven innovations in the biomedical sector: Opportunities in stable IP regime for shared success. *Frontiers in Artificial Intelligence*, *7*, 1372161. DOI: 10.3389/frai.2024.1372161

Prasad, K. R., Karanam, S. R., Ganesh, D., Liyakat, K. K. S., Talasila, V., & Purushotham, P. (2024). AI in public-private partnership for IT infrastructure development. *The Journal of High Technology Management Research*, *35*(1), 100496. DOI: 10.1016/j.hitech.2024.100496

Prilliadi, H. (2024). *Harnessing AI for ASEAN's future*. https://www.eria.org/uploads/Harnessing-AI-for-ASEAN%E2%80%99s-Future.pdf

Qiang, R. E. N., & Jing, D. U. (2024). Harmonizing innovation and regulation: The EU Artificial Intelligence Act in the international trade context. *Computer Law & Security Review*, *54*, 106028. DOI: 10.1016/j.clsr.2024.106028

Qu, C., & Kim, E. (2025). Artificial-Intelligence-Enabled Innovation Ecosystems: A Novel Triple-Layer Framework for Micro, Small, and Medium-Sized Enterprises in the Chinese Apparel-Manufacturing Industry. *Sustainability*, *17*(11), 5019.

Radaelli, D., Di Maria, S., Jakovski, Z., Alempijevic, D., Al-Habash, I., Concato, M., Bolcato, M., & D'Errico, S. (2024). Advancing patient safety: The future of artificial intelligence in mitigating healthcare-associated infections: A systematic review. *Healthcare (Basel, Switzerland)*, *12*(19), 1996. DOI: 10.3390/healthcare12191996

Radanliev, P. (2025). AI ethics: Integrating transparency, fairness, and privacy in AI development. *Applied Artificial Intelligence*, *39*(1), 2463722. DOI: 10.1080/08839514.2025.2463722

Radu, R. (2021). Steering the governance of artificial intelligence: National strategies in perspective. *Policy and Society*, *40*(2), 178–193. DOI: 10.1080/14494035.2021.1929728

Ravikumar, A. Olimbaevich, I. R., Mashkhura, S., & Musayeva, S. (2025). Transforming Healthcare with Large Language Models and AI agents. In Advances in Computational Intelligence and Robotics (pp. 51–82). IGI Global Scientific Publishing. https://doi.org/DOI: 10.4018/979-8-3373-2008-3.ch003

Ravikumar, R. N., Aarthi, S., Ruzimova, F., & Mamadiyarov, Z. (2025). Training and development in AI-driven education scaling solutions. In *Advances in Computational Intelligence and Robotics* (pp. 267–298). IGI Global Scientific Publishing. https://doi.org/DOI: 10.4018/979-8-3373-2185-1.ch010

Ravikumar, R. S., Manujakshi, Aarthi, S., Urazbaeva, Y., & Tamilselvi, S. (2025). Navigating data privacy, security, and regulatory challenges in healthcare AI ensuring fairness, bias mitigation, interpretability, and trust. In Transformative Role of Transformer Models in Healthcare (pp. 25–54). IGI Global Scientific Publishing. https://doi.org/DOI: 10.4018/979-8-3373-2038-0.ch002

Ravikumar, R. N., & Aarthi, S. (2025a). AI-powered synergistic robotics and IoT ecosystems for predictive and preventive healthcare. In *Robotics and IoT Synergy in Next-Generation Healthcare* (pp. 1–32). IGI Global Scientific Publishing., DOI: 10.4018/979-8-3373-5447-7.ch001

Ravikumar, R. N., & Aarthi, S. (2025b). Federated Learning and privacy-preserving search. In *Role of Library Resources for Higher Education in the Digital Era* (pp. 71–108). IGI Global Scientific Publishing., DOI: 10.4018/979-8-3373-3005-1.ch004

Ravikumar, R. N., Aarthi, S., Nadarajan, S., Masharipova, G., Mamadiyarov, Z., & Tamilselvi, S. (2025). Big data and cloud computing for climate-oriented remote sensing. In *Advances in Geospatial Technologies* (pp. 165–196). IGI Global Scientific Publishing., DOI: 10.4018/979-8-3373-3501-8.ch006

Rosienkiewicz, M., Helman, J., Cholewa, M., Molasy, M., Górecka, A., Kohen-Vacs, D., & Benis, A. (2024). Enhancing technology-focused entrepreneurship in higher education institutions ecosystem: Implementing innovation models in international projects. *Education Sciences*, *14*(7), 797.

Rossoni, A. L., de Vasconcellos, E. P. G., & de Castilho Rossoni, R. L. (2024). Barriers and facilitators of university-industry collaboration for research, development and innovation: A systematic review. *Management Review Quarterly*, *74*(3), 1841–1877. DOI: 10.1007/s11301-023-00349-1

Rubén Cukierman, U. (2025). The Triple Helix of Knowledge: Synergies and Potentialities among Engineering, Art, and Education. *International Journal of Engineering Pedagogy*, *15*(5).

Sadykova, A., Berikkhanova, A., Atabekova, B., Sholpankulova, G., & Abdykhalykova, Z. (2025, February). Social partnerships among academia, industry, and government in education: A bibliometric analysis. [). Frontiers Media SA.]. *Frontiers in Education*, *10*, 1516358.

Said, N. A., & Abdullah, Z. (2024). The Triple Helix of Innovation: A Case Study of the Role and Social Relations of Universities, Industry and Government. *Akademika*, *94*(3), 283–299.

Salas-Pilco, S. Z. (2021). Comparison of national artificial intelligence (AI): Strategic policies and priorities. In *Towards an international political economy of artificial intelligence* (pp. 195–217). Springer International Publishing., DOI: 10.1007/978-3-030-74420-5_9

Sam, M. (2025). Optimizing Data Governance via Triple Helix Model: A Systematic Review and Bibliometric Analysis. *Public Governance Practices in the Age of AI*, 327-354.

Samperio Sánchez, F. (2023). The Gestation of a Triple Helix in Queretaro, Its Contribution to the Formation of the Global Value Chain of the Aerospace Industry and the Type of Upgrading That Powers. In *Global Value Chains in Latin America: Experiences of Transformations* (pp. 251–285). Springer Nature Switzerland.

Sargiotis, D. (2024). Data Governance Frameworks: Models and Best Practices. In *Data Governance: A Guide* (pp. 165-195). Cham: Springer Nature Switzerland. https://doi.org/DOI: 10.1007/978-3-031-67268-2_4

Sasi, A. (2025). Decoding the Indian data governance model: Relooking at aadhaar. *Social Sciences & Humanities Open*, *11*, 101408. DOI: 10.1016/j.ssaho.2025.101408

Saudi Data and AI Authority (SDAIA). (2022). *National strategy for data and artificial intelligence*. https://www.sdaia.gov.sa

Saudi Data and AI Authority (SDAIA). (2023). *Personal data protection law*. https://www.sdaia.gov.sa

Schebesch, K. B., Soim, H. F., & Blaga, R. L. (2024). The triple-helix model as foundation of innovative entrepreneurial ecosystems. *Journal of Ethics in Entrepreneurship and Technology*, *4*(2), 104–129.

Senthil, B. A., Prema, R. K., & Sharif, L. S. (2025). Industry-Academia Partnerships: Bridging the Gap for R&D Success. In *Evolving Landscapes of Research and Development: Trends, Challenges, and Opportunities* (pp. 191-208). IGI Global Scientific Publishing.

Sharma, A. K., & Sharma, R. (2025). Governance in the age of artificial intelligence: A comparative analysis of policy framework in BRICS nations. *AI Magazine*, *46*(2). Advance online publication. DOI: 10.1002/aaai.70010

Sharma, M., & Singh, A. (2024a). Embracing Technological Innovation: A Review of Hi-Tech Services in Hospitality Industry. *Evergreen*, *11*(4), 2818–2830. DOI: 10.5109/7326926

Sharma, R., Sachdeva, T., Singh, A., & Nadda, V. (2024). A New Era of Engagement and Satisfaction: Transforming Customer Experience With AI-Driven Technologies. In Nadda, V., Tyagi, P., Singh, A., & Singh, V. (Eds.), *AI Innovations in Service and Tourism Marketing* (pp. 1–16). IGI Global., DOI: 10.4018/979-8-3693-7909-7.ch001

Sharma, R., & Singh, A. (2024b). Use of Digital Technology in Improving Quality Education: A Global Perspectives and Trends. In Nadda, V., Tyagi, P., Moniz Vieira, R., & Tyagi, P. (Eds.), *Implementing Sustainable Development Goals in the Service Sector* (pp. 14–26). IGI Global., DOI: 10.4018/979-8-3693-2065-5.ch002

Sharma, S. (2024). The role of government in regulating Ai for economic benefit. *ShodhKosh: Journal of Visual and Performing Arts*, *5*(1). Advance online publication. DOI: 10.29121/shodhkosh.v5.i1.2024.1659

Shin, B., Rask, M., & Kahma, N. (2023). Measuring the Quadruple Helix in social media: A case study of university–industry collaboration. *Technological Forecasting and Social Change*, *194*, 122711.

Shyiramunda, T., & van den Bersselaar, D. (2024). Local community development and higher education institutions: Moving from the triple helix to the quadruple helix model. *International Review of Education*, *70*(1), 51–85.

Sigfrids, A., Leikas, J., Salo-Pöntinen, H., & Koskimies, E. (2023). Human-centricity in AI governance: A systemic approach. *Frontiers in Artificial Intelligence*, *6*, 976887. DOI: 10.3389/frai.2023.976887

Singh, A., & Bathla, G. (2023). Fostering Creativity and Innovation: Tourism and Hospitality Perspective. In P. Tyagi, V. Nadda, V. Bharti, & E. Kemer (Eds.), Embracing Business Sustainability through Innovation and Creativity in the Service Sector (pp. 70-83). IGI Global.

Singh, A., & Kumar, V. (2025a). Organizational Innovation and Adaptation in Hospitality and Tourism: Strategies for Resilience and Leadership. In C. Ramos, T. Costa, R. Madeira, & J. Ferreira do Rosário (Eds.), Open Innovation and Technology in Tourism and Hospitality (pp. 355-372). IGI Global Scientific Publishing. https://doi.org/DOI: 10.4018/979-8-3693-8633-0.ch018

Singh, A., & Kumar, V. (2025b). User-Centered Hospitality: UI/UX as the New Frontier in Hotel and Restaurant Innovation. In C. Ramos, T. Costa, R. Madeira, & J. Ferreira do Rosário (Eds.), Open Innovation and Technology in Tourism and Hospitality (pp. 395-410). IGI Global Scientific Publishing. https://doi.org/DOI: 10.4018/979-8-3693-8633-0.ch020

Singh, A. (2022). Conceptual framework on Smart Learning Environment- An Indian perspective. *Journal of Education and Law*, (25). Advance online publication. DOI: 10.1344/REYD2022.25.36706

Singh, A. (2024a). Virtual Research Collaboration and Technology Application: Drivers, Motivations, and Constraints. In Chakraborty, S. (Ed.), *Challenges of Globalization and Inclusivity in Academic Research* (pp. 250–258). IGI Global., DOI: 10.4018/979-8-3693-1371-8.ch016

Singh, A. (2024c). Endorsing Gamification Pedagogy for Nurturing Employability Skills in Higher Education Institutions (HEI). In Membrive, V. (Ed.), *Practices and Implementation of Gamification in Higher Education* (pp. 172–183). IGI Global Scientific Publishing., DOI: 10.4018/979-8-3693-0716-8.ch008

Singh, A. (2024d). Impact of E-learning on Student Motivation in Higher Education Institutions: An Indian Perspective. *Journal of Education and Law*, (29). Advance online publication. DOI: 10.1344/REYD2024.29.43214

Singh, A. (2024e). Students Wellbeing and Performance in Higher Education Institutions. In Aloka, P. (Ed.), *Factors Impacting Student Well-Being and Coping Tactics* (pp. 1–12). IGI Global Scientific Publishing., DOI: 10.4018/979-8-3693-8860-0.ch001

Singh, A. (2025). Integrating Artificial Intelligence in Enhancing Cultural Tourism Experiences. In Albattat, A. (Ed.), *Technological Innovation in Global Cultural Tourism* (pp. 23–40). IGI Global Scientific Publishing., DOI: 10.4018/979-8-3693-3196-5.ch002

Singh, A., & Hassan, S. C. (2024). Service Innovation Through Blockchain Technology in the Tourism and Hospitality Industry: Applications, Trends, and Benefits. In Singh, S. (Ed.), *Service Innovations in Tourism: Metaverse, Immersive Technologies, and Digital Twin* (pp. 205–214). IGI Global., DOI: 10.4018/979-8-3693-1103-5.ch010

Singh, A., & Kumar, P. (2024). E-Learning Ecosystem in Higher Education Institutions: Trends and Practices. In Al Husseiny, F., & Munna, A. (Eds.), *Preparing Students for the Future Educational Paradigm* (pp. 1–18). IGI Global Scientific Publishing., DOI: 10.4018/979-8-3693-1536-1.ch001

Singh, A., & Sihmar, P. (2025). Higher Education Institution Sustainability: Role of Green Human Resource Management. In Adu-Gyamfi, M., Boateng, F., & Atiku, S. (Eds.), *Green HRM Awareness and Training in Higher Education Institutions* (pp. 1–14). IGI Global Scientific Publishing., DOI: 10.4018/979-8-3693-2956-6.ch001

Singh, A., Singh, D., & Chhikara, S. (2024). Online Learning: Challenges and Suggestions to Enhance Student Engagement in Higher Education Institutions. In Naidoo, V., & Verma, R. (Eds.), *Reshaping Entrepreneurial Education Within an Industry 4.0 Context* (pp. 59–80). IGI Global Scientific Publishing., DOI: 10.4018/979-8-3693-0409-9.ch004

Singh, V., & Singh, A. (2024). Revolutionizing the Hospitality Industry: How chatGPT Empowers Future Hoteliers. In Bansal, R., Ngah, A., Chakir, A., & Pruthi, N. (Eds.), *Leveraging ChatGPT and Artificial Intelligence for Effective Customer Engagement* (pp. 192–203). IGI Global., DOI: 10.4018/979-8-3693-0815-8.ch011

Singla, B., Afridi, S., Vayolipoyil, S., Ahmed, T., Afzaal, S., Saleem, K., Zobia Malik, M. T., & Qudsia, M. (2025). The evolving role of artificial intelligence in medical science: Advancing diagnostics, clinical decision-making, and research. *Cureus*, *17*(9), e91514. DOI: 10.7759/cureus.91514

Siregar, P. D. (2024). *Problem payung hukum dalam penggunaan artificial intelligence.* https://www.hukumonline.com/berita/a/problem-payung-hukum-dalam-penggunaan-artificial-intelligence-lt66d4b01adeaf2/

Sophia, L. I. (2025). The social harms of AI-generated fake news: Addressing deepfake and AI political manipulation. *Digital Society & Virtual Governance*, *1*(1), 72–88. DOI: 10.6914/dsvg.010105

Stephens, R. J. S. (2025). Quadruple Helix co-creation and cities: Behavioral and institutional changes in innovation capacities and cultures. *Cities (London, England)*, *157*, 105579.

Subrahmanyam, S. (2025). Strategic Collaboration and Partnerships in R&D for Innovation. In *Research and Development Practices in Innovation* (pp. 283–314). IGI Global Scientific Publishing.

Su, C. Y., Lin, B. W., & Chen, C. J. (2015). Technological knowledge co-creation strategies in the world of open innovation. *Innovation*, *17*(4), 485–507.

Suminar, T., Sutarto, J., Raharjo, T. J., Kisworo, B., Cahyani, A. D., & Raharjo, S. R. (2025). Development of a Triple Helix-Based Course and Training Management Model to Accelerate the Transformation of Work Competencies in the Era of Disruption. *TEM Journal*, *14*(3), 2537.

Tagliazucchi, G., Della Santa, S., & Gherardini, F. (2024). Design of a living lab for autonomous driving: An investigation under the lens of the triple helix model. *The Journal of Technology Transfer*, *49*(3), 876–899.

Tanveer, U., Hoang, T. G., Ishaq, S., & Khalid, R. U. (2025). Public-private partnerships as catalysts for digital transformation and circular economy: Insights from developing countries. *Technological Forecasting and Social Change*, *219*. Advance online publication. DOI: 10.1016/j.techfore.2025.124270

Ten Holter, C. (2022). Participatory design: Lessons and directions for responsible research and innovation. *Journal of Responsible Innovation*, *9*(2), 275–290. DOI: 10.1080/23299460.2022.2041801

Thomas, D. O., Nwaichi, E. O., & Umunna, A. O. (2024, October). Enhancing Workplace Safety Through Innovation and Human Factors Engineering: A Collaborative Approach Among Academia, Industry, and Government. In *Triple Helix Nigeria SciBiz Annual Conference* (pp. 117-139). Cham: Springer Nature Switzerland.

Thomas, D. O., Nwaichi, E. O., & Umunna, A. O. (2025, March). Enhancing Workplace Safety Through. In *Triple Helix Nigeria SciBiz Annual Conference 2024: THN SciBiz* (p. 117). Springer Nature.

Thorpe, M., Healy, C., & Olsen, D. (2025). Bridging workforce skills gaps in rural America amid 'the great resignation'by leveraging a triple helix collaboration. *Industry and Higher Education*, *39*(2), 198–211.

Tidjon, L. N., & Khomh, F. (2022). The different faces of AI ethics across the world: A principle-to-practice gap analysis. *IEEE Transactions on Artificial Intelligence*, *4*(4), 820–839. DOI: 10.1109/TAI.2022.3225132

Tiernan, P., Costello, E., Donlon, E., Parysz, M., & Scriney, M. (2023). Information and Media Literacy in the Age of AI: Options for the Future. *Education Sciences, 13*(9), 906. DOI: 10.3390/educsci13090906

Tokopedia-UI AI Center of Excellence. (2024). *AI and data innovation booklet.* Tokopedia-Universitas Indonesia. https://tokopedia-ai.cs.ui.ac.id/booklet/

Tutak, M., & Brodny, J. (2025). Stakeholder collaboration and open innovation in smart cities: A Quattro Helix model for technological and social transformation. *Journal of Open Innovation, 11*(3). Advance online publication. DOI: 10.1016/j.joitmc.2025.100594

UNESCO. (2021). *Recommendation on the ethics of artificial intelligence.* UNESCO Publishing. https://www.unesco.org/en/artificial-intelligence/ethics

UNESCO. (2023). *Guidance for generative AI in education and research.* UNESCO Publishing. https://www.unesco.org/en/articles/guidance-generative-ai-education-and-research

UNESCO. (2025). *Artificial intelligence readiness in Indonesia: Progress, policy, and potential.* https://unesdoc.unesco.org/ark:/48223/pf0000392317

United Nations Conference on Trade and Development. (2024). *Digital economy report 2024: The role of AI in trade and development.* https://unctad.org/system/files/official-document/ditctsce2024d2_en.pdf

University of Staffordshire. U. K., Adebayo, A. S., Chukwurah, N., Dish Network CO USA, L., Oluwaseun Ajayi, O., & University of the Cumberlands, U. S. A. (2025). Artificial Intelligence and Machine Learning algorithms for advanced threat detection and cybersecurity risk mitigation strategies. Engineering and Technology Journal, 10(03). https://doi.org/DOI: 10.47191/etj/v10i03.18

Uppuluri, P. C., & Yang, C. W. (2025). The Emergence of Foundation Models in U.S. Radiology: A Narrative Review of Clinical Utility, Safety, and Evaluation. *Academic Radiology*. Advance online publication. DOI: 10.1016/j.acra.2025.10.063

Van Dijk, M. P. (2025). Triple Helix approach to innovation in Rwanda's agriculture resulted in a partnership between educational institutions and a private firm producing clean seed potatoes. *Journal of Agribusiness in Developing and Emerging Economies, 15*(4), 832–848.

Variety Intelligence Platform. (2024a). *Generative AI, celebrity deepfakes, and digital replicas: Special report.* https://variety.com/vip-special-reports/generative-ai-celebrity-deepfakes-digital-replicas-special-report-1236218083/

Variety Intelligence Platform. (2024b). *Creative consent and data ethics in AI model training: AI training – consent & content report.* https://read-vip.variety.com/html5/reader/production/default.aspx?pubname=&edid=f72ee533-d63a-40af-969f-8b05af56de44

Ver. (2024). *Kecerdasan buatan (AI) sebagai objek hukum vs subjek hukum dalam pelindungan kekayaan intelektual.* https://www.dgip.go.id/index.php/artikel/detail-artikel-berita/kecerdasan-buatan-ai-sebagai-objek-hukum-vs-subjek-hukum-dalam-pelindungan-kekayaan-intelektual?kategori=liputan-humas

Viale, R., & Cucchiarini, V. (2025). Behavioral Triple Helix for Innovation. Triple Helix, 1(aop), 1-23.

Villacis, A. H., & Badruddoza, S. (2023). Using artificial intelligence to predict and prevent future food insecurity. *Georgetown Journal of International Affairs, 24*(2), 191–197. DOI: 10.1353/gia.2023.a913645

Vision 2030. (2016). *Saudi Vision 2030.* https://www.vision2030.gov.sa

Walter, Y. (2024). Managing the race to the moon: Global policy and governance in Artificial Intelligence regulation—A contemporary overview and an analysis of socioeconomic consequences. *Discover Artificial Intelligence, 4*(1). Advance online publication. DOI: 10.1007/s44163-024-00109-4

Wang, L., Ni, Y., Zhao, Y., & Chen, Y. (2024). The triple helix collaboration: Lessons from a Chinese provincial innovation ecosystem. *Chinese Management Studies, 18*(4), 1276–1289. DOI: 10.1108/cms-08-2023-0391

Wang, S. (2025). The application and challenges of artificial intelligence in personalized learning for higher education. *Lecture Notes in Education Psychology and Public Media, 106*(1), 164–170. DOI: 10.54254/2753-7048/2025.cb25753

Wang, T., Suo, B., Jiang, J., & Jia, W. (2025). A triple helix model analysis of China's regional industry-university-research collaborative innovation in low-carbon technologies. *International Journal of Climate Change Strategies and Management, 17*(1), 846–866.

Wawak, S., Teixeira Domingues, J. P., & Sampaio, P. (2024). Quality 4.0 in higher education: Reinventing academic-industry-government collaboration during disruptive times. *The TQM Journal, 36*(6), 1569–1590.

Weidenfeld, A., & Anusik, J. (2025). Exploring the systemic qualities and institutions of a Triple Helix municipal knowledge network. *European Planning Studies, 33*(12), 2184–2206.

Wirz, C. D., Demuth, J. L., Bostrom, A., Cains, M. G., Ebert-Uphoff, I., Gagne, D. J., Schumacher, A., McGovern, A., & Madlambayan, D. (2025). (Re)Conceptualizing trustworthy AI: A foundation for change. In *Artificial Intelligence* (Vol. 342). Elsevier B.V., DOI: 10.1016/j.artint.2025.104309

Wu, S., Shi, C., Leung, Y. F., Otake, Y., Konishi, C., Zhou, M., Tao, Y., Cao, Z., & Nakamura, T. (2025). Perspectives: LLM agents reshaping the foundation of geotechnical problem-solving. *Geodata and AI, 4,* 100036. DOI: 10.1016/j.geoai.2025.100036

Wu, X., Zheng, Y., & Wang, X. (2025). Government–Industry–Academia Collaboration for Sustainable Autonomous Vehicle Development: A Qualitative Case Study in Suzhou, China. *Sustainability, 17*(12), 5348.

Xia, S., Zhou, Y., Wang, Z., He, Q., & Parry, G. (2025). Enhancing green innovation through university–industry collaboration and artificial intelligence: Insights from regional innovation systems in China. *The Journal of Technology Transfer*, •••, 1–29.

Xin, P., Arshad, N. I., Mohamad, U. H., Huang, Y., & Su, S. J. (2025). Reframing the Triple Helix for Sustainability: A Mechanism-Based Framework for University–Industry–Government Collaboration in Global Innovation Systems. *European Journal of Education*, *60*(4), e70361.

Xiong, W., Song, Y., & Fu, H. Z. (2025). The diversity and Triple Helix interactions among universities, industries and governments: Case of climate change field. *Scientometrics*, •••, 1–26.

Yang, B. B., & Park, S. D. (2025). Evolving Innovation Ecosystems: Longitudinal Insights into the Triple Helix Model and Enterprise Innovation in China. *SAGE Open*, *15*(4), 21582440251393200.

Yang, Z., Cui, X., & Song, Z. (2023). Predicting sepsis onset in ICU using machine learning models: A systematic review and meta-analysis. *BMC Infectious Diseases*, *23*(1), 635. DOI: 10.1186/s12879-023-08614-0

Yazıcı, A. M. (2023). The quintuple helix, industrial 5.0, and society 5.0. In *Digitalization, Sustainable Development, and Industry 5.0: An Organizational Model for Twin Transitions* (pp. 317-336). Emerald Publishing Limited.

Yelpaala, K., Gibbons, M. C., Vigil, I. M., Leaño, J., McCall, T., Opara, I., Zink, A., Nunez-Smith, M., Mukherjee, B., & Ranney, M. (2025). The Role of data in Public Health and health Innovation: Perspectives on social determinants of health, community-based data approaches, and AI. Journal of Medical Internet Research, 27(v27i1e78794), e78794. https://doi.org/DOI: 10.2196/78794

Yessimova, S., Rakhymzhanov, Y., Spanova, B., Baizhanova, S., Seidakhmetov, M., Yessenova, A., & Altynbassov, B. (2024). Strengthening the Nexus: Policy and Legislative Reforms for University-Industry Collaboration in Kazakhstan. *Theoretical and Practical Research in Economic Fields*, *15*(1), 136–144.

Yu, W., He, H., Song, S., Zhang, J., Dai, L., Zheng, L., & Letaief, K. B. (2025). AI and Deep Learning for Terahertz Ultra-Massive MIMO: From Model-Driven Approaches to Foundation Models. *Engineering*. Advance online publication. DOI: 10.1016/j.eng.2025.07.032

Zadegan, M. G., Ghazinoory, S., & Nasri, S. (2025). The triple helix model of innovation and sustainable development goals: A literature review. *Sustainable Development*. Advance online publication. DOI: 10.1002/sd.70041

Zhang, L., Banihashemi, S., Zhu, L., Molavi, H., Odacioglu, E., & Shan, M. (2024). A scientometric analysis of knowledge transfer partnerships in digital transformation. In *Journal of Open Innovation: Technology, Market, and Complexity* (Vol. 10, Issue 3). Elsevier B.V. https://doi.org/DOI: 10.1016/j.joitmc.2024.100325

Zhang, B., Anderljung, M., Kahn, L., Dreksler, N., Horowitz, M. C., & Dafoe, A. (2021). Ethics and governance of artificial intelligence: Evidence from a survey of machine learning researchers. *Journal of Artificial Intelligence Research*, *71*. Advance online publication. DOI: 10.1613/jair.1.12895

Zhang, X., & Tan, Y. (2025). Digital Empowerment: Unlocking the “synergy barrier” of government-enterprise-public air pollution control. *Energy Reports*, *13*, 4846–4865. DOI: 10.1016/j.egyr.2025.04.036

Zhao Yi, Z. Y., Guo Qian, G. Q., & Fu Rao, F. R. (2025). University-Industry Collaborative Innovation for County-Level Prosperity-Driven Industries: Dynamic Mechanisms and Implementation Pathways. *University-Industry Collaborative Innovation for County-Level Prosperity-Driven Industries. Dynamic Mechanisms and Implementation Pathways*, *2*(11), 172–177.

Zhao, X., Wang, L., & Chen, L. (2024, February). Industry and Education Integration for Chinese University of Applied Science and Technology, Based on the Triple Helix Theory. In *3rd International Conference on Education, Language and Art (ICELA 2023)* (pp. 316-328). Atlantis Press.

Zhou, C. (2008). Emergence of the entrepreneurial university in evolution of the triple helix. *Journal of Technology Management in China*, *3*(1), 109–126. DOI: 10.1108/17468770810851539

Zhou, J., & Wang, M. (2023). The role of government-industry-academia partnership in business incubation: Evidence from new R&D institutions in China. *Technology in Society*, *72*, 102194.

Zhuang, T., Oh, M., & Kimura, K. (2025). Modernizing higher education with industrial forces in Asia: A comparative study of discourse of university-industry collaboration in China, Japan and Singapore. *Asia Pacific Education Review*, *26*(1), 195–210.

Zhuang, T., & Zhou, H. (2023). Developing a synergistic approach to engineering education: China's national policies on university–industry educational collaboration. *Asia Pacific Education Review*, *24*(1), 145–165.

Zhuang, T., Zhou, H., & Sun, Q. (2024). Ushering in industrial forces for teaching-focused university-industry collaboration in China: A resource-dependence perspective. *Studies in Higher Education*, *49*(12), 2357–2375.

Zhu, X., Weigel, P., Baloh, J., Nataliansyah, M., Gunn, N., & Mueller, K. (2019). Mobilising cross-sector collaborations to improve population health in US rural communities: A qualitative study. *BMJ Open*, *9*(11), e030983. DOI: 10.1136/bmjopen-2019-030983

Zhu, Y. P., & Park, H. W. (2025). Publication, collaboration, citation performance, and triple helix innovation gene of artificial intelligence research in the communication field: Comparing Asia to the rest of the world. *Journal of the Knowledge Economy*, *16*(2), 10308–10328.

Zirpoli, C. T. (2025). *Artificial intelligence and intellectual property rights: Emerging policy challenges* (CRS Legal Sidebar No. LSB10922). https://www.congress.gov/crs-product/LSB10922

About the Contributors

Mohieddine Rahmouni, Ph.D., is an Associate Professor of Economics and Quantitative Methods at the Applied College, King Faisal University (Al-Ahsa, Saudi Arabia), and at the High School of Economic and Commercial Sciences of Tunis (ESSECT), University of Tunis, Tunisia. He earned his Ph.D. in Economics through a joint program between the University of Montesquieu Bordeaux-IV (now University of Bordeaux), France, and the University of Tunis. His research focuses on innovation economics, applied econometrics, productivity, and industrial dynamics, with particular emphasis on economic development in emerging economies. Dr. Rahmouni has published in leading international journals, including Structural Change and Economic Dynamics, the Journal of Industrial and Business Economics, and the International Journal of Innovation and Technology Management. His work examines external knowledge sources, innovation drivers, and the policy impacts shaping firm-level performance. Actively engaged in global academic and policy communities, Dr. Rahmouni contributes to informing innovation policy in the Global South, positioning him as a key voice in advancing studies on university government partnerships and innovation ecosystems.

Mossab Saud Alholiby is an Associate Professor of Educational Leadership at the College of Education, King Faisal University, Al-Ahsa, Saudi Arabia. He earned his Ph.D. in Educational Management from the University of Glasgow in 2018, with a thesis on enhancing quality assurance in Saudi higher education through educational and e-management perspectives. His research interests include higher education leadership, quality assurance, educational management, digital leadership, and technology-enhanced learning. Dr. Alholiby has published widely in international and regional journals, including the Journal of Industrial and Business Economics, International Journal of Leadership in Education, and Administrative Sciences. His scholarship explores academic leadership, innovation in higher education, and governance practices, with a particular focus on the role of education in advancing sustainable development.

Ben Othman Soufiene is an Assistant Professor of computer science at the King Faisal University from 2025. He received his Ph.D. degree in computer science from Manouba University in 2016 for his dissertation on “Secure data aggregation in wireless sensor networks. He also holds M.S. degrees from the Monastir University in 2012. My research interests focus on the Internet of Medical Things, Wireless Body Sensor Networks, Wireless Networks, Artificial Intelligence, Machine Learning and Big Data. Dr. Ben Othman has published more than 140 papers at reputed international journals, conferences, and book chapters. He is an Editorial Board Member in the different Journals and Conferences. He serves as an associate editor/academic editor for international journals including IEEE Access, IEEE Sensors, IEEE Internet of Things, Elsevier, Springer, Taylor & Francis, IGI, IET, Telecommunication Computing Electronics and Control, and Wiley. Dr. Ben Othman is a Technical Program Committee Member for more than a dozen of international conferences.

Ashraf Alam currently holds the position of Research Faculty at the Centre of Excellence in Public Policy, Sustainability and ESG Research, housed within the Faculty of Law and Policy Studies at Alliance University, Bangalore. Renowned for his transdisciplinary acumen spanning education, technology, and policy studies, Dr. Ashraf has been distinguished as one of the World’s Top 2% Scientists by Stanford University and Elsevier. His prolific academic output includes over fifty SCOPUS-indexed publications and more than one hundred conference presentations at esteemed national and international academic forums. His educational trajectory reflects both depth and versatility: a Ph.D. in Education from the Indian Institute of Technology (IIT) Kharagpur, an M.Ed. with a concentration in Mathematics Education, and a B.S. in Computer Science from the University of Delhi. He also holds postgraduate degrees in Public Administration (M.A.) and Mathematics (M.Sc.), supplemented by a suite of postgraduate diplomas in Higher Education, Guidance and Counselling, Educational Technology, Criminology and Police Administration, and Value Education. Dr. Ashraf is an active participant in global scholarly discourse. As Associate Editor of Frontiers in Education, he plays a pivotal role in curating and guiding intellectual contributions across the Educational, Pedagogical, and Learning Sciences. Concurrently, he serves as Founder and Director of Academic Chronicles Private Limited, where he orchestrates editorial board formation and develops strategic frameworks for peer-reviewed publishing in the Social, Behavioural, and Humanistic Sciences. His research has been disseminated through elite academic platforms, including Elsevier, Springer,

Taylor & Francis, Wiley, Routledge, Sage, Emerald, and IEEE, and addresses a remarkably diverse array of topics such as pedagogical theories, educational administration, educational psychology, educational sociology, educational policy, technology-integrated learning, mathematics education, educational philosophy, educational technology, teacher education, and AI/ML in learning environments. Dr. Ashraf's scholarly rigor is further demonstrated by his success in qualifying multiple prestigious examinations including UGC-NET-JRF in both Education and Adult and Continuing Education, UGC- NET in Public Administration, and GATE in Humanities and Social Sciences. At the heart of Dr. Ashraf's intellectual ethos lies a steadfast belief in education as a catalytic and emancipatory force capable of engendering social justice, human flourishing, societal progress, and sustainable transformation. His recent explorations into 'Happiness Engineering' and holistic well- being in school ecosystems articulate a vision of education that transcends instrumentalist paradigms, prioritizing emotional intelligence, global consciousness, empathy, and psychosocial resilience among learners. His research agenda seeks to conceive educational praxis through the affordances of inclusive digital learning, gamified instructional design, and artificial intelligence (AIEd), thereby constructing robust, ethically grounded frameworks for 21st century education. At Alliance University, Dr. Ashraf remains committed to architecting pedagogical models that not only cultivate intellectual dexterity and cognitive excellence but also prepare learners for morally responsive leadership, intellectual nimbleness, and responsible global citizenship in an increasingly volatile, uncertain, complex, and ambiguous (VUCA) world.

Azamat Ali is an Associate Professor in the School of Liberal and Creative Arts (Journalism and Mass Communication) at Lovely Professional University, Punjab, India. He earned his Ph.D. from the Central University of Gujarat, Gandhinagar, and a M.Sc. in Science Communication from Devi Ahilya Vishwavidyalaya, Indore. His research interests span emerging technologies, development communication, public policy, and health and science communication. Dr. Ali research is directed toward bridging the divide between scientific innovation and societal application, with a particular focus on harnessing the transformative potential of emerging technologies to drive innovation, address developmental challenges, and enhance societal wellbeing.

Silambarasan G possesses a comprehensive academic foundation, holding a Bachelor of Computer Applications (BCA) and a Master of Computer Applications (MCA), and is currently pursuing a Ph.D. (Full-Time) in the Department of Computer Science at Periyar University, Salem, Tamil Nadu, India. With over 08 years of teaching experience and 02 years of industry exposure, he has consistently demonstrated excellence in both academic and technical domains. His professional journey reflects a strong commitment to research, innovation, and pedagogical advancement in the rapidly evolving field of computer science. Renowned for his expertise in network administration, system architecture, virtualization, and emerging computing technologies, Silambarasan G continues to contribute significantly to the integration of theory and practical application. His academic and research pursuits exemplify a passion for technological innovation and a steadfast dedication to advancing the frontiers of computer science education.

Nasiba Jumaniyazova is a faculty member in the Department of Psychology at Mamun University, Khiva, Uzbekistan. She is engaged in teaching and academic activities related to psychological science, human behavior, and educational psychology. Her academic interests include cognitive and developmental psychology, student mental well-being, and the application of psychological principles in educational settings. She is committed to fostering students' analytical thinking, emotional intelligence, and academic growth through learner-centered instruction. Nasiba Jumaniyazova actively contributes to academic and institutional initiatives aimed at strengthening psychology education and promoting research-informed teaching practices in higher education.

Nazira Kurbanova is a faculty member in the Department of Pedagogy and Psychology at Termez University of Economics and Service, Termez, Uzbekistan. She is engaged in teaching and academic activities related to educational psychology, pedagogy, and learner development. Her academic interests include learner-centered teaching approaches, motivation in education, classroom psychology, and contemporary pedagogical practices in higher education. She is committed to fostering supportive and inclusive learning environments that enhance students' cognitive, emotional, and social development. Nazira Kurbanova actively contributes to academic and institutional initiatives aimed at improving teaching quality and advancing pedagogical effectiveness.

Azalia Primadita Muchransyah, Ph.D., is a filmmaker, writer, and scholar from Indonesia. She received her doctorate in Media Study from the University at Buffalo, SUNY, in 2021. Her research and creative interests span media studies, film studies and production, documentary and hybrid forms, HIV studies, feminist studies, and media activism in Indonesia. Her dissertation explored alternative documentary production and distribution to examine the paradoxes of HIV advocacy from a media ecology perspective. A two-time Fulbright grantee, she has received awards including the UB Three Minute Dissertation Award and fellowships from the Gender Institute and the Mark Diamond Research Fund. Her recent publications address topics such as AI filmmaking, the metaverse, the comparison between professional and smartphone cameras, and alternative film screening venues. She was nominated for the Citra Award for Best Animated Short Film at Festival Film Indonesia 2022 for Nusa Antara, an animated documentary that has since screened internationally.

Ravikumar R. N. is currently a Postdoctoral researcher at Universiti Malaysia Perlis, Malaysia. Also, working as an Associate Professor in the department of Computer Engineering at Marwadi University, Rajkot, Gujarat. He has 12+ years of national and international teaching experience. He completed his PhD at Amity University, Rajasthan, M.E at VMRF Deemed University, B.E at Anna University, Chennai. He is the co-founder of the Research Activities Club at Marwadi University and trains students on research activities, which leads to the publication of 7 Scopus/SCI journals, 20 Book chapters, 25 Conference papers, and 10 patents. His specialization is ML, DL, Federated Learning, Recommendation Systems, and Optimization Techniques.

Aarthi S is a dedicated Assistant Professor in Computer Science with over six years of teaching experience. She is currently pursuing her Ph.D. at Marwadi University, Gujarat, and holds an M.Phil. and MCA from Bharathiar University, Tamil Nadu. Throughout her academic career, Aarthi has specialized in programming languages such as C++, Java, and C, and contributed to research in recommender systems and AI-related data privacy. She has published journal articles, contributed to book chapters, and actively participated in technical workshops. Known for her student mentorship and engagement in academic events, Aarthi remains committed to fostering innovation and excellence in computer science education.

Karimov Eyyub Sevdim is a Professor in the Department of Humanities at Azerbaijan Technical University, Baku, Azerbaijan. He is actively engaged in teaching and research in the humanities, with academic interests that include cultural studies, philosophy, and interdisciplinary approaches to social and technical education. His scholarly work contributes to the integration of humanistic perspectives within technical and engineering education. Karimov Eyyub Sevdim participates in academic research, curriculum development, and international collaboration initiatives aimed at advancing humanities scholarship in higher education.

Gautam Shivaraj, with a comprehensive academic background including a Bachelor's in Mechanical Engineering, Master of Engineering Management (Australia), MBA and also pursuing Ph.D., brings an impressive 06 years of teaching experience alongside a brief stint in the industry of 3 years. Currently serving as an Assistant Professor at the Adarsh Institute of Management and Information

Technology in Bangalore, Karnataka, India, he has distinguished himself in the academic and research fields. Prof.Gautam Shivaraj professional journey is a testament to his dedication to academia, research, in the evolving world.

Amrik Singh is working as Professor and HOD in the School of Hotel Management and Tourism at Lovely Professional University, Punjab, India. He obtained his Ph.D. degree in Hotel Management from Kurukshetra University, Haryana, India. He has published 115 Scopus-indexed publications. He has published 12 patents, and 01 patent has been granted in the inter-disciplinary domain. Dr. Amrik Singh participated and acted as a resource person in various national and international conferences, seminars, research workshops, and industry talks. He has published 20 books with IGI Global Publication, Emerald Publication, Bentham Publication, Nova Publication etc., on trending areas such as Food waste, Artificial Intelligence, Mountain Tourism, Virtual tourism, Healthcare Tourism, Guest behavior in tourism and hospitality. His area of research interest are Accommodation management, sustainability, Green practices, Human Resource Management in Hospitality, Artificial Intelligence, AR VR in hospitality, Hotel pricing, Employee Disability, Work life balance, women empowerment etc. He is currently guiding 8 Ph.D. scholars, and 5 Ph.D. scholars have been awarded Ph.D.

Bakhritdinova Dilobar Zaynitdinovna is a faculty member in the Department of Primary Education at Shakhrsabz State Pedagogical Institute, Uzbekistan. She is engaged in teaching and academic activities focused on primary education pedagogy, curriculum planning, and learner-centered instructional strategies. Her academic interests include innovative teaching methods, classroom management, formative assessment, and inclusive practices in primary education. She is committed to strengthening foundational learning outcomes and supporting the professional development of future primary school teachers. Bakhritdinova Dilobar Zaynitdinovna actively contributes to academic and institutional initiatives aimed at enhancing the quality and effectiveness of primary teacher education.

Index

A

C

D

E

G

H

V

www.ingramcontent.com/pod-product-compliance
Lightning Source LLC
LaVergne TN
LVHW081526300926
849161LV00006B/1316